MUMBAI FABLES

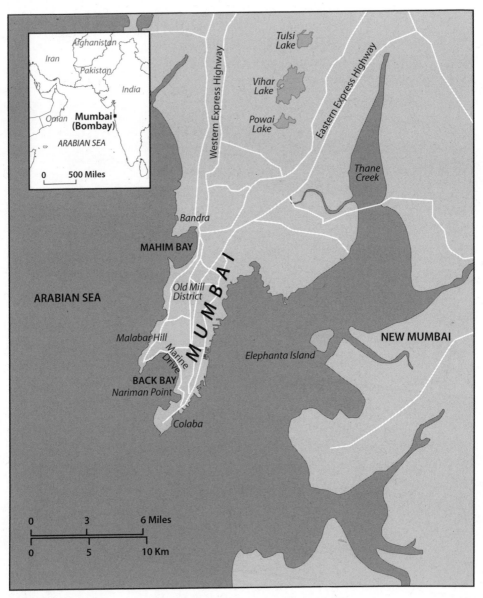

Frontispiece. Mumbai. Courtesy: Tsering W. Shawa

MUMBAI FABLES

Gyan Prakash

PRINCETON UNIVERSITY PRESS
PRINCETON AND OXFORD

Library of Congress Cataloging-in-Publication Data

Prakash, Gyan, 1952–
Mumbai fables / Gyan Prakash.
p.   cm.
Includes bibliographical references and index.
ISBN 978-0-691-14284-5 (hardcover : alk. paper)
1. Bombay (India)—Civilization. 2. Bombay (India)—History.
3. Bombay (India)--Biography. I. Title.
DS486.B7P73 2010
954'.792—dc22   2010012510

British Library Cataloging-in-Publication Data is available

This book has been composed in Minion Pro

Printed on acid-free paper. ∞

Printed in Canada

1   2   3   4   5   6   7   8   9   10

For Aruna

Contents

Illustrations

FIGURES

PLATES

1

THE MYTHIC CITY

It is just before two o'clock in the afternoon in April, the hottest month of the year. A tiny speck appears in a cloudless Poona sky, moving steadily toward the Tower of Silence, the funerary place where the Zoroastrians expose their dead to be consumed by birds of prey. It is not an eagle; nor is it a crow, for it could never fly that high. As the speck approaches the tower, its outline grows larger. It is a small aircraft, its silver body gleaming in the bright sun. After flying high above the Parsi place of the dead, the plane disappears into the horizon only to double back. This time, it heads determinedly to the tower, hovers low over it, and then suddenly swoops down recklessly. Just when it seems sure to plunge into the ground, the plane rights itself and flies upside down in large circles. A bright object drops from the aircraft into the well of the tower, illuminating the structure containing a heap of skeletons and dead bodies. As the light from the bright flare reveals this gruesome sight, the plane suddenly rights itself and hovers directly overhead. The clock strikes two. A camera shutter clicks.

The click of the camera shakes the Zoroastrian world. The Parsi head priest of the Deccan region, taking an afternoon nap, immediately senses that foreign eyes have violated the sacred universe of his religion. Parsi priests, who are performing a ritual at their Fire Temple, feel their throats dry up abruptly and are unable to continue their chants. As the muslin-covered body of a dead Parsi is being prepared for its final journey to the tower, the deceased's mother suddenly lets out a piercing shriek. When the sacred fire burning at a Zoroastrian temple bursts into sparks, the assembled priests agree that a vital energy has escaped the holy ball of fire.

Thus begins "Tower of Silence," an unpublished novel written in 1927 by Phiroshaw Jamsetjee Chevalier (Chaiwala),[1] a Parsi from Bombay.* After setting the scene of this grave sacrilege to the Zoroastrian faith, the novel shifts to London. On the street outside the office of the journal *The Graphic* is a large touring Rolls-Royce, richly upholstered and fitted with silver fixtures. In it sits a tanned young man in a finely tailored suit, with a monocle in his left eye. He is Beram, a Parsi who blends "the knowledge of the shrewd East" with that of the West and is a master practitioner of hypnotism and the occult. He is in London to hunt down and kill those who have defiled his religion—the pilot who flew the plane over the tower, the photographer who clicked the snapshot, and the editor who published it in *The Graphic*. This locks him in a battle of wits with Sexton Blake, the famous 1920s fictional British detective, and his assistant Tinker, who are employed by the magazine. As Beram goes about systematically ferreting out his intended victims, with Blake and Tinker in pursuit, the novel traverses London, Manchester, Liverpool, Burma, Rawalpindi, and Bombay. It concludes with Parsi honor restored.

In Chaiwala's thrilling fable of Parsi revenge, the protagonists slip in and out of disguises and secret cellars. They follow tantalizing clues and leave deliberately misleading traces, practicing occult tricks and hypnotism to gain an advantage in their quest. Magic and

---

* Bombay/Mumbai: Unless I am referring to the period after 1995, when Bombay was officially renamed as Mumbai, I use the name Bombay, as the city was called, for most of the period covered by the book.

sorcery, however, operate in a thoroughly modern environment. Industrial modernity, in the form of planes, trains, and automobiles, figure prominently. The high-altitude camera and the illustrated magazine reflect a world of image production and circulation. The novel travels easily between Britain and India and comfortably inhabits British popular culture. Imperial geography underwrites this space. Colonialism conjoins Britain, India, and Burma and produces the cosmopolitan cultural milieu that the novelist presents as entirely natural. Beram dwells in this environment while proudly asserting his religious identity. He is no rootless cosmopolitan but a modern subject, deeply attached to his community. His quarrel with the pilot, the photographer, and the editor is not anticolonial. Chaiwala mentions the Gandhian movement against British rule, but Beram expresses no nationalist sentiments; his sole motivation is to right the wrong done to his faith by modernity's excesses, by its insatiable appetite to erase all differences and violate all taboos. He represents a form of cosmopolitanism that is based on an acknowledgment of cultural differences.

The novel bears the marks of its time, but it also presents a picture of Bombay that persists. This is evident as much in the depiction of the city, where Beram and Sexton Blake play their cat-and-mouse game, as in the whole imaginative texture of the novel. A Bombay man himself, Chaiwala celebrates the city's mythic image when he describes it as "gay and cosmopolitan," a heady mix of diverse cultures and a fast life. Its existence as a modern city, as a spatial and social labyrinth, can be read in the detective novel form. The sensibilities and portraits associated with Bombay are inherent in the novel's geographic space, in its characters and their actions.

When I came upon Chaiwala's typescript in the British Library, I found its fictions and myths resonate with my childhood image of Bombay. Cities live in our imagination. As Jonathan Raban remarks, "The soft city of illusion, myth, aspiration, nightmare, is as real, maybe more real, than the hard city one can locate on maps in statistics, in monographs on urban sociology and demography and architecture."[2] This is how Bombay, or Mumbai, as it is now officially known, artlessly entered my life. Bombay is not my hometown. I was born more than a thousand miles away in a small town named Hazaribagh. I grew up in Patna and New Delhi and have lived in the United States for many years. Mine is not an immigrant's nostalgia for the hometown left behind, but I have hungered for the city since my childhood. Its physical remoteness served only to heighten its lure as a mythic place of discovery, to sustain the fantasy of exploring what was beyond my reach, what was "out there."

This desire for the city was created largely by Bombay cinema. Nearly everyone I knew in Patna loved Hindi films. Young women wore clothes and styled their hair according to their favorite heroines. The neighborhood toughs copied the flashy clothes of film villains, even memorizing and mouthing their dialogues, such as a line attributed to the actor Ajit instructing his sidekick: "Robert, Usko Hamlet wala poison de do; to be se not to be ho jayega" (Robert, give him Hamlet's poison: from "to be" he will become "not to be"). No one knew which film this was from, or indeed if it was from a film at all. Ajit's villainous characters were so ridiculously overdrawn that he attracted a campy following that would often invent dialogues. Then there were Patna's own Dev Anand brothers, all three of whom styled their hair with a puff, in the manner of their film-star idol. Emulating their hero, they wore their shirt collars raised rakishly and walked in the actor's signature zigzag fashion—trouser legs flapping, upper body swaying, and arms swinging across the body. Like many others, I remember the comedian Johnny Walker crooning in Mohammed Rafi's voice, "Yeh hai Bambai meri jaan" (It's Bombay, Darling) to the tune of "Oh My Darling, Clementine," in *CID* (1956).

Hindi cinema stood for Bombay, even if the city appeared only fleetingly on-screen, and then too as a corrupt and soulless opposite of the simplicity and warmth of the village. I understand now that underlying our fascination with Bombay was the desire for modern life. Of course, the word *modernity* was not in our vocabulary then; we spoke of Bombay's charms with signs and gestures, with wistful looks and sighs, expressing desires for self-fashioning and deprived pleasures. We knew of New York, Paris, and London, but they were foreign places, holding no emotional resonance. To us, the most familiar large city was Calcutta, in the neighboring province of West Bengal. Many, particularly the poor, from my province of Bihar went there to work. But the proverbial Bengali cultural arrogance was a hurdle in developing any lasting love or longing for their city. New Delhi was just a dull seat of government, heavily laden with a bureaucratic ethos, and Madras was too culturally and linguistically remote. Although far away, it was Bombay that held the promise of exciting newness and unlimited possibilities. It reached out across the physical and cultural distance to stir desires and kindle imaginations. Even my father was not immune to Bombay's magnetism. When he built the family house in Hazaribagh, the facade was modeled on the Marine Drive Art Deco apartment buildings that he had seen in photographs.

The Bombay tabloid *Blitz* epitomized the city's mischievously modern spirit. The only one of its kind in India at the time, this provocative weekly unabashedly presented itself as the voice of the citizenry, excoriating officialdom with over-the-top reports and articles. Adopting the loud and brash character of its larger-than-life Parsi editor, Russi Karanjia, the tabloid was identified with the city. So was Behram Contractor, known by his pen name Busybee, who wrote his popular and characteristically witty "Round and About" columns, first in the *Evening News of India* and subsequently in *Mid-Day*, before eventually settling on *Afternoon Courier and Despatch*, a tabloid he founded and edited. Poking gentle fun at everyone while offending no one, Busybee became known and loved as a classic Bombay figure—at home in its metropolitan chaos while remaining alive to the absurdities of its everyday life. Similarly playfully critical was Gangadhar Gadgil. Trained as an economist, he wrote

1.1. Mario's Bombay. Source: *Illustrated Weekly of India*, October 18, 1970.

both in Marathi and in English with equal facility and prolificacy, his satirical eye alighting on an eclectic choice of subjects—from an encounter with pickpockets in the city to the experience of traveling in its crowded trains to the obsessions and practices of tea drinking in Bombay.[3]

And then there was Mario Miranda, whose cartoons on the pages of the *Illustrated Weekly of India* leaped out at you with their wit and biting commentary. He gave us memorable city figures—Miss Fonseca, the buxom Anglo-Indian secretary; the office clerk Godbole; the corrupt and rotund politician Bundaldass; the seductive actress Miss Rajni Nimbupani; and the Catholic girl Petrification Pereira. Using the cartoon form, Mario's pictorial illustrations were works of art that depicted Bombay's mongrel and chaotic world with humor and acute observations.

The *Illustrated Weekly*, which featured Mario's art, and *Femina*, both owned by the Times group, were two widely circulated magazines that also disseminated the city's metropolitan image. The

Weekly lived up to its promise, featuring stories with photographs that showcased modern life. Whether they were accounts of dance bands, cabaret acts, architecture, cinema, and art or famous murder cases, exposés of brothels, illegal gambling, or the manufacture of illicit liquor in the Prohibition era, the magazine covered them all with lavish illustrations. The popular glossy women's magazine *Femina,* which started publication in 1959, featured mainly articles on style, health and beauty, relationships, and celebrities. Its vibrant pages flaunted the latest trends in clothes, cosmetics, and home furnishings. Its splashy coverage and proud sponsorship of the annual Miss India contest paraded Bombay's trendy fashion sense. Addressed as it was to the English-reading public, there was no doubt about *Femina*'s elitism. But this only added verve to Bombay's image as a place of high style.

Philip Knightley, the Australian journalist, writes of the excitement of the Bombay of the early 1960s.[4] He arrived in the city on a voyage from Britain via Basra, intending to lay over only until a ship was ready to sail to his home country. But he stayed for two years, working for a literary journal. Unaware that the journal was funded by the CIA—a fact he discovered only years later—Knightley ended up playing an unwitting role in a Cold War cloak-and-dagger drama when the KGB also tried to recruit him. In retrospect, he saw the international espionage angle as part of Bombay's dynamic milieu. "Everyone seemed to be on the move," he remembers, "even though they did not know where to."[5]

Harry Roskolenko, an American writer who also made his way to the Island City in the sixties, thought that Bombay was the world's most open city after Tokyo. What he meant by "open" is manifest in the title of his book. *Bombay after Dark* is a racy travel account that he published under the pen name Allen V. Ross. The book describes his sexual romp through Bombay, including the experience of a young college student "pressing her rubbery young body against mine" in a temple during a religious celebration and of his "water circus" with an Anglo-Indian woman in the Arabian Sea.[6] Though he finds that vice and commerce are "natural handmaidens," the book is not a judgmental account of the flesh trade but a celebration of "a man's city, sensual and open to pleasure." *Bombay by Night*, a book published a decade later by the *Blitz* crime reporter Captain F. D. Colaabavala, adopts a shocked tone, but it too offers a titillating, voyeuristic account of Bombay as a haven for erotic pleasure. While purporting to expose vice, the book invites you to do a little "undercover research" in "Bombay after Dark," promising that no matter what your desire, taste, or mood, you will find what you want in India's commercial capital, "where the history of commerce is often written on the bedsprings."[7]

Such accounts of sex and vice sketched a free-spirited city, a palace of pleasures. A photograph published in newspapers and magazines in 1974 served only to reconfirm the city's freewheeling spirit. It showed a woman streaking on a busy Bombay street in broad daylight. The nude photograph attracted much attention because the woman was Protima Bedi, a glamorous model and the wife of the handsome model and rising film star Kabir Bedi. The fashionable couple was frequently in the news. In her posthumously published memoir, Bedi acknowledged that the nude photograph was genuine, but she alleged that it had been taken while she was walking naked on a beach in Goa and was then superimposed on a Bombay street to produce the sensational copy. A rival account is that the streaking was staged to gain publicity for the launch of *Cine Blitz*, a new film magazine.[8] Whatever the truth, no one questioned the photograph's authenticity because it played into Protima Bedi's image as a model with a swinging lifestyle. The shocking picture also contributed to Bombay's mythology as a city with an uninhibited and audacious ethos, a place where the "iron cage" of the dull routines—the familiar and regular—of modern life was shaken loose with the energy and excitement of transgression.

If films, newspapers, and magazines broadcast Bombay in glamorous, sunny hues, they also narrated tales of its dark side. These impressions were powerfully amplified by the lyrics of several film songs penned by progressive poets that inveighed against the unjust social order. So, while Johnny Walker romps on the breathtaking Marine Drive in the film *CID*, sweet-talking his girlfriend in the voice of playback singer Mohammed Rafi, the song warns of the perils that await the unwary in Bombay and offers a biting critique of the industrial city's soullessness: "Kahin building, Kahin tramen, Kahin motor, Kahin mill, milta hai yahan sub kuch, ek milta nahin dil, insaan ka hai nahin namo-nishan" (In this city of buildings and trams, motorcars and mills, everything is available except a heart and humanity). Though the song speaks of a callous city habitat in vivid and richly textured lyrics, it also offers hope. Johnny Walker's girlfriend responds to his evocation of Bombay's capriciousness and contradictions by rewording the song's idiomatic refrain. In place of "Ai dil hai mushkil jeena yahan" (It is hard to survive here), she sings "Ai dil hai aasaan jeena yahan, suno Mister, suno Bandhu, Yeh hai Bombay meri jaan" (O gentlemen, O my friends, living here is easy, it's Bombay, darling). She does not deny his sentiments about hypocrisy and injustice in the city but counters them with an optimistic one of her own. There is a sense of confidence and optimism, even appreciation for the city, despite its conflicts and contradictions. References to the Hindi-speaking "Bandhu" (friend) and the English-speaking "Mister" suggest a feeling of belonging in Bombay's socially and linguistically mongrel world.

Ironically, even as the song celebrated Bombay's mongrel world, a political movement for the creation of the linguistic province of Maharashtra, including the fabled city, was heating up. This was followed by the rise of the Bal Thackeray–led Shiv Sena, a nativist party named after Shivaji, the seventeenth-century Maratha warrior. The Sena's growing influence signaled the eclipse of the radical aspirations that socialist lyricists expressed. The challenge came not just from the Sena's right-wing populism but also from political stirrings among the formerly "untouchable" castes. The strong protests against centuries-old caste discrimination included the rejection of the name "untouchable" because it carried the stigma of the Brahmanic caste hierarchy. Demanding equality, justice, and dignity, the leaders of the discriminated castes called their group Dalit (the Oppressed). Like the African Americans' proud embrace of the term "Black" during the 1960s, the adoption of a new name signified an insurgent consciousness. The parallel with African American militancy and its influence went even further when the poet Namdeo Dhasal formed the Dalit Panthers in 1972, a powerful group of writers. The Panthers penned insurgent poetry and prose that challenged the centuries of discrimination and exploitation the oppressed castes had suffered.

The Dalit Panthers added to the sense of crisis that gripped the city in the 1970s as sharp challenges from below tested the governing political and social order. The populist mobilization against elected governments, led by the Gandhian socialist Jai Prakash Narayan, and the National Emergency that Indira Gandhi declared in 1975 pointed to the erosion of liberal democracy and constitutional politics. National events and political crises bore down on Bombay, taking the shine off its image. But what gave the city's portrait a decidedly dark turn were the Hindu-Muslim riots of 1992–93. The riots were followed by a series of bomb blasts—ten in all—on March 12, 1993.

The communal violence and the explosions left many wondering if Bombay's cosmopolitanism had been just a facade, now as charred as the buildings damaged by the explosions. After all, Mumbai is no ordinary city. An island city of nearly twelve million, according to the 2001 census, it is the *ur*-modern metropolis in India. Kolkata (Calcutta), Chennai (Madras), and Delhi are also major Indian cities, but unlike them Mumbai flaunts its image as a cosmopolitan metropolis by transcending its regional geography. The map locates it in Maharashtra—the cartographic fact is the product of political agitation in the 1950s—and Marathi-speaking Hindus constitute the largest group. However, the city's population remains dazzlingly diverse.

Attracted by the city's position as the hub of manufacturing, finance, trade, advertising, media, and the film industry, people from all over India have washed up on the island. They speak different languages—Marathi, Gujarati, Hindi, Urdu, Bengali, Tamil, Malayalam, English—and practice different faiths—Hinduism, Islam, Christianity, Zoroastrianism, Jainism, Judaism. Historically, immigrants from villages and small towns have managed their assimilation into the modern metropolis by maintaining their native tongues and cultures in their homes and neighborhoods. Mumbai's map is a jigsaw puzzle of distinct neighborhoods marked by community, language, religion, dress, and cuisine. As a means of communicating across differences, the city has even concocted a hybrid but wonderfully expressive vernacular for everyday communication—Bambaiya.

For a metropolis that prided itself on its cultural diversity and that staked its claim on being a modern capitalist city where the worship of Mammon trumped the worship of all other gods, the communal riots and bomb blasts appeared atavistic. When the Shiv Sena–led government officially renamed Bombay Mumbai in 1995, the rechristening seemed to formalize the transformation that had already occurred.

The breakdown of the cosmopolitan ideal occurred against the background of a runaway growth in population and the closure of textile mills and deindustrialization, which together dismantled the image of the old Bombay. Where once the city had hummed to the rhythm of its cotton mills and docks, now there was the cacophony of the postindustrial megalopolis. Working-class politics that had once formed a vital part of city life now barely breathed, leaving the toilers unorganized and defenseless. State policies and urban government had done little to relieve, let alone improve, the condition of those who struggled to survive. Armies of poor migrants, slum dwellers, hawkers, and petty entrepreneurs occupied the city's streets, pavements, and open spaces. Mumbai appeared under siege, imperiled by spatial mutations and occupation by the uncivil masses, a wasteland of broken modernist dreams. Currently it enjoys the dubious distinction of being home to Asia's largest slum, Dharavi.

Sudhir Patwardhan, a leading Bombay painter, poignantly registers the anxiety caused by urban change. Patwardhan, a politically conscious artist, had made a name for himself as a social realist painter of the city during the 1970s and the 1980s. A radiologist by profession, he had used his penetrating vision to focus on figures set against Bombay's social and spatial contexts. The destruction of working-class politics, followed by the 1992–93 communal riots and the ruination of liberal ideals, introduced a discerible change in his art.[9] His *Lower Parel* (2001) depicts the space of the old mill district worked over by deindustrialization and globalization. In *Riot* (1996), we see communal vitriol at its rawest. The image of society as a collective recedes.

If Patwardhan paints a violence-ridden, splintered city, writers depict Mumbai as a place stalked by corrupt politicians, shady real estate tycoons, bribed policemen, brutal underworld bosses, and compromised film stars.[10] Mumbai pulsates, but to the throbbing beat of greed, ambition, jealousy, anger, communal passions, and underworld energies. Suketu Mehta's "maximum city" is a place bursting with not just urban desires but also urban problems.[11] Here and there, Mehta finds honest and straightforward characters, but his city is a cabinet of curiosities peopled by violent policemen, vicious killers, crazed communal rioters, brutal underworld foot soldiers, and troubled but kindhearted beer-bar dancers.

In 2002 *Outlook*, a popular newsmagazine, published an issue on the city that stated, "Yes, Mumbai exists, but India's most liberal, economically vibrant, multicultural metropolis is no more."[12] The lead article recited killer statistics and facts. The population, already a "scary 11 million," was estimated to reach 28.5 million by 2015, making Mumbai the world's most populous city; the infrastructure in this city of slums and high-rises has already reached a breaking point, and the suburban trains are packed four to five times their capacity.[13] A picture of Queen's Necklace, Marine Drive's signature nighttime image, on the magazine's cover was emblazoned with a bold title: "Bombay: The Death of a Great City."

Literary writings on Mumbai register the anguish over what has occurred. Salman Rushdie's *Midnight's Children* (1983) portrays the Bombay of his childhood as an island of raucous and colorful coexistence of different communities. In *The Moor's Last Sigh* (1995), however, the Island City is lashed by angry tides of ethnic strife churned up by cynical and corrupt politicians and businessmen. The chaotic but robust coexistence of different communities and cultures now appears as a remote figment of the city's imagination. In Rohinton Mistry's 2002 novel, *Family Matters*, a character called Mr. Kapur desperately seeks to recapture the spirit of the shining city on the sea, "a tropical Camelot, a golden place where races and religions lived in peace and amity."[14] But he despairs of ever resurrecting his tropical Camelot: "Nothing is left now except to talk of graves, of worms and epitaphs. ... Let us sit upon these chairs and tell sad stories of the death of cities."

Events in the twenty-first century appear to give credence to the prophecies of Mumbai's demise. On July 26, 2005, the rain gods attacked Mumbai with relentless intensity. Over thirty-nine inches of monsoon rain lashed the city within a twenty-four-hour period, submerging some areas under fifteen feet of water. Transportation came to a standstill, flights were canceled, the stock exchange was closed, and schools and colleges were shut down. People in the streets tried to wade or swim to safety. Over four hundred people drowned or were killed in stampedes while trying to escape the onrushing water.

When I arrived in the city on July 29, the affected neighborhoods were still slushy. Cars and motorcycles stood forlornly, covered in mud. A sense of the wet, mildewed aftermath hung in the air. The brightly lit shops on the main streets could fool you into believing that nothing had happened. But the garbage piled on the sidewalks broke this air of eerie normality. Mumbai's streets are not clean at the best of times. But this was not the usual litter and trash; it was heaps of household garbage refuse and commercial merchandise covered by a rotting, deep black sludge. It was as if the water had forced the city to bring its innards out into the open, exposing its decaying, putrid secret.

The idea of a city destroyed by a deluge is the stuff of myths. The 2005 flood evoked just such a primeval image, of nature biting back, punishing humans, its fury leveling their prized creation—the city. The urban government and infrastructure appeared defenseless against the wrath of the celestial powers. Just a few months earlier, business and political elites had been retailing dreams of turning Mumbai into a "world-class" city, of transforming it into another Shanghai. But those dreams had literally gone down the clogged drains. Monsoon waterlogging is commonplace, but this was a frighteningly different sight; the city was sinking inch by inch.

Mumbai's confidence was shattered. Every time it rained over the next few days, one could detect anxious looks. This was unusual, for the monsoon is always greeted with happiness in India. In the countryside, a timely monsoon augurs a good crop, and in the cities it spells relief from the searing summer heat, but the experience of that terrible Tuesday had changed Mumbai's disposition. It was as if the urban motion arrested by the flood had spilled onto people's nerves and battered their psyches. Mumbai appeared imperiled; it was no longer a dream city but a nightmare.

A Bhojpuri music video called *Museebat mein Bambai* (Bombay in Trouble) conveys the gloomy mood.[15] A mournful ballad, serving as the background score to images of the flood, tells us:

Kahal ja la Bambai kabo sute la nahin
Kabo ruke la nahin
Kabo thake la nahin

It is said that Bombay never sleeps
Never stops
Never tires

Cutting to visuals of cars and trains screeching to a halt, a voice intones:

> Lekin ai bhaiyya chabbis July din mangalwaar ko
> Bambai ruk bhi gayil
> Bambai thak bhi gayil

> But Brother, on Tuesday 26 July
> Bombay stopped
> Bombay tired

A little later, accompanied by images of people repeatedly trying to make calls on their mobile phones:

> Band hoi gayile sabke phonwa mobile
> Bambai pe jaise baadalwa tooti aayee
> Bijli katal tab le bhayil ba andheriya

> Every mobile phone went silent
> When the cloudbursts struck Bombay
> Darkness prevailed when the power went out

As the ballad relates the city's sudden collapse, it locates the catastrophe in the abrupt failure of the machinic city. One would think that the experience of floods and their destructive force would be familiar to rural immigrants. After all, almost every year the monsoon submerges roads and villages in the countryside. But Mumbai? How could anyone imagine a devastating flood here? It was as if the country, banished by urban modernity, had stormed back to the city with the rage of the repressed.

A year later, just as the city had recovered its spirits, signs of trouble reappeared. In early July 2006, the monsoon pelted the city with high-velocity winds and heavy rains. There was a sense of déjà vu. Frustration with both the city and nature boiled over. The authorities were excoriated for their inaction in spite of the previous year's terrible events, and a newspaper columnist threatened to file a lawsuit—against the monsoon! No sooner had the ground dried than on Sunday, July 9, the Shiv Sena, Mumbai's nativist party, went on a rampage. Seeking vengeance for the alleged desecration of the statue of Meenatai Thackeray, the wife of their supreme leader, Bal Thackeray, the Sena mobs stopped traffic, burned vehicles, smashed shop windows, and shut down Mumbai. The shuttered city trembled helplessly in ghostly silence.

Two days later, on July 11, the silence was shattered by a series of terrifying bomb blasts in Mumbai's commuter trains, within minutes of each other. They occurred with sickening regularity—6:24, Khar; 6:25, Jogeshwari; 6:25, Mahim; 6:26, Borivli; 6:27, Bandra; 6:30, Matunga; and 6:31, Mira Road. With all local train service suspended in the city, everyone took to the roads. Cars, taxis, buses, trucks, and auto rickshaws blared their horns as they snaked through streets clogged with pedestrians. Traffic slowed to a halt on highways packed with panic-stricken people who, in desperation and with no alternatives, had decided to walk home. The commuter-hour traffic jam escalated into an exodus.

The television networks flashed images of mangled bodies, severed limbs, blood-soaked bags, shoes, umbrellas, and newspapers belonging to either the victims or those who had escaped the carnage. Frightened survivors spoke of their brush with death and the pain of seeing their fellow passengers consumed by the explosions. The hospitals were choked with the injured and their grieving relatives and friends. Politicians and officials appeared on television to condemn the blasts and to reassure the public that the administration was acting to help the victims and to catch the perpetrators. Television "experts" speculated that the culprits were Kashmiri militants and jihadi terrorists, masterminded by Pakistan's intelligence agency. The next morning, screaming newspaper headlines promptly named the tragedy 7/11, as if the American 9/11 had become the global frame for viewing violence.[16]

In spite of attempts to process the carnage as a story of terrorism and statecraft, the dominant response at the experiential level was confusion and a mixture of fear, grief, trauma, and fatalism. Account after account in newspapers and conversations on the street highlighted the suddenness of the experience. One moment a person was standing at the doorway of the packed compartment talking to a friend, the next he found himself sprawled on the tracks, with no memory of what had occurred in between. Some passengers in the second-class compartment remembered hearing a loud blast before they were caught in the stampede to escape from the mangled smoke-filled compartments. Many were so paralyzed by the shock of the deafening blast that they remained rooted to their seats, moving only when other fleeing passengers ushered them out. One survivor said that when he heard the blast, at first he thought that it was an earthquake. Before losing consciousness, he was convinced that he was going to die but then was saved by the slum dwellers who live along the tracks. Another recounted how a young woman collapsed when she saw the lifeless body of her husband pulled out from the train. They had been married for only six months.

The city was shaken. Wild speculations and alarming rumors flew rapidly. There were reports of a panicked citizenry taking to vigilante actions. A mob attacked four men who were thought to be carrying suspicious-looking packages; they turned out to be North Indian immigrants looking for jobs, and the dangerous-looking parcels contained nothing more lethal than their lunch. Commuters picked on people they thought were loitering suspiciously, and bomb squads were summoned to inspect numerous harmless abandoned bags and packages. Suspicion and fear became the common currency.

Two years later, the terrorist attacks on November 26, 2008, reignited the fear and the sense of catastrophe. For nearly three days, the terrorists ran amok, holding and killing hostages at the Taj Mahal Hotel, the Trident Hotel, and the Jewish Center at Nariman House. They rained bullets on unsuspecting commuters at the crowded Chhatrapati Shivaji Terminus (formerly Victoria Terminus) and shot at the staff and patrons of the popular Leopold Café. Although the brutal assault on civilians was confined to particular locations in South Mumbai, bomb explosions and shootings elsewhere created an impression of roving terror squads. By the time the security forces rescued the hostages and killed all but one of the attackers, at least 164 civilians and police personnel lay dead.

Unlike the deluge of 2005 or even the 2006 train blasts, the terrorist assault on the city was catapulted into a geopolitical event. Part of the reason was the presence of foreigners in the two luxury hotels. The attack on the Jewish Center with Israeli citizens also ensured international coverage. The around-the-clock television broadcast of the three-day ordeal circulated the brutal drama widely, turning it into a global media event. The carnage at the train station that claimed the lives of many ordinary citizens became a mere footnote to the attention showered on the Taj, the Trident, and Nariman House. Hysterical on-the-spot reports by television correspondents, frenzied news anchors, and heated talk shows whipped up fear and paranoia. As the media reported details about the attackers' Pakistani origins, their hijacking of an Indian fishing vessel on the high seas, and the details of their murderous actions, Pakistan bashing and war talk became common.

While those who were held hostage, killed, and injured were subjected to unspeakable horror, for the rest of the city the event was a media experience. The spectacular images of flames engulfing the historic Taj and the bloody battle between the security forces and the terrorists produced intense fear and anger. The police, ordinarily reviled for its corruption and ridiculed as incompetent, suddenly rose in the public's estimation. The fallen policemen became instant heroes, and the security forces personnel were showered with bouquets and garlands. The verbal brickbats were reserved for the politicians.

In the media-generated frenzy, the fury against politicians was second only to the rage against Pakistan. Reports on the apparent ease with which the terrorists had sailed into the city, the unpreparedness of the police, their inadequate equipment, and the three-day bloodbath whipped up antipolitician hysteria. A socialite-cum-journalist coined the slogan "Enough is enough" and directed it against politicians, which went viral. The slogan resonated particularly with the South Mumbai elites, who rarely bother to vote. They loudly proclaimed that the people had had enough of vote banks and slogan mongering; the need of the hour was accountability for the security failures. This opinion received prominent coverage in the media, and banners attacking politicians went up at key venues.

Underlying the antipolitician sentiment was a desire for politics as administration. This sentiment expressed frustration with the messiness of democracy and construed politics to mean the clean and efficient management of society. Even though this emotion was stirred up by the elites, it found resonance in the general public's widespread dissatisfaction with politics—its dysfunction, cynicism, and corruption and its power brokering and influence peddling. Sensing the hostile mood, the politicians made themselves scarce. Even the Shiv Sena, which is usually first out of the gates in going after all things Pakistani, chose to remain invisible.

The terrorist attacks once again brought forward the frame of "crisis" to represent Mumbai's condition. Only this time, it appeared larger, graver than on previous occasions; Mumbai's problems became national and international. Underlying this sense of mortal crisis was an apprehension of total dysfunction expressed in the public's antipolitician reaction. Mumbai could not even govern itself.

In light of the recent events, the dystopic mood about Mumbai's future is understandable. It is a mood that echoes the current discourse among urban theorists who speak of the city as a thing of the past, its identity overrun and scrambled by explosive urbanization. There is no doubt that urbanization is a central force in the contemporary world. According to UN estimates, the world's urban population has risen from 30 percent in 1950 to 47 percent in 2000, and it is expected to reach 60 percent by 2030.[17] Much of the developed world has been predominantly urban at least since the early twentieth century as a result of capitalist industrialization and colonial and imperial expansion. The recent spurt in urbanization, therefore, is concentrated in the developing regions of the world. Mexico City, São Paulo, and Mumbai are experiencing explosive growth, outstripping the populations of cities such as London, Paris, and even New York. If Mumbai points to the future of urban civilization on the planet, Suketu Mehta writes, "God help us."[18]

The spurt in urbanization is a matter not just of numbers but also of changes in the urban form. Suburbanization and "edge" cities encapsulate the transformation in the urban landscape in North America. Paris is no longer just the city that Baron Haussmann built but includes the towns connected to it by roadways, airports, and metro lines. The megacities of the developing world, swollen with rural immigrants, are burgeoning with slums and squatter settlements, pointing to the increasing urbanization of poverty and raising the specter of a "planet of slums."[19] As the urban network extends to fill the spaces between the city and the countryside, we can no longer speak of a strict divide between the two. Increasingly, there are regional urban complexes, huge urban corridors (for example, the one connecting Hong Kong to Guangzhou), and not the earlier city-hinterland configuration. Cities are no longer internally coherent and bounded entities but parts of vast urban networks that are often regional and global in scale.

Urban theorists contend that capitalist globalization has also overwhelmed the modernist city of the nineteenth and early twentieth centuries.[20] Prototypical political movements and ideologies nursed in the heyday of modernist cities have lost their appeal, and new informational networks and "pirate modernity" have marginalized old urban solidarities.[21] As globalization produces different kinds of legal regimes and citizens, new hierarchies of cities and urban dwellers, it poses a new set of questions for citizenship, identity, and politics.[22] The nonlegal basis of urban existence and politics in the slums and squatter settlements of the global south mocks the classic ideal of the city as the space of civil society and rational discourse.[23] Never realized in practice even in European cities, this ideal lies in ruins. The contemporary urbanization and its global processes and representations have destroyed the halo of this modernist urbanism. Today it is difficult to sustain the paradigmatic notion of modern cities as unified formations, securely located within their national borders and with clearly legible politics and society.

The media theorist Paul Virilio had predicted the dissolution of the city by media and communication.[24] But it was left to the architect and urban theorist Rem Koolhaas to celebrate the death of the modernist city and hail the emergent urban form—the "Generic City." Writing in 1988, Koolhaas, the enfant terrible of urban theory, emphasized a shift from the center to the periphery, of fragmentation, and of spontaneous processes and described his research on the contemporary city as "a retro-active manifesto for the yet to be recognized beauty of the twentieth-century urban landscape."[25] He followed this up by announcing and celebrating the arrival of "generic cities," urban spaces indistinguishable from one another and modeled on the contemporary airport.[26] Koolhaas argued that like these airports, the emergent "generic cities" will look like one another—the same constellation of shopping malls and spatial arrangements, the same lack of uniqueness. Architecture and urban design will be uniform, freed of the weight of history and tradition. The generic city will be like a Hollywood studio lot, constantly destroyed and rebuilt.

Koolhaas's nightmare scenario is meant to provoke, but there is a grain of truth in his interpretation and predictions. It is undeniable that certain generic urban forms and architectural designs are visible in city after city across the world. Shopping malls, cafés, restaurants, multiplex theaters, entertainment complexes, tall office towers, and apartment buildings dot the urban landscape worldwide. These are spaces that invoke a feeling of placelessness.

Drive through Shenzhen, the special economic zone in Mainland China, across from Hong Kong. Mile after mile, you will come across fields of office and residential towers sporting a uniform style. Cafés, restaurants, and art spaces with a global look are springing up even in the old *hutong* areas of Beijing, now refurbished as traditional neighborhood theme parks. Walk into a mall in Tardeo or Andheri, or eat in the chic restaurants of Colaba and Bandra offering Mediterranean or nouvelle cuisines, and you could forget that you are in Mumbai. Coffeehouses filled with young cappuccino sippers dressed in generic global styles and fast-food chains crowded with families have become familiar sights, displacing the Irani cafés that have served the city's working and lower middle classes since the early twentieth century.

Gleaming apartment and office buildings that tower over tenements and slums in the old mill districts promise to transport the tenements' occupants away from the grim ground reality of Mumbai's poverty and grime. Media and advertising relentlessly express aspirations of global lifestyles and consumption. Place these developments alongside new infrastructure projects, including the recently commissioned Bandra-Worli Sealink, which is seen as a harbinger of developments to come that will lift Mumbai out of its communications misery, and you come face to face with the urban elites' dream of turning Mumbai into Shanghai. Never mind that many planners see these projects as exacerbating the overburdened north-south axis of the city. There is also the fact that, unlike China, India is a democracy. Thus, Mumbai's robust activism functions as a brake on the drive to impose from above the fantasy of a global city. Still, this does not prevent the elite from pushing for forms that look toward the "generic city." In fact, the Chinese example inspires builders and planner-bureaucrats to circumvent public scrutiny while promoting their schemes of malls, apartment and office towers, entertainment complexes, and infrastructures.

Urban change is indisputable, but the narratives of change from Bombay to Mumbai and the rise and fall of the city are deeply flawed. They conceive change as the transformation of one historical stage to another, from the bounded unity of the city of industrial capitalism to the "generic city" of globalization, from modernity to postmodernity, from cosmopolitanism to communalism. However flawed, you cannot miss the widespread presence of this narrative. Pick up recent novels on the city, read nonfiction writings, turn the pages in newspaper and magazine files, talk to people, and you will be confronted with a story that purports to tell us what the city was as Bombay and what it has become as Mumbai.

This narrative is widely shared and deeply believed because it presents itself as historical fact. The nostalgic "tropical Camelot" and the dystopic city of slums appear as compelling bookends of Mumbai's story because they seem to have the force of historical truth. In fact, it is a trick of history, inviting us to believe its Bombay-to-Mumbai tale as an objective reading of the past when it is a fable. To accept it at its face value is to get ensnared in the fabulous spell that history casts. What requires examination is the history of this fable. What enabled the composition of the city's image as a "tropical Camelot" in the past, and what has produced the picture of the dysfunctional, out-of-control city of the present?

To ask what lies behind the very powerful fable about the city's past and its present is to excavate the history of Mumbai's life as a "soft city"; it is to examine what permitted the telling of certain stories and not others. My goal is not to strip fact from fiction, not to oppose the "real" to the myth, but to reveal the historical circumstances portrayed and hidden by the stories and images produced in the past and the present. I am interested in uncovering the backstories of Mumbai's history because they reveal its experience as a modern city, as a society built from scratch. To some extent, all modern cities are patched-up societies composed of strangers. This is all the more the case with Mumbai, a city of immigrants that was sired by colonial conquest. What did it mean for people belonging to different castes, different religions, different regions, speaking different languages, to work and live together as a society? How was the image of the cosmopolitan city composed to represent the patchwork of its ethnic and cultural multiplicity, at what cost, and how did it unravel? What social fantasies and imaginations has the city repressed and expressed through the course of its history? The backstories behind the fable promise to reveal Mumbai's experience of the modern city *as* society.

Now that the images of the cosmopolitan city lie shattered, deprived of the "aura" that they enjoyed in their own time, a new historical understanding of the past becomes possible. The fables of the city can be unraveled to reveal how they came to be. We can cast a fresh look at the remains of its Portuguese history and at the monumental structures erected by the British, turn over the soil of reclaimed lands, and read between the lines of official and unofficial documents. The shuttered textile mills, now overrun by residential and commercial towers, invite a fresh scrutiny of the enchantments of industrial progress that they once exuded and the aspirations and desires they stifled. The yellowing newspaper records and archival documents, the travel writings, social commentaries, and political treatises that exist outside their time promise to reveal what was masked in the past.

The whole city is open for an archaeological excavation, for turning over the material remains of its history to disclose what remains hidden under the weight of the petrified myths.[27] We can now uncover the historical experiences of forging a modern collective of different religions, classes, castes, and languages and undo the fables to lay bare the history of the city *as* society.

With these thoughts in my head, I hit the streets of Mumbai.

2

THE COLONIAL GOTHIC

Bombay, Bombay
O my dear slut
I may say a good-bye
But not before
I take you
in multiple ways
Not before
I will pin you down
here and how
thus and thus.
—Namdeo Dhasal, "Mumbai, Mumbai My Dear Slut"

Bombay is now officially Mumbai.[1] The colonial era is abolished, dismissed as history. I encountered the most visible expression of the postcolonial abolition of the city's colonial past in the ubiquitous presence of Shivaji, the seventeenth-century Maratha warrior and a national and regional cultural icon. Public spaces named after him abound. Victoria Terminus, the late-nineteenth-century railway station with its ornate riot of roofs, towers, and domes in the Gothic Revival style, is now called Chhatrapati Shivaji Terminus, and the airport is named after him. A striking statue of the warrior, mounted on his horse, sword in hand, stands near the Gateway of India. The

Maratha chieftain could never have imagined that his seventeenth-century wars with the Mughal Empire would one day earn him a place in the gateways to a modern city. But there he is, miraculously installed as the city's icon, greeting visitors, commuters, and passersby today with the memory of centuries ago.

Soon after I encountered Shivaji on his horse at the Gateway, I discovered that he had stood earlier at Kala Ghoda (Black Horse), a spot once occupied by a huge equestrian statue in bronze of King Edward VII. In 1965 political activists defaced and removed the foreign emperor's likeness, vacating the space for the nationalist hero. After reclaiming and occupying Kala Ghoda for the nation, Shivaji rode away to the symbolically more important Gateway while the vanquished King Edward was relegated to a museum. Many streets, squares, and public buildings that once sported European names now wear Maharashtrian and national ones. The colonial era met with its final ignominy when Kala Ghoda became an undistinguished parking lot.

But looks can be deceiving. Legends abound that the vanquished king lives on. While the city sleeps, he rises from the grave of history to defend himself. Night after night, he slips out of the museum and rides on his horse to engage Shivaji in duels. Their battles take them all over the city, fighting for neighborhood after neighborhood. They clash swords astride their horses and on foot, but always to a stalemate. When morning breaks, Shivaji returns to his triumphant Gateway home and King Edward to the museum, both vowing to resume their duel.

Colonialism has been dispatched to the museum, and the postcolonial present summons Shivaji, Mahatma Gandhi, Bhagat Singh, Dadabhai Naoroji, and other regional and national icons to provide a different cultural significance to the city's topography. But all this effort at erasing history cannot expunge Mumbai's colonial past. Like King Edward, the colonial past refuses to be consigned to the museum. To begin with, the physical form of the city invites reflections on its colonial origin. Mumbai, it is said, stands on lands reclaimed from the Arabian Sea, as if the city had some prior claims on what lay buried underwater. In fact, the Island City occupies lands stolen from the sea. The deluge of July 2005 was a brutal reminder of the fact that the city represents the colonization of nature by culture. But this is not all there is to Mumbai's parasitical foundation.

The city's built environment also bears the marks of its colonial birth and development. In a country with settlements going back several millennia, Mumbai boasts of no ancient monument—no fort, palace, temple, or mosque—from the deep past. The monuments from the era of European trade and conquest are another matter; they bear testimony to Mumbai's doubly colonial history, pointing out that the seizure of lands from the sea for the urban settlement went hand in hand with the conquest of the territory and the people by European colonialism.

The period of Portuguese conquest is visible in the Roman Catholic churches scattered across the city. The signs of the Portuguese past, however, are mere footnotes to the massive presence of British colonialism, which is evident, most of all, in the Fort area of South Bombay. Here, a Portuguese-era gateway and sundial survive, but their presence is dwarfed by the outlines of the British-built colonial city. They outgrew the Fort, a castle surrounded by rampart walls that the East India Company constructed after they took over the Bombay islands from the Portuguese in 1688. To accommodate the growing settlement, the British tore down the rampart walls in 1862, starting a building boom in the late nineteenth century. In today's map you can easily distinguish the outlines of the colonial city that grew out of the Fort.

At its center is the imposing neoclassical Town Hall, housing the Asiatic Society Library, which leads westward to the circular Horniman (formerly Elphinstone) Circle garden and buildings complex, and then on to Hutatma Chowk (formerly Flora Fountain), Veer Nariman Road (formerly Churchgate Street), and the Arabian Sea. Close to the Town Hall stands the old Customs House, which, along

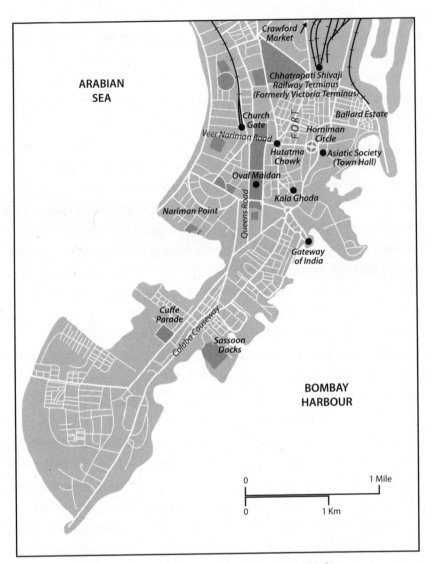

Within the map:

ARABIAN
SEA

Crawford
Market

Chhatrapati Shivaji
Railway Terminus
(Formerly Victoria Terminus)

Church
Gate

Ballard Estate

Veer Nariman Road

FORT

Horniman
Circle

Hutatma
Chowk

Asiatic Society
(Town Hall)

Oval Maidan

Kala Ghoda

Nariman Point

Queens Road

Gateway
of India

Cuffe
Parade

Colaba Causeway

Sassoon
Docks

BOMBAY
HARBOUR

0   1 Mile

0   1 Km

2.1. The Fort and its environs. Courtesy: Tsering W. Shawa

with the dockyard wall on Bhagat Singh Road (formerly Dockyard Road), calls to mind the era of European trade and conquest. Farther south and just beyond where the Fort walls once stood is the Gateway of India, built on the eastern waterfront to commemorate the visit of the Prince of Wales to the city in 1911. Farther south are the Colaba Causeway and Sassoon Docks, which represent the city's growth beyond the Fort walls, as do the cluster of Gothic Revival structures along the Maidan, and the arcaded commercial strip on Dadabhai Naoroji Road leading north to Chhatrapati Shivaji Terminus (formerly Victoria Terminus) and Crawford Market. Also in the north, on the eastern waterfront and beyond the old fort ramparts, is the Ballard Estate, a majestic European-style early-twentieth-century business district.

These signs of the colonial past, however, lack their gloss. The once-thriving ports on the eastern waterfront have lost much of their business to the port on the mainland. The cotton mills that sprang to life in the late nineteenth century, turning Bombay into an industrial city, are now frozen in silence. The Fort area no longer has the orderly urban form that it once enjoyed. Hawkers occupy the arcaded walkways. Riotous signboards cover the face of ornamented buildings. The pressure from heritage activists has succeeded to some extent in restoring the original structures and facades, but the colonial past appears without its aura. Indeed, the keystone heads embellishing the cleaned-up and restored archways draw attention only to their being out of time. The absent statue of King Edward VII in Kala Ghoda points to the ruination of colonial mastery. The parade of Gothic Revival architecture in South Bombay appears out of joint. In their afterlives, the colonial monuments and remnants exist without the halo that once gave them power.

Undoubtedly, Mumbai has changed. Portuguese rule ended long ago, and the British left in 1947. With Europeans gone, the city is now under Indian control. By Indianizing street and building names, by officially renaming Bombay Mumbai, the postcolonial present suggests that colonial control is over. Charting transformations primarily in terms of native-versus-alien rule, however, is to miss the histories lodged in the city's doubly parasitical birth and development. It assumes that the colonial past can be bleached out of Mumbai's historical existence as a metropolis and neatly appropriated by the postcolonial era. But the Dalit poet Namdeo Dhasal's eloquent rage, his searing accusation that the city is a slut, one that enchants only to deceive, draws attention to a deeper meaning of colonial oppression, one that did not end with the British departure. He exhorts us to revisit the Island City's past to disclose Mumbai's history as culture's triumph over nature; to see that its life as an emblem of cosmopolitan modernity is also an account of oppression and exploitation. His vengeful fury obliges us to ask: How did colonization come to represent the triumph of human artifice? What was involved in turning seven islets on the Arabian Sea into the modern Island City? How were its enchantments produced? What were the horrors that they concealed? With Dhasal's accusing finger as my guide, I set out to unearth this story of conquest and exploitation, of urban horror and oppression, in Mumbai's heroic narrative as a modern city.

THE CONQUEST OF THE ISLAND OF LOVE

The story begins in 1498. On May 20 Vasco da Gama landed in Calicut on the southwestern coast of India, seeking Christians and spices. The ruler, the zamorin of Calicut, rebuffed him. Undeterred, Gama returned for two more voyages. Thus began the era of European trade and conquest that would unite East and West and bring Bombay into the colonial world. The Portuguese spearheaded this venture, following Gama's historic voyage with repeated assaults on the western shores of the subcontinent. Francisco de Almeida, the first Portuguese viceroy, carried out a raid on Bombay in 1509, seizing cattle and killing local residents. The next two decades witnessed repeated raids on Bombay that thrust the Portuguese into hostilities with the chieftains of Gujarat's Muslim ruler, who claimed authority over these territories. Nuno da Cunha, the Portuguese governor-general of India, assaulted Bassein in 1532 with a fleet of one hundred vessels. Accompanied and blessed by Franciscan monks, Cunha led his soldiers into battle and seized the Bassein fort. He celebrated the victory in a mosque with fifty casks of wine and biscuits, tarts, beef, boiled ham, and cheese. Impressed with Portuguese power and hoping to enlist their aid against Mughal incursions, the Gujarat sultan conceded defeat and signed a treaty surrendering authority over Bassein, its dependent territories, and its seas to the king of Portugal.

The new rulers built their headquarters at Bassein, from where they ruled Bombay, which was then seven separate islets—Colaba, Old Woman's Island, Bombaim or Bom Bahia, Mazagaon, Parel, Worli, and Mahim. People on the islands lived by fishing, rice and coconut farming, and trading. They worshiped a number of different goddesses; among them was Mumba, the goddess from whose name the names Bombay and Mumbai are derived. The islands were covered with groves, and game was plentiful. The Portuguese called their newly acquired possession *a ilha da boa vida*, or the island of good life.

Writing in 1900, Gerson da Cunha, an early historian of Bombay, speculated that this idyllic image was the source of the mythical Island of Love in the Lusiads, the great sixteenth-century Portuguese epic poem. Composed by Luíz Vaz de Camões, "the Portuguese Virgil," the poem is an ode to the voyages made by his compatriots. In the epic, the Island of Love appears as a magical place created by Venus with the assistance of Cupid and the Nereids for the reception of mariners. On this miraculous island, beautiful nymphs await the heroic but weary seaman to rejuvenate them after their arduous oceanic journeys around the world.

Like others, Cunha acknowledges that the magical island is an allegory and that it is not located in the Indian seas. Yet, he speculates that Camões's imagination may well have drawn from the charming descriptions of the island penned by others, including his friend Garcia da Orta, the distinguished botanist. If this fictional image had a material reference, he argues, it must have been Bombay, not St. Helena, Angevida, or Zanzibar, as others have suggested. "Here was an island, as if floating on water in the midst of a beautiful group of is-

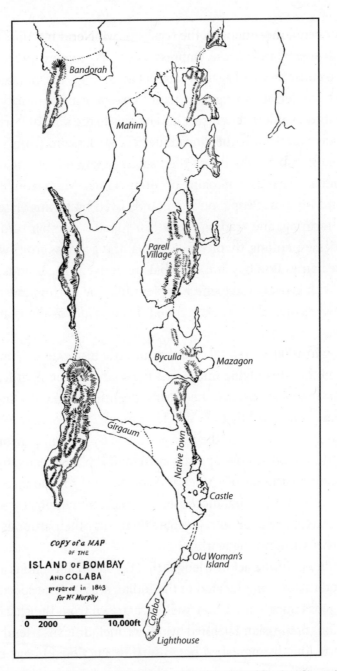

Copy of a MAP
OF THE
ISLAND OF BOMBAY
AND COLABA
prepared in 1843
for Mr Murphy

0   2000   10,000ft

Bandorah

Mahim

Parell
Village

Byculla

Mazagon

Girgaum

Native Town

Castle

Old Woman's
Island

Colaba

Lighthouse

2.2. Seven Islands. Source: S. M. Edwardes, *The Gazetteer of Bombay City and Island*, vol.
1 (Bombay: Times Press, 1909)

lands, not peopled perhaps by the Nymphs, the Nereids and Naiads, but by winsome Kôlis of the Negrito type, with the sea all around, and rivers, springs, trees, and mountains in the adjacent islands."[2]

Whether or not the island of good life was the source of the imagined paradise that Venus created, the Portuguese painted it in pastoral, soothing colors. They coveted the life of plenitude offered by its abundant rice, game, and fish. The conquerors rewarded their distinguished servants by leasing them fiefs, but there was no substantial immigration from Portugal. A century after the conquest, only eleven Portuguese families lived on the islands. Among the local population, the majority were Kolis, who subsisted primarily by fishing and farming. Garcia da Orta also mentions the Kunbis, who lived by agriculture; the Malis (gardeners); the Prabhus, who worked as accountants and merchants; the Bhandaris, who acted as peons; the Banias and the Parsis; and the lower-caste Deres or Farazes, "who eat everything, even dead things," and were "despised and hated by all."[3] There was also a small group of Muslims called the Naitias, whose Arab and Persian ancestors had married Hindu women on the Konkan Coast.

Conquest did not transform economic life; people continued to farm and fish. But the winds of change were unmistakable, and they blew with the force of religious fanaticism. Vasco da Gama is reported to have proclaimed that he had come in search of Christians and spices. The first order of business, then, was proselytization. The Franciscans, the Dominicans, and the Jesuits fanned out on the islands, destroying temples and mosques and building churches. The Franciscans built the church of St. Michael at Mahim. The Jesuits followed suit with the church of St. Andrew in Bandra. Churches in Sion, Dadar, Mazagaon, and Parel followed as the two orders vied with each other to spread Christianity. They were considerably strengthened by the king of Portugal's order in 1549 that civil authorities support the church. With its coffers overflowing, ecclesiastical power soared. It used this power to build churches and monasteries with forced labor and compelled many Kolis, Prabhus, Bhandaris, and Mahars to convert.

The Jesuits were especially zealous. They not only forced the Prabhus to convert but also used them as their subordinate agents to oppress the Brahmans.[4] The Brahmans posed a threat because they were suspected of inciting the converts to return to their ancestral faith. The Portuguese saw the Brahman endorsement of the annual ritual of bathing in the river to purify the soul as a deliberate provocation. According to their records, the Jesuits retaliated by planting crosses all along the river.[5] To avoid the crosses, the Brahmans retreated to an isolated lake. Incensed, the Jesuits sent musketeers and horsemen accompanied by civil authorities to disperse the bathers. Everyone fled, except for an ascetic covered in tiger skin. Speaking in Portuguese, he claimed that he was only emulating St. John the Baptist. The tables had turned. The Hindu convert to Christianity had ended up converting Christianity to Hinduism. The Jesuits were furious. They responded by demolishing the temple by the lake, smashing the idols, and slaughtering a cow, sprinkling its polluting blood in the water.

Subsequent history has written over this legacy of forced conversion and coerced labor but has not erased it completely. The traces of this legacy can be found in the presence of a small but noticeable Roman Catholic community, churches, and Portuguese street and neighborhood names. They remind us that although the Portuguese pioneered the European maritime route to India, their main concern was Christianity. While they searched for Christians, others voyaged on the sea route they had charted to seek the riches of the East. In 1583 the first English traders set foot on the western shores of the subcontinent. Three decades later, the East India Company established a foothold in Surat. From there, they eyed the natural advantages of Bombay as a naval base. Joined by the Dutch, they attacked Bombay in 1626, torching the manor house that was originally built by Garcia da Orta.

Bombay's modern birth occurred in this crucible of European overseas conquest. The Portuguese contributed, by first seizing the "island of good life" and then gifting it as a dowry to the English when Catherine of Braganza married Charles II in 1661. Seven years later, when the Crown leased Bombay to the East India Company, conquest was rewritten as lawful possession. Now that the Portuguese were history, a new chapter opened in Bombay's modern life— its growth as a port city under the company.

BLACK GOLD AND KING COTTON

Under the British, Bombay developed its reputation as a city of commerce, a dynamic trading and banking center serviced by merchants belonging to different communities. It is a well-deserved reputation, and one that rings true even today despite the recent rise in communal tension. Go to any bazaar in the city, and you will find a medley of castes and communities eagerly transacting business. But the sordid origins of this mercantile cosmopolitanism involved ruthless profiteering from opium, cotton, and labor.

Soon after acquiring the island, the East India Company's first order of business was to build Bombay Castle on the site where Garcia da Orta's Manor House had once stood. A few decades after the company shifted its headquarters from Surat to Bombay in 1686 to escape the bruising Maratha attacks, the Fort became a well-defended walled town. It had fortified gates, a bastion that could mount several cannons, a marine force to defend the dockyard, and St. Thomas Church, where the Europeans could pray. The British nurtured the fortified town as a commercial center by encouraging merchants from Gujarat to migrate to their settlement. Among these, none were more prominent than the Parsis.[6] The Zoroastrians had never been traders; after fleeing from Persia in the eighth century to escape Muslim persecution, they settled as agriculturists in Gujarat. The network of European trade, however, drew them into the world of commerce. They developed close ties to the company in Surat, acting as interpreters and agents, provisioning and building ships for the Europeans. When the company shifted its headquarters to Bombay, they followed and quickly became the most important and wealthy mercantile community. They were not alone. Hindu and Jain merchants of the Bania caste and Muslims of the Bohra, Khoja, and Memon communities from Gujarat flocked to exploit the opportunities that the new colonial settlement offered. The merchants settled in separate enclaves in the Bazaar Gate area at the northern end of the Fort, which developed as the "native" town, a mix of houses and bazaars. The British lived in the south, with the east-west axis of Churchgate Street forming the boundary between Europeans and Indians.

Bombay flourished with the influx of immigrants, with many settling beyond the walls of the crowded fortified town. However, it remained a remote British outpost for much of the eighteenth century. It was poorly connected with the mainland to the east, which remained under Maratha sway until the early nineteenth century. It experienced exponential growth only after the abolition of the East India Company's monopoly in 1813, which sparked a rapid rise in trade. Close on its heels came the victory over the Marathas in 1818, which brought much of western India under company rule and opened up central India to British control. With private European traders now trawling for Eastern riches, and vast new territories opened for exploitation, Bombay's growth prospects improved dramatically.

The turn in fortunes came with the growing trade in opium to China. Since the late eighteenth century, the company had developed a system of opium cultivation in eastern India under its monopoly. It would auction the produce in Calcutta for transportation to China, where it was sold to pay for Chinese tea and silk. Encouraged by the growing trade, private merchants circumvented company monopoly and procured opium from Malwa in central India, shipping it from Daman, a port held by the Portuguese. The British countered by encouraging traders to bring the Malwa opium to Bombay.

The city's merchants seized the opportunity. Attracted by the high profit margins, they took to the opium trade with great vigor. According to a historian, early Victorian Bombay became an "opium city."[7] By the 1820s the city surpassed Calcutta in bullion remittances from China.[8] Revenue from opium strengthened the colonial government's monetary reserves, paid for part of the costs of the empire, and filled the coffers of Bombay's mercantile communities. The Parsis took the lead. They already had a close relationship with the company as brokers, interpreters, distillers, and shipbuilders, and they enjoyed close business ties with European firms.[9] They had also established a presence in China. The Readymoney family's involvement with the China trade, for example, began as early as 1756. They owned several ships and amassed great wealth, acquiring their surname on account of their readiness to advance money.[10] Similarly, the Camas and the Wadias also developed a long-standing presence in the China trade.

The king of the opium trade, however, was Sir Jamsetjee Jejeebhoy, whose name is ubiquitous in the city's public spaces. Few remember that the man whose name graces the famous art school Sir J. J. School of Art and the popular Sir J. J. Hospital earned his exalted place through drug trafficking. Nor is it often mentioned that the opium traffic was part of Britain's illustrious "civilizing mission" to uplift the natives through the taste of free trade. Jejeebhoy certainly enjoyed the taste of it. Born to a poor artisan family in Bombay in 1783, his rags-to-riches story is the stuff that has made up the Island City's mythic life as the city of gold. He grew up in Navsari, Gujarat, and returned to Bombay at the age of sixteen, after losing both parents in quick succession. For three years he worked at his uncle's shop, counting and selling empty bottles. He made his first trip to China in 1800 as an accounts clerk for another Parsi merchant.[11] On his second voyage, he traveled as his uncle's partner. In 1805 his fourth voyage aboard the *Brunswick* was eventful. The French captured the ship in July on its way to China. After several months of adventures aboard the ship as it sailed to Ceylon (Sri Lanka,) Malagasy (Madagascar), and the Cape of Good Hope, Jejeebhoy finally made his way back to Calcutta in December on a Danish vessel. This misadventure cost him dearly—the French confiscated his cargo and robbed him of his belongings—but it had one profitable outcome. Aboard the *Brunswick,* he met the ship's assistant surgeon, William Jardine, who, in partnership with James Matheson, would go on to found Jardine Matheson and Company in 1832. As this firm quickly became the dominant force in Canton, its principal supplier of opium turned out to be none other than Jardine's fellow captive on the *Brunswick.* Jejeebhoy had not let captivity and financial loss dampen his enthusiasm for the China trade. He made one final trip to Canton in 1807. Seven years later, he acquired the first of his fleet of seven ships and began chartering several more to service his expanding business. His wanderlust and determination paid off. The orphan from Navsari had become a merchant prince. As his biographer remarks, the "rolling stone had gathered golden moss!"[12]

Jamsetjee was far from being the lone profiteer from the lucrative opium trade. The commerce was vast, and many drank from the deep well of the drug trade profits—Europeans, Parsis, Hindu Banias and Marwaris, and Konkani Muslims. Among the largest dealers were names that, like Jejeebhoy, still adorn public spaces and buildings in Bombay—the Wadias, the Cowasjis, Motichund Aminchund, Khemchund Motichund, and others. These men combined their interlocking interests in cotton, opium, banking, brokerage, and shipping to become great merchant princes of the city. Their drive in pursuing commercial opportunities and the fortunes that they amassed helped to establish Bombay's image as a place of untold wealth. In fact, they owed their wealth to Bombay's particular colonial history.

Unlike Bengal and Madras, the territories of western India were not under the control of the East India Company until well into the nineteenth century, thus offering Indian merchants an opening. This also suited the British, who depended on indigenous merchants for their needs in the isolated fort town of Bombay and for servicing cotton and opium exports to China. By the mid-nineteenth century, Bombay had developed into a thriving port city. Its population rose from 162,000 in 1826 to 566,000 in 1849.[13] However, the conditions for Indian merchants were changing. The British shipping interests, enjoying official patronage and access to dominant international networks of finance, edged out the indigenous shipowners. With a similar advantage, the British managing agencies also narrowed the opportunities for Indian merchants in the China trade. Ever resourceful, Indian capital sought alternative opportunities. It turned to cotton mills.

Parsi merchants began exporting cotton to Lancashire in the early nineteenth century. Jamsetjee had reportedly made huge profits in this trade during the Napoleonic Wars.[14] However, Lancashire preferred the long-stapled American supply to the short-stapled Indian variety. The big break came during the American Civil War in the 1860s when, starved of supplies, Lancashire turned to Indian raw cotton. "The produce of all the great cotton fields of India," wrote Sir Richard Temple, "found its way to Bombay in order to be exported to England with all possible dispatch, while the high prices ruled and the blockade of the South American ports lasted."[15] According to one estimate, this sudden turn in fortune added £70 to £75 million to Bombay's wealth.[16]

Joint-stock companies, banks, insurance firms, and financial schemes proliferated to ride the sudden tidal wave of wealth. A speculative flame enveloped the city as brokers tried to gain an advantage by attempting to obtain intelligence on the latest prices in Liverpool. While Europeans gathered in the stock exchange, Indian brokers with no fixed offices milled around at the junction of Meadows Street and Rampart Row, seeking shade under fig trees or "paper umbrellas of the Chinese type."[17] Stoking the fire was Premchund Roychund, a successful Bania merchant whose skills in high finance had won him close ties with the city's leading European businessmen and access to predictions in the Liverpool cotton market.[18] Using these to his advantage, Roychund established agencies in cotton-growing districts and amassed a fortune. He stimulated such speculation in shares that he earned the title of "Supreme Pontiff of Speculation."[19]

But the boom was short-lived. The cessation of the American Civil War brought cotton prices crashing down. The wild fluctuations only underlined the difficulty Indian cotton traders faced. As in the China trade, Indian cotton-export merchants had to cope with the entry of well-financed European agency houses with better market information and access to insurance facilities. Their entry forced Indian capital to play a subordinate role. The nimble Parsi merchants responded by establishing cotton mills. As Raj Chandavarkar points out, this was not a case of linear progression from trade to industry but a defensive reaction by their subordination to the larger and more resourceful expatriate capital.[20] Cotton mills offered the advantages of diversification. When raw cotton prices turned unfavorable, the cotton traders could easily switch to the manufacture of yarn for export to China, deploying the raw cotton stock according to market conditions. Supplies became readily available with the opening of the railways in the 1850s and their extension in the following decades, connecting Bombay to the cotton-growing areas of the Deccan.

Once again it was a Parsi, Kavasji Nanabhai Davar, who established the first cotton-spinning mill in 1854. His Bombay Weaving and Spinning Company was a joint-stock firm, with its one hundred shares owned largely by Parsi merchants. Soon afterward, Manakji Nasarvanji Petit, a successful China trader, established the Oriental Spinning and Weaving Company. Other Parsi merchants followed— Byramjee Jejeebhoy, Mancherji Naoroji Banaji, the Camas, and the

Wadias. Though dominant, the Parsis were not alone. The Bhatia magnate Varjivandas Madhavdas was another notable player. So was the family of David Sassoon, the Baghdadi Jew, who, fleeing persecution in Baghdad, arrived in Bombay via Persia in 1832. He rose very quickly up the ranks of Bombay's mercantile elite, establishing a countinghouse and warehouse. Advancing money to other traders and trading in commodities, he soon became a force in the China trade. As his business prospered, he became an equal to the leading Parsi merchants. His son, Abdullah, known later as Sir Albert Sassoon, established a cotton-weaving and spinning mill and built the Sassoon Docks in 1875, then the largest in the city. Later he moved to England, earned a baronet, and married into the Rothschild family.

The Sassoons profited from the rapid growth of the cotton industry in Bombay. The number of mills grew from 1854, when the first mill was founded, to 28 by 1875, when they employed over 13,000 workers. Two decades later, there were 70 mills employing nearly 76,000 workers, and by 1925, there were 82 mills with 148,000 workers.[21] The growth was largely due to the demand in the China yarn market. In response, the Bombay mills expanded their yarn output. Spinning forged ahead, but looms lagged behind. This was also because, under the colonial government, India was one of the most open markets for cotton textiles. Faced with the competition from Lancashire in the domestic woven-goods market, Bombay took refuge in the China market for yarn. This lopsided growth was not its only weakness. As Chandavarkar astutely suggests, the industry as a whole rested on shaky foundations.[22] He argues that the inception of cotton mills did not represent a structural transformation in the Indian economy. Rather, it was a defensive measure to spread the risks in view of the growing stranglehold of European firms in trade. This meant that the industry operated under several constraints. The narrow industrialization of the economy limited the purchasing power of the domestic market, exposing cotton mills to the fluctuations in international trade. The limited indus-

2.3. Raw cotton for Bombay mills. Courtesy: British Library Board, photo 364/12 (42).

trial base also meant that the mills were dependent on the import of expensive machinery from overseas.

The upshot of the constraints under which the cotton industry developed was that it depended on the supply of cheap labor for profitability. Thousands of migrants from the immediate hinterland and beyond flocked to the city. Most came from the Deccan and Konkan areas, particularly the Ratnagiri District. Migrants from the United Provinces began to swell the workers' ranks in the 1880s, and their number increased substantially in the twentieth century.[23] The flow of rural migrants was not due to any fundamental structural transformation in the countryside. It was not as if large numbers of peasants were suddenly thrown off the land and became an agricultural proletariat. Rather, the slow but relentless demographic and commercial pressure on the countryside drove many to the city to seek a livelihood to supplement the family income in the village. The presence of this cheap pool of labor allowed the mill owners to employ as much as 28 percent of the labor force in Bombay on a daily basis.[24] The use of casual labor on such a scale was not conducive to developing a skilled and stable workforce, but it permitted the owners to adjust their production according to market fluctuations. Of course, workers paid the price for this flexibility, another sordid secret of Bombay's rise as an industrial city.

By the early twentieth century, the city's population was nearly a million, of whom only a quarter had been born in the city.[25] The mills, located in central Bombay, employed only 18 percent of the population, but the share of industrial employment as a whole was over 30 percent.[26] Many more worked as general laborers and domestic servants and in trades such as petty grocers, peddlers, hawkers, tailors, cobblers, and barbers. Religious and linguistic diversity marked this teeming immigrant population. The Hindus were dominant, constituting 65 percent of the population in 1901, and Muslims made up 20 percent, followed by smaller percentages of Christians, Zoroastrians, Jains, and Jews.[27] The gross figures on religion, however, conceal the city's true diversity, for religious communities were made up of different linguistic groups. Slightly more than 50 percent of the population spoke Marathi, 27 percent were Gujarati speakers, and nearly 15 percent spoke Hindi and Urdu, followed by smaller proportions of other language groups.[28]

This dazzling mélange of communities and tongues imparted an image of openness and promise to Bombay. The city teemed with industrialists, merchants, bankers, brokers, shipping agents, shopkeepers, artisans, clerks, mill hands, dockworkers, and casual laborers. The mills and dockyards hummed with activity, and the jangle of money filled the air in company offices and bazaars. With the toil and sweat of immigrant workers, the city's businessmen amassed great fortunes. Bombay became the city of gold.

With the city rising as a hub of colonial trade and industry, its physical shape changed. Lands and seas were colonized to accommodate a growing urban society. Municipal administration and modern transportation produced a new map of the city, which burst out beyond the Fort. The British celebrated Bombay's rise as a modern city by dressing the new public buildings in Gothic Revival architecture, thus underscoring the imperial genealogy of its modernity.

The Portuguese had mooted the idea of reclaiming lands submerged under the sea, but this process began in earnest only under the East India Company. Under the governorship of William Hornby, the British constructed an embankment on Worli Creek. Completed in 1784, the Hornby Vellard protected the low-lying areas of the island from flooding during high tide and opened the way for subsequent reclamations. By 1838 these reclamations, the filling of breaches and the construction of bunds and roadways, had joined the seven islets into a single island. The boom in the cotton trade in the 1860s in response to the American Civil War produced a commercial delirium that unleashed a mania of reclamation projects. Speculative companies sprang into existence, and the government swung into action to advance Bombay's eastern and western foreshores, which, until 1860, according to James Maclean's *Guide to Bombay*, "was one foul cesspool, sewers discharging on the road, rocks used only for the purposes of nature."[29] The bottom fell out of the cotton boom with the end of the American Civil War in 1865, but the city was transformed by the reclamation ventures. Swamps were drained, ditches and tanks were filled, and the ocean was beaten back. By 1872 reclamations had added four million square yards to the city, increasing the island's area from eighteen to twenty-two square miles.[30]

Vital to the expansion and transformation of urban space was the governorship of Bartle Frere from 1862 to 1867. Frere's reign was short, but he was an energetic imperialist and urban planner whose ambitious plans for Bombay's development had long-lasting effects. He began by ordering the demolition of the rampart walls as soon as he took office. The order recognized the fact that the city had outgrown its origins as a garrison town. The fortifications no longer served any purpose, and the only function that the ditches performed was to store stagnant and foul water that bred disease. Thus, following Frere's order, the Apollo, Bazaar, and Church Gates were demolished. The walls were leveled, and trenches were filled. The integration of the Fort with the rest of the island sent land values soaring, encouraging further reclamations. Swamps were drained, tanks and quarries were sealed, and flats were raised to the level of roads. These measures opened up lands for mills and workers' chawls, or tenements. Simultaneously, the government built new roads, widened old ones, and completed the construction of overbridges.[31]

"A new Bombay arose, phoenix like from the debris of the old fort," write Sharada Dwivedi and Rahul Mehrotra.[32] They point to the Elphinstone (now Horniman) Circle as the first remarkable piece of new urban form to emerge. It was built on the site of the Bombay Green, a large open space in the old town. The plan for converting this space into a circle had originated before Frere's tenure, but it was he who sanctioned its development. The land was bought by the municipality, which sold it at a profit as building lots to English mercantile firms, who then developed the garbage-strewn open space into a striking garden complex. When completed in 1872, the complex incorporated the neoclassical Town Hall. It consisted of a circular central garden surrounded by architecturally unified buildings with uniform facades and covered arcades at the ground level.

The razing of the ramparts also opened up the Esplanade, the vast open space outside the walls that had hitherto provided the military with a clear firing range from the Fort. Once freed from the military's claim, the government allotted the land for building lots and wide roads. The large unbroken stretch was divided into four

2.4. View of Elphinstone Circle from Town Hall. Courtesy: British Library Board, photo 2/3 (7)

maidans—Azad and Cross in the north, Oval and Cooperage in the south. During the next few decades, a succession of public buildings extending from south to north rose up along the maidans. Frere had called for the construction of such buildings to enhance the image of the colonial government and to exercise its authority more effectively.[33] Once constructed, these Gothic Revival buildings confidently looked outward to the Arabian Sea and assertively staged the city as an imperial spectacle.

Much has changed in and around the southern core of the city, but Gothic buildings from the late nineteenth century still stand at attention as you walk up the old Esplanade.[34] The Gothic parade begins with the elephantine Secretariat, designed by General Henry St Clair Wilkins. Housing the administration until the 1950s, its Venetian Gothic style expressed the remoteness of colonial power. Next come the Bombay University buildings, set in neatly manicured lawns. They include the university library in yellow sandstone topped by the soaring Rajabai Clock Tower. The clock tower, which invokes London's Big Ben, was built with funds donated by Premchund Roy-

2.5. The Gothic parade. Courtesy: British Library Board, photo 807/1(2).

chund, the wealthy nineteenth-century cotton merchant and broker, and is named after his mother. This is followed by the High Court, its weighty authority cast in a fortresslike structure (though curiously a one-eyed monkey holding the scales of justice stands on one of the pillars). The Public Works Office and the Bombay, Baroda, and Central Indian Railway headquarters, designed in what is called Oriental Gothic, complete the Gothic procession. However, the desire to dress the colonial space in Gothic garb is evident elsewhere too. You can spot it in the towers and onion domes of the Bombay Municipal Corporation Building. It is also evident in the arcaded walkways on Hornby Road (now Dadabhai Naoroji Road) that leads up to Victoria Terminus, the high point of Bombay Gothic. Designed by F. W. Stevens, this lavish knot of towers, domes, spires, cornices, and gargoyles was completed in 1888.

Built at the intersection of major roads with the docks and harbor behind it, Victoria Terminus encapsulated the essence of Bombay's transformation. As a major railway station, it expressed the city's industrial and commercial underpinnings. This was underscored by a series of sculptures placed on the exterior—*Commerce*, *Agriculture*, and *Engineering*. The figure of Progress atop the central dome, carry-

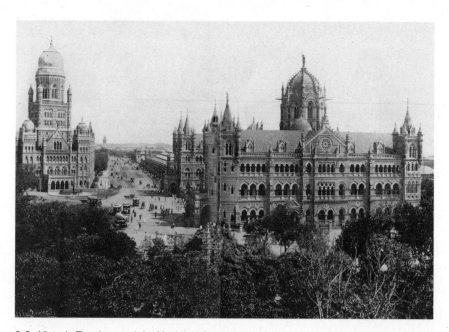

2.6. Victoria Terminus and the Municipal Corporation. Courtesy: Sharada Dwivedi and Rahul Mehrotra, *Bombay: The Cities Within* (Bombay: India Book House, 1995).

ing a copper gilt flaming torch in her right hand and a winged wheel in her left, clearly proclaims the underlying ideology.[35] While projecting the colonizing power of capitalist commerce and industry, the richly sculptured Gothic architecture of Victoria Terminus also expressed British colonial power over the city.

The transformation that began with Frere's demolition of the Fort's walls was contemporaneous with Baron Haussmann's redevelopment of Paris and the construction of the Ringstrasse in Vienna.[36] As in Europe, the construction program created the new spatial complex of the modern city of Bombay. However, there was one major difference. Bombay was a colonial city. This meant that its urban projects epitomized and represented their colonial conditions. Industrialization, built on the backs of cheap labor and appallingly inadequate housing and public infrastructure facilities, went hand in hand with grand building projects. The preindustrial Gothic buildings functioned not so much to screen the shaky industrial edifice

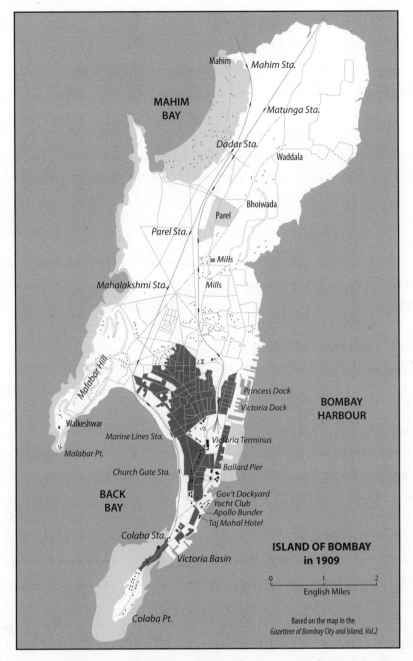

MAHIM
BAY

Mahim   Mahim Sta.

Matunga Sta.

Dadar Sta.

Waddala

Bhoiwada

Parel

Parel Sta.

Mills

Mahalakshmi Sta.   Mills

Malabar Hill

Princess Dock

Victoria Dock

BOMBAY
HARBOUR

Walkeshwar

Marine Lines Sta.

Victoria Terminus

Malabar Pt.

Church Gate Sta.   Ballard Pier

BACK
BAY

Gov't Dockyard
Yacht Club
Apollo Bunder
Taj Mahal Hotel

Colaba Sta.

ISLAND OF BOMBAY
in 1909

Victoria Basin

0   1   2
English Miles

Colaba Pt.

Based on the map in the
Gazetteer of Bombay City and Island, Vol.2

2.7. The Island City in 1909. Source: S. M. Edwardes, *The Gazetteer of Bombay City and Island*, vol. 2 (Bombay: Times Press, 1909).

as to project it in the image of a European city. Architectural styles and sculptural designs fashioned from ransacking the European past were not merely decorative but expressions of colonial urbanism. The imperial spectacle they produced was no myth, no mere illusion to be set against the reality of the city. On the contrary, Elphinstone Circle and the Gothic buildings, together with British street names, intersections marked by statues, and fountains commemorating European figures and cultural symbols staged the modern city as a colonial city. No wonder, a Briton remarked in 1899, that Bombay was "a proud and comely city," a place where "the Briton feels himself a greater man."[37]

The European city in the colony in which the Britons took pride radiated the alluring images of European civilization and civic consciousness. Its residents were expected to earn their livelihood in docks, mills, and assorted capitalist institutions and to function under the colonial authority encased in Gothic Revival architecture. They were to settle their disputes in British courts, study in Western-style schools and colleges, travel on new roadways and railways, write letters delivered by the postal system, stroll in its arcaded walkways, relax and play sports on the maidans, and value the public space of fountains and squares marked by the statues of imperial figures. There was never any doubt that entry into this urban order was conditional on the acceptance of colonial authority, that alien power and culture underpinned the public space of avenues, parks, educational institutions, and learned societies. There was also little likelihood that the poor could live the ideal of colonial urbanism, but then this ideal was staged as the pedagogic model that the natives were expected to learn from and emulate.

The indigenous elites were quick to learn from the colonial model, none more rapidly and completely than the Parsis. Even as they zealously maintained their religion and identity, their homes were furnished in European style, they dressed in English clothes, their education was Western, and cricket, golf, tennis, and bridge became their pastimes. Identifying with the British, they also bought into the colonial urban ideal. They contributed handsomely to various charities and donated funds for several public institutions. The evidence of their philanthropic investment in the city is visible all over Bombay today; several neighborhoods, squares, statues, and public buildings are named after the nineteenth-century Parsi families—Sir J. J. School of Art, J. J. Hospital, Petit Library, Jehangir Art Gallery, and many others. Equally prominent in contributing to this imaginary were the Sassoons, who used their wealth to fund a number of charitable projects. They founded synagogues and established the Sassoon Mechanics Institute—rechristened in 1938 as the David Sassoon Library and Reading Room—to foster the knowledge of mechanical models and architectural design. Today, a regular flow of patrons can be seen in the library, consulting its impressive rare book collection and enjoying a cool retreat from the scorching summer sun in its splendid Venetian Gothic building. Evidently less appreciated is the considerable contribution the family made to the erection of the colossal King Edward statue at Kala Ghoda, which few even know about.

This imperial city of Gothic architecture and European culture was built upon and enabled another form of colonization—the colonization of nature. As the breaches were filled, embankments were built, lands were reclaimed, roadways and tramways were laid, buildings and mills were constructed, and new urban institutions arose, the physical space was treated as an abstract object that could be manipulated and reshaped at will. This involved the repression of the existing meanings of particular cultural significance that people attached to specific spaces.

The story of this colonization of meanings can be gleaned from Govind Narayan Madgavkar's Marathi text *Mumbaichi Varnan*.[38] Written in 1863, his eyewitness account of Bombay as it was undergoing far-reaching transformations is the first full description of the city in any language. Writing of the construction of the Worli embankment,

Madgavkar recounts an oral tradition preserved in a *bakhar*, the traditional chronicle. According to the bakhar, the embankment kept collapsing during its construction. The Indian engineer who was entrusted with the task of supervising the construction had a dream in which the goddesses Mahalaxmi, Mahakali, and Mahasaraswati appeared. They commanded him to retrieve their idols, which lay buried in the seabed, and install them in a temple. When the engineer followed the divine orders, building the Mahalaxmi temple, the goddesses blessed the construction of the embankment.[39] Such stories appear frequently in Madgavkar's text. Sometimes, as in the case of the Worli embankment, they relate to reclaimed land; at other times to temples, shrines, and particular neighborhoods. He declares the legends fanciful and unverifiable by the standards of historiography, but recounts them nevertheless while offering an admiring description of the city's progress under the British. It is as if the existing meanings of land and neighborhoods, subordinated and reduced to rubble by the onward march of colonial modernity, rise up as ghosts to extract a revenge on the rationalist chronicler's text of progress.

URBAN PICTURES

Since Max Weber, it is customary to view modern life as disenchanted, freed of gods and myth. But what was colonial Bombay if not enchanted? The physical, social, and political geography forged by colonization in the double sense became its "natural" landscape. To its inhabitants, the city looked, felt, and smelled like a new environment. It was different from the towns and urban life that most immigrants had encountered elsewhere. The modern city's infrastructure, technology, institutions, neighborhoods, society, and daily life presented a novel sight and experience. The newness of its "second nature," the everyday reality that its institutions and the built environment had forged, became objects of wonder and reflection.

Bombay's rapidly changing visual landscape fostered a form of urban writing that described the city in terms of images. This phenomenon was similar to the flânerie that Walter Benjamin wrote about so compellingly in his reflections on Charles Baudelaire and in the fragmentary observations contained in his *Arcades*.[40] Writers in Bombay also depicted the city as a collection of pictures, reading its buildings, streets, traffic, and social groups as visual signatures of "second nature." They portrayed Bombay at the level of the everyday, identifying the existence of the modern city in the portraits of its daily routines. But they acted less as realist witnesses and more as myth-makers. Offering the observer's view of the cityscape rather than the subjective experience of the urban dweller, they produced hyperbolic and extravagant descriptions, presenting Bombay as a happening place. There is a guidebook quality to their writings.

Consider, for example, Sir Dinshaw Wacha's (1844–1936) *Shells from the Sands of Bombay*, which contains his recollections of the city between 1860 and 1875 and a survey of Bombay's history.[41] Born in the city and educated at Elphinstone College, Wacha lived through the period of Bombay's expansion and building boom. He worked as an accountant in the mills and became one of the most prominent Parsi politicians of his time. He was a founding member of the Indian National Congress, serving as its president in 1901, and a member of the Bombay and Imperial Legislative Councils. A moderate nationalist who deeply appreciated the British presence, he was knighted in 1917.

Wacha was also a prolific writer, whose works register the deep impression left by the urban form of Bombay that the British and Indian elites had assembled. He described in great detail and with palpable affection the founding of the mint, post office, police, civil and criminal courts, railways, telegraph, mills, trading houses, chamber of commerce, and Western educational institutions. These institutions have become so much of an accepted part of our world that it is now difficult to appreciate the spell cast by their newness during his time. For him, the modern city of sanitary works and piped water supply unfolding before his eyes was an object of wonder. He even penned a book of over four hundred pages on the history of the Bombay Municipal Corporation.[42]

Referring to the introduction of the railways and telegraph, "two marvels of applied science discovered by the occidental mind and implanted on the Oriental soil," he wrote: "Let the reader stretch his imagination and ruminate on the condition of semi-darkness which was prevalent in all India."[43] Describing the development of the postal system, he called it a "glorious evolution." He noted the introduction of undreamed-of facilities—money orders, post savings banks, postal insurance, and the postcard. "And yet one's appetite grows on what it feeds. Here we are in the year of grace 1920, clamoring for a bi-weekly mail and still further improvements and facilities."[44] The construction of wet docks and the pioneering role the Sassoons played in building the Sassoon Docks merited fulsome praise.[45] Open sewers and drains received severe strictures.[46] As one reads his breathless praise and stern criticisms, it becomes clear that the urban form forged by colonial modernization had become firmly lodged in his consciousness.

But Wacha was no mere chronicler of Britain's work in India. He wrote as an urbanite, deeply conscious of his city as a distinct form of social existence. As much as he admired the changes the British introduced, his primary concern was their impact on the city. Watching Bombay transform before his eyes convinced him it was no longer just a colonial outpost but also a dynamic city that had assumed a life of its own. Though developed and shaped by alien rule, it had a vitality and an identity derived from commerce. It was an upstart city, a parvenu, whose buildings lacked the stately dignity that only the possession of a deep past could provide.[47] So strongly rooted was the city in the worship of commerce that its temples and mosques inspired neither reverence nor awe, neither beauty nor joy.[48] Instead, Bombay was defined by its newness.

The consciousness of newness was reflected not only in Wacha's rapturous attention to the establishment of the railways, docks, and municipal government but also in his readings of the signs of modern urban life. He wrote, for example, of "air eating" by the Parsis on the maidan, a wide expanse of green that stretched beyond the fort walls.[49] Here, groups of young and old, "but almost all of the sterner sex," could be seen sitting on China mats in circles. In the middle a large lantern or an oil lamp would shed its light on the "air-eating" group. The men on mats played cards or chess and engaged in the "*goube-mouche* of the day, replete with town gossip and light criticism on men and things happening during the day." Another group could be seen listening with keen curiosity and bated breath to the thrilling legends of ancient Persian heroes read by a Parsi priest or layperson well versed in Gujarati and Persian. While adults amused themselves in these activities, "boys and girls, in their silk frocks, and quaint caps of *kinkob* from Surat, or embroidered in Berlin wool, would carry on their gambols all innocent in their happiness." Vendors, also Parsi, would move from group to group, selling sugarcane by "calling out 'Ganderi, goolab ganderi'" (Sugarcane, rosy sugarcane).

We should not think of Wacha's remembrances of evenings on the maidan and the brisk trade in English toys as a compendium of meaningless facts. The quotidian, Henri Lefebvre writes, is where people are born, live, and die. "They live well or ill; but they live in everyday life."[50] The routines and objects of daily life are forms in which society is produced and reproduced. It was precisely the existence of the city *as* society at the level of the everyday that Wacha sought to capture in the images of daily occurrences on the maidan. The descriptions of China mats, silk frocks, and caps were not mere decorative flourishes but visual signs in which he read the city's existence. He identified these signs in the public spaces of the city, reading maidans, streets, shops, theaters—including places of "vulgar entertainment by the popular classes"—and eating establishments as visible expressions of the changing city. The meticulous cataloging of objects and places served to portray an order behind the surface of seeming flux and clutter.

The rapturous representation of the kaleidoscopic but orderly city was also a prominent strain in Govind Narayan Madgavkar's description of Bombay. Presenting his account of the city as an eyewitness portrayal of a visitor, he noted with wonder the sight of the dazzling range of communities that lived in the city. Offering an early portrait of Bombay as a cosmopolitan city, he wrote that just "the Marathi language comes in thirty or forty dialects" and estimated that there were about a hundred fifty varieties of Hindus. "Then there are other communities—Parsis, Muslims, Jews, Arabs, ... etc. In addition, the English, Portuguese, French, Dutch, Turks, Germans, Armenians, Chinese and such other hat-wearers are visible in all directions."[51] He reported a man from Konkan dumbstruck by the sight of the city. "Amazing! Your Mumbai is just like Paradise. If one doesn't visit Mumbai at least once in a lifetime, life is not worth having lived."[52] Hari Narayan Apte's 1889 novel described a woman's expression of awe and wonder at the scale and style of buildings, the mills, "the chimneys touching the sky," and the sheer size of the city. "I had imagined Bombay only as a city far greater than Poona. ... But the reality was incredible. What carriages! What tramways! O no! All was quite unimaginable."[53]

The visual medley and the intense stimuli in the crowded bazaars of Indian neighborhoods were captivating. Madgavkar wrote enthusiastically about the neighborhood of Dongri and Bhendi Bazaar, where Muslim merchants of the Kutchi, Memon, Khoja, and Bohra communities predominated. "One can experience many unique sights and sounds in these areas—a profusion of workshops—splendid shops—closely packed houses—crowds of people—goods of all kinds being transported—the jangling of pole-slings—noisy vehicles, shouts and screams of labourers—and a variety of goods being transported in carts."[54] He represents the bazaars in Kalbadevi, Bhuleshwar, Null, and elsewhere as a richly embroidered urban tapestry—shops of businessmen and moneylenders, someone selling sweets while others hawk cloth, an oil mill here and a stable there, shops with Chinese bangles and trinkets made of lac, a soda-water factory, vendors selling Kashmiri shawls, jewelers, and perfume sellers.

Such readings and celebrations of the buildings, bazaars, streets, alleys, and crowds offered the idling flaneur's observation of urban variety. Absent from them was the depiction of the perplexing, disquieting experience of the modern city. This task was left to the writers on crime. Walter Benjamin suggested that the detective shares with the flaneur an attention to minute visual details.[55] While the literary observer is fascinated by aesthetic concerns, and the detective is driven by the motive to solve crimes, both gather and read visual details as codes that unlock the meaning of their respective stories. One can witness this feature in a book published in 1896, detailing the work of Sardar Mir Abdul Ali, a police detective.[56] Its author, Naoroji M. Dumasia, was a reporter for the newspaper *Bombay Gazette*. This is not surprising, for newspapers were, after all, in the forefront of fashioning the observations of the everyday life of the city.

Dumasia opens a section entitled "Criminal Life in Bombay" by describing the Island City as a thriving metropolis, "the gateway of all sorts of adventurous people who visit the country." He follows this with a caution: "As we pass through the busy bazaars of Bombay, and look upon its teeming masses of people of every nation, we little dream of the crime that exists, of the various kinds of villainy that are continually being practiced there." The experience of being swindled and cheated is common. "What stranger to Bombay, or indeed any other Indian town, has not discovered after, perhaps, he has gone home chuckling with the idea that he has driven an excellent bargain, that he has after all been tricked by the wily Borah, who sleepy though he may appear as he lazily smokes his hookah by his shop floor, serenely indifferent to all that is going around him, is much more wide-awake than he looks."[57]

In Dumasia's account, the city was deceptive; its complexity and appearance concealed what went on under the surface. To survive in this environment, one had to read the signs correctly; read them wrong, and you were likely to be duped. This is what happened to a Marwari merchant who was sitting one afternoon in his shop in the bazaar.[58] A landau, "drawn by a pair of well-caparisoned horses, stopped at his door." Out from the carriage stepped a "Hindu lady, who, from her rich dress and the servants who accompanied her, appeared to be connected in some way with the house of a Native Chief." The lady bought small amounts of jewelry and then left. She reappeared by herself some days later and asked for a loan of Rs 10,000, which, according to her, she urgently needed to buy a house in Bombay. When the merchant balked at lending such a large sum to a stranger, she offered to place as security jewelry worth Rs 50,000. The Marwari agreed and visited her house, where, after showing the jewelry to the satisfaction of the merchant, she ordered the jewelry sealed in a bundle. The merchant was to keep this sealed bundle for three months, during which the loan would accrue an interest of 5 percent per month. If the lady failed to repay the principal along with interest at the end of three months, the Marwari was free to break the seal and keep the jewelry. A document was drawn up, both parties signed the agreement, and the Marwari handed over Rs 10,000.

Some days later, the Marwari became alarmed when a friend laughed upon being told about the excellent deal he had struck with the lady. The friend said that she was no lady from the house of a native chief but a notorious city woman called Amba. The Marwari broke the seal and opened the bundle. It contained stones all right, but none was precious. The lady had somehow substituted common bits of road metal covered in mud for the jewelry before sealing the bundle. The crestfallen Marwari filed a criminal complaint. Although the police later apprehended Amba, she was acquitted for lack of evidence.

The sight of a carriage drawn by "well-caparisoned horses," the dazzle of jewelry, the staged appearance of servants, and the seeming assurance of the signed document and the sealed bundle had misled the Marwari. If this was an example of misreading signs at one's own peril, the detective's work in solving a double murder showed how reading them correctly could uncover hidden details.[59] This was the case in the investigations following the brutal murders of a "Mogul merchant" and his wife in 1884 in Umerkhadi, a densely populated neighborhood in the eastern part of the city. At about two o'clock in the morning of June 25, an assailant entered the bedroom of the couple's house, extinguished the lights, and cut through the mosquito net with a knife. The merchant's wife woke up when she felt a hand on her body. Her screams woke her husband. A scuffle followed. When the wife cried "Thief, thief," the assailant turned to her and said in Persian, "Father is burnt, *you also* raise cries." Then he stabbed her. Her cries roused the neighbors, but the assailant escaped capture. The merchant, who was also stabbed, and his wife were rushed to the hospital, where, after giving depositions, they died.

The case was assigned to Sardar Mir Abdul Ali. Based on the words the assailant directed at the merchant's wife, Sardar Ali surmised that she knew her attacker and that the assailant spoke Persian. The detective began by inquiring about the skullcap and the cloak the intruder left behind. He discovered that on the morning of the murder, people in Null Bazaar had seen a Mogul with torn clothes. The man was not wearing a skullcap and cloak, but they remembered him wearing both on the previous evening. After further inquiries, the detective discovered that a "certain Mogul," Haji Mirza Aga, had once been deeply smitten with the merchant's wife and had wanted to marry her. When the woman's brother turned down his marriage proposal, Aga went on a pilgrimage to Karbala, hoping that this pious act would win him the family's approval. But in his absence, his beloved was married off to the merchant. The murder of the merchant was his brutal revenge, and he killed his beloved in outrage for raising the alarm. Sardar Ali apprehended Aga and built the case against him by gathering visual evidence to support the prosecution's story of the murderous vengeance of a disappointed lover.

Dumasia's accounts of crimes and their detection shared with other urban writings an attention to the minute visual details of everyday life. Of course, their purposes were different. Wacha's wondrous depiction of "air eating" on the maidan, and Madgavkar's portrait of the dazzling diversity and stimuli on the streets, sought to capture what was exciting and intoxicating. Dumasia's stories of crime, by contrast, aimed to uncover what lay underneath the shiny glitter. But common to all was a concern with visuality. This was because urban change was experienced as a transformation in the way the modern city looked.

COLONIAL EYES

There is a hint of the exotic in Parsi and Marathi descriptions of the city. The exotic in their writings, however, refers to the novelty of the everyday sights and sounds of Bombay's urban life. The Europeans, on the other hand, viewed the Indian as the exotic because they saw the city through a colonial prism. Bombay, after all, was a colonial city. Its spatial divisions and order encoded racial dominance. While the nucleus of the European population lived in the south, Indians were clustered north of the old fortified town, with the east-west line of Churchgate Street demarcating the boundary between the natives and the foreigners. This basic division persisted even after the fort walls came down in 1862. Over time, however, class came to mute racial divisions as wealthy Indian merchants and industrialists built houses in European areas. Broad avenues and spacious houses set in gardens characterized the European areas, where elite Indians also built grand bungalows. No Europeans lived in the native quarters, which were crowded, mixed-use neighborhoods where the Indian merchants both lived and worked.

Europeans felt proud of the "comely city" in the south with its gardens, bungalows, and public buildings dressed in neo-Gothic architecture, but they did not think of it as exotic. Its feel was comfortingly familiar. The expression of their wonder at Bombay's modern urban life was reserved for the city's Indian quarters. Their snapshots of these areas represented Bombay's modern everyday life in images of otherness. The product of colonial modernity appeared as the timeless East. Thus, nearly four decades after the fort walls came down, a Briton wrote about the dramatic change in the landscape as one crossed over from the British to the Indian areas. It was as if a magician had suddenly turned his ring, he remarked. The old was new, the plain was colored, and the East had swallowed up the West. "Cross one street and you are suddenly plunged in the native town. In your nostrils is the smell of the East. . . . The decoration henceforth is its people. The windows are frames for women, the streets become wedges of men."[60]

S. M. Edwardes, who had served as Bombay's police commissioner, wrote a series of ethnographic sketches, highlighting the charming colors of the "native" quaters. Originally printed in the *Times of India* under the pen name of Etonensis, they were later published as a book. Here, too, the focus is visual. Thus, he writes of the dazzling tides of humans rolling through the city streets every morning, of Memon and Khoja women in green and gold or pink and yellow *kurta* and *izzar*, strolling with their children dressed in all hues of the rainbow. The accent in these descriptions is on capturing ethnic groups in their characteristic dress, colors, and sounds. He depicts "sleek Hindus from northern India in soft Muslin and neat colored turbans; Gujarathis [*sic*] in red headgear, Cutchi seafarers, descendants of the pirates of dead centuries. . . . Bombay Mahomedans of the lower class with their long white shirts, white trousers and skull-caps of silk and brocade; there too every type of

European from the almost albino to the swarthy Italian."[61] There are Arabs, Africans, Afghans, Persians, and Malays, all in their ethnic dresses. The portrait of an array of communities is followed by a description of the medley of sounds—the rattle of trams, the hymn of fakirs, the cry of "Allaho Akbar," the shouts of the vendors. While the faithful wend their way home, "bands of cheerful millhands hasten past you to the mills, and are followed by files of Koli fisherfolk,—the men unclad and red-hatted, with heavy creels, the women tight-girt[ed] and flower-decked, bearing their headloads of shining fish at a trot towards the market."[62]

The evening brings forth images of "rich black-coated Persian merchants, picturesque full-bearded Moulvis, smart sepoys from Hindustan, gold-turbaned and shrewd-eyed Memon traders, ruddy Jats from Multan, high-cheeked Sidis, heavily-dressed Bukharas, Arabs, Afghans and pallid embroiderers from Surat."[63] Then there are mill hands returning from their daily labor, merchants going home, beggars, hawkers, fruit sellers, and sweetmeat sellers milling about, crowds entering shops, and groups on the thresholds of coffee vendors.

Edwardes then invites the reader to enter the shadows of the night in the city. Make your way through a squalid lane to a house covered in darkness, walk to the end of the passageway, lift the greasy curtain, and you are in an opium den, where the flotsam and jetsam of the city gather to purchase nightly oblivion for a modest sum.[64] Or wander down one of the arteries of the city, enter a double-storied tumbledown house, walk up the stairs, and enter a room carpeted with cheap date-leaf mats and a faded polychromed dhurry. You are in a "Kasumba" saloon, where a woman nurses "an elderly and peevish Lothario with a cup of sago-milk gruel, which the opium-eaters consider such a delicacy." After everyone has had their fill, an elderly Muslim in shabby clothes recites stories interspersed with quotations from Persian poets and culled from *A Thousand and One Nights.*[65] The police commissioner then introduces you to Nur Jan, who sits in her *diwankhana* "like some delicate flower cradled on a crystal lake." She is a courtesan, a dancer and singer who sings Hindustani melodies and even some old English roundelays. Her delicate hands, great dark eyes, little ivory feet, and courteous bearing captivate him. He learns that Nur Jan came from a respectable family in Calcutta, went to school, and learned English but fell on hard times and ended up in Bombay, where she earns a living with her singing.[66]

Like the other urban writers we encountered above, Edwardes reads the city visually. But there is a vital difference. Whereas Wacha and Madgavkar saw the exotic in Bombay's modernity, in its intoxicating hustle and bustle, Edwardes writes about the "sleek Hindus" and "rich black-coated Persian merchants" and invites you to the opium den. His snapshots of daily life transport the reader to an exotic place of another kind. The imperial flaneur's eyes see strangeness not in Bombay's modern industrial life, which finds scarcely a mention, but in its rich mix of communities, in the colorful tapestry of different ethnic types. Each person's ethnicity is identified by his or her dress, language, or behavior. Edwardes skillfully enlists ethnographic description and situates different ethnic types in particular spaces to evoke a sense of the place. Streets and alleys emerge invested with deeply resonant cultural meanings, as a locus for the dance of timeless traditions. This was the colonial way of rendering familiar the strangeness of modern urban life.

URBAN HORROR

Bombay's modern urban life may have been a spectacle, but the sights were not always shining and enchanting. When colonial officials turned their eye to the mill districts, they saw squalor and degradation. Pride in the comely city gave way to horror and revulsion at the sight of the dark, ill-ventilated tenements packed with impoverished workers and set amid cesspools of filth and disease.

2.8. A chawl. Courtesy: Sharada Dwivedi and Rahul Mehrotra, *Bombay: The Cities Within* (Bombay: India Book House, 1995)

Land was abundant in the city, but neither the capitalists nor colonial authorities were willing to spend enough money to build inexpensive and adequate transportation. This forced workers to live close to work, where land was at a premium. Seeing opportunities for profits with little investment, landlords recklessly erected slums and tenements. The chawl, a Marathi word meaning "room or house fronted by a corridor," was the defining emblem of the overcrowded working-class space.

Initially, mill owners and private builders built these tenements. A typical chawl was a two- or three-storied building, each floor consisting of a row of single rooms sharing a common balcony. Each room had a small *mori*, a space for a faucet or for storing water in vessels. The common toilet and bathing facilities were on the ground floor. Each room, measuring six square meters or less, housed five to ten people. Lucky was the family who had sole occupancy of the room, for the scarcity of working-class housing frequently forced multiple households to cram into the tiny cubicle. Equally common was the sight of a single chawl room packed tight with several men. The immigrants were predominantly male. So, when they arrived in the city without their families, these men from the countryside used their village and kin ties to find work and a place to live. This often meant somehow squeezing into a room already filled to capacity by their kinsmen. Every inch of space, including verandas, was rented to immigrants from the countryside.

The jam-packed chawl became a symbol of Bombay's working-class space. Patrick Geddes remarked that the chawls were not for "housing, but warehousing people."[67] Those not lucky enough to be warehoused in chawls found roofs over their heads in makeshift dwellings fabricated with corrugated iron, flattened tins, and wooden planks or found refuge on the sidewalk. This was the lot of casual laborers, hawkers, peddlers, cobblers, tailors, and domestic servants. With no access to the mill chawls, and with their employment conditions even more unsteady than those of industrial workers, these laborers were forced to improvise living quarters for which the term *housing* was largely a euphemism.

The government recognized the wretchedness of working-class housing.[68] In fact, colonial officials themselves drew dark pictures of the poor, packed in dense clusters of overcrowded and poorly ventilated chawls and slums that were set between narrow lanes and open drains, stables and warehouses. But what the British observers saw is as striking as what they did not, or could not, see. There is a Dickensian impulse in their focus on squalor and misery but none of the English novelist's insight that industrialization was directly responsible for the wretched, inhuman conditions.[69] Their imperial blinders prevented the recognition that the hellish landscape was produced by the colonial economy; they could not see that the economic relations that British power imposed rendered the precarious mill industry critically dependent on the exploitation of cheap labor. To them, the workers' appalling living conditions had nothing to do with British rule; it was a matter of civic facilities' lagging behind industrial growth or simply a result of Indian unsanitary habits.

In developing as a colonial outpost and as a hub in the colonial exploitation of Indian resources, Bombay had acquired the facade of a European city. But outside the elite precincts, the island had developed other urban forms. Gillian Tindall, in her evocative biography of colonial Bombay, calls these forms "non-European." She writes that "every mill that has been built has created mud-shanties somewhere near at hand; every block of flats that has been built, from the ponderous 'Hindustan Chambers' or 'Dharbanga Mansions' of the high Edwardian era to the glass towers of the present, has attracted into the city yet more up-country people with country standards and country ways."[70] This is true, but classifying them as "non-European" conceals their lives as the other side of modernity, which she implicitly identifies in the twin birth of mills and mud shanties. Slums and tenements were not alien to modern Bombay but its intimate other; they held up a mirror to elite spaces, reflecting the grotesque other side of colonial and capitalist spatialization.

Undoubtedly, a difference in spatial patterns was a common feature in colonial cities from Bombay to Algiers.[71] As one moved from the space of the rulers to that occupied by the ruled, the population density and urban forms changed. However, the "white" and "black" towns were neither homogeneous nor radically set apart; nor could they be. The very logic of colonial power required interactions, blurred boundaries, and scrambled spatial patterns. The separation was in the colonial mind. It was precisely because social and spatial borders were regularly crossed that colonial ideology seized on the wretchedness of chawls and slums to deny that the mill districts could ever form part of the "comely" city that made the Briton proud.

The colonial eye not only failed to see the intimate connection between the two cites but also could not penetrate the gloomy lens of misery and horror to see the lives the workers lived in their dismal chawls and slums. With social and cultural ingenuity, the working-class immigrants forged strategies to survive and fashion an urban life in Bombay. They coped with their uncertain and difficult circumstances by maintaining their rural links. Many returned annually to their villages to help with harvesting and used connections based on the village, caste, and kin in finding their feet in the city. Male workers from the same village grouped together to rent a room. Caste and kin members could be persuaded to make a few feet of space available in their crowded single-room tenements. The social patterns of the working-class neighborhood imparted the appearance of a village. Not surprisingly, the mill district became known as Girangaon, the village of the mills.

The village was a powerful ideal for migrants who dreamed of returning one day permanently to the village.[72] It was their way of negotiating the difficult conditions in the city. The social and cultural resonance of the rural forms in the urban setting did not signify the persistence of tradition in the face of modernity.[73] Workers summoned "traditions" to manage the conditions of urban modernity; they erected villagelike structures in response to housing and labor conditions in the modern city. If mud shanties were born as the mill's inseparable twin, then the village also emerged as an aspect of the city's formation. Instead of following the ordered sequence of tradition and modernity, Bombay developed by intertwining and interweaving different histories. Migrants from near and far traversed and marked the urban landscape with the footprints of the village, language, ethnicity, region, and religion. An integral aspect of colonial urbanism, the packed chawls and their "village life" equally nurtured and sustained the spell of Bombay's industrial modernity.

THE CITY OF THE DEAD

It was the late summer of 1896. The year had been one of the hottest recorded over fifty-one years. The monsoon lasted only half its normal duration, but the downpour was heavy. A concentrated rainfall of fifteen inches above the average lashed the city during this truncated monsoon season. The ground was moist, and the drains overflowed with sewage. Masses of wet grain rotted in dark granaries.[74] The atmosphere was ripe for disaster in poor neighborhoods where Bombay's working classes huddled in dark, crowded, poorly ventilated, and ramshackle buildings, jammed together without consideration for drainage or ventilation. The streets were heaped with garbage. Several lodging houses had no plinths at all; the ground floors were frequently below the level of the streets, over which flowed the deadly soup of rushing rainwaters mixed with sewage. Cesspools of human waste and animal refuse accumulated right outside living quarters and soaked into the ground.[75]

Dr. Acacio Gabriel Viegas was first to ring the alarm bell. A Goan graduate of Grant Medical College, Dr. Viegas's dispensary was located in Mandvi in the Port Trust Estate. It was a poor neighborhood of narrow and overcrowded streets, with buildings piled atop each other and filth accumulating in its sewers.[76] The drains were silted and blocked up with buckets of night soil that were routinely emptied into the nearby gullies. The night soil found its way into the blocked drains, along with urine and sewage from the privies and sullage water. The worried doctor raised his concerns about these conditions at the Municipal Corporation meetings. Then, at noon on September 18, 1896, he was asked to see a patient, Lukmibai. He learned that she had not slept for three days. She was comatose and yet could be roused easily. Her eyes were bloodshot, and she had a glandular swelling the size of an orange in her femoral region. Her temperature was 104.2, with a pulse rate of 140. There was nothing to explain the femoral bubo. He prescribed diaphoretics, salicylate of soda, and quinine, but her condition worsened in the evening. When he went to see her the next day, she was dead. Surprised by the rapidity of her death, he suspected that this might be a case of bubonic plague.

On September 19, Dr. Viegas saw another patient who also presented with a high temperature, developed a bubo, and died within a day. He was now convinced that bubonic plague was raging in the neighborhood. Reports of fifty to sixty deaths following similar symptoms confirmed his diagnosis, which he promptly brought to the municipal commissioner's attention. The government summoned Waldemar Haffkine, the famous Russian Jewish epidemiologist from Calcutta, whose bacteriological examination established that the city had a plague epidemic on its hands. Official investigations reported armies of rats infected with the disease moving from area to area, spreading the epidemic. Mortality figures mounted; the average number of deaths for the last three months of the year was well over fifteen hundred per week.

In *Bleak House*, Dickens predicts that the wicked force of disease and moral depravity bred in the foul Tom-all-Alone slum "shall work its retribution, through every order of society, up to the proudest of the proud, and to the highest of the high."[77] Colonial officials shuddered with something of that fear as they struggled to contain the epidemic and keep the sanitary workers from fleeing. Meanwhile, their measures to segregate and hospitalize the plague victims provoked widespread opposition. Shut out from decisions that affected them, the poor residents of the city were suspicious of the government's motives. A rumor spread that hospitalized people were being killed. On October 10 mill workers gathered outside the Arthur Road Hospital and threatened to demolish it. Two weeks later, a thousand of them returned and attacked the hospital with sticks and stones.[78] As the epidemic continued unabated toward the end of the year, the panic spread. People mobbed the railway stations, desperately trying to escape. Nearly four hundred thousand people—almost half of the city's population—fled. Bombay became the "City of the Dead."[79]

The plague epidemic of 1896–97 demonstrated that the commitment of the British to the city's welfare was limited to questions of order—order for colonial governance and for the operation of laissez-faire capitalism. The epidemic threatened the security of the colonial order and the industrial economy. The British could no longer pre-

2.9. Plague inspections. Courtesy: British Library Board, photo 311/1 (110).

tend that all was well with the urban edifice. While the well-heeled
European residents from the central parts took flight to the healthy
air of neighborhoods such as Malabar Hill, the government established the Bombay City Improvement Trust in 1898 to tackle problems of housing and urban infrastructure.

The trust's establishment and its activities signaled a redirection
of colonial urbanism. This occurred against the background of a
general shift in the colonial state's functions by the early twentieth
century. By this time, the energies of the state throughout the colonial world were increasingly directed toward managing and developing a healthy and productive subject population. To achieve
this end, the state acted upon its colonial subjects, known and enu-
merated through census operations, by enacting and implementing public health laws; by building roads and railways that trans-

ported the population to work in factories, plantations, and mines; and by laying the framework of institutions and regulations to govern the urban dwellers in towns and cities that had developed as nodes in the imperial network of the capitalist economy. Such a mode of managing the insertion of colonies in the capitalist world economy meant that the exercise of imperial power could not be limited to the assertion of sovereignty; indeed, imperial sovereignty had to be expressed and realized in configuring and governing colonial life. Ruling Bombay now meant governing the life of the subject population—improving sanitation and general hygiene, decongesting crowded neighborhoods, upgrading housing, and developing the infrastructure to shape Bombay into a productive, healthy, and efficient urban society.

By exploding through the complacent and self-satisfied images of growth and development, the bubonic plague forced the government to rethink its urban policies. But official inquiries looked only for the epidemiological causes of the plague. The government recognized, as Dr. Viegas insisted, that the dreadful sanitary conditions in the Bombay Port Trust chawls had bred the disease. However, it could not acknowledge that the underlying cause was colonial rule. The unsanitary and disease-prone living conditions, after all, were the result of the industrialization-on-the-cheap forced upon by colonialism. Its response, therefore, was to deal with the symptoms—the segregation and removal of victims to the hospital. Victimized by the epidemic nurtured by colonial industrialization, the workers whose toil had built the city were now subjected to the full force of the government's despotic power. In Albert Camus' *The Plague*, the solidarity of the people against the depredations of the epidemic in the mythical city of Oran in colonial Algeria stands as an allegory for the struggle against fascism and war in Europe. In Bombay, the residents did not gather in solidarity; instead, they took to their heels. They were not just fleeing dying rats.

THE GOTHIC CITY

We know only two roads
One which leads to the factory
And the other,
Which leads to the Crematorium
. . . .
My father withered away toiling
So will I, and will my little ones?
Perhaps, they too face such sad nights
Wrapped in coils of darkness.
My heart wells up,
Seeks an outlet;
For it was my father
Who sculpted your epic in stone.
—Narayan Surve, "Mumbai"

The Portuguese are long gone now, the British have packed their bags and left, and yet the experience of the city as a colonizing force persists.[80] Dalit writings brilliantly and powerfully portray the image of the metropolis as an urban monster that devours the toiling classes, whose labor and sweat produced it. The city appears as an oppressor, a whore. It ensnares the oppressed into its fold with its promise of livelihood and freedom, only to squeeze and smother them. In his autobiographical novel, the Dalit writer Daya Pawar writes that "a mad attraction for Bombay was deeply entrenched in my blood," but he wonders, after all these years, "what has this city really given me."

As a I seek a place to merely rest my heart at the end of a hard day, all I have to come back to is a wretched hell that this city can offer ... the life I see from a distance, the life of indulgence that I can see from afar is different. She appears as a temptress (Mahanagari), an illusion ... like a ruby in a ring. It dazzles me, beckons me. But I can never escape the realization that this dazzling ruby has always eluded me.[81]

This is not the traditional romantic critique of the city. There is no nostalgia for the imagined warmth and solidarity of the village. The perspective is entirely urban, and it springs from a history of the city whose promise has been built upon conquest.

Capital comes into the world, Marx wrote, dripping from head to toe in blood and dirt. This is how capital came to life in Bombay, not by sprouting from its soil but by colonizing it with the force of the conqueror's sword. Conquest carried with it alluring representations. As the Portuguese looked for Christian souls in Bombay, they termed it "the island of good life." Under the British, profits from the opium and cotton trade and wealth amassed from the labor of immigrants turned Bombay into the fabled city of gold. Bombay spilled out beyond the Fort by appropriating lands from the sea under the legal fiction of reclamation. Colonial domination over the land and its people combined with the conquest of nature by culture to forcefully produce a double colonization. Imperial power dressed this doubly colonized city in Gothic Revival architecture, enlisting an imagined European Middle Ages to establish its claims. All this elaborate subterfuge served the interests of capitalist industrialization and colonial power. Urban writers experienced the new urban landscape as "second nature" and tried to make sense of it by reading its visual fragments.

Deprived of the context that lent it a glow, the history of colonial Bombay now appears in dark hues. This is not just hindsight, but an understanding that emerges because the passage of time has set aside the spell of "second nature." The sight today of buildings named after merchant princes, who accumulated their wealth from the opium trade, no longer inspires awe. The post office and sewage works do not captivate us as they once did Dinshaw Wacha; now familiar and creaking under the pressure of popular growth, they appear ordinary and unremarkable. This is not to say that the historical imagination of the city as a dazzling metropolis of opportunity and cultural multiplicity is false, but that it concealed Bombay's Gothic life of power and oppression in its own time. By displacing King Edward, Shivaji's statue presents Mumbai's history as an embodiment of unbroken Maratha and national glory and achievement. But can Mumbai usurp Bombay's enchanting history without also inheriting its record of oppression? Can the postcolonial present appropriate the colonial past's bewitching charm without also owning up to the enduring effects of double colonization, to its history as one that enchants only to devour? The bodies of the plague victims say no, and the Dalit writers say no—not until the city oppresses those who nurture it.

3

THE CITY ON THE SEA

Marine Drive is no ordinary place. Mumbai's residents, who do not need much prodding to rattle off the problems facing their city, change their disposition the moment the panoramic boulevard on the Arabian Sea enters the discussion. Their eyes turn dreamy and their speech slows down in midsentence as they voice the name in hushed and unhurried tones—M-a-r-i-n-e D-r-i-v-e. Utter the name slowly, clear up spaces before and after it, and you also might feel its aura.

Running along Mumbai's arcing southwestern shoreline, Marine Drive calls to mind the visual drama of the city by the sea. This is where one can observe the imagination to create the city as a society of immense openness—open to the sea, exposed to influences from far and wide, a dream city of cosmopolitan desire. The grandeur of the curving boulevard as it extends northward from Nariman Point and disappears into Malabar Hill evokes Mumbai's ambition as a city of human artifice. Even the ocean does not appear in its natural form but comes into view framed by the curving shoreline dredged into shape by industrial technology. As this shoreline extends southward, a towering mass of buildings seems to rise up from the sea. This projecting arc of steel and concrete, extending from the office structures of Nariman Point to the luxury high-rise apartments on Cuffe Pa-

3.1. Marine Drive in the early 1950s. Photo by A. L. Syed. Courtesy: Sharada Dwivedi and Rahul Mehrotra, *Bombay: The Cities Within* (Bombay: India Book House, 1995).

rade, stands on lands reclaimed—amid tales of greed and corruption—from the sea in the 1970s. Only the ramshackle huts of the Koli fishing community break up the solid continuity of the industrial mastery of the sea.

Standing in stark contrast to the brash high-rises of the 1970s is the faded glory of the Art Deco buildings from the 1930s—also built on reclaimed lands—that line one side of the boulevard and look out confidently onto the Arabian Sea. The sea has avenged its loss by blasting the surface of Art Deco architecture with unsightly blotches of mildew. On the other side of the roadway, a promenade, flanked by a retaining wall reinforced by strange-looking concrete tetrapods, forms the border between the built space of the city and the blue waters of the Arabian Sea. When night falls and envelops Mumbai's pulsating life in the mystery of darkness, the dance of lights on Marine Drive stages the nocturnal drama of the city by the sea. One can trace the city come to life by the clusters of glowing lights all the way from Marine Drive to distant Malabar Hill. On the boulevard itself, the streetlights form a luminous curve, often referred to as the Queen's Necklace in a bid to evoke something poetic from the glitter of industrial technology.

Marine Drive invites you to Mumbai's imagined life as a spectacle of modernity, as an ideal of modern urban life. Here, heavy police patrols and the physical layout, which is designed to facilitate the flow of traffic, have kept urban sprawl at bay. The sweeping boulevard and the sites visible from it clearly demarcate the city into orderly spaces, public and private, work and leisure. The layout locates family life in apartments, business life in office towers, tourists and visitors in hotels, entertainment and leisure on the promenade and Chowpatty Beach, and the flow of modern traffic on the roadways. Set against the background of the limitless ocean, this methodical arrangement of urban life enhances the power of human artifice and ambition in Mumbai's constitution. Here, the city is dressed in its finest to present itself as an incarnation of the good life. The squalor of slums, the violence of poverty and homelessness, the wretched effects of staggering inequality, and the oppression of power are tucked away from sight. All one is invited to see is the utopia promised by the city on the sea.

It is a compelling image, endlessly reproduced and circulated in postcards, books, and magazines. Above all, it is the Hindi cinema

3.2. Rain-drenched romance on Marine Drive in *Kala Bazaar*. Source: Navketan Films.

of the 1950s—Raj Kapoor's tramp films and the crime melodramas starring Dev Anand—that disseminated this picture far and wide. Raj Khosla's *CID* (1956), for example, represents it as a classic Bombay mise-en-scène. As the film shows the comedian Johnny Walker prancing on the sidewalk, singing what was to become Mumbai's rhapsody, "Ai Dil Hai Mushkil Jeena Yahan" (O Gentle Heart, Life Is an Uphill Struggle Here), we see a tableau of urban forms, characters, and life—the apartment buildings, the medley of traffic, the crowd, the hustle and bustle of the street, and people taking a break from the turbulence of metropolitan living by relaxing on the promenade. In Vijay Anand's *Kala Bazaar* (1960), the boulevard surges with romantic passion as waves crash against the seaside wall and rains cascade down on the lovers against the background track of "Rimjhim Ke Taraane Leke Aai Barsaat" (Here Comes the Soft Rain with Its Melody of Joy). The sweeping seaside boulevard has it all— the turmoil, the glitter, the darkness, and the romance.

As an emblem of Mumbai, Marine Drive evokes an epic narrative. Since it stands, like much of the Island City, on land that once lay under water, the whole dance of metropolitan life on its stage appears as a product of heroic modernity. We are invited to see the city as an expression of human artifice, of nature bent to the will of culture. How did this captivating picture emerge? What does it express, and what does it conceal? As a historian, I must dig to discover what lies beneath it, to unearth the topography of the alluring image of the city on the sea. What better place to begin this archaeology of Mumbai's image as a modern city than Marine Drive?

PLOTTING THE DREAMSCAPE

When the plague epidemic hit Bombay in 1896–97, the British could no longer pretend that all was well with the urban edifice. While the well-heeled European residents from the central parts took flight to the healthy air of neighborhoods such as Malabar Hill, the Bombay City Improvement Trust undertook a number of projects and introduced building-design regulations and standards to shape the city's urban form over the next three decades.[1] It began restructuring congested neighborhoods and building working-class tenements, and it built roads to improve traffic flow and circulation. The trust's most visible effort to shape Bombay's urban form was the Cuffe Parade reclamation on the southern end of the western seashore. Completed in 1905 and named after T. W. Cuffe, a member of the Improvement Trust, the parade was developed as an upscale residential area. Its showpiece was a row of Edwardian bungalows and villas that looked out to the sea across the promenade. Today the promenade does not exist; it was swallowed up by the reclamation of the 1970s. The tall residential towers that rose on the reclaimed New Cuffe Parade stole the sea view from the older bungalows and villas, which have given way almost entirely to apartment blocks. But the old residents still fondly recall the way it was—the graceful homes, strolls on the promenade, views of the ocean.

Cuffe Parade's successful realization of the ideal of upper-class urban life spurred the government to become more ambitious. It resuscitated the plan to reclaim the Backbay—so called because it was on the other side of the bay—which had first surfaced in the speculative bubble of the 1860s. The plan had lost its fizz when the bubble burst. Periodically, the government returned to the idea, but only in 1909, when flush with the success of the Improvement Trust's projects, was fresh life breathed into the reclamation plan. After officials consulted with the city's mill-owning and merchant elite, the government passed a resolution on urban policy. The decision was to earmark the western shores for the wealthy, and Salsette in the north for the middle classes, while punching through the congested central parts of the city to build arterial roads connecting the upper- and middle-class areas to the business district in the Fort, and to the magnificent commercial precinct of Ballard Estate then being built by the Bombay Port Trust on reclaimed lands on the east.

Thus began the first act in the drama that was to be staged on the city's western foreshores. The plan to rob the sea for the rich began modestly, starting with the shuffling of bureaucratic memos on reclaiming lands on the Backbay for the wealthy classes who desired sea-facing residences in close proximity to the business district.[2] The scheme gathered momentum in 1912 when the government hired the engineering firm of Messrs. Lowther, Kidd and Company to prepare estimates for reclaiming 1,145 acres in the Backbay and 124 acres on the east side of Colaba for military purposes.[3] Two years later, the Bombay Development Committee, appointed by the government to recommend plans for the city's growth, reconsidered the scheme. Over two years of meetings, it invited and received written statements and oral testimonies from government officials, leading merchants, and industrialists. When it was all over in 1914, the committee submitted a report with a set of recommendations. Among these was a suggestion to reclaim lands on the Backbay.[4] Less grandiose than previous proposals, the committee's recommendation nevertheless was reclamation as part of a plan to accommodate public buildings and to improve the urban environment. The government hesitated because of the cost involved, but this evaporated when two private consortiums joined hands in January 1918 to bid for the reclamation project. The offer convinced the government of the reclamation's financial feasibility.[5] The government concluded that if the project was profitable, why allow private individuals to reap the benefit? Why not use the profits for the general good? The land-grab scheme now wore the veil of "public" purpose.

When Sir George Lloyd arrived in December 1918 as the governor of Bombay, the Backbay reclamation once more rose high on the agenda as a desirable and profitable scheme for the government to undertake to relieve the pressure on housing in the city. Somehow, the government convinced itself that providing land for upper-class residences would relieve overcrowding in the working-class neighborhoods. This fantastic make-believe had already been established by the colonial government's written proceedings, which in lieu of popular representation, served as the legitimate basis for policy making. Lloyd had to look no further than the official records to arrive at the conclusion that reclamation was a bold measure to tackle Bombay's urban blight.

In fixing his sights on reclamation, Lloyd invoked the justification already well entrenched in the official discourse: the housing shortage. Lord Montagu, the secretary of state for India, had spoken forcefully of the urgent problem of housing for the poor when the governor met him in London prior to his departure for Bombay. Charged to deal speedily with the housing problem, Lloyd wrote to Montagu soon after he arrived in India. He complained that wartime migration had worsened the problem of congestion. The Improvement Trust had tried to open up existing neighborhoods and to develop new areas for construction, but these efforts were frustrated by

Indians, who refused, unless forced, to move out of their congested neighborhoods near bazaars and temples. According to Lloyd, the problem was that the native landed interests dominated the municipality and did not want any increase in the housing stock lest it lower the rents. The nationalists, in his view, only added fuel to the fire by backing up these vested interests.[6]

The solution, then, was to circumvent the Municipal Corporation altogether. Speaking in the Bombay Legislative Council in 1920, Lloyd listed the bold steps needed—improving the water supply, drainage, sewage, roads, schools, and housing—to bring the city up to the standard that would do it credit. For this purpose, he proposed the establishment of the Development Directorate.[7] This was a canny move. It took Lloyd's showpiece Backbay project out of the public scrutiny by the Municipal Council's Indian members, whose motives he distrusted. The ambitious imperialist that he was, Lloyd believed that for a public welfare project to succeed, the public must be shut out.

The plot thickened as the government hired Sir George Buchanan, who had done reclamation work on the Rangoon River and at Basra, as a consulting engineer. In 1919 Buchanan submitted a report on the scheme prepared by Lowther, Kidd and Company in 1912, estimating that the project would take about six years to complete at a cost of about Rs 37 million. This was an increase of a mere 10 percent over Kidd's 1912 estimate—a gross underestimate that later was to haunt him and the project. He also approved a dredger that was designed for soft clay, not the stiff clay that Kidd had identified as present in the harbor—another grievous mistake that would later bedevil the reclamation.

Greedily eyeing the huge profit of £20 million promised by the high land values that had prevailed since the war, the government did not look too closely at Buchanan's report. Enough time had passed. Now was the moment to act. So thought Lord Montagu, who wrote that any delay in starting the Backbay reclamation would be scandalous.[8] Following the scheme's approval by the secretary of state in May 1920, a bill was introduced in the Bombay Legislative Council in August 1920 entrusting the Development Department with carrying out the reclamation and other urban projects. In 1921 Buchanan's firm was appointed as consulting engineers, and work finally began on a project that the colonial ideology had miraculously posited as the panacea for Bombay's housing shortage.

THE PLOT UNRAVELS

A quarry was opened some twenty miles away at Kandivli for the construction of a retaining seawall from Colaba to Marine Lines. The dredger, the "Sir George Lloyd," commenced dredging the projected filling of twenty-five million cubic yards. The sight and sound of construction sent the colonial urban imagination soaring. In 1924 the British town planner W. R. Davidge published an article detailing the plan he had prepared for the reclaimed land.[9]

Reaffirming the colonial make-believe that the reclamation aimed to solve the city's housing problem, Davidge also drew on all its latent fantasies. The fiction that seaside reclamation would address the problems of housing and public hygiene, long articulated in colonial documents, was now given full expression in his Backbay dreamscape. He visualized an imposing seaside complex of public buildings and office premises, grouped around shady quadrangles modeled after Gray's Inn and Oxford colleges. A broad open space, lined with palm trees, was to run along the whole length of the reclamation, ending in a public building at the southern end of the vista, while the northern end was to be directed toward the Rajabai Clock Tower, built by Sir George Gilbert Scott in 1865. Residential quarters laid out in neatly lined rectangular plots were to occupy the remainder of the area.

It was a grand vision of the city on the sea, an elegant picture of wealth and power. But the poor were nowhere to be seen in Da-

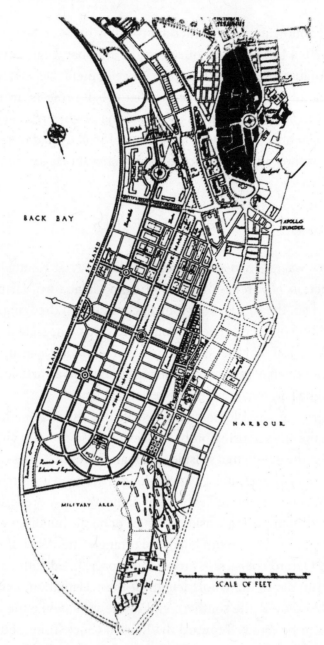

BACK BAY

APOLLO BUNDER

HARBOUR

MILITARY AREA

SCALE OF FEET

3.3. Davidge's plan. Source: W. R. Davidge, "The Development of Bombay," *Town Planning Review* 10, no. 4 (1924): 273–79.

vidge's dreamland. Their lives, the way they used space, appeared only through images of congestion, disease, filth, and fetid smells, which served as alibis for the proposed plans. The neatly and harmoniously organized buildings, parks, trees, and roads, offered as solutions to the social problem of poverty and exploitation, did not reserve any space for the poor. It was a vision from above that divided physical spaces and drew geometrical shapes to produce a visually compelling plan of society, formulated and executed by disinterested experts and administrators.

Consider, for example, the book *Development in Bombay*, published in 1924 by the government. Written by S. Nihal Singh, it began by stating that Bombay was at a crucial point in its life as an urban community. The Island City had grown tremendously since its beginnings as seven islets. Trade, commerce, and industry had turned it into a bustling metropolis. But its laissez-faire growth had also created spots of incredible ugliness—the living hell of chawls, the congested neighborhoods and bazaars, and the foul and fetid lanes. George Lloyd's administration and the Development Department had embarked on such an audacious plan precisely to meet the challenge posed by this haphazard growth. Predictably, Singh described the Backbay reclamation as a spectacular attempt to remake the urban community, writing enthusiastically of its grand design. Enthralled by the picture of a four-mile-long seawall running from Colaba to the Marine Lines, he envisioned it as defying and mocking the crashing waves. He wrote of hearing the rumble following a series of deafening explosions, of falling rocks at Kandivli, where the mountain's nose was being cut off to spite the sea. The projected dredging of twenty-five million cubic yards of mud and the advanced science of engineering manifest in the pile-driving machine and the dredger "Sir George Lloyd" left him awestruck.[10] Written in breathless tones, the book celebrated the Backbay reclamation as a daring assault on nature by forces of urban planning and technology to remake Bombay's urban community. Photographs of the stone quarry, the work in progress at the reclamation site, the dredger, and the seawall going up offered an image of the heroic efforts by labor and technology to tame the sea.

The praise was premature, for the Backbay plan was soon plunged into a crisis. If even the best-laid plans often go awry, then poorly drawn ones are destined to come undone. Contrary to the official propaganda, the reclamation was planned with stunning casualness. The details of the staggering mistakes and oversights became apparent and caused great official embarrassment the moment the plans were scrutinized. An official inquiry in 1926 determined that George Buchanan's plans were plagued with problems from the very beginning. He had so wildly underestimated the project's cost that within a year of the plan's approval, the budget was revised upward to Rs 70 million from Buchanan's original estimate of Rs 37 million—an 89 percent increase![11]

Even more disastrous was his approval of the purchase of the dredger "Sir George Lloyd" from Messrs. Simon and Company. Kidd's 1912 report had ruled out dredging the Backbay because of its rocky bed and high tides and had recommended fillings from the harbor, where the soil was of stiff clay. Buchanan accepted Kidd's report but went on to approve Simon and Company's specification of the dredger, which was designed to dredge 2,000 cubic yards per hour of soft, not stiff, clay. He overlooked this specification and estimated that the "Sir George Lloyd," along with the booster "Colaba," would deliver 2,000 cubic yards per hour from the harbor to the Backbay, over 15 hours of pumping time per day, for 170 days a year for five years, to complete the project.[12] Astonishingly, he conducted no check borings to test the harbor bed. Nor did he make the dredger's approval conditional on its successful testing on the harbor. As the manufacturer's representative acknowledged in his testimony before the inquiry committee, he did not test the dredger on the harbor because he knew that the harbor's stiff clay would not permit it to produce 2,000 cubic yards of fill per hour.[13] Indeed, the manufacturer did not even guarantee that its dredger would achieve the planned target of 2,000 cubic yards, but only that it "may be expected to meet your requirements."[14]

Naturally, disaster struck. To begin with, the dredger and the booster sat idle for twenty-one months after their purchase because there were no lagoons ready for them to fill. When they finally started dredging at the end of 1922, no one checked their output for a year. Measurements were finally taken in July 1924, but it was discovered that the sea had refused to cooperate. Its stiff clay permitted the dredger to scour only 1,020, not 2,000, cubic yards per hour. The next year, the results were even more disappointing. This was not all. Inquiries also revealed that a significant portion of the filling had escaped through the porous seawall.[15] Suddenly, the project's completion appeared decades away, and the costs seemed prohibitive, particularly because land prices had fallen off sharply since their wartime highs.

THE MUCKRAKER'S MOMENT

The grand plan was now a grand mess; a magnificent urban vision had become a visible illustration of official incompetence, mismanagement, and allegedly a lot more. The Backbay Enquiry Committee confirmed that the project was in disarray. But even before the official pronouncement, the whole scheme had been publicly declared a failure. Indeed, it was in response to a sustained public campaign against the scheme that the government was forced to institute an inquiry committee.

Leading the campaign was the fiery nationalist Khurshed Framji Nariman. A Parsi lawyer and a prominent congressman, he began his public criticism of the Development Department by writing columns in the nationalist newspaper the *Bombay Chronicle*. He wrote regularly on development scandals under the byline Development

Scandal Monger, and he carried his scandalmongering into the Legislative Council, to which he was elected in 1922–23. The Development Department was the chosen object of his ire because he believed, rightly, that the government created it to execute the reclamation and other schemes without any public scrutiny. If the government had hoped to bury the scandal of the reclamation's despotic birth in its supposedly intrinsic appeal as a public good, then it had overlooked Nariman's nationalist fervor. For no sooner was he elected to the Legislative Council than Nariman was railing against the Development Department and the reclamation scheme. He demanded an unofficial and public inquiry in 1924. The government responded by appointing an advisory committee, which he refused to join because it was not permitted to examine the workings of the department. While the majority report blamed Sir George Buchanan for the failures of the reclamation scheme, the minority report, authored by Indian members, held the government responsible for embarking on the scheme without legislative scrutiny. The graceful bay had been ruined and turned into a "Lord Lloyd lake for breeding mosquitoes," the minority concluded.[16] Nariman was not satisfied with this indictment. When the council assembled for a session in March 1925, he usurped the stage, denouncing the department and the scheme at length. Charging the possibly criminal misuse of funds, he spoke darkly of "ugly rumours" of payoffs to high officials.[17]

The charges stung. The department's spokesman, Sir Lawless Hepper, replied that much had been made of "trifling mistakes." Taking exception to the charges against public servants, he acidly remarked that if Nariman saw corruption too readily, it was probably because he encountered it all too often in his environment. Nariman cried foul, taking great offense at Hepper's insinuation that he was acting like a despicable anonymous letter writer. When Hepper withdrew his remarks, a triumphant Nariman proceeded to reiterate his charges and offered to prove every one of them.

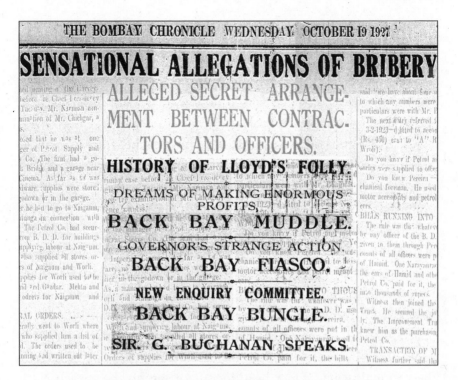

3.4. "Back Bay Bungle." Source: *Bombay Chronicle*, 1927–28

All this high drama would not have mattered much had it remained confined to the cloistered council. But Nariman, determined to dig out the reclamation's buried history and expose it as truth, carried out a vigorous campaign in the press. His main vehicle was the *Bombay Chronicle*, a nationalist newspaper edited by B. G. Horniman, the anticolonial Irishman. Day after day, the *Chronicle* published articles attacking the reclamation and the Development Department. Sir George Lloyd's prize venture became "Lloyd's Follies," "Back Bay Bungle," and "Back Bay Muddle."

The opposition to the scheme received powerful support from the landed interests, who feared that the supply of reclaimed lands would depress the rental market. Wealthy magnates, whose contract bids the government had spurned, also joined the nationalist bandwagon to assail the reclamation. In bold letters, the *Chronicle* announced public meetings, usually held at the Gaiety Theatre, opposite the Victoria Terminus station, for their strongly worded denunciations. Leading magnates of the city attended and spoke at these meetings, but the star was Nariman, who thundered against the government for its "vandalism" on the Backbay.[18]

Nariman's rhetoric was combative and designed to provoke. To be sure, nationalist politics had been around for a few decades, and it had become increasingly assertive. But western-educated Parsi politicians of Nariman's class had traditionally spoken in reverential tones about British rule, suggesting only greater representation of Indians in the administration. But here was Nariman, dressed immaculately in three-piece suits—no coarse homespun nationalist uniform for him—ratcheting up the nationalist rhetoric several notches in flawless English. The scandal of colonial government was out in the open, revealed in public meetings and emblazoned in the pages of the *Bombay Chronicle*. "Bring Offenders to Book" screamed the nationalist newspaper headline, reporting on the speech Nariman had delivered at a public meeting organized by the Bombay Provincial Congress.[19] So effective was Nariman's *Chronicle* campaign that a hapless Buchanan felt compelled to plead his defense to the newspaper.

If the government had thought that the establishment of an official inquiry would quiet the relentless din of criticisms, it had thought wrong. Nariman immediately denounced the inquiry committee as a mask to cover up the failures.[20] And when the Backbay Enquiry Committee started its work, its proceedings served only to provide additional grist to the nationalist mill. The first day that Sir Lawless Hepper, the director of the Development Department, appeared before the committee to give evidence, the *Chronicle* had a field day. The story ran under the headlines "A Mad Venture," "A Huge Hoax," and "Public Hoodwinked from Day to Day." The paper reported some "startling disclosures" and gleefully noted Hepper's "damaging" admission that his reports on the project's progress had been misleading. Referring to the blame that he placed on Buchanan, the paper asked: "Lloyd's 'Folly' or Buchanan's 'Blunders'"?[21] The next day Hepper heaped blame for the project's problems on Lloyd's desire to stage the reclamation as an impressive spectacle.[22] The *Chronicle* was only too happy to place the blame squarely on the shoulders of the former governor rather than allow the government to make the engineer the scapegoat.

The inquiry committee's proceedings had helped to make the reclamation such a riveting scandal that even the staid and reliably pro-British *Times of India* jumped into the fray with the storyline "Sensational Revelations in Back Bay Inquiry."[23] But nothing was more sensational than Nariman's appearance before the committee. The *Chronicle* reported in big, bold letters: "Mr. Nariman Speaks Out." Delivering his testimony with great style to a packed room, Nariman blamed Sir George Lloyd and his government's violation of constitutional principles, rather than Sir George Buchanan's incompetence, for the reclamation's failure. Once again, he repeated the charges of corruption and favoritism, prompting Sir Frederick Hopkinson, a member of the committee, to accuse him of wasting its time. An angry Nariman gathered his papers and threatened to leave, but he was dissuaded by the chairman and others. The *Chronicle* reported Nariman's triumph in this stormy drama with satisfaction and then proceeded to recount the hard-hitting charges that he went on to hurl at the administration. One exposure of hidden malfeasance followed another—the tampering with indents, the payment of secret commissions to high officials, the hushing up of the bungle, the hoodwinking of the public, and the abuse of the scheme as a free pasture for foreigners.[24] It took five newspaper pages to chronicle Nariman's dramatic performance.

Outraged, the British officials decided, foolishly, to prosecute Nariman for defamation. To be sure, they were exceedingly aggrieved. Had they not undertaken the reclamation with the loftiest of motives? Lord Lloyd, in his appearance before the committee, had reiterated that it was the scarcity of affordable and hygienic housing that had been uppermost in his mind. Admittedly, there had been mistakes. But the person to blame for the most consequential ones was Sir George Buchanan. After all, he was the expert on whose advice they had depended. As for other mistakes, they were trifling. In any case, who was this upstart Nariman?

A few days after Nariman's testimony, Sir Hopkinson, the committee member, felt so stung by the charges leveled against his compatriots that he used Hepper's appearance before the committee to bring down the nationalist. "Is Mr. Nariman what is known here as a pleader?" he asked Hepper. Unstated in the question was that Nariman was no barrister, but only a lowly pleader. Having established this fact, he proceeded to ask: "As such is it partly his professional business to defend criminals in the Police Court?" When Hepper answered that it was, he gleefully flung some mud on Nariman: "Some of his charges are so extraordinary that I venture to suggest that possibly his point of view is somewhat clouded by his professional activities, particularly criminal."[25] If Nariman had accused the government officials of corruption, the Hopkinson-Hepper masquerade at the inquiry concluded, it must surely be because graft was rife in the circles in which he moved.

On November 6, 1926, the *Chronicle* announced in bold headlines that the government of India, with the strong recommendation of the Bombay government, had sanctioned the prosecution of Nariman for defamation. The permission to prosecute was requested by Thomas Harvey, a superintending engineer in the Development Department, who claimed that Nariman's testimony before the Backbay Enquiry Committee had defamed him.[26] Three days later, Nariman was decisively reelected to the Legislative Council, topping the polls.[27] The government's decision had turned Nariman into a martyr.

Nariman played the martyr with consummate skill when the trial opened on December 4, 1926. He used the proceedings in the Police

Court, which lasted all of the next year, to stage himself as a fearless citizen determined to expose the Backbay scheme as a scandal. Acting as his own defense lawyer, he sparred with, tormented, and ridiculed the prosecution's witnesses and solicitors. Relishing his role as a muckraker, he dramatically repeated his allegations, accused the prosecution of suppressing documents, and charged the government with trying to silence criticism. The pages of the *Bombay Chronicle* presented the proceedings as gripping drama. Its reports frequently began with a description of the courtroom swarming with lawyers and laymen eager to see the show. In bold headlines, it announced fresh revelations of bogus payments, secret commissions, collusion between administrators and contractors, and official misconduct.[28] In the courtroom, Nariman seized on the admission of every minor mistake and every misstatement by the government and prosecution witnesses to paint a dark picture of official wrongdoing and deceit. The *Chronicle* followed suit.

Nariman's successful self-staging as an intrepid critic of the government in the courtroom and the press reached its climax on January 27, 1928. On that day, the presidency magistrate's exhaustive judgment cleared him of libel charges. Nariman was judged to have made his allegations of "ugly rumours" in good faith and not personally against the complainant. The government stood humbled. The *Chronicle* proclaimed in big bold letters: "Nariman Triumphant."[29] He had challenged the British and won. A "monster" public meeting on Chowpatty, attended by a thoroughly "cosmopolitan" crowd that included women, feted him.[30] The *Chronicle* printed letters celebrating his victory, and Nariman's supporters published a book that chronicled the origin of the libel case and its prosecution, with all the relevant documents, including the sixty-page judgment.[31] Nariman was declared a hero.

But besides the encomiums to Nariman, the whole episode inaugurated a vigorous public discussion. To be sure, the "public" was restricted to the Western-educated elites conversant in English. Still, there is no denying the importance of the circulation of those "ugly rumours" in the press. Nariman's dramatic recitation of rumors and allegations before the inquiry committee and the Police Court, prominently published by the *Bombay Chronicle*, showcased the reclamation as an issue of public interest. It did not matter that nationalists and disgruntled merchants and landlords had orchestrated the press coverage and public meetings; the result was to establish the idea that the city was an object of public interest. The government could not fail to take notice of this development and prosecuted Nariman precisely for this reason, though it ended up enhancing his reputation.

The government had painted the reclamation as a bold attempt to solve the problem of the housing shortage. Deeply convinced of its own role as a guarantor of the public interest, it had shut out public scrutiny to realize the dream of a neatly organized complex of public buildings, private residences, and gardens on the western foreshore. The government assumed that everyone would be dazzled by the mesmerizing dreamscape. But Nariman had other ideas. He dug beneath the glossy image to unearth the truth in the detritus of its financial and administrative failures. He pried and picked through official documents and discovered the muck of colonial despotism. Nariman exposed official highhandedness and corruption only to place colonialism on trial. According to him, the underlying cause of graft and incompetence was the arbitrary exercise of British power. The real scandal, the muckraker charged, was colonialism.

Nariman battered the Backbay fantasy. Even the government had to admit that the dream had gone sour and curtailed the scale of the reclamation. Only two blocks each on the northern and southern ends were to be fully reclaimed; the middle portions were to be left for the future.[32] The incompletion told the story of the flawed birth of the city on the sea, of its emergence as an expression of colonial fantasy.

But it would take more than the heroic efforts of Nariman to kill the fantasy. Once the dust had settled on the controversy and the land market had recovered from its slump in the early 1930s, the government was back to greedily eyeing the Backbay as a source of profits. As it set about leasing land, the desire for making the most of the opportunity induced a sudden amnesia about W. R. Davidge's grand plan of parks, avenues, and public buildings. Even Claude Batley's alternative plan, which proposed buildings around central gardens, did not meet with its approval; instead, the government opted to maximize its gains by dividing the land into small blocks, with narrow lanes running between them.[33] Appropriately enough, Art Deco came along to sculpt the commercial motive with its design motifs. The second act in the staging of the Marine Drive myth commenced.

Art Deco was launched by the 1925 Exposition internationale des arts décoratifs et industriels moderne in Paris. Following the Paris exhibition, this vibrant new style spread worldwide during the 1920s and the 1930s. The term *Art Deco* was not used then; it was only in the 1960s that the name began to be widely applied to label an eclectic range of designs in architecture, fine art, textiles, everyday objects, film, and photography inspired by this modern style. The "decorative" style varied greatly, yet underneath the heterogeneity, there was a common spirit.

Spurred by technological improvements in the production and utilization of electric power, transportation and communication, manufactures of new materials, and the application of new organizational forms, capitalism's worldwide reach achieved an unprecedented breadth and depth during the interwar years. The invasion of capitalist social relations and mass-produced consumer goods in everyday life was accompanied by their aestheticization. Art Deco was an expression of this aesthetic turn of capitalism, playing a powerful role in binding commerce with design.[34] Unlike avant-garde, or modernist, art, it was not utopian but pragmatic; it championed novelty without being radical. Nurtured by the interwar social and technological changes, it advanced capitalist modernity by adding a fashionable gloss to the context and objects of everyday life.

Though rarely produced by machines, Art Deco admired the machine age. This was discernible in its incorporation of industrial symbolism in design—clean and simple shapes, the use of plastics and other man-made materials, the emphasis on surface effects, and the use of decorative motifs without being ornamental. Its pragmatic bent and the lack of a formal theory meant that it could accommodate motifs from exotic cultures and far-flung areas to expand and renew its decorative repertoire. Such a flexible mode of appropriating the old and the exotic into the new dovetailed perfectly with capitalism's remorseless expansion and produced a rich design vocabulary. Buildings, furnishings, textiles, and items of everyday use designed in Art Deco style came to exude an aura of wealth and luxury, elegance and cosmopolitan sophistication. This was appealing to the aspirations of industrialists, businessmen, and the middle classes spawned by industrial capitalism.[35]

While mass production and the flush of commodities for mass consumption leveled society into a horizontal order of consumers, Art Deco projected capitalist modernity in the image of an elitist, fashionable lifestyle. With the dirt, grime, and exploitation tucked away from view, capitalism appeared in the surface glitter of Art Deco. The shimmering aesthetics of this new style contributed greatly to the exuberance of the Roaring Twenties in the United States. New York built the Chrysler and Empire State buildings under its influence, and Miami acquired its image as an affluent beach resort from its parade of Art Deco buildings on South Beach. This high-spirited style drew from a variety of sources—from Bauhaus to Cubism to Constructivism to Art Nouveau to Modernism to Futurism—and it swept through the world from Europe to Cuba to Latin America to Australia.

A center of trade and industry, Bombay was primed for an Art Deco makeover. The city was also the center of the architectural profession in India. Unlike other parts of the country, the government was not the only patron of architecture. The prosperous mercantile and upper classes offered architects the opportunity to design buildings suited to urban life—spacious homes and apartments, offices and shops, cinemas and commercial establishments. Many of the city's British and Indian architects were trained in foreign institutions and were familiar with contemporary European and American idioms in architecture and design.[36]

Not surprisingly, then, the Indian Institute of Architects, founded in Bombay in 1929, played a prominent role in disseminating Art Deco. In November 1937 it organized the Ideal Home Exhibition in Bombay. Held over twelve days, the exhibit at the Town Hall attracted one hundred thousand visitors, leading the *Journal of the Indian Institute of Architects (JIIA)* to declare it a success. Outlining the goal of the exhibit, the president of the institute asked: "Have you noticed how annoying it is, if the ashtray is not placed within the comfortable reach of your hand as you sit well back in the deep armchair? How often have we all entered a dark room and fumbled despairing for a switch? Or stumbled unexpectedly upon a step that has absolutely no right to be there?"[37] These are little things, he added, but when enlarged they become enormous blunders. To demonstrate how to avoid these blunders and offer efficient and well-thought-out models, the exhibit displayed the ideal arrangements for a living room, bedroom, kitchen and pantry, bathroom, and office space. New building materials and methods, furniture, products of interior decoration, and appliances like radios and refrigerators were showcased (see fig. 3.5).[38] The ideal home in modern life meant rational arrangements and beautiful objects. The future was here, and the exhibition promised to transport visitors to this beautifully lit and appointed world on the wings of technology.

3.5. Ideal Home Exhibition. Source: *Journal of Indian Institute of Architects* (January 1938).

Having grown and prospered with capitalist modernization, the architects were understandably fascinated with Art Deco's fashionable rendering of industrial modernity. They heartily endorsed the reinforced concrete construction (RCC) that formed the material basis of Art Deco architecture. An unsigned article in *JIIA* lauded the artistic possibilities opened by Snowcrete white cement. Comparing concrete to sculptor's clay, it extolled the "truly artistic and colourful manner" in which the architect was able to mold buildings to meet structural requirements, environmental needs, and "the artistic tastes of the most critical clients."[39] The trade journal of concrete manufacturers agreed. In an editorial, the journal championed RCC as a form with unlimited structural possibilities. "In steel and concrete we have the two greatest structural units the world has known—steel in tension, concrete in compression." The combination of the two, it added, had revolutionized design. "Gone are the heavy and thick walls, piers and abutments—gone, in fact, are the construction principles of dead materials—stone, brick and mass concrete—their places being taken by small steel columns, beams and reinforced concrete—materials that never sleep nor rest, but enable us to span any reasonable distance or space and to support and transmit weights to positions as required."[40] The *Indian Concrete Journal* followed up this breathless prose in praise of RCC with advertisements for Snowcrete and Colorcrete in issue after issue. Art, commerce, and publicity came together to sell an aesthetic image of industrial modernity.

The projection of a stylish and technologically advanced life was addressed to the Westernized elites, whose tastes the architects were already transforming by the early 1930s. In Malabar and Cumbala Hills, they built attractive Art Deco homes for the rich. Other parts of the city, including the Fort, Apollo Bunder, Colaba, Dadar, and Mahim, also witnessed the erection of office buildings, homes, and apartment blocks built in the style.[41] But the most concentrated cluster of Art Deco buildings came up on Marine Drive and the Oval Maidan. By the mid-1930s, water mains, sewage, and telephone and electrical lines were being laid; work had begun on building a forty-foot-wide road and a ten-foot-wide pavement on the splendid Marine Drive.[42] As land prices rose and the government began selling plots on the Oval Maidan and the Backbay reclamation, there was a spurt in building construction.[43] Special building regulations were issued to achieve uniformity of scale and spatial organization, giving the area a distinct look.

By 1940 the construction of Marine Drive was complete. It was, the *Indian Concrete Journal* proclaimed, the "finest promenade in the East, built in concrete."[44] Lining the drive were Art Deco apartment blocks, looking out to the Arabian Sea. Behind them, on Queens Road, were also modern buildings of steel and concrete, staring across the Oval Maidan at the medievalism of the Gothic Revival buildings. The new-built form represented an architectural shift from Victorianism to modernity. Made with reinforced concrete and brick-filled stucco facades, these buildings, unlike Victorian structures, did not erect columns or beams for decoration; instead, they used a smooth, unbroken, and continuous building surface to create a modern

3.6. Art Deco apartments on Marine Drive. Photo by A. L. Syed. Courtesy: Sharada Dwivedi and Rahul Mehrotra, *Bombay: The Cities Within* (Bombay: India Book House, 1995).

image.[45] The repeated use of simple vertical and horizontal patterns and the uniform scale of windows and doors suggested industrial design. Unlike the monumentalism of the Gothic Revival, the curved and stamped form of Art Deco signified the dynamism and rationalism of industrial capitalism. This display of industrial symbolism by the sea, the juxtaposition of human artifice and nature, provided Marine Drive with its special appeal. Whereas the bungalows and villas on Cuffe Parade and the Art Deco mansions on Malabar and Cumbala hills exuded a sense of leisurely seaside life, the apartment blocks on the western foreshore drew nature and industry together in a compact to create Marine Drive's enchantment.

As important as the stylistic shift was the change in the living pattern that apartment complexes represented. Unlike the traditional joint-family homes, apartments signaled single-unit households. For the *JIIA*, this was part of a general modernization of life. Raised with an international outlook, the newspapers, automobiles, and cinema, the young, according to the *JIIA*, were no longer satisfied with the slow pace of acquiring a traditional family household; they wanted a home, and they wanted it now.[46] The apartment blocks were not lifeless buildings but projections of desire—a desire for a bourgeois life. They envisioned single-unit families—relieved of the burden of the traditional household and its retinue of servants—living independently and freely. Technology made this social imaginary possible. Reinforced concrete construction permitted the building of multistory residential blocks at relatively low cost. Electric fans allowed the ceiling height to be lowered, since the *punkah* operated by a servant was no longer required. The availability of refrigerators, modern cooking appliances, and other household gadgets meant that the number of servants could be reduced. Art Deco orchestrated these technological developments into a style that put a luster on the social form of apartment living produced by industrial modernity.

The centerpieces of the Art Deco glorification of modernity were the grand new cinema theaters: Regal, Eros, and Metro.[47] Situated on the most visible corner of Colaba Causeway, the Regal was owned by Framji Sidhwa, a Parsi businessman, and designed by Charles Stevens Jr., the son of F. W. Stevens, the architect of Bombay's magnificent Gothic Revival buildings. With a simple, streamlined facade, a curved form, an underground parking garage, a bar, two soda fountains, and a gorgeous interior designed by the Czech artist Karl Schara, this 1,200-seat theater opened in 1933 and received an enthusiastic response from Bombay's elite. Five years later, the Eros opened across from Churchgate Station, on a triangular site on reclaimed land. Owned by S. C. Cambata, also a Parsi businessman, it was designed by Bhedwar and Sorabji Architects. After settling on a design, Cambata went on a six-month world tour, during which he visited more than one thousand theaters to learn the refinements that could be made to his plan. On his return, he proudly noted that most theater owners told him the Eros's design was more advanced than anything they knew.[48]

The four-story shiplike building had a stepped-up octagonal tower in front, with walls swept into curves to create an impression of motion and length. White-veined black marble and sleek chrome-

3.7. Eros Cinema. Courtesy: Sharada Dwivedi and Rahul Mehrotra, *Bombay: The Cities Within* (Bombay: India Book House, 1995).

plated metalwork added a rich grandeur to the imposing three-story entry foyer, while silver-painted murals depicting the process of filmmaking decorated the auditorium walls. This flamboyant encasing of modern technological entertainment, in layers of resplendent luxury, could also be witnessed in the Metro, a theater owned by Metro Goldwyn Mayer. It was designed by Thomas W. Lamb of New York, in association with the Bombay architectural firm Ditchburn and Mistri. Located on the border between the city's European and Indian districts, the Metro represented an attempt to draw a broader cinema audience, with its entrance through a brightly lit tower leading into the gorgeous two-story lobby with Italian marble floors.

As in the West, the surge in Art Deco's popularity in Bombay went hand in hand with the burgeoning capitalism of the interwar period. Louis Bromfield's best-selling novel, *Night in Bombay* (1939), registers this connection, noting that all the "American firms in Bombay had launched into marble and *art moderne*."[49] But the rage to dress industrial modernity in the new aesthetics had its limits. In the staggeringly unequal society of the colonial metropolis, the vast population of poor workers and casual laborers could not even dream of making the beautiful Art Deco objects a part of their daily lives. Only the elites could afford to be lured by the fantasy of the novel life that the new designs promised. This included, in addition to the Europeans, the rulers of the so-called Native States, that is, those principalities that enjoyed nominal internal autonomy under British rule. Shorn of real power but left with their coffers intact, these decorative chiefs expressed their hollow majesty in pomp and splendor. They hunted, played sports, bred racehorses, traveled, and collected and patronized European art objects. Art Deco's decorative motifs struck a chord in their lifestyle. They built their Bombay mansions and apartment blocks in this style, which they visited regularly for shopping and the races and en route to Europe.[50]

The new style's deepest impact, however, was felt among Bombay's princes of commerce and industry. Bombay was a colonial metropolis, but it was here, more than anywhere else, that Indian merchants and industrialists possessed substantial resources and exerted great influence. The wartime interruption of commerce with Britain had offered business opportunities that they eagerly exploited to carve out a position, one they never completely relinquished once the hostilities were over. Enriched and emboldened by their economic expansion, these commercial and industrial magnates assumed a prominent role in the city, financing the construction of apartment blocks, office buildings, and cinema theaters. Bombay's modernity acquired an Art Deco gloss.

Art Deco's exuberant spirit broke from the stern and monumental medievalism of the colonial Gothic. The new style was meant to "reflect the image of the modern, ocean voyaging/jet-setting, international Indian, emerged from the shackles of backwardness and ignorance, seeking his place in the New World as an equal."[51] It rejected both colonial aesthetics and the anti-industrialism of Gandhian nationalism. Prominent architects like G. B. Mhatre adopted Art Deco as a modern style without any explicit ideological reference. For him, it was a form of aesthetic modernism that was fashioned in relation to international influences and styles, deployed to introduce industrial designs and methods in architecture. In this sense, Deco's adoption and adaptation to Bombay heralded an Indian modern, nursed by capital, and not by anticolonial nationalism. Out of this aesthetic modernism, deeply rooted in the promise of the industrial age and confidently engaged with Western culture, emerged Bombay's mythic image in the 1930s and the 1940s as a metropolis on the move, a swinging city. Art Deco not only rescued the city from the muck of the Backbay but also applied on it the shining polish of industrial modernity.

THE SHINING, SWINGING CITY

The winds of cultural change were also in the air. The improvements in transportation enabled a regular flow of visitors who brought with them contemporary European culture and fashion. The city's hotels and theaters regularly hosted performances of Western music, with the luxurious Taj Mahal Hotel serving as the top venue. Opened in 1903 by Sir Jamsetji Tata, apparently in response to the insult of being denied entry to a Europeans-only hotel, the Taj was the city's best and most opulently appointed hotel. In 1907 it permanently engaged the Taj Mahal Orchestra.[52] In 1930 it hired its first foreign band. A few years later, it became the Mecca for the city's jazz aficionados. African American jazz musicians from the United States, by way of Paris and Shanghai, descended on the Island City. These included star trumpeters like Crickett Smith and Bill Coleman, the famous tenor-sax stylist Castor McCord, the ace drummer Oliver Tines, and the versatile Leon Abbey Band. The sounds of their trumpets, saxo-

3.8. The Crickett Smith Band, Taj Mahal Hotel, 1936. Courtesy: Naresh Fernandes.

phones, drums, pianos, and clarinets, showcased at the Taj, also became the craze at other venues, such as the nearby Green's and Majestic. Indian bands, manned largely by Goans, took enthusiastically to the enthralling new sounds from New Orleans and Chicago.

Jazz, ballroom dancing, cabarets, and the screening of Hollywood films created an atmosphere of fun, fashion, and frivolity that was receptive to the lure of Art Deco modernity.[53] Advertisements in newspapers and magazines, promoting Western culture and entertainment, portrayed the city as an exciting place. Typical advertisements in the May 1936 issue of the *Illustrated Weekly of India*, for example, invited readers to the screening of Charlie Chaplin's *Modern Times*, playing simultaneously at the Regal and the Capitol to "cope with the rush," and to watch "Love-Making Sothern Style" (punning on the actress Ann Sothern's name) in *The Girl Friend* at Central. The Taj enticed those looking for exciting entertainment with a "non-stop cocktail dance" to the sounds of Crickett Smith

3.9. Teddy and His Plantation Quartet, Taj Mahal Hotel, 1939. Courtesy: Naresh Fernandes.

and the Raj Symphonians and Leon Abbey and His Boys.[54] The use of clever copywriting and illustrations to wrap entertainment choices in an attractive package formed part of the broader tendency to aestheticize commerce.

Boxed classified advertisements continued to appear in print, but purple prose, eye-catching graphics, and illustrations gained favor. J. Walter Thompson (JWT), who had the General Motors account, set up shop in Bombay in 1929, soon becoming the leading agency under the creative eye of E. J. Peter Felden.[55] The artists and copywriters of JWT's agency, as well as other agencies such as Stronach and Lintas, showcased the novelty and design of buildings, furniture, bathroom fixtures, lighting, automobiles and tires, and everyday objects. In putting a glossy sheen on the products, they infused advertising with the aesthetic spirit of Art Deco. Appropriately, Tata Steel also got into the act, using Art Deco motifs to emboss its image in advertisement (see plate 1). Advertisers also began to use cinema.

JWT, for example, produced a twenty-minute film in 1931 showing a Chevrolet racing against the Deccan Queen train from Poona to Bombay and winning!

Cinema added to the image of exuberance. Beginning with the sensational exhibition of *cinématographie* by the Lumière Brothers at the Watson Hotel on July 7, 1896, cinema had come a long way in the city. In 1913 Dadasaheb Phalke had screened the first Indian motion picture, and Western films were a regular feature of entertainment. By 1926–27 the Bombay Presidency had the largest number of cinema theaters—seventy-seven—in the colonial territory, of which twenty were in the city.[56] Foreign films, chiefly from Hollywood, dominated at this time, constituting nearly 85 percent of the footage until 1927–28. But the production of Indian films was growing. The arrival of sound proved to be their trump card. After the first synchronized sound film, *Alam Ara* in 1931, Indian films, using Indian music and languages, developed a large market that foreign-language films could not enter. Studios were established in different parts of India. Increasingly producing films in Hindi—the biggest market—Bombay emerged as the leading center.

The Indian film industry grew, but Hollywood and European films continued to be screened, and Indian cinema developed in conversation with its Western counterparts. Like them, it projected the novelty and excitement of the new industrial medium. Even though many of the early film stories were derived from Indian mythology, they addressed their audience through a modern medium. For example, Phalke's *Raja Harishchandra* (1913), which was inspired by the *Life of Christ*, told a mythological tale, but it did so with industrial technology. It was also not long before modern settings appeared alongside mythological themes in Indian films. Chandulal Shah made several box-office hits in Hindi, including *Devoted Wife* (1932)—a remake with sound of his 1925 film *Gun Sundari* (Why Husbands Go Astray)—*Typist Girl* (1932), and *Miss 1933* (1933), which placed elements of Westernized urban life and modern technological products in an Indian setting.[57] Himansu Rai established Bombay Talkies in 1934, drawing on his experience of working with German producers. Starring Devika Rani and using German and British technicians, Rai began to produce a steady stream of films with modern themes.

Cinema signified not just industrial modernity but also its thrill and excitement. The stunt films of the 1920s expressed this phenomenon most fully, none more so than those starring Master Vithal. The publicity material often called Vithal an "Indian Douglas Fairbanks." Fairbanks's name offered commercial advantages, and America represented a better face of the West than the colonial British, but this was not a simple case of Hollywood influence; Indian stunt films drew on deeply rooted traditions of physical culture and performance.[58] These were often encased in Hindu religious ideas, but they also had a secular presence in such activities as wrestling and bodybuilding. Nationalism had also secularized Hindu discourses on the body, championing physical discipline and vigor as signs of nation building. Though stunt films drew on a mix of religious and secular discourses, the long-term tendency was toward secularization. As the religious gave way to the secular and the mythological to the historical, cinema projected stunt as pure excitement.

The exhilarating spirit of stunt found its most spectacular and popular expression in Wadia Movietone's Fearless Nadia series.[59] The unlikely stardom of Mary Evans, also known as Fearless Nadia, began with *Hunterwali*, or *The Lady with the Whip* (1935). Born in 1908 in Perth to a Greek mother and a British father, she came to India in 1911. After Evans's father's death in 1915, her mother lived in Bombay, before moving to Peshawar. It was in Peshawar that Mary Evans became a fan of Pearl White films and learned dancing and horse riding. Returning to Bombay in 1926 with a baby boy in tow and finding office work too dull, she tried to earn a living by dancing, singing, and the circus. She also adopted the name Nadia.

In 1934 Nadia met J.B.H. Wadia and his younger brother, Homi Wadia. The Wadias belonged to a wealthy Parsi family in Bombay.

J.B.H. had studied English literature and law but was a film buff from a young age. His decision to become a filmmaker created a crisis in the respectable Parsi family. "How dare I ever entertain the very idea of plunging into a 'low' profession like film making? How could I ever think of becoming a home wrecker?"[60] But he won his mother's acquiescence and even managed to calm the frayed family nerves when his younger brother, Homi, decided to join him in the despised profession. The brothers were passionate about cinema. A fan of Douglas Fairbanks, J.B.H. made sure that he met the Hollywood star when he visited the city in the 1920s. He acquired the Indian distribution rights to *The Mark of Zorro* and went on to adapt it as *Diler Daku*, or *Thunderbolt*. Not content with adapting it once, he remade the action film as *Dilruba Daku*, or *Amazon*, this time with a Bengali actress in the lead as an avenger with a mask and sword.

The Wadias' taste for stunt films also proved to be commercially profitable. Action films ran to packed houses in the mill-district cinemas. But even then, they could not have predicted that the blue-eyed, buxom blonde they had first met in 1934 would become a box-office queen a year later. They initially tried her out in small roles in a few films. Then, in 1935, they chose her as the star of *Hunterwali*, a film inspired by *The Mark of Zorro* and *The Perils of Pauline*. The film was a box-office hit and catapulted the masked avenger Nadia into instant stardom. From then on, there was no stopping Fearless Nadia. A stream of films flowed—*Miss Frontier Mail* (1936), *Hurricane Hansa* (1937), *Lutaru Lalna* (1938), *Punjab Mail* (1939), *Diamond Queen* (1940), *Bambaiwali* (1941), and many others. In each one, the plump but athletic blonde essayed the role of a confident, self-sufficient woman who fought injustice vigorously and decisively. Each one was a hit.

Nadia was white and spoke Hindi poorly. Yet, she became a Hindi film star. Typically, Western women in Indian films appeared as ultramodern and corrupt vamps. But the Wadias were careful to define her as an Indian whose whiteness signified cosmopolitanism.[61]

3.10. Fearless Nadia. Courtesy: Wadia Movietone / Roy Wadia.

She could beat up evil Indian men, and yet arouse no nationalist backlash because cultural modernity, rather than race, defined her identity. In fact, her whiteness was a plus. She could be shown scantily dressed and seen acting in nontraditional ways. The modern action queen in skimpy, tight shorts was an attractive commodity. The swashbuckling blonde who beat up evil men, cracked a whip, swung from chandeliers, rode on top of speeding trains, and fought lions was a thoroughly modern woman. Unmarried on- and off-screen, Fearless Nadia projected an image of independence that sidestepped the alternatives of the whore and the housewife presented to women in contemporary Hindi cinema. Even as her heroic exploits resonated with the traditional figure of the brave *veerangana* (female warrior), she exuded the autonomy and individuality of a modern woman. Her stunts were sensational. Technology—planes, trains, and automobiles—figured prominently in her films. The whole package radiated the thrills of industrial modernity, circulated widely by the mass medium of cinema, itself an industrial form. While the elites had their beautiful Art Deco buildings and objects, ballroom dances, cabaret, and jazz, the masses were treated to the excitement of the action queen's stunts.

THE OTHER SIDE OF EDEN

"Yes, Bombay was fantastic and romantic and extraordinary things happened there, if you didn't notice the coolies, the women and the children sleeping on sidewalks and in gutters as you drove home from a good party about sunrise." So observes Bill Wainright, the American protagonist in Bromfield's *Night in Bombay* as his ship docks in the city.[62] Later, traveling in a taxi through the poor quarters of the city, he notes the difference between those and the elite world of the Taj Hotel and Malabar Hill. It was full of "smells and sweat and dust." "The district grew shabbier, the houses a little taller, the burning streets filled with sweating people. The smells of garlic and cow dung and filth became overpowering." He wonders: "How do people manage to keep alive in such a world? How do children ever survive?"[63]

No one could miss the contrast between the fashionable, elite precincts and the mill district. Time and again, British officials depicted the poor living on top of each other in chawls, somehow squeezing out space and air in extremely congested and poorly ventilated quarters to survive in the big city.[64] They often commented on the dank and dark tenements and on the puddles of water and sewage festering all around their living quarters. When visiting them for inspections, the filth and the stench would "compel a hurried exit."[65] The stench, the dirt, and the diseases of the tenements cast the mill districts in the official eye as the other city, set apart from the elite precincts, yet receiving the benefits of progress and civilization. They failed to see the dismal tenements as reflections of the particular conditions of Bombay's industrialization, the other side of progress. It was as if the poor were fated to live in wretched dwellings. Their lot was the chawls, just as the rich were destined to soak up the Art Deco style, with no structural connection between the two opposite fortunes. All that could be done was to build more tenements and call it development.

Accordingly, at the same time that it used the alibi of a housing shortage to undertake the Backbay reclamation, the government built tenements for the workers in the central districts of the city, the largest cluster being the Bombay Development Department (BDD) chawls at Worli. Constructed without consulting either architects or the intended residents, these three- to five-story chawls were cheerless structures in concrete, or at least so thought the workers, who initially refused to occupy them. The renowned Bombay architect Claude Batley described them in the 1930s as "single-room tenements with concrete-louvered verandahs, from which neither heaven nor earth could be seen."[66] Whatever the architectural judgment, the chawl as working-class housing had acquired the status of normality in Bombay's spatial map. Official reports on tenement construction displayed none of the breathless enthusiasm that they reserved for the Backbay buildings; with a matter-of-fact tone, they dryly listed the number of rooms built, the facilities provided, and their occupancy. The 1931 census came close to expressing an airy optimism when it applauded the rise in the number of chawls as a significant improvement. If the municipal rules could only ensure that the design of chawls would include a satisfactory number of privies and faucets on each floor, then what could be better for workers and the lower middle classes than the development of these tenements?[67] This was the extent of fervor that the colonial officials could work up for workers' housing.

The densely packed chawls were distorted reflections of the apartment buildings. If the working-class tenements were a form of industrial housing, a way of massing one living space atop another, so were the apartments. The difference was that the apartments on Queen's Road and Marine Drive were significantly more spacious and comfortable, dressed up to add a fashionable, aesthetic gloss to industrial modernity. But the secret of this polished surface of the metropolis could be found in the dimly lit and densely packed chawls. Capitalism had forced architecture and town planning to design beautiful buildings and objects for the elite to cover over the ugly reality of workers "warehoused" in oppressive tenements.

Likewise, the swinging and shining milieu of music and entertainment had another side. In the brothels of Kamathipura, the flesh trade was brisk and sordid. Beginning first as a neighborhood where European prostitutes were concentrated, by the end of the nineteenth century it had become the city's red-light district. According to the census,[68] the number of prostitutes in 1931 was 1,136, which appears to be a gross underestimate. Official figures counted only the prostitutes in registered brothels, excluding those who operated outside the law. Being a port city and an industrial center with a skewed sex ratio among its immigrants—eighty-one males per one hundred females in 1931[69]—Bombay probably had a much larger number of prostitutes. Certainly, anecdotal evidence portrays Kamathipura as a thriving and populous red-light district. In addition to prostitutes, brothel keepers and pimps crowded the area. Many of the brothels had barred doors on the ground floor, making the prostitutes appear as caged women.

Kamathipura was a far cry from the Taj bar where Bromfield found bartenders mixing gimlets and gin slings and serving chotapegs "in quantities vast enough to float a ship," and where "'advanced' Indian girls and Russian and German tarts danced odd versions of what they believed to be the latest American dances."[70] No, the American novelist would not have found the fake baroness Stefani there, speaking English in an East European accent while prospecting for women suitable for her rich clients in Paris. But Kamathipura was also fashioned by industrial modernity. Though it lacked the sophistication of the Taj, Marine Drive, and Malabar Hill, the red-light district also gained sustenance from Bombay's industry and trade, catering to mill workers and other underclasses. Like the rest of the city, the brothels were also cosmopolitan, made up of the flotsam and jetsam that washed ashore the Island City. Greeks, East Europeans, Levantines, women of assorted European descent, and Arab women described as belonging to the "Jewesses" caste found their way to the brothels in the city.[71] They probably ended up in the establishments on Safed Gulli (White Lane) in Kamathipura, which served European sailors and soldiers. Indian prostitutes, who were initially scattered over the mill districts, occupied other streets in the area. They were drawn from all over—Punjab, Sind, Kashmir, Goa, Karnataka, and many other places.[72]

The bleak chawls and the sordid Kamathipura do not usually enter the picture of the city on the sea composed by the sweeping promenade of Marine Drive, the aesthetics of Art Deco, and the hot sounds of jazz. Claude Batley, the well-known Bombay architect and urbanist, spoke feelingly about the abysmal living conditions of the poor in the government-constructed chawls. But he too was inspired by the possibilities opened by the Backbay reclamation. Speaking in 1934, he criticized the government plan and proposed that "the front of the Marine Parade from Colaba to Chowpatty should be a great, wide sea-front with recessed lawns on its East side, with rides, drives and a promenade so that all may realize again that Bombay is by the sea."[73] It is another matter that the government did not follow his advice, but the point is that Batley was not immune to the charm of the image of the city on the sea. Nor did he see it vitally connected to the reality of the chawls, which he condemned.

Even Nariman, who earned his spurs exposing the Backbay scandal, did not view the two as structurally related. His target was colonial despotism. Focused on unearthing the murky secret of the Raj, he could not fathom the force of what was unfolding before him. It was not just colonial power, but industrial modernity, now clad in aesthetic modernism. The appeal extended even to the working classes, which responded enthusiastically to the thrill of Fearless Nadia.

The package of Art Deco architecture and objects, fashion, entertainment, and cinema was seductive. It offered a dreamworld of human and technological mastery of nature. Caught up in its allure, the city columnist for the *Illustrated Weekly of India* published an article tellingly entitled "A Jungle Mind Looks at Bombay."[74] It recounted the visit of Bhendu, a member of the Bhil "jungle tribe," to Bombay. The crowd did not faze Bhendu, but he "stood on the pavement grinning with amazement and threw sly glances at the tops of several of the city's landmarks." Most of all, cinema startled him. As soon as he entered the theater, Bhendu rushed to the door to escape, asking: "Why the darkness?" He refused to believe that *tamasha* (traditional Indian theater) could be performed in the dark. Coaxed to return, Bhendu sat high up on the tilted edge of his seat. "I explained how the seat sprung back and Bhendu stood up several times to study the wonders of that tip-up chair." To "Bhendu's credit," he sat "like a gentleman" through the whole performance, clicking his tongue "during a particularly exciting part of the film." After the show, Bhendu noted that he would have difficulty explaining "the wonderful piece of magic" he had witnessed to his fellow villagers. Finally, the author, suitably satisfied with his experiment of showing the magic of the city and cinema to Bhendu, asked him if he would like to work and live in Bombay. "Bhendu did a surprising thing. He put his finger to his nose and shook his head emphatically."

Bhendu was able to resist the seduction of the modern city and technology despite the shock experience. Not so the author of the article; he was more bewitched by the charms of industrial modernity than the "jungle tribe" visitor to Bombay. Indeed, so powerful was the enchantment that even Nariman's exposés were ignored. Years later, an area on the Backbay was named after him. Later still, adding insult to injury, yet another scandal-riddled reclamation was also christened after him. But meanwhile, industrial modernity forged ahead, and the City on the Sea went on to stage its magical visual drama.

4

THE COSMOPOLIS AND THE NATION

On October 9, 1947, a young Muslim woman committed suicide in Bombay. She was married to a police constable who was adamant that they move to newly created Pakistan. The husband was persistent, but so was the wife in refusing to snap the deep ties to the land of her childhood and ancestors. Finally, tired of his stubborn insistence, she hung herself by a rope fastened to the ceiling of their home.[1]

Tragic though it was, the Muslim woman's death pales in comparison with the scale of the displacements and killings that marked the unruly end of the Raj. Between half a million to a million people lost their lives in the butchery that greeted the British decision to partition the colonial territory into the independent states of India and Pakistan. Over twelve million Hindus and Muslims were uprooted from their homes, forced to relocate to a state where their coreligionists were in the majority. Punjab and Bengal bore the brunt of the Partition carnage. In Bombay, where the 1941 Hindu and Muslim populations were 68 and 17 percent, respectively, the riots never reached the scale of other areas. Still, the politics of Partition and Independence cast a pall on Bombay's multicultural world.

Like Istanbul under the Ottomans and Vienna under the Austro-Hungarian Empire, Bombay owed its cosmopolitan nature to imperialism. What brought together its inhabitants was not their common humanity but their subjection to the British Raj. The imperial cosmopolis was deeply hierarchical; it was underwritten by concepts of racial and cultural superiority and required subordination to imposed authority. But it did not demand a common, homogeneous identity among its subjects. On the contrary, it thrived on differentiating and dividing the subject population. Not so nationalism. In challenging imperialism, it pressed the nation's claim as the most fundamental of all identities. Jawaharlal Nehru famously viewed India as unity in diversity, but diversity was subordinate to unity. A person was an *Indian* first, and only then a Hindu, Muslim, or Christian. Religion, region, and language added color and texture but did not fundamentally contribute to national identity, which was unmarked and undivided. So it was with the idea of Pakistan. The central assumption was that a Muslim was a *Pakistani* first, and only then anything else. This demand for loyalty to the modern nation-state over everything else left little room for those who took their other affiliations as seriously as they did the nation.

The Muslim policeman's wife in Bombay committed suicide when faced with this meaning of identity imposed by the change from empire to nation. Fortunately, not many others took this fatal step. Nevertheless, the politics of nationalism challenged the cosmopolitanism of the colonial metropolis. Bombay's multiethnic and polyglot world of radical politics, literature, film, and art felt the pressure to choose between a religious and a national identity. Saadat Hasan Manto, the brilliant Urdu writer, whose searing Partition short stories have no equal, was unable to cope. In 1948 he bade farewell to the city he loved and migrated to Pakistan. He died there in 1955, at the age of forty-three, consumed by alcohol, loneliness, penury, and a lack of critical recognition. Others, such as Ismat Chugtai and Khwaja Ahmed Abbas, refused to choose between their faith and the nation. They elected to remain in Bombay. Writers and intellectuals like them, many of whom were Muslim, rejected the entanglement of national freedom with communal violence and rebuffed an exclusivist definition of the nation. This is a story of the city that they made, the cosmopolitan world they inhabited and sought to project in the changed context of national citizenship.

THE WRITERLY CITY

By the 1930s, Bombay was the place to be if you were a writer, an artist, or a radical political activist. Already a preeminent center of commerce and industry, the Backbay reclamation and the Improvement Trust's housing and transportation projects had imparted it the urban form of a metropolis by the early thirties. The colonial invocation of medieval authority by Gothic Revival buildings now faced the internationalist aspirations of Art Deco's industrial modernity. The resumption of international travel and migration after World War I reenergized the city's links to the world. The elites heard swing and jazz sounds in clubs and restaurants and watched Hollywood films in the new Art Deco theaters. The world of workers in chawls and slums lay far away from the cosmopolitan glitter of the elites, but there too the winds of change were blowing. While the Congress activists mobilized working-class neighborhoods for nationalist agitations, the Communists organized the mill hands for militant industrial actions. Politically energized by anticolonialism and Marxism, many middle-class intellectuals found stimulation in the modern metropolitan milieu of Bombay. Writers and artists from North India flocked to the city, seeking opportunities to practice their craft in newspapers, literary journals, and the growing film industry.

Saadat Hasan Manto came to Bombay in 1936. Of Kashmiri descent, he was born in 1912 in Punjab and grew up in the Sikh holy city of Amritsar, where his father, a judge in colonial service, was posted.[2] His father married twice and had twelve children, Manto being the youngest child of his father's second wife. Living in constant dread of his short-tempered father and feeling neglected and ignored by the rest of the family except his mother, he struck out in a free-spirited direction. Manto loved to read but failed his high school matriculation examination twice—including Urdu, of all subjects. Although he barely passed in his third attempt, he showed no interest in further studies, failing his intermediate examinations twice. He drifted for a while, loafing on the streets, gambling, drinking, consuming marijuana, visiting graveyards to commune with the spirits of Sufi saints, and hanging out with friends, listening to classical Hindustani music. While living this bohemian life, Manto found a mentor in Bari Alig, the editor of an Urdu journal, who kindled his interest in modern European literature. He read Victor Hugo, Gogol, Gorky, Chekhov, Pushkin, Oscar Wilde, Maupassant, and Somerset Maugham. While plying himself with liquor, he also published Urdu translations of Hugo's *The Last Day of a Condemned Man* and Oscar Wilde's *Vera*. Manto even tried to revive his failed academic career by enrolling in Aligarh Muslim University in 1934. But a false diagnosis of tuberculosis limited his university education to a mere nine months. More important, it was writing, and not a formal education, that consumed his attention. Before he was twenty-four years old, he had published Urdu translations of European authors, penned a short story and film reviews, and become acquainted with Marxist ideas through his mentor, Bari Alig.

Fittingly, a footloose and rebellious man who had found his direction in modern literary pursuits gravitated to Bombay in 1936. With the death of his father a few years earlier and a dependent mother, money was tight. When Manto received an offer from Bombay to edit the Urdu film journal *Mussawar*, he promptly accepted. For the next twelve years, he lived almost continuously in Bombay, except for an eighteen-month period in 1941–42 when he worked for All India Radio in Delhi. Over a hundred radio plays written by him were broadcast. It was in Delhi that he came to know other Urdu writers, such as Krishan Chander and Upendra Nath Ashk. Although it was a productive time, Manto found the imperial capital too slow and dull. He returned to Bombay and worked for several film companies over the next five years, writing stories for the screen. He also continued publishing short-story collections that he had begun with *Aatishpare* in 1936, followed by *Manto Ke Afsane* (1940) and *Dhuan* (1941). While writing for films, he published *Afsane Aur Dramme* (1943) and *Chughd* (1948), the last appearing shortly after he left for Pakistan. Between 1934 and 1947, he published nearly seventy stories.

Manto is justly celebrated for his Partition short stories. Although the stories sketch unsparing portraits of ordinary people as willing executioners, they also draw attention to the little acts of humanity practiced by flawed individuals. This concern with the ordinary, the flawed, the minor, the social outcast, was enduring in Manto. He was a classic flaneur, writing about the everyday experiences of the people who lived in his neighborhood. Above all, he was drawn to the urban reality. Breaking from the sentimentalism and romanticism of traditional Urdu literature, he sketched modern urban life in sparkling prose. The pointed and pithy short story was his chosen form to chronicle the city, to depict the drama of modernity in the small details of life on the street.

"Mammad Bhai" is one such delightful tale about the street.[3] It is set in the time when Manto first moved to Bombay and lived in a rented room in Arab Gulli, located in the heart of the city's red-light district. The tone is nonjudgmental and affectionate. He starts with a montage of the street. In short but vivid strokes, he brings to life a picture of the hustle and bustle of the neighborhood—the cinema employees soliciting viewers with bells, people getting oil massages, and, of course, prostitutes of every possible nationality and price. The story centers on Mammad Bhai, a neighborhood Dada (gangster) with a heart of gold. Manto does not pull punches on the nature of his profession and the fear he arouses among the people. But it turns out that the fierce Mammad Bhai, always armed with a menacing knife, is also a kind neighborhood patron. When Manto, who places himself in the story as the narrator, is struck with malaria, shivering with fever in his room for days with no one to take care of him, the dreaded Dada pays him a visit. Manto has never met him before. Nonetheless, Mammad Bhai arrives with his posse to check on his health. Twirling his alarming "Kaiser Wilhelm" handlebar mustache and stroking his razor-sharp knife, the gangster reprimands Manto for not contacting him. A doctor is summoned. He is ordered to treat Manto free of charge and threatened with dire consequences if his patient does not survive.

Fortunately for the doctor, Manto does recover. But the exercise of raw street power, albeit for benign purposes, soon hits its limits when Mammad Bhai is charged with the murder of a man who had raped a prostitute's daughter. An uneducated tough who strikes fear in the red-light district, he is filled with anxiety about his court appearance. The confidence gained from the street deserts the gangster and his posse when faced with the weighty authority of the court. At the suggestion of many, including Manto, he shaves his menacing mustache to look respectable in the court. His anxiety is unfounded, as no witness is willing to testify against him. When the judge acquits Mammad Bhai but exiles him from the city, it is not the banishment that the Dada mourns. Rather, he is stricken with remorse on losing his mustache. The story poignantly marks the limits of Mammad Bhai's very being, his street-born confidence and power, in the loss of his mustache.

"Naya Qanoon" (New Constitution) also deals with the restricted power of the street, though in the context of modern politics.[4] The setting is Lahore, and the protagonist is Mangu, the coachman. Though uneducated, Mangu picks up stray bits of information from his passengers and is considered a knowledgeable man in his subaltern circle. One day he hears from his passengers that a new constitution will come into effect on April 1, which will end the power of the Goras (Whites). Mangu does not know or understand that the new constitution refers to the Government of India Act of 1935, passed by the colonial government in response to the nationalist movement that was meant to devolve power. Instead, he conflates conversations about the new constitution and the Soviet Union to infer a connection between the two and concludes that the "Russian king" has ordered the inauguration of a new regime. The new constitution will terminate the rule of the whites, whom he hates because of their racial arrogance, and will inaugurate wholesale social changes. April 1 arrives. Mangu spots an Englishman, recognizing him as the same drunken Gora who had once beaten him. The coachman is brimming with self-assurance. But when he behaves haughtily, the Englishman strikes him with his cane. Mangu responds by delivering a solid thrashing to the Gora. The police appear and promptly drag Mangu away, ignoring his screams of "New Constitution, New Constitution!"

In the story, the street appears as a space of self-fashioning. Thus, picking up and mixing together bits of information from his passengers, the coachman fancies himself a knowledgeable person, about to achieve full freedom of expression. But the confrontation with authority brutally clarifies the political and social limits of his self-fashioned world. Manto excels at showcasing both the soaring possibilities and crushing limits of modern urban life. He treats urban society as an exciting constellation of multiplicity, mixture, and unpredictability, bringing to the surface its ironies and contradictions. But even as he chronicles these possibilities and paradoxes, Manto cannot remain immune from them; they enter and disturb the flaneur's observing self. We can witness the shadow cast by the romance of modern urban life on Manto the narrator in "Babu Gopinath."[5]

Babu Gopinath, a rich Hindu merchant from Lahore, comes to Bombay in 1940. His entourage includes a few hangers-on, who regularly fleece him, and two courtesans, one of whom is Zeenat, a young Kashmiri woman. The rich merchant has two passions: the company of courtesans and Sufi shrines. He is perfectly aware that "in kothas [courtesans' establishments], parents prostitute their daughters, and in shrines, men prostitute God."[6] Yet, Babu Gopinath says to Manto, he is willing to spend time in both because both are places of illusion, fit for a man seeking to deceive himself. The only thing he is sure about is that his money is going to run out soon. Before that happens, he is determined to find a suitable husband for Zeenat, the woman he loves. When a rich Sindhi landlord falls in love with Zeenat, he arranges the marriage. Manto is invited to the wedding, where he sees Zeenat dressed in a fine bridal dress. At the sight of a flower-bedecked bridal bed prepared for the courtesan, Manto bursts out laughing. In spite of his modern, broad-minded outlook, he cannot resist judging the courtesan. The sight of the virginal bed stumps the flaneur's celebration of the impure, the lowly, and the ironic. His laugh, the cruel laughter of tradition, which shows he is unable to accept the irony of the courtesan's desire for matrimonial respectability, makes Zeenat burst into tears. Babu Gopinath comforts her, casts a disappointed look at the chastened chronicler of modern society, and leaves the room with tears glistening in his eyes.

To Manto's credit, the story ennobles Babu Gopinath and Zeenat and casts a critical eye on his own narrow-mindedness. In story after story, Manto engages with the humanity of courtesans, prostitutes, and their paramours. The street is his hunting ground, and the people on the fringe of society his dramatis personae. With sensitivity, he explores the world of street toughs, pimps, and hustlers. Unsparing in unmasking the respectable, Manto treats the disreputable with sympathy. He does not judge their profession; nor is his prose wrapped in the language of reform. He writes with a humanist impulse, one that illuminates the self that emerges in the struggle to negotiate with the demands of modern life. Stable families and kinship ties play no role in his portrait of the city. His urban society is formed in daily exchanges and chance interactions between strangers. No single identity of religion, class, gender, or language acts as the sole determinant of the self in the city. Hindus, Muslims, Sikhs, Christians, and Jews interact without any prior philosophy of cosmopolitanism guiding their exchanges. Rather, it is the vortex of money, occupation, friendship, and desire that brings them together without diluting their religious identities. In Manto's stories, there is a celebration of the diversity and vitality, the randomness and motion, of everyday modern city life.

Manto lived his urban imagination. Interactions and friendships across religious boundaries marked his life in Bombay. This remained true even after he achieved fame and riches and moved from his Arab Gulli room to a flat in Byculla, where he lived with his wife after their marriage in 1940. Prostitutes, courtesans, and pimps continued to inhabit his stories. When he achieved literary recognition and started writing for films, his circle of friends came to include writers and artists who had also gravitated to Bombay and to cinema. Among them was Ismat Chugtai (1915–91), later lauded as a feminist writer.

Like Manto, Chugtai was also fiercely independent and unconventional. She grew up in a large family (the ninth of ten children), first in Agra, and subsequently in Aligarh. The family was well off, and Chugtai grew up surrounded by servants. Her father, a judicial magistrate in colonial service, was a progressive man, and the family had easy relations with their Hindu neighbors. But there were limits. Despite neighborly exchanges, the Hindus considered Muslims ritually polluting, and for all its progressivism, Chugtai's own family saw nothing wrong with the lot of their servants. Most of all, what irked her was the differential treatment of girls. Fortunately, growing up in the company of her brothers, Chugtai seized the freedom that the boys enjoyed. One of her elder brothers took her under his wing and introduced his sister to history, geography, and literature. She started translating English novels into Urdu and also wrote (by her own admission) "filthy" short stories.[7] When they were discovered, Chugtai disowned her creations, claiming they were translations. This setback did not dim her rebelliousness. Her heroine was Rashid Jahan (1905–52), whose story had appeared in the Urdu collection

Angaarey (Embers). Published in 1932, this collection caused a stir. Muslim clerics and conservatives denounced it as blasphemous and obscene. Under their pressure, the British government banned the anthology. Such strident admonitions and the ban only enhanced *Angaarey*'s radical status and turned Jahan into a feminist literary icon.[8] Drawing strength from this example of a deep churning in the Muslim middle class, Chugtai rebelled against the gendered double standard of her milieu. She rejected an arranged marriage, earned a BA degree, trained as a teacher at Aligarh Muslim University, and became the headmistress of a girls' school. She moved to Bombay after marrying Shaheed Lateef, a filmmaker. After initially working in the colonial education service, she resigned her position to become a full-time writer, publishing in Urdu journals and writing scripts for films.

In Bombay, Chugtai became part of the literary circle that had turned the city into an intellectual hub. It is no surprise that she and Manto got on like a house on fire from the very first time they met. It was a friendship of the intellect. Both were iconoclasts, opinionated, and argumentative, their exchanges full of high-voltage disagreements over ideas high and low; but they also had genuine affection for each other. Chugtai became very close to Manto and his wife, Safia.

The bond between the two writers became even stronger when both were charged with obscenity in their writings. In 1942 Chugtai had published "Lihaaf" (Quilt).[9] The story is about the neglected wife of an aristocrat who prefers to spend his time in the company of handsome young men. The unhappy wife finds comfort under the quilt in the company of her maid. The scene of her physical and emotional fulfillment is reported through the eyes of the wife's young niece. The girl wakes up at night and notices that the quilt covering her aunt and the maid is moving. She does not understand her aunt's lesbian relationship, but the reader does. This was cause enough for her majesty's government, apparently egged on by the conservative Muslims of Lahore, to charge her with obscenity. Chugtai was no defender of homosexual relationships and was not proud of having written a story that had won her such notoriety. Consequently, she was not exactly thrilled that the obscenity charge brought attention to "Lihaaf."[10]

Manto, on the other hand, wore the obscenity charge as a badge of honor. Two of his stories, "Boo" (Odor) and "Kaali Shalwaar" (Black Trousers), were on trial.[11] The two stories are very different. The first concerned male sexuality, which expressed masculine desire in the fetish for the odor of an earthy, unrefined woman. The second was a story about a prostitute in Delhi, whose desire for a pair of black trousers is used by Manto to reflect on urban society and sexual politics. Not only was Manto unrepentant about these stories, he tried to convince Chugtai that "Lihaaf" was her best work.[12] Both traveled to Lahore for the trial. The Muslim conservative elite of Lahore tried to pressure Chugtai to confess to the crime of obscenity, but she resisted. Manto was his irrepressible self. When a witness testified that he found the word "bosom" obscene, Manto shot up from his chair and asked sarcastically if he should call a woman's breasts "peanuts." The court tittered. The charges were thrown out, and the duo returned triumphantly to Bombay.[13]

The friendship between Manto and Chugtai, cemented by their obscenity trials, was expressive of the space Bombay afforded for relationships based on literature and art. In their different ways, both writers explored the functioning of modern social relationships, of desire and sexuality. The city and its film industry offered them opportunities for their literary pursuits. To read the accounts of their arguments over philosophy and literature, their friendly quarrels over small matters, their everyday comings and goings, is to appreciate the social exchanges and ties that Bombay provided to the life of literature, art, and commerce.[14]

Manto and Chugtai were not the only ones inhabiting and exploring Bombay's modern life. Several other Urdu writers, including Krishan Chander (1914–77), made the city their home. Like Manto and Chugtai, Chander also wrote scripts for films. Whereas Hindi writers looked down on cinema in their quest for pure forms, Urdu writers, both Hindu and Muslim, found a receptive audience and a new medium for their work in films. The desire to address a mass audience in a popular, accessible language fell in line with their literary quest to explore new forms to represent modern experiences and question customary norms. The film industry also offered lucrative and steady employment. In the 1940s, the industry was organized in a studio system. Each studio had a stable of writers, who were paid a regular monthly salary to write stories and scenes. Of course, not every writer or intellectual drifted into the film world. There was, for example, Mulk Raj Anand (1905–2004), who returned from London in 1946 to live in Bombay, with his literary fame already established by his social realist novels in English—*Untouchable* (1935) and *Coolie* (1936).

Intellectuals and artists were drawn to Bombay's pulsating modernity, but they also viewed it as deeply contradictory. If the city's promise of progress and freedom attracted them, they were repelled by its depredations and injustices. Theirs was not a belief in idyllic progress. Even as they represented and criticized caste, gender, and class inequalities with new eyes and excoriated religion and religious divisions as backward, the writers and artists also strove to uncover the oppressions of colonialism and capitalism. As much as they broke from inherited norms and dogmas, these intellectuals also brought to light the dark and dense reality hidden by the glitter of modernity. Intellectuals influenced by this progressivism congregated in Bombay, turning it into a hothouse of radical art and ideas. Giving this milieu a political direction and organization were the

Communist-led Progressive Writers' Association (PWA) and Indian People's Theatre Association (IPTA).

The PWA's origins went back to *Angaarey*'s publication in 1932. This anthology included short stories by Rashid Jahan, Sajjad Zaheer (1905–73), Ahmed Ali (1910–94), and Mahmuduzzafar (1908–56). Remembering the *Angaarey* group of writers, Ali writes that they "shared a love of sombreros, bright shirts, and contrasting ties, collecting candlesticks and gargoyles, Bach and Beethoven, and an admiration for James Joyce and D. H. Lawrence and the *New Writing* poets, as well as Chekhov and Gorky."[15] The group combined a youthful, cosmopolitan outlook combined with a predilection for realism and a desire to expose social injustices and "outmoded" beliefs and customs.

To this broadly progressive outlook, Zaheer gave a political and organizational shape. Zaheer, the son of a High Court judge, was initially educated in Lucknow and earned a bachelor's degree at Oxford in 1932. While in England, he turned to Marxism. Like many intellectuals of his generation, Zaheer was alarmed by the rise of the Nazis in Germany and Europe's drift toward militarism.[16] Politically energized by anti-Fascist struggles in Europe, Zaheer and several like-minded aspiring writers decided to form a literary association. The kindly owner of a Chinese restaurant in London offered them the use of a small, unventilated room at the back of his establishment for a meeting. A group of thirty-five (mostly students from Oxford, Cambridge, and London) met at the Nanking Restaurant on Denmark Street in November 1934 to discuss a manifesto. Drafted by Mulk Raj Anand, it called for rescuing literature and other arts from "the priestly, academic and decadent classes in whose hands they have degenerated so long" and "to bring the arts into the closest touch with the people."[17] The aspiring writers met periodically in London to discuss literary works, but it was clear to Zaheer that he had to make connections with progressive writers in India. Thus, after completing his law degree, he set sail for India.

The All India Progressive Writers' Association held its first meeting in Lucknow in April 1936.[18] The choice of Lucknow was not accidental. The Congress was also meeting in the city, and Jawaharlal Nehru was to preside over its session. As a left-wing nationalist, Nehru qualified as an ally according to the Comintern's united front strategy. Nehru warmly greeted the PWA's formation. Messages of support also came from the Bengali writer and Nobel laureate Rabindranath Tagore. The only disquieting note was struck by the near absence of Hindi writers. With the Hindi-versus-Urdu controversy raging in North India, they were wary of the prominence of Urdu writers in the PWA. The Hindi writers' absence was made up for by the presence of Premchand (1880–1936). The noted Hindi-Urdu writer, who was then at the peak of his literary fame, was elected as the president, and Zaheer as the secretary-general of the association.

Though Zaheer was a member of the Communist Party of India (CPI), the PWA was not just a front organization. Many writers who were influenced by progressive and socialist ideas were neither CPI members nor followers. Indeed, a tension between didactic and creative tendencies was present from the PWA's inception. But all these writers expressed a genuine social and intellectual ferment. Modernity had brought with it a critique of customary authority and religion and sparked a reevaluation of traditional aesthetic forms. The encounter with European literature and philosophy shaped their critical outlook and literary practice, providing them with a sense of belonging to a cosmopolitan political and literary world. The PWA seized on the changing literary and intellectual milieu to move the writers in the direction of socialist realism. Under its influence, the Urdu writers, for example, shifted the focus of their aesthetic attention. "The rose still bloomed in the spring, the cup of wine still passed around, the bulbul still sang songs of love," but the suffering of the romantic lover was transformed into the plight of humanity.[19] They penned poems of incitement and anger, in a language that had become far more direct. Of course, not everyone followed the credo of socialist realism, but the commitment to engage with the "real" was widely shared. This "real" in India was colonial. The progressive writers did not approach this reality as simpleminded nationalists; they saw the nation as a horizon of social equality and communal harmony. This was in line with the broad goals of the Communists, whose stewardship of the PWA provided the literary milieu with an organized coherence.

The PWA enjoyed a significant presence in Bombay. Chugtai, Krishan Chander, Majrooh Sultanpuri, Ali Sardar Jafri, Sahir Ludhianvi, Kaifi Azmi, Josh Malihabadi, all were actively involved. They were some of the most talented Urdu writers and poets, who went on to achieve great fame as film lyricists and scriptwriters. Their circle extended to gifted writers spread all across North India. Manto was friendly with several PWA writers but remained deeply skeptical of the political orientation of Progressives. His short story "Taraqqi-pasand" (The Progressive) pokes fun at them as superficial intellectuals captive to the sound of the English word *progressive*. He was to write later that the Progressives were apparatchiks, bent on turning "a poem into a machine and a machine into a poem."[20] Notwithstanding his hostility to socialist realism, Manto's writings engaged with the social inequities of the world around him. Progressivism was in the air, and Manto breathed it, even if he turned up his nose at its political prescriptions. Many of his fellow writers in the city did not share his suspicion. Marxism appealed to intellectuals who wished for national freedom to mean something more than the mere end of British rule.

The presence of the CPI headquarters in Bombay and the influence of its powerful trade unions added to the sway of progressivism among intellectuals. The party headquarters on Sandhurst Road was run like a commune under P. C. Joshi, the CPI's charismatic secretary. Joshi had a particular talent in interacting with artists and intellectuals. It was largely under his direction that the IPTA, founded in 1942, went on to quickly become a powerful cultural movement.

The Communist attempt to organize artists was part of the Comintern's response to political developments in Europe. The Reichstag fire, the Nazi rise to power, and the persecution of Communists had convinced it of the need for the widest possible mobilization against fascism. The Nazi attack on the Soviet Union in 1941 demonstrated the virtue of the united-front strategy all the more urgently.

The favorable response to a workers' theater group in Bangalore inspired some intellectuals in Bombay to gather in the Taj Mahal Hotel to form a similar cultural group. But "the proletarian theatre was apparently stifled in the air-conditioned atmosphere of the far-from-proletarian Taj!"[21] In February 1942 another attempt was made, which met with more success. A committee—"ranging from the deepest Red to the bluest Blue blood"—was formed. Among others, it included Lt. Col. S. S. Sokhey, the director of Haffkine Institute, "who divides his study tours between snakes, dance, and Marxism"; Mrs. Wadia, a wealthy socialite; and Anil de Silva, the socialist daughter of a Sri Lankan government minister.[22] The new organization was inspired by the Little Theatre movement in England, the WPA Federal Theater Project in the United States, and the Chinese theatrical productions against Japanese occupation. IPTA aimed to deploy the popular theatrical and musical traditions as "the expression and the organizer of our people's struggles for freedom, economic justice and a democratic culture."[23] The physicist Homi J. Bhabha, later regarded as the founder of the nuclear establishment in India, was a member of IPTA and is the one who named the organization.

Bombay became an important hub of IPTA, attracting radical writers, poets, musicians, journalists, and film artists, as well as a number of cultural activists from the working-class districts. Its inaugural performance on May Day in 1943 was a play written by a working-class activist. IPTA also staged *Yeh Kiska Khoon Hai?* (Whose Blood Is This?), a play watched by over four thousand workers, written by the Urdu writer Ali Sardar Jafri. The performance ended with all the actors coming on the stage, singing:

Woh duniya, duniya kya hogi, jis duniya mein Swaraj na ho?
Woh azaadi, azaadi kya, jis mein mazdoor ka raj na ho?

What will be that world, a world that is not free?
What is that freedom, where workers don't rule?[24]

IPTA held film screenings, one of which showed a Soviet woman making a parachute jump. The audience responded with cries of "Stalin Zindabad" (Long Live Stalin). Paul Robeson's portrayal of an African American miner apparently elicited interest among workers about the life of miners in the West. Working-class activists such as D. N. Gavankar and Anna Bhau Sathe drew on folk theater to write Marathi plays that were staged in working-class districts. Khwaja Ahmed Abbas wrote a Hindustani anti-Fascist fantasy titled *Yeh Amrit Hai* (This Is Nectar), which was also staged in working-class districts.[25]

Abbas (1914–87) belonged to a Muslim middle-class family from Panipat, a town near Delhi. He received his college education at Aligarh Muslim University, the educational Mecca of modern Muslims. At Aligarh, he started writing for newspapers and became enchanted with Nehru and his socialist ideas. In 1934 he made his first journey to Bombay, a city he had read about in novels and short stories. He records the excitement of the immigrant's arrival in the city: "As the train thundered past the local station platforms, there were dark clouds in the horizon. It was raining somewhere. Excitement piled upon excitement as we recognized, from hearsay, some of the suburban stations—Andheri, Bandra, Dadar. ... Bombay, it has been said, is not a city, it is a state of mind. It is the state of a young man's mind, exciting and excitable, exuberant and effervescent, dynamic and dramatic."[26] After working as an intern for a few months in the nationalist newspaper *Bombay Chronicle*, he returned to Aligarh to complete his law degree. But the Bombay bug had bitten him for good. He returned a year later to work for the *Bombay Chronicle* and made the city his home.

Living in the city, the news of the formation of the PWA gladdened Abbas's heart. Although he was a journalist who wrote in English, he also had an abiding interest in Urdu literature and later wrote literary works in Hindustani. He became one of the founding members of IPTA and was commissioned to write a Hindustani play for North Indian mill workers. He wrote *Zubeida*, which was directed by Balraj Sahni (1913–73), who was to become a celebrated film actor.

Sahni grew up in a Punjabi family in Rawalpindi, then a British military cantonment town. His father ran a successful clothing business, but Sahni's interest ran in a different direction. Like many other young people in Rawalpindi, he was besotted by cinema.[27] This love persisted while he studied at Lahore. He saw both Hollywood and Hindi films and acted in plays while earning a master's degree in English literature in 1934. At loose ends after his university education but determined not to be in the family business, he wrote Hindi short stories, became a teacher in Tagore's Shantiniketan, and then jumped to Sevagram, Gandhi's ashram in 1939. Both Shantiniketan and Sevagram were centers of experimentation in search of new forms of art, culture, and education. Drawn by this heady atmosphere, Sahni and his wife, Damyanti, spent nearly three years working on the experiments to formulate a new language of Indian art and education. But they were not done yet with searching for a purpose in life.

A job offer from the BBC took the couple to London, where they worked in its Hindi service. London overawed Sahni, who spent a good part of his salary visiting strip clubs and watching films. It was only the outbreak of the war that awoke him to politics. He saw Soviet films, read Marxism, and met writers and intellectuals such as T. S. Eliot, George Orwell, Harold Laski, Lionel Fielden, and Gilbert Harding.[28] After soaking in the intellectual life of London, the Sahnis returned to India in 1944, making Bombay their home.

Sahni ran into Chetan Anand, an acquaintance from Lahore, who was now in Bombay, working on a film. The chance meeting introduced him to the film industry. Sahni describes how the studios were working overtime to produce films, and educated young men and women were joining the industry. Famous writers and poets such as Krishan Chander, Manto, Upendra Nath Ashk, Josh Malihabadi, and Bhagwati Charan Varma were writing screenplays and songs and earning fabulous sums. Chetan Anand offered acting roles to both Sahni and his wife. The couple, along with their young daughter, moved in with Anand in his rented bungalow in Pali Hill, Bandra, a big rambling house surrounded by mango groves. Anand lived there with his wife and his two brothers—Vijay Anand, who was later to make his name as a successful director, and Dev Anand, who went on to become a huge star. Like Sahni, Chetan Anand was also a Punjabi. After completing his BA in Lahore, he went to London to study for the competitive Indian Civil Service examinations. Instead, he took part in BBC programs, attended seminars, and reveled in the intellectual atmosphere of the city. On his return, he taught briefly at Doon School, but his love of theater and film drew him to Bombay in 1943.[29]

Chetan Anand's Pali Hill bungalow was a salon for artists. His wife, Uma Anand, ran an open house, frequented by aspiring writers, poets, actors, filmmakers, and artists. "Life at 41 Pali Hill resounded with ideas; scripts being discussed; Kamleshwar painting, Zohra dancing, everybody arguing, reading and discussing."[30] Chetan Anand and Sahni also went downtown every day to breathe in the heady atmosphere of the India Coffee House at Flora Fountain, where they would run into writers, journalists, painters, and dancers. "The occupants of the next table might be spiritedly defending the Congress policies, while the one in front of you was likely to be a communist or a socialist stronghold! Naturally, all these budding geniuses were accompanied by their girlfriends, who hung on every word they uttered! The whole atmosphere in that cafe used to be charged with emotion and you felt a mood of expectancy in the air."[31]

A chance glance at a newspaper advertisement announcing that People's Theatre was to stage a play took Sahni and Chetan Anand to an IPTA meeting.[32] Abbas conducted the meeting, attended by twenty-thirty young men and women. Without getting Sahni's prior consent, Abbas announced that "Comrade Balraj Sahni" was going to direct his play *Zubeida*. Sahni was taken aback by this sudden anointment, but since nothing was happening to his film career, he decided to take up the challenge. He recruited Chetan and his brother Dev Anand as actors, but on the day of the performance, Chetan suddenly took ill, forcing Sahni to play the lead role. The play was about a young Muslim girl who casts aside her veil to take up relief work for cholera victims. The high point of the performance was the appearance of her bridegroom, who rode a horse down the aisle of the auditorium. The play was a great success and was performed several times.

IPTA became a fixture in the city. It staged plays and performances in the working-class districts as well as before middle-class audiences. Its reputation grew, and noted theater and film actors, such as Prithviraj Kapoor, maintained a sympathetic and supportive relationship to its activities. Leading actors, writers, musicians, and dancers who went on to great fame and fortune were involved in its performances. Chetan Anand's *Neecha Nagar* (Lowly City), for example, won the Palme d'Or at the Cannes Film Festival in 1946. Written by Abbas, with music composed by Ravi Shankar, the film tells the story of the nonviolent struggle of the underclasses against the rich. *Neecha Nagar* combines a social realist story with a cinematic style of set design and lighting that was clearly influenced by German Expressionism. Abbas also wrote *Dr. Kotnis ki Amar Kahani* (The Immortal Journey of Dr. Kotnis). It was directed by and starred V. Shantaram, a legendary name in Marathi and Hindi films. The film told the story of a young Indian doctor who goes to China to help Chinese troops fighting the Japanese invasion. IPTA itself also produced a film, *Dharti ke Lal* (Children of the Earth), in 1946. Directed and cowritten by Abbas, it was based on Krishan Chander's novella *Anndaata*. Also a social realist film, *Dharti ke Lal* was the story of a poor family's struggle to survive during the devastating Bengal famine of 1943. It starred Zohra Sehgal and Sahni, but the film flopped at the box office.

Notwithstanding the *Dharti ke Lal* setback, IPTA and the PWA remained an influential presence in the city. In spite of the frequent contortions in its strategy, the CPI, under P. C. Joshi's stewardship, was remarkably successful in nursing the youthful enthusiasm for radical change. Margaret C. Godley, a British social worker visiting Bombay at that time, described the party headquarters as "a large, shabby set of offices in a shabby street" but "the abode of the young & eager, all working hard in a veritable hive of activity." The activists were occupied in preparing the Communist newspaper and propaganda material in English and Indian languages. Amid all this feverish activity, Godley spotted Joshi's wife looking after her baby, "which lay chuckling in bed, surrounded by Communist slogans."[33] The party office functioned as a commune, a place of politics and sociability, where the young activists talked, argued, wrote, and organized for the revolution while living a communal life along with their families.

The CPI attracted intellectuals ranging from working-class artists to upper-class journalists and writers who had been educated and traveled abroad. Among them was the couple Romesh and Raj Thapar. Both were privileged Punjabis from Lahore, who were married in Bombay in 1945 when Romesh returned from England. They resided in Breach Candy, in the elite Mafatlal Park block of flats by the seashore, boasting a lawn and a swimming pool. Their three-bedroom flat, which came with a garage and servants' quarters, became a hub of activity. "People flowed in and out all hours of the day and night, staying to eat and drink even when we were not there. The cook had a standing order of dinner for five."[34] After dinner, the Thapars and their guests would sit outside on the grass until the early hours of the morning, talking and discussing ideas.

Marxism was often quoted in conversations, with no one in the midst of frenzied arguments ever being conscious of "the obvious incongruity of holding a juicy job in a foreign firm on the one hand and entertaining ideas of communism on the other." Accusations of being a Menshevik and a reactionary flew fast and easy. The couple's social list included Frank Moraes, the editor of the *Times of India*, where Romesh Thapar worked. The Goan editor, with "slurringly British" speech," took Romesh regularly to his weekly dinners at Raj Bhavan, the Communist Party headquarters on Sandhurst Road. The celebrated social realist author Mulk Raj Anand once came to stay in their flat for a month. But Raj Thapar's excitement turned to disappointment because the novelist was then preoccupied with "a grand passion with the rather remarkable and attractive Anil De Silva,"[35] while his English wife remained in London. The couple's Communist friends included Mohan Kumarmangalam and his sister Parvati Krishnan, who belonged to a distinguished Tamil political family and had been to school and university abroad. "Parvati could move in and out of any drawing room, clad in white cotton, holding her own," and Mohan's "eyes were forever twinkling, never dimmed by communist ideology or by living in the urine-smelling commune at Raj Bhavan."[36]

Raj Thapar's no-holds-barred memoir is peppered with catty remarks about people and deeply affected by her elite status—the "urine-smelling" party headquarters frequently throws her upper-class nose out of joint. Nevertheless, she paints a vivid picture of the intellectual and political ferment in the city. Bombay seemed to hold the promise of a new India, and to the educated elite of Thapar's generation, Nehru was the symbol of a modern India. But even more inspiring was Marxism, which enchanted both Raj and Romesh. She found herself "moving naturally and effortlessly, almost sleepwalking, towards the communists, who were as much part of the social elite of Bombay at the time as anyone else."[37] When Rajni Palme Dutt, the legendary leader of the British Communist Party, visited India in

4.1. Happy times: Chugtai (2nd from the left) with other Progressives. Source: *Eve's Weekly*, August 6–12, 1983

1946, he obviously could not stay at the "urine-smelling" Raj Bhavan. So the party arranged for the Thapars to host him. J.R.D. Tata sent a message through a mutual friend that he wanted to meet Dutt, or RPD, as he was known. "So I asked Jeh [JRD] and his wife Thelma, for dinner one night." It was an uncomfortable evening, with RPD and JRD repeatedly thrusting swords at each other.

Sucked into the exciting whirlpool of Communist political and intellectual vision, Raj and Romesh became active in party activities. Raj even started working in the reviled party headquarters, where, to her great relief, she found that she was not discriminated against for her Westernized background. She came to admire Joshi for his knack at picking talented artists. Romesh became active in IPTA, which was running into financial difficulties. To raise money, Mulk Raj Anand adapted Clifford Odets's *Waiting for Lefty* for the Indian scene. Godley, the British social worker, described the performance as good—"more for the sincerity & impassioned enthusiasm of the actors than for the quality of acting."[38] Romesh took to playing the role of the eternal worker with such gusto that he changed Odets's words after every evening performance. The audience was far from working class, but so were the actors. One female actor, when asked what socialism meant, said "going to parties."[39]

"Going to parties" expresses the range of socialism's promise. To politically conscious writers and activists, Marxism provided a general horizon for progressive art and politics. But even some of the elite were caught up in its charm. And at the center of this Communist promise of a new dawn, of modern society, art, cinema, and literature was Bombay. Writers, film and theater actors and directors, and musicians saw India's future in progressivism and gave a progressive cast to the city, until communal riots shattered the dream.

COSMOPOLIS LOST

In March 1946 the British government sent a cabinet mission to India with a plan to transfer power. It held talks with the Congress and the Muslim League and proposed independence under dominion status to a united India, composed of a three-tier federation. The central government was to be a limited one, with power restricted to foreign relations, communications, defense, and unionwide finances. India was to consist of three major groups of provinces: Group A, comprising the Hindu-majority provinces of the Bombay Presidency, Madras, the United Provinces, Bihar, Orissa, and the Central Provinces; Group B, to include the Muslim-majority provinces of the Punjab, Sind, the North-West Frontier, and Baluchistan; and Group C, containing the Muslim-majority Bengal and the Hindu-majority Assam. Barring powers conceded to the central government, the three groups were proposed as virtually autonomous. Both the Congress and the Muslim League accepted the plan. However, Nehru announced that the Congress had agreed to participate only in the Constituent Assembly, and that it would be free to amend these arrangements as it saw fit. Jinnah, the Muslim League leader, saw this as a betrayal and believed that Nehru's position meant that minority interests would be placed at the hands of the majority. Faced with this crisis, the cabinet mission proposed the subcontinent's division into India and Pakistan. Nehru and Gandhi rejected the division. After a Muslim League meeting in Bombay, Jinnah announced on July 27 that he accepted the partition plan and called for Muslims to observe August 16 as "Direct Action" Day. The country plunged into bloody Hindu-Muslim riots, with the "Calcutta killings" consuming nearly six thousand lives.

In Bombay the Muslim League observed Direct Action Day on August 16 by closing all Muslim schools and colleges and shuttering their neighborhoods. Muslim workers also stayed away from mills. However, the day passed off peacefully, with no retaliatory violence in response to the "Calcutta killings."[40] But the idyll did not last. Serious communal disturbances broke out on the afternoon of September 1, when Muslims began to hoist black flags. At some places, sandals, brooms, Gandhi caps, and felt hats were also hung. In response, the Hindus hoisted Congress flags. The commissioner of police issued a curfew order and prohibited meetings, assemblies, and processions. Despite the presence of troops, who were called out, and in spite of the twenty-four-hour curfew, organized violence and stabbings occurred over two days. The city was quiet for a while, but communal clashes resumed ten days later.

Hindu-Muslim riots were not new to Bombay. In the bloody riots of 1893, Hindu and Muslim street gangs fought pitched battles.[41] In 1929 there was another serious outbreak of communal violence, following unfounded rumors that Pathans (Pashtuns from Afghanistan who lived in the city as moneylenders, traders, and security guards) were snatching children and spiriting them away in a red car. As school after school reported falling attendance due to the fear of kidnapping, the Pathans were attacked. As moneylenders and as muscle for mill owners, they were easy targets. Despite the government's efforts to squelch the rumor, the Pathans faced the murderous wrath of Hindu mill workers fearful of the danger to their children. Retaliatory violence followed, making the mill districts a scene of assaults and counterassaults.[42] Three years later, Hindus and Muslims were at each other's throats again in and around the mill districts. The Muslim isolation from the Congress-led nationalist agitation created communal tension in the city. Stray incidents of stone throwing lit the fuse, leading to full-scale riots that consumed 133 Hindu and 83 Muslim lives between May and July 1932.[43] Four years later, communal violence returned, sparked by a dispute over the construction of a raised platform for worship by Hindus next to a mosque. In a cruel validation of Gandhi's repudiation of the biblical retributive justice of an eye for an eye, the killing of forty-seven Hindus was matched by the murder of forty-seven Muslims.[44]

What distinguished the bloodshed of 1946 and 1947 was that it was sparked by events and purported developments elsewhere in British India, and not local incidents.[45] The circulation of the false rumors—that the Muslim League planned to forcibly convert Hindus or that Nehru had been shot and injured—raised the communal temperature. Exaggerated accounts of the massacre of Hindus in East Bengal and stories of atrocities on Muslims in North India provoked clashes. Attacks on Muslim mill workers were followed by retaliatory violence on the Hindus. There were rival black-flag demonstrations, strikes, stabbings, and violent disturbances that lasted up to three days at a time.[46] The violence and tension prevailed for the rest of the year and well into 1947 as reports and rumors of violence and mass displacements continued to circulate.

A. C. Clow, the governor of Bombay Presidency, noted with satisfaction that nothing like the "Bombay riots" had occurred,[47] but the communal frenzy could not but cast a pall on Bombay. "The city was divided between 'Hindu Bombay' and 'Muslim Bombay.'" No Muslim ventured into a Hindu area, and no Hindu would stray into a Muslim area. Writing about the climate of fear, Abbas recounts seeing a killing that was to haunt him for years. A hoodlum in a Hindu neighborhood spied a man dressed in kurta pajama and concluded by this clothing that he was a Muslim. He pounced on him from the back and stabbed him. As he wiped his bloody knife clean on the clothes of the man he had slain, a doubt appeared to cross his mind. He tugged open the pajama cord and saw that the man was uncircumcised. The killer clasped his knife and uttered "Mishtake ho gaya!" (Oh, a mistake!)[48]

Manto found the communal tension in the city unbearable. August 14, 1947, the day of Partition and the day before Independence, was celebrated with great fanfare in the city, with cries of "Long Live India" and "Long Live Pakistan" reverberating in the streets. Manto was unable to decide which was his country even as he agonized about people dying. "Where were they going to inter the bones which had been stripped of the flesh of religion by vultures and birds of prey? ... When we were colonial subjects, we could dream of freedom, but now that we were free, what would our dreams be?"[49] Bombay Talkies, the studio where he was employed, had begun receiving hate mail threatening arson and murder because it employed Muslims. The studio owners were unconcerned, but the communal enmity worried Manto. One day in January 1948, he packed his bags and left for Pakistan. The only person who knew that he was leaving was his close friend Shyam. When they had a parting drink of brandy, Shyam threw his arms around him and said affectionately, "Swine." Tearfully, Manto replied, "Pakistani swine." Shyam accompanied him to the port, and Manto sailed for Karachi.[50]

Chugtai was deeply disappointed. She writes that Manto had once suggested that she also move to Pakistan. According to her, he said: "There's a bright future for us in Pakistan. People there will get bungalows of those who have fled, and we'll be in a better position there to get things done, we'll make rapid progress."[51] Chugtai thought that

Manto was a coward for preparing to take advantage of those who had been forced to flee.

Chugtai judges him too harshly. It was a difficult time, and people made decisions to stay or move under trying conditions. It is perhaps more fruitful to view the move to Pakistan in light of Aamir Mufti's reading of Manto's ambivalent relationship to national culture. He suggests that the prominence of the prostitute and the brothel in his stories is a sign of a larger theme in Manto—the subordinate relationship of the minority to the majority, the subaltern to the dominant. "The insistent irony of Manto's stories, his characteristic irreverence for all cultural and political pieties and solemnities, and his elevation of doubt and 'betrayal' to something like the imperatives of an ethical life" meant that he could not be accommodated within a nationalist aesthetics.[52] His short stories were destined to remain a minor figure to the epic form of the nation. As a writer, he did not have an easy time in the new nation of Pakistan.

However, Manto went on to pen some of the most powerful short stories ever written on the Partition violence. Among them is the poignant "Toba Tek Singh."[53] It concerns a lunatic who refuses to choose either India or Pakistan as his country. The story uses lunacy as an allegory for the madness of the subcontinent's division and the maniacal desire for modern nation-states. So illogical are the new nations that even a lunatic finds them unacceptable. Manto was interested not in the politics of the nation-state as such but in its effects on the textures and feelings of everyday life.

In his delightful sketch of his friend Shyam, Manto writes about the effect of the politics of the state on friendship. It is abundantly clear that the two enjoyed a warm friendship. Shyam, a handsome film star with a love for drink, women, and books, was just the kind of person Manto adored. They drank together and helped each other out with money, and Manto was privy to the ups and downs in Shyam's numerous affairs. One time during the Partition violence, Manto and Shyam were listening to the plight of Sikh refugees forced to flee the killings in Punjab. Manto could see that his friend was deeply moved, and so he asked Shyam: "I am a Muslim, don't you feel like murdering me?" "Not now," Shyam answered gravely, "but when I was listening to the atrocities the Muslims had committed ... I could have murdered you." Manto was shocked and thought that he could have murdered Shyam at that moment. "But later when I thought about it—and between then and now there is a world of difference— I suddenly understood the basis of these riots in which thousands of innocent Hindus and Muslims were killed every day."[54]

Yet another account of "then and now" is his story "Mozail," set in a Bombay torn apart by the Partition.[55] The story showcases the city as a space of diversity, of chance encounters and affinities between strangers, of beastly violence and little acts of redemption. It opens with the protagonist, Tarlochan, a Sikh, worrying about the safety of his fiancée, Kirpal, whose family lives in a Muslim neighborhood. In his mind, he is cursing Kirpal's brother, whom he has implored several times to move the family to safety. But the brother scoffed at the idea: "This is not Amritsar or Lahore. ... It is Bombay." Tarlochan's thoughts move from Kirpal to Mozail, a Jewish woman who had lived in his building and whom he had loved. He remembers Mozail making fun of his religion when he asked her if she loved him. When he implored her to marry him, she laughed and responded that she would if he cut his hair and shaved his beard. He complied. But on the day they were to marry, she ran off with another man. Tarlochan suffered greatly but recovered. He started growing his hair and beard again and fell in love with Kirpal. Now, he worries that he will lose her too. Suddenly, he recognizes the sound of the wooden sandals that Mozail used to wear. She is back. They talk, and Tarlochan tells her that he is concerned about Kirpal. Ignoring his protests, Mozail drags him to Kirpal's house. A bloody attack is in progress. Mozail rescues Kirpal by handing her the gown she is wearing, which identifies her as a Jew. Kirpal escapes with her life, but Mozail dies, naked.

In a few pages, Manto lays out the diverse social geography of the city, its multiple religions, and its chance interactions, setting up the bonds of religion against the ties of humanity. Mozail, a member of the classic minority and otherwise unreliable, stands for values that neither religion nor the state embodies. Manto resists sentimentalism and lofty humanism by portraying Mozail as flawed. She has no feminine modesty—she never wears underwear—she ridicules Tarlochan's religion, strings him along, and double-times him. Yet, such are the attachments formed by urban life that she sacrifices her life for Tarlochan's beloved. Manto left Bombay, unable to cope with its communal tension, and yet he remained wedded to his imagination of the city *as* society. Later, he wrote this ode to the city:

> My heart is steeped in sorrow today. A strange melancholy has descended on me. Four and a half years ago, when I said goodbye to my second home Bombay, I had felt the same way. I was sad at leaving a place where I had spent so many days of hardworking life. That piece of land had offered shelter to a family reject and it had said to me, "You can be happy here on two pennies a day or on ten thousand rupees a day, if you wish. You can do what you want. No one will find fault with you. Nor will anyone subject you to moralizing. You alone will have to accomplish the most difficult tasks and you alone will have to make every important decision of your life. You may live on the footpath or in a magnificent palace; it will not matter in the least to me. You may leave or you may stay, it will make no difference to me. I am where I am and this is where I will remain."
>
> After living there for twelve years I find myself in Pakistan. I am here because of what I learnt there. If I leave and go elsewhere, I will remain the way I am. I am a walking, talking Bombay. ... I loved that city then and I love it today.

The intellectuals and artists of the city who had dreamed of a cosmopolitan nation of justice and freedom were left reeling by the blood-soaked birth of India and Pakistan. In his regular "Last Page" column in the *Bombay Chronicle*, Abbas wrote about the loss of his sense of humor. Where was it? "Perhaps, it was drowned in the rivers of blood, Hindu blood and Muslim blood, your blood and mine, that have been flowing in the streets of Calcutta, in Noakhali, in Bihar, in the U.P., the Punjab and North-West Frontier Province, not to mention the occasional bloody spurts in the streets of our own Bombay."[56] Chugtai wrote: "Communal violence and freedom became so muddled that it was difficult to distinguish between the two. ... The hearts that had been singing were hushed, the dancing feet were stilled."[57] The poet Josh Malihabadi asked:

This measuring, this cutting, this wanton devastation
The drowning of swimmers, the helplessness of the fighters,
What shall we call autumn if this is spring?

A distraught Jan Nisar Akhtar discovered:

The flower lost its colour the moment it was touched
The garland had yet to be braided when it came undone
The goblet hadn't touched the lips when it was shattered
It's not my dreams that have been looted and pillaged, it is me.[58]

The Progressives responded to the communal bloodbath by organizing writers and artists to spread the message of harmony. The PWA and IPTA mobilized several theater groups and cultural associations in a unity procession that marched through the city. Prithviraj Kapoor, accompanied by his sons, Raj and Shammi Kapoor, who were to become film stars in the following decade, were in the rally, beating a drum. Balraj Sahni, Chetan Anand, Dev Anand, and Prem Dhawan spread the message of communal harmony from an IPTA truck. The Urdu writers Sajjad Zaheer, Ali Sardar Jafri, Kaifi Azmi,

Sahir Ludhianvi, and Majrooh Sultanpuri joined the procession for peace.[59] Abbas wrote a play, *Main Kaun Hoon?* (Who Am I?), drawing on his experience of a "mistaken" killing. The play was staged multiple times to promote the message of communal harmony. Krishan Chander was like a man possessed, writing story after story, and a novel, *Hum Vehshi Hain* (We Are Savages), on communal violence.

It was difficult to pick up the pieces after the trauma of 1946–47. The about-turns in the CPI's strategy did not help. Its support of the demand for Pakistan on the grounds of self-determination, followed by an overnight conversion to the cause of India's unity, were confusing. The loyal party members went along with the twists and turns, but others were not so compliant. Abbas wrote: "My Communist friends, who have always ridiculed me for my sentimental *petite bourgeoisie* faith in the unity of India and hostility to the idea of Pakistan, who were ready to divide India into two or twenty pieces in pursuance of their theory of self-determination, have suddenly become fanatical believers in the unity of India."[60] Asking himself who killed India, he answered that Hindu and Muslim fanatics did, the Communist Party did.

The PWA continued to function, but its fire had been doused. The new nation-state responded with repression to yet another of the CPI's strategic about-turns, calling Indian independence a hoax and launching an armed peasant insurrection in Telangana. As the state consolidated itself under Nehru, fiercely putting down challenges to its authority, including those from the Communists, the Progressive writers fell into disarray. Instead of their grand vision of politically committed writers engaged with worker and peasant struggles, writing stories and poems that outlined a diverse nation of justice and freedom, they had to content themselves with films. The Progressives, who were already firmly entrenched in Bombay's film world, became the leading scriptwriters and lyricists.

It was because of the Progressive writers' well-established position that a socially conscious cinema developed in the 1950s. This period is considered the golden age of Hindi films, a time when cinema spoke to the common concerns of the people. Progressive poets such as Sahir Ludhianvi wrote angry and searing critiques of society. In the 1957 film *Pyaasa* (The Thirsty One), Ludhianvi asks the national leadership:

Ye kooche, ye neelam-ghar dilkashi ke
Ye lut-te hue karvaan zindagi ke
Kahaan hai, kahaan hai, muhaafiz khudi ke?
Jinhen naaz hai Hind par voh kahaan hai?

These streets, these auction houses of pleasure
These looted caravans of life
Where are they, the guardians of selfhood?
Those who are proud of India, where are they?[61]

Sahir, Majrooh Sultanpuri, Shailendra, Pradeep, Prem Dhawan, Rajinder Singh Bedi, Abbas, and many others wrote songs and stories that shaped the cinema of the 1950s. But film was a medium of mass entertainment. It was a business. This was all the more the case after the war boom, which brought an influx of producers involved with films in Hindi, which had emerged as something approximating a "national" language. Hindi cinema, eclipsing films in other languages, held the promise of providing the largest return on investment. As new producers seized on this chance, stars' salaries soared. Formula became king. Eric Barnow and S. Krishnaswamy, in their authoritative history of Hindi cinema, state: "A formula, as dictated by the exhibitor and distributor, called for one or two major stars, at least half a dozen songs, and a few dances."[62] The story became less important and was deployed primarily as a vehicle to exploit the stars' appeal.

An equally relevant factor was the existence of the new nation-state and nationalist sentiments. The Partition had been a traumatic experience, but Nehru's government had moved on to nation building, with the state seen as a vital instrument in modernizing India.

What would our dreams be, Manto had asked, now that colonial rule was over? The Progressives in the film industry had to answer this question against the background of cinema's role as mass entertainment and the ideological shadow of the new nation-state.

They answered Manto's question by writing socially conscious lyrics and stories, but the postnational conjuncture also witnessed a coming to terms with the new nation-state. This is evident in the two "tramp" films of the 1950s written by Abbas and starring Raj Kapoor: *Awara* (1951), or The Vagrant, and *Shree 420* (1955), or Mr. 420. Both were great commercial successes, and Kapoor became one of the most popular stars of the 1950s. In these films, Abbas attempts to articulate progressive themes within the commercial imperatives of Hindi cinema. Working with stars and containing songs that have endured, Abbas's films portray the subjecthood of the citizen in the nation-state.[63]

Awara is an Oedipal drama between Raj, played by Kapoor, and his father, Judge Raghunath, played by his real-life father, Prithviraj Kapoor. The judge is a reformist who has defied feudal norms by marrying a widow. He believes, however, that heredity has a determining influence; the son of a criminal can be only a criminal, and one born to a gentleman will also be a gentleman. In accordance with his belief, he convicts the son of a criminal who is trying to reform himself and has been falsely accused of rape. The son takes revenge by kidnapping the judge's wife, but he frees her when he learns that she is pregnant. But Judge Raghunath suspects that she has been defiled and throws his pregnant wife out of the house. Poor but honest, she struggles hard to raise her son on the mean streets of Bombay, hoping that he will one day become a lawyer like his father. However, Raj is thrown out of school when his mother is unable to pay his tuition fees. He is seduced into a life of crime and makes his living from "import-export."

Raj is a delightful, Chaplinesque "awara" (vagabond), happy with his life on the streets, singing "Awara hoon" (I Am a Vagabond) in

4.2. The vagabond Raj Kapoor in *Awara*. Source: R.K. Films.

lyrics penned by the Progressive poet Shailendra. After a chance encounter with a childhood sweetheart, Rita, played by the star Nargis, he tries to mend his ways. Rita happens to be an orphan who is Judge Raghunath's ward and a lawyer. Raj is charged for the murder of the gangster who had kidnapped his mother and had induced him to follow a life of crime. This is not all. He is also booked for the attempted murder of Judge Raghunath. Rita acts as Raj's defense attorney in her guardian's court and makes a stirring defense, arguing that Raj is not a born criminal but a victim of his social circumstances. All ends well when his real identity as the judge's son is revealed.

The professed theme of the film is heredity versus environment, but at the center of it is the vagrant's reform from a figure on the social margins to an upstanding citizen of the nation. Although it is society that produces the vagrant, it is not radical social change but a return to the affective fold of the family that enacts his transformation. The film highlights the role of social inequality in producing the outlaw but suggests that his redemption lies in the rule of law softened with a heart. Now that colonial rule has ended, the agenda of transforming society is left to its conscience. Abbas shifts the radical agenda of the Progressives into the register of affect and morality. Gone is the language of revolution, and in comes the vocabulary of individual choice and responsibility to rescue Raj from his vagrancy.

The commercial success of *Awara* was followed by an even bigger box-office hit, *Shree 420*. The opening song of the film, which became an overnight chart buster, offers a cosmopolitan anthem of the nation:

Mera joota hai Japaani
Yeh patloon Englishtaani
Sir pe lal topi russi
Phir bhi dil hai Hindustani.

My shoes are Japanese
These trousers are English
The red hat on my head is Russian
But my heart remains Indian.

A Chaplinesque Raj, an unemployed graduate from a small town, comes to Bombay, joyously declaring himself a member of the cosmopolitan world of nations. The sight of the big city—its traffic snarls and the hurrying crowd—bewilders the immigrant. He asks for directions, but no one answers him. Frustrated, he asks a beggar, "Is everyone deaf in Bombay?" The beggar replies: "Deaf and blind. They hear nothing but the jingling of money. This is Bombay, my brother, Bombay! Here the buildings are made of cement and the hearts of stone. Stone! Only one god is worshipped here and that is money!" This sets up the tale of the innocent, common citizen, done in by the heartless city of money. Playing on the classic nationalist exaltation of the village and the representation of the city as alien and corrupting, Raj becomes a cardsharp. He conquers the city with the tricks that it teaches him and enters a world of wealth and glamour.

4.3. A beggar explains Bombay to Raj Kapoor in *Shree 420*. Source: R.K. Films.

The film's title plays on section 420 of the Indian Penal Code, which deals with fraud, to highlight what the capitalist city forces the common person to become. Bombay brings Raj close to two women. One is Maya, or Illusion, a Westernized vamp, who draws him toward money and desire. The other is the woman he loves. She is Vidya, or Knowledge, modestly dressed, an identifiably Hindu woman, and a schoolteacher. Vidya is shocked when she learns about the source of Raj's wealth. She accuses him of selling his soul for the false world of glitter. He is unmoved by her critique of commodification. But when an unscrupulous businessman tries to defraud the homeless by promising them housing, Raj's conscience is awakened. He outwits the crooked capitalist and becomes a hero to the masses.

The film mobilizes the progressive themes of capitalist exploitation and injustice to set up the resolution in the victory of human values. The savior of the masses is the educated citizen Raj, who speaks and acts on their behalf. The exaltation of the hero coincided with Raj Kapoor's elevation as one of the biggest stars in Hindi cinema.

The commercial imperatives of the film industry worked in tandem with the nonrevolutionary ideology of Nehru's India. *Shree 420* provides a progressive critique of social inequality and capitalist power while presenting humanist reform as the path forward using a deeply moral tone. Instead of radical change, the film offers individual responsibility and the law, softened by a heart, as the means to combat the temptations and illicit desires of modernity. Significantly, the film ends with Raj pointing in the direction of planned housing. The radical urban imagination has made peace with the nation-state.

But this is not the whole story. The writers and the artists who had breathed Bombay's exhilarating air were no narrow-minded nationalists. They played with the nationalist contrast between the simple village and the corrupt city, between Vidya and Maya, adopting a moral tone strikingly different from the heady and hedonistic mood of Fearless Nadia's stunt films. But they based their moral-humanist drama on Bombay's multifaceted life. The city was the symbol of both the challenges and the promises of modern life. Accordingly, the trials and tribulations of the modern national subject were to be played out in the city. It was also here that the citizen, who was neither Hindu nor Muslim but a subject of the modern nation, could seek freedom and justice. This national subject was cosmopolitan. He wore Japanese shoes, English trousers, and a Russian hat while remaining Indian at heart. The song privileges the nation as the "heart" of identity but positions this Indianness in the wider world.

It was in Bombay that the modern and cosmopolitan social world of the Indian could be best represented. Thus, the crime melodramas of the 1950s, starring Dev Anand, are frequently located in the city. Stylishly dressed and personifying urban cool, Anand always appeared as an utterly modern character. The films, shot in the noir style of shadows and highlights, showcase the modernity of the city—its spatial organization in buildings, open streets and dark lanes, brightly lit clubs, and shadowy dens of gangsters. Modern urban types—the taxi driver, the pickpocket, the trickster, the club dancer, the street urchin, the shopkeeper, the stylish city slicker, the villain in trench coat and hat, and the smart police detective— appear in film after film.

Taxi Driver (1954), for example, parades Bombay's irreducibly diverse social milieu. A pivotal location in the film is a club for workingmen—Doston ka Adda (Friends' Hangout)—shown serving only nonalcoholic drinks such as Coca-Cola in Prohibition-era Bombay. Dev Anand, playing a Hindu taxi driver named Mangal —called Hero by his friends — frequents the club after work. His best friend, Mastana, played by Johnny Walker, is a Muslim (going by his own name in the film), who also treats it as a meeting place. D'Mello, a Christian, owns the club. His employees include the Anglo-Indian Mrs. Thomas, who plays the piano, and her beautiful daughter Sylvie, a singer and dancer. Breaking from the standard depictions of Christians and Westernized Indians as alien and portending trouble, the film treats them as ordinary city dwellers. Sylvie fleeces rich men who entertain her at the fancy Taj Hotel, but she is no prostitute; she is simply another urban trickster who loves to have a good time. In the club, she maintains an easy and harmlessly flirtatious relationship with men. D'Mello is in love with her, but she fancies Hero. Though the rakishly charming taxi driver does not love Sylvie, he treats her respectfully and as a friend.

The affectionate interactions between Sylvie and Hero in an atmosphere of easy communication across gender and religious identities infuse the club with emotional and social significance. This is captured in a sequence in which Sylvie tries to charm a hard-to-get Hero with seductive dancing and singing. The scene breaks from the Hindi film convention that presents women as objects of male seduction, unless they are vamps who flaunt their wanton sexuality to ensnare men. Sylvie is no vamp, but a modern woman confidently pursuing the man of her dreams. Undeterred by the failure to enchant Hero, she continues with her performance of enticement (fig. 4.4). The band—which includes Sylvie's Anglo-Indian mother on

4.4. Bombay's cosmopolitan world in *Taxi Driver*. Source: Navketan Films.

the piano, her young brothers playing a clarinet and maracas, and a Goan Christian-looking man on the guitar—plays on, backing her bold spirit. The men in the audience, including Hero, look on indulgently at her playful flirtation. The mood is easy and tolerant. A picture of urban conviviality and openness, Doston ka Adda appears as a microcosm of Bombay's culturally hybrid and modern world.

If Bombay's Indian world is cosmopolitan, it is also full of vicious predators. Gangsters and gamblers prey on innocent city dwellers. Unscrupulous men lie in wait to entice and coerce poor women into the flesh trade. Street toughs extort the vulnerable, and slumlords terrorize their poor tenants. While highlighting Bombay's perils, these crime melodramas also accept them as given. *Baazi* (1951), for example, opens with Dev Anand in a gambling den. He is a small-time gambler with uncanny skills. His urgent need for money drives him to participate in a big-time gambling racket that already exists. *CID* (1956) opens with a petty pickpocket, played by Johnny Walker, who ends up witnessing a murder while slinking into a newspaper

4.5. Love and freedom in Bombay—Dev Anand and Kalpana Kartik in *Taxi Driver*. Source: Navketan Films.

office to steal typewriters. In the film, the CID detective (Anand) is up against an established crime mafia run by a respectable business-man who doubles as a criminal mastermind, with a beautiful moll and murderous henchmen at his command. Of course, the crimi-nals are always caught in the end. If the hero takes to crime, it is only because he is poor and unemployed, and, in any case, eventually he finds his way to the right path because of love. Like the tramp films, law, leavened by morality and affection, wins in the end.

The thematic victory of law and morality must be placed against the celebration of the city. Bombay may be perilous, but it is also the place where the heroine played by Kalpana Kartik in *Taxi Driver* seeks refuge from an arranged marriage in the village. She finds love—Dev Anand—and a career as a singer in the film indus-try. The dark city is also the shining city, a place of glamour and fortune, of opportunity and freedom, of cosmopolitan culture and bourgeois self-fashioning. If the artists have made peace with the nation-state, they have also accepted the capitalist city as their mise-en-scène, their here and now.

5

THE TABLOID AND THE CITY

It was April 27, 1959. As the day wore on, the oppressive humidity hung like a pall over the city. Deputy Commissioner John Lobo of the Bombay City Police was in his office, planning to escape the sweltering heat with a family holiday in the cool Nilgiri Hills.[1] But police work intervened. Lobo recalls that he had spent a typical busy day at his Crime Branch, CID (Criminal Investigation Department), office in the hulking police commissioner's building. The daily routine of discussing business with the commissioner over a cup of tea had ended at around 5:00 p.m., when the phone rang. Commander Samuel of the Indian Navy was on the line.

> "Commander Nanavati is coming to see you. He was down at my residence."
> "What's the problem?"
> "He has had a quarrel with a person and has shot at him."

A short time later, he received another call, this one from Deputy Inspector Gautam of Gamdevi Police Station.

> "There has been a shooting incident. A Mr. Ahuja has been fatally injured. We are proceeding to the spot and will get back to you."

A little later, he heard a voice outside his office, asking "Lobo sahib ka kamra kahan hai?" (Where is Mr. Lobo's office?). A tall, handsome gentleman dressed in white shirt and slacks walked in and introduced himself as Commander Nanavati. He appeared to Lobo like a man in a hurry to unburden himself of something weighing on him.

"I have shot a man."
"He is dead. I have just received a message from Gamdevi Police Station."

Commander Nanavati turned pale on hearing this. There was a pause. It was Lobo who broke the silence.

"Would you like a cup of tea?"
"Just a glass of water."

Lobo then gathered from Commander Nanavati that the shooting had occurred over an affair between the commander's wife, Sylvia, and the man who now lay dead. As Lobo puts it, it was a case of "the eternal triangle that sometimes upsets a marriage." Based on Nanavati's statements, the police retrieved a revolver and some unspent ammunition from his car. Lobo then placed the commander under arrest.

"Ordinarily, undertrials in police custody are lodged in police lock-ups. We felt Nanavati could be shown some consideration and accommodated him in one of our office-rooms."

Later, Lobo describes the "feverish activity" at the Jeevan Jyot apartment building of the victim as the Gamdevi police officers investigated the scene of the crime. They noted the shattered glass in the nine-by-six bathroom, the bloodstains on the wall and door handle, and, lying on the floor, "the empty brown envelope bearing the name 'Lt.-Commander K. M. Nanavati.'" Recalling the murder scene years later, Lobo could not resist a philosophical observation: "The evil that men do lives after them—it leaves 'footprints on the sands of time.'"

Thus began the sensational Nanavati case that consumed the city. It had all the ingredients of a thrilling drama—extramarital sex, jealousy, and murder. It also had compelling and cosmopolitan dramatis personae—Kawas Maneckshaw Nanavati, an upright Parsi naval officer; Sylvia, his beautiful English wife; and a rich, swinging Sindhi bachelor, Prem Bhagwandas Ahuja. The locus of the drama was decidedly upscale. The Nanavatis lived in elegant Cuffe Parade, and Ahuja's posh apartment building on Nepean Sea Road (ironically named Jeevan Jyot, or Flame of Life) was in the exclusive Malabar Hill neighborhood. This upper-class geography cast the case as a story about the cosmopolitan elite in the city. The murder case was fought all the way from the trial in the Bombay Sessions Court to the final appeal in the Supreme Court in Delhi, with renowned lawyers battling on opposite sides. It was also destined to make legal history as the last jury trial in India.[2]

The case received relentless press attention throughout the nearly three years of legal wrangling in the courts. The story even made the pages of *Time* and the *New Yorker*.[3] Facts and opinions surrounding it entered everyday conversation and popular culture in India. So great and lasting was the public impact of the case that even when it disappeared from the front pages of newspapers, the interest in the event never waned. In 1963 a Hindi film loosely based on the incident, *Yeh Raaste Hain Pyaar Ke* (These Are the Pathways to Love), opened in theaters. Ten years later, *Achanak* (Suddenly), another Hindi film based on the Nanavati story, was released. It appears as a vignette in Salman Rushdie's *Midnight's Children* and forms the central arc of Indra Sinha's sprawling novel *The Death of Mr. Love*.[4] In 2002 the *Hindustan Times Tabloid* ran a special on the case, reminding its readers of the compelling cast of characters, the captivating legal drama, and its sensational impact on popular culture. It revisited all the lurid details and gossip surrounding the case. Retailed once again was Ahuja's image as a Don Juan, cooing seductively into the ears of one of the several women he wooed: "The meaning of my name is Love—Prem."[5]

Half a century after Nanavati pumped three bullets into the body of his wife's lover, the event continues to retain its sensational appeal. I return to the case to examine the postcolonial city that the legal and mass cultural spectacle brought into sharp focus. At the center of this new culture of sensation produced by the outsize media attention was the portrait of a cosmopolitan society. The case's multiethnic and sophisticated cast of characters evoked Bombay's mythic image. The fact that an Englishwoman was involved never raised an eyebrow. There was no insinuation (one very likely today) that she lacked the cultural values of India and exhibited the lax morals of Western women. At that time, the fact that Sylvia lived in Bombay and was married to a Parsi seemed totally natural. It was as if nothing had changed in the city, as if the Partition violence had done nothing to tarnish its myth of openness. In fact, a lot had changed. British rule had ended a little over a decade ago, and Bombay was no longer a colonial metropolis. Now, writers, artists, and filmmakers had to imagine the promise of the city in the context of the nation. The picture of the cosmopolitan milieu broadcast by the trial also had to contend with the legal system, ideology, and politics of a free India. In revisiting the case, my goal is to examine this changing city and to draw out the murder trial's effects on the politics of the city; specifically, I am interested in its contribution to the development of populist politics, that is, the politics of the "people."

MEET THE PRESS

Almost single-handedly responsible for turning Ahuja's murder into a gripping and enduring event in popular culture was the spunky

Bombay tabloid *Blitz*. For nearly two and a half years after the trial opened on September 23, 1959, *Blitz* covered the case with outsize and relentless attention. With bold front-page headlines, photographs, scoops, special features, boxed reports, and gossip, *Blitz* dramatized the case as a soap opera of morality and patriotism and played it on the stage of mass culture. The three chief protagonists were—a dashingly handsome naval officer devoted to the nation; his beautiful but impressionable wife; and an ultramodern, wealthy, and wily Lothario, who had wronged not just Nanavati but India itself by seducing a married woman while her husband sailed the seas in defense of the nation. There was also a fourth protagonist—*Blitz* and its dapper and dynamic Clark Gable look-alike, the Parsi editor Russi K. Karanjia, a well-known figure in the city. Under his direction, *Blitz* audaciously framed and broadcast the case of a murder in the city as an event of nationwide importance. Splicing lurid details and courtroom drama into a moral and patriotic story line, it staged the Nanavati case as a riveting media event, the first of its kind in India.

When Ahuja's murder occurred, *Blitz* was already established as a widely read Bombay tabloid. From its inception in 1941, it quickly became known for sensational stories under its colorful and larger-than-life founder-editor, Karanjia. With an irrepressible drive to unearth and spice up stories, Karanjia fashioned *Blitz* into a popular tabloid known for its irreverence and outsize confidence. A sign hanging outside his office read: "You don't have to be crazy to work here, but it helps."[6]

Born in 1912, Karanjia belonged to an upper-class family.[7] His father was an ophthalmic surgeon who had trained in Edinburgh. His mother came from a wealthy family from Quetta and had been educated by an English governess. The family lived opposite the famous Orient Club on Chowpatty Beach in Quetta Terrace, a wedding gift to the couple by Karanjia's maternal grandfather. As was typical with upper-class Parsis, his upbringing was Western. The hand-wound gramophone played records of Enrico Caruso, Fernando Gusso, and

Lawrence Tibbett. A grand piano, the surgeon's wedding gift to his wife, occupied nearly one-third of the living room in the sprawling apartment. At the frequent parties hosted by his mother, tea would be offered in the finest china and served to the upper-crust guests by a liveried butler. The evening would invariably include his mother playing Beethoven's *Moonlight Sonata* and his younger brother singing "The Lost Chord," Gounod's "Ave Maria," or Schubert's "Serenade."

Growing up in an elite Parsi family, Karanjia was expected to go on to Cambridge University and pursue a career in the Indian Civil Service after his education in Bombay's St. Xavier's High School and Wilson College.[8] But an innocent prank changed his life. While waiting to qualify for admission into Cambridge, Karanjia engaged in a back-and-forth exchange of letters under different pseudonyms in the "Letters to the Editor" column of the *Times of India*. When Ivor Jehu, the deputy editor, discovered his identity, he offered him a job with the newspaper, which Karanjia accepted. Recognizing his potential, the paper sent him to London to apprentice with the *Evening Standard*. But he was soon bored with the staid *Standard*, gravitating instead to the excitement of the tabloid the *Daily Mirror*.

When he returned to India, Karanjia was dismayed to find himself relegated to the background while the management groomed Frank Moraes as the first Indian editor of the *Times of India*. He left the *Times* and went on to briefly edit the *Sunday Standard* and the short-lived *Morning Standard*. After leaving the *Morning Standard*, he assembled a group to start a tabloid of his own. The group included Dinkar V. Nadkarni, who had earned a reputation in journalism by penning sensational crime stories in the *Bombay Sentinel*, edited by the veteran Irish journalist and longtime advocate of Indian nationalism Benjamin Guy Horniman; Zahir Babar Kureishi, who wrote a popular column under the pen name of ZABAK; and Nadir Boman-Behram, who was to look after the advertising and business side of things. The tabloid, launched from an old Apollo Street building in the Fort, was introduced as "our BLITZ, India's BLITZ against Hitler."[9] Within four months of the inaugural issue, the circulation had reached twenty thousand; twenty-five years later, the "people's paper" claimed a readership of one million.[10]

Blitz both inhabited and defined Bombay's dynamic urban milieu. As a newsweekly, it drew on the Island City's highly developed bourgeois public sphere. A key element of this sphere was the city's newspapers, where Bombay's public life appeared as news and photographs. Like all newspapers, Bombay's press served a crucial function in making the city legible. Typically, newspaper readers confront their public world in reports on politics and economics, descriptions of social engagements, crime stories, announcements of job vacancies and tender notices, advertisements of products and entertainment, film and theater reviews, and accounts of sporting events. In an important sense, newspapers bring the public sphere to life for their readers and function as agents that act upon it. It has been said that in modern city life, the secular ritual of reading the newspaper replaces the Morning Prayer. It is safe to say that Bombay's illiterate and poor citizens did not practice this secular ritual. The public life rendered real by the newspapers lay beyond them. What is more, the English language dominated the lettered world brought into view by newspapers. In this English-scripted public world, the *Times of India* was preeminent. Sober and elitist, it carried a whiff of the formality inherited from its colonial past.

In contrast, *Blitz* adopted a populist and nationalist mantle. What it lost by publishing in English it tried to gain by deploying a radical ideology. It espoused socialism and planning, and identified the cause of the nation with anti-imperialist internationalism. The tabloid lauded Afro-Asian solidarity against the capitalist West, and loudly and regularly unveiled dark CIA plots against India and Third World leaders. Columnists with Communist sympathies—Ramesh Sanghvi, A. Raghavan, and K. A. Abbas—contributed to the leftist flavor. Karanjia reveled in playing the champion of the Third World cause against American interests. A characteristic example of his posture was the front-page story in the early sixties headlined "Editor Karanjia Crashed US Curtain into Cuba."[11] The report, datelined Havana, triumphantly noted his arrival in Cuba at Fidel Castro's invitation in spite of the denial of a transit visa by the United States to permit him to fly via New York. When the Egyptian president Gamal Abdel Nasser visited the city in 1960, *Blitz* declared: "President Nasser Captivates the Heart of Bombay!"[12] Five years later, Nasser bestowed Karanjia with the Republican Order of Merit, the highest award given to a foreigner. Exultantly, *Blitz* reported that despite torrential rain, thousands of Bombay's citizens turned out to felicitate Karanjia.[13]

Blitz's political viewpoint closely echoed that of its idol, Nehru, who also viewed a robust national identity and anti-imperialist cosmopolitanism as complementary. Indeed, the endorsement of Afro-Asian solidarity, the admiration for the Soviet Union, the distrust of the United States, and the support for socialism and planning formed parts of an ideology that was widely shared in the decolonized world during the fifties and sixties. In this respect, *Blitz* was not unusual.

But Karanjia's journalistic creation was no ordinary left-nationalist fare. True, anti-imperialism and socialism were its watchwords, but it espoused populist rather than class politics. In line with Third World radicalism, *Blitz* frequently denounced capitalists and championed socialism, but it regarded class as an element, not the whole of the political division. The battle lines were clear. The "people," a homogeneous category constructed out of a socially heterogeneous population, stood on one side. Socialism and anti-imperialism were seen to serve the "people," and the cause was entrusted with the leader, Jawaharlal Nehru. On the other side were the corrupt, the profiteers, big business, their right-wing political patrons, and communal politicians who divided the "people" along religious lines. *Blitz* saw its mission as one of carrying the battle of the people into the English-dominated public sphere. With hard-hitting, two-fisted reports, it saw itself smashing open the arena of public opinion monopolized by the procapitalist and proimperialist elites.

To brashly insert the politics of the collective people, *Blitz* openly and warmly extolled Nehru and skewered those it saw as undermining his leadership with its signature muckraking, over-the-top stories. Among the unlucky politicians to draw its fire was Morarji Desai, the conservative Congress leader who was elected as the chief minister of Bombay in 1952 and was to become India's prime minister in 1977. *Blitz* assailed him as a power-hungry hypocrite who had become the chief minister through a subterfuge.[14] It scorned his persona of incorruptibility and moral rectitude and taunted his orders on Prohibition by calling illicit liquor "Morarjin" and Morarjuice."[15] Never missing an opportunity to denounce him as an autocratic enemy of the people, it published stories that claimed to expose his abuse of power, patronage of big business and profiteers, and vindictiveness toward his critics, most notably Karanjia and *Blitz*. Desai's greatest defect, in the tabloid's eyes, was that he feigned loyalty to Nehru while harboring ambitions to succeed, if not replace, him as prime minister.

Blitz thrived on controversy, and Karanjia was frequently embroiled in defamation suits, which the tabloid wore as badges of honor. This is precisely what happened in the so-called Chester Bowles Forgery Case, which once again pitted Karanjia against Desai. The saga began in July 1952 when Karanjia published an interview with Chester Bowles, the U.S. ambassador to India.[16] Apparently, this irked D. F. Karaka, the Oxford-educated Parsi editor of the rival Bombay tabloid, *Current*. On October 1, 1952, *Current* published purported copies of letters exchanged between Karanjia and Bowles. In one letter that Karanjia allegedly wrote to Bowles, he complains of *Blitz*'s financial difficulties, asks for help in getting American advertisements, and requests that the ambassador meet some of his Communist friends. In the purported reply, Bowles expresses his readiness to meet Karanjia's friends. *Current* charged that the letters exposed Karanjia's secret desire to be a "Washington patriot."[17] Karanjia thundered in reply: "A MONSTROUS LIE ... Illustrated with Shameless Forgery."[18] He denied writing such a letter or receiving the one attributed to Bowles. The American ambassador also called the letters forged and denounced *Current* as irresponsible for publishing a smear.

The Desai government ordered a probe and ended up filing charges against Karanjia. It was alleged that Karanjia had fabricated the forgeries and conspired to get them published in *Current* in order to embarrass Karaka. *Blitz* covered the trial with its usual repertoire of bold headlines and blow-by-blow accounts of the proceedings. It expressed outraged innocence and dropped dark hints of a conspiracy hatched by Republicans and McCarthyites against the Democrat Bowles and the progressive Karanjia. After the testimonies and cross-examination of numerous witnesses, the scrutiny of typewriter fonts and letterheads, and legal jousting by the prosecution and the defense, Karanjia was exonerated. The government appealed the decision to the High Court, but its plea was dismissed. The headline in *Blitz* exclaimed: "KARANJIA DOUBLY ACQUITTED, INNOCENCE DOUBLY PROVED."[19]

Never one to shy away from self-publicity, Karanjia cut a flamboyant figure. His tabloid frequently carried his pictures, now speaking at a meeting, now exchanging pleasantries with political and cultural celebrities. He brashly promoted himself and his paper. During his long editorship of *Blitz*, he took many controversial and unpredictable positions. He railed against the powerful but was not averse to cozying up to those at the top. Despite his self-professed radicalism, he was an open admirer of Jawaharlal Nehru and his daughter, Indira Gandhi. He professed republican sentiments but lauded the shah of Iran as the ruler over the ancient homeland of his Parsi community. An ardent rationalist, he became a devotee of Satya Sai Baba, the god man whom he had previously denounced for retailing mumbo jumbo. Such a figure naturally cut a divisive figure. There were

Right from 1951, when Karanjia visited China as the deputy leader of the first Indian delegation to be invited by Mao's regime, almost all the Chinese leaders including the Chinese Premier, Chou En-lai (above), granted long and exhaustive interviews to Karanjia. Yet BLITZ did not hesitate to deal an editorial "bloody nose" to the Chinese when they betrayed India-China friendship.

BLITZ
ASIA'S FOREMOST NEWSMAGAZINE
EVERY SATURDAY   PRICE 25

"Suezide No. 2" In
The Caribbean...?

HAVANA (Cuba)

**YANKS PLOT
4-STAGE WAR
ON CUBA!**
CASTRO TELLS BLITZ...

Karanjia was the first editor to interview Cuba's great revolutionary Prime Minister Fidel Castro, forcing the American and European press to take a back seat and quote extensively from Karanjia's talks with the Cuban leader exposing the US power-politics and highlighting Cuba's freedom fight.

...Biographer
of Revolutionaries

5.1. Karanjia with revolutionaries. Source: Homi D. Mistry, ed., *Blitz: Four Fighting Decades* (Bombay: Blitz Publications, 1981).

hushed rumors in the city that he was on the take from the KGB, that he was a blackmailer and a hypocrite. The rumors only served to make him more interestingly colorful and controversial, and his tabloid the purveyor of a sensational public culture.

Central to *Blitz*'s self-representation as a radical paper of the people was its tabloid form. The tabloid is a classic urban form that claims to render legible the anonymous reality of everyday life in the modern metropolis in its bold and sensational headlines. It professes to reveal the mystery of the goings-on in the backrooms of power and money and expose the real motivations and desires of all and sundry. The city becomes real. Adopting this stance, *Blitz* dispensed with the convention of dispassionate observation and balanced opinion and assumed a charged tone from the very beginning. The tabloid reveled in its self-proclaimed role as a racket buster, exposing truths concealed by the powerful and fearlessly advocating the interests of the people.

In 1945, for example, D. V. Nadkarni, *Blitz*'s chief racket buster, wrote a series of sensational stories on the textile shortage. These accounts claimed to uncover the hidden hand of the big wholesale dealers who, with the alleged help of government officials, were hoarding textile stocks to drive up the price while representing the shortage as the result of a natural scarcity.[20] This was not unusual. Week after week, *Blitz* exposed truths allegedly buried beneath the surface of random and fragmentary events. The embezzlement of public funds, prostitution rackets, sordid stories of seduction and sex in the name of spiritualism, dark political designs behind high-sounding rhetoric, and the fleecing of the poor by rich industrialists and property developers, all were staples in the weekly. Even its sports column, called "Knock Out," took on the racket-busting posture. It was written by A.F.S. Talyarkhan, whose bearded, pipe-in-mouth photograph on the page appeared to lend gravity to the charges of malfeasance that he leveled against the sports authorities. The poor performance of Indian athletes in international competitions, he alleged, could be explained by the petty squabbles and power grabbing of officials behind the scenes. Of course, no tabloid can be complete without pinups. Thus, the last page always carried a pinup that greeted the reader with a witty caption, for example, "Nalini makes a winsome bather, But will someone blow off the lather!" Beside the titillating photograph, there was always the "Last Page," written by K. A. Abbas, a journalist, screenplay writer, and film director. His column offered a man-about-town view of the world, commenting, venting against, and exposing the machinations of the powerful.

In *Blitz*'s world, there was nothing mysterious about reality. Once it had wiped the mist off the surface-level mystery and decoded the outward face of events, the exposed reality always appeared rational, a product of the relentlessly instrumental and banal pursuits of money and power. The scandal lay in the fact that people wrapped their ruthlessly rational motivations and actions in tissues of lies and deceptions. This required a careful scrutiny of the misleading exteriority of events. The journalist had to act as a detective and plunge into the rough-and-tumble of life. He had to examine seemingly disconnected fragments to decipher hidden connections and detect clues to the underlying reality. In this process, the journalist-as detective functioned as an author who produced written and illustrative political and social texts that claimed to depict modernity's imperceptible reality.

Bombay acquired a textual and photographic face in *Blitz*'s news accounts and images that sought to represent reality in its surface-level expressions. No grand philosophy or concept defined this depiction of reality. Rather, the tabloid identified the phenomena in the empirical material itself, in the exemplary spaces and activities of modern life. It traced the contours of Bombay's daily life on its streets and neighborhoods, restaurants and cinema theaters, textile factories and neighborhoods, docks and shipping offices, and municipal institutions and public parks. Warnings of "Death-Trap for Promenaders at Marine Drive Seafront" and exposures of "Super-Market in Sex: Where Vice Is Sold on Department-Store Basis" or "Bombay Municipality Creates Slums" formed the stuff of *Blitz*'s Bombay.[21]

These stories of the city's dark side did not signify cultural pessimism or despair. If anything, *Blitz* always expressed supreme confidence in modern life. Showing no nostalgia for the imagined harmony of the countryside, it openly embraced the gritty, conflict-ridden, and urban milieu of Bombay. While it uncovered tales of greed for money and power, it also provided glamorous accounts of film personalities and celebrated popular struggles for justice. On its pages, the city appeared as an immense and exciting mix of multilayered, contradictory, and restless lives. Everything seemed to be in motion. Fortunes were being made and lost, swindles were being plotted and exposed, and big dreams were being dreamed and shattered. People jostled for space and heroically struggled for survival and justice. Against the shadow of its dark side, Bombay's metropolitan life glittered on the pages of *Blitz*.

The Nanavati trial was a godsend for *Blitz*. It provided an opportunity to project the case as a drama of the politics of the "people" on the sensational surface of the tabloid pages. *Blitz* seized the opening and framed the trial as a titillating urban drama of national significance. Interestingly, although Nanavati belonged to Karanjia's Parsi community, *Blitz* never highlighted the ethnic dimension. It did not extol Nanavati's Parsi origins or comment negatively on Ahuja's Sindhi identity. Nor did it read any dark conspiracy in Sylvia's English origins despite the tabloid's penchant for discovering neocolonial designs on India. The tabloid presented the story as a moral and political scandal, as a case of the nation's betrayal by the seductive and corrupt influence of the rich.

THE TRIAL

The trial opened on the afternoon of September 23, 1959, in the packed District and Sessions Court of Judge R. B. Mehta, the first legal venue entrusted to try a murder case.[22] The nine-member jury consisted of two Parsis, one Anglo-Indian, a Christian, and five Hindus. Representing the government, Chief Public Prosecutor C. M. Trivedi charged Nanavati with intentionally causing Ahuja's death, an offense under section 302 of the Indian Penal Code. Commander Nanavati, resplendent in his naval uniform, pleaded not guilty. Leading the defense team was Karl J. Khandalawala, a famous criminal lawyer, equally well known as an expert on Indian painting and sculpture.

During the month-long trial, which included a dramatic visit by the judge, the jury, and the counsels to the murder scene, the following facts were established. Nanavati, a highly regarded naval officer, had married Sylvia in England in 1949. After his return to Bombay, the couple had three children and lived in a Cuffe Parade flat in Colaba. In 1956 another naval officer's wife introduced Sylvia to Prem Ahuja, a thirty-one-year-old, curly-haired, and handsome businessman. A bachelor, Ahuja lived with his unmarried sister Mamie and three servants in a large apartment on Nepean Sea Road in posh Malabar Hill. Like many Sindhis of the Hindu community, Ahuja's family had fled Karachi after the Partition in 1947. In Bombay he had built a successful car dealership called Universal Motors, which sold Willys Jeeps. Ahuja's acquaintance with Sylvia turned into an affair while Nanavati spent long periods at sea, away from home.

On April 18, 1959, when Nanavati returned home, he found his wife inexplicably cold toward him. On April 27 the couple woke up early, took the dog to a veterinary surgeon, bought tickets for an afternoon cinema show, did some shopping at Crawford Market, and returned home. At breakfast, Nanavati asked Sylvia if there was a reason for her cold behavior, but she did not reply. Nanavati asked again after lunch, but she told him to stay away when he approached her. Finally, when he asked if she loved someone else, Sylvia confessed that she loved Ahuja and had been unfaithful. Stunned, Nanavati asked if she was willing to give up her lover. She did not respond. Meanwhile, the children were waiting to go to the cinema. Nanavati drove Sylvia, the children, and a neighbor's child to the Metro Theatre for the afternoon show of *Tom's Thumb*, promising to pick them up after the film at 6 p.m. But things took a different turn.

Nanavati drove straight to his ship at the naval docks and obtained a revolver with six rounds of ammunition, telling the naval authorities that he needed the gun for personal protection. He then drove to Universal Motors on Peddar Road. When he was told that Ahuja had gone home for lunch, the commander drove to Malabar Hill. He parked in the driveway of Jeevan Jyot and went up to Ahuja's second-floor apartment, carrying the fully loaded revolver in an envelope. He rang the doorbell at around 4:20 in the afternoon. Anjani Rapa, the bearer who answered the door, told him that Ahuja was in the bedroom. Before the bedroom door closed behind Nanavati, Deepak Sampath, the cook, saw Ahuja standing in front of the bathroom mirror, combing his hair.

Less than a minute later, the servants heard the sound of two shots, followed by a third shot accompanied by a loud noise—the clatter of breaking glass. The servants, followed by Mamie Ahuja, who was resting in her bedroom, rushed to Ahuja's room, where they found Nanavati standing with a revolver in his hand. Ahuja, clad only with a towel around his waist, lay prostrate on the bathroom floor. A bewildered Mamie asked what had happened. The commander did not reply. Instead, pointing the gun at the servants and asking them to stand clear, he walked out. Downstairs, the guard of the building tried to stop him, but Nanavati drove off, saying he was going to the police station. As he did not know the location of the police station, he drove instead to the residence of the provost marshal of the navy, Commander Samuel. "Something terrible has happened. I have shot one man." With this confession, he handed over the keys to his apartment and asked Commander Samuel to give them to his wife at the Metro Theatre. Commander Samuel then phoned Deputy Commissioner Lobo, and Nanavati surrendered to the police.

These, in a nutshell, were the facts. The prosecution produced twenty-four witnesses and marshaled forensic evidence to prove that Ahuja's murder was premeditated. Testifying for the prosecution, Lobo was about to recount the sequence of events leading up to Nanavati's surrender and confessional statement, when he was stopped. The problem was that the confession was not admissible because it had not been obtained under a judicial magistrate's supervision. After huddling for a quick conference with the counsels to consider this issue, the judge instructed Lobo to submit his evidence in writing. Lobo wrote his submission in dialogue form, which was entered in the case record, with the confession placed in brackets and excluded.[23] However, his testimony that Nanavati had appeared in his office dressed in white shirt and slacks, which were without bloodstains or any tears, backed up the prosecution's contention that the naval officer had shot Ahuja from a distance and killed him intentionally.

The defense offered thirteen witnesses of its own, cross-examined the prosecution testimonies, and furnished its own forensic experts to prove that the death was accidental. Its star witnesses were Sylvia and Commander Nanavati himself. For two days, Nanavati was on the witness stand, reiterating that he had not killed Ahuja intentionally. He claimed that he had gone to Ahuja to ask him if he was prepared to marry Sylvia and take care of the children. But instead of a rational discussion, a heated exchange and physical struggle followed. The gun went off in the course of the struggle. "If I had intended to kill the deceased (Ahuja), I would have riddled him with bullets as he was standing in front of the dressing table."[24] Asked why he had procured the gun, Nanavati stated that he wanted the weapon so he could shoot himself.[25] Sylvia testified in support of the defense theory of an accidental shooting. Described as often restless in the witness stand, her eyes moist with tears, she acknowledged her affair with Ahuja. It was infatuation, the remorseful wife claimed. He had seduced her with the promise of marriage but had seemed to be backing away. That is why she had kept silent when Nanavati asked if Ahuja was prepared to marry her. She testified that her silence left Nanavati stunned and disoriented. The defense elicited this testimony to establish that the knowledge of the affair left Nanavati dazed and suicidal, that the anxiety about the future of his wife and children gnawed at him, and that he went to Ahuja to ask him about his intentions, not to kill him.[26]

Emily Hahn, the *New Yorker* correspondent who witnessed part of the trial, describes the drama vividly. The street leading to the courthouse was jam-packed. The spectators were "mostly women, who had, I thought, taken considerable trouble to make themselves look nice." Women also lined the gallery leading up to the courtroom, carrying garlands for the commander. Viewers crammed the benches—"lots of women, most of them glamorous looking types," one "dressed up as if she were going to the opera." Hahn spotted Nanavati in a spotless, starchy white uniform bedecked with medals and wearing an expression of "polite indifference."[27]

The *Times of India*, the premier Bombay daily, covered the trial in detail from the very start. Day after day, it reported the trial proceedings. Naturally, Nanavati's and Sylvia's testimonies received prominent attention, as did the defense portrait of Ahuja as a liquor-loving philanderer. But it also paid ample attention to the less dramatic aspects of the proceedings. Its overall approach was sober and balanced. Treating the case as a crime story, albeit a prominent one, the *Times* stuck to factual reporting, eschewing screaming headlines and colorful language.

As a weekly, *Blitz* obviously could not provide a daily account of the trial. Therefore, it was slow to pick up on the story. It filed its first report well into the trial. The editorial staff had reluctantly accepted that the weekly was at a disadvantage in relation to the dailies in covering the trial's day-by-day developments. But Karanjia would have none of it. "Go ahead, go ahead. Start working right now. Money does not matter, but we want a front-page smasher."[28] The staff sprang into action. *Blitz* published a boxed item on October 10, 1959, entitled "The Nanavati Trial in a Nutshell."

In keeping with its format as a weekly, *Blitz* presented the summary of the trial's daily proceedings as a story. Also, its tabloid format meant that its predilection was to ferret out a scandal beneath the surface, find a drama buried in the cold recitation of facts. Thus, while its synopsis of the prosecution's case was factual, the report on the defense plea was another matter. In contrast to the *Times*'s straightforward account, *Blitz* spiced up its summary of the defense case with verbatim quotations from Nanavati's deposition. The commander had deposed that he found his wife tense and unresponsive to his affectionate touch on April 27.

"Do you still love me?" he asked. No reply.

"Are you in love with someone else?" he asked again. No reply.

"Have you been faithful to me?" Sylvia shook her head to indicate "No." To Nanavati, "this looked like the end of the world." He decided to shoot himself.

Nanavati, however, wanted to know from Ahuja whether he was "prepared to marry Sylvia and look after the children." He went to INS "Mysore" and secured a service revolver.

When Nanavati walked into Ahuja's bedroom and asked him "Are you going to marry Sylvia and look after the kids," Ahuja nastily replied, "Do I have to marry every woman that I sleep with. . . . Get the hell out of here. . . ."

When Nanavati retorted, "By God, I am going to thrash you for this" and raised his hands to fight, Ahuja made a sudden grab for the envelope containing the revolver, which Nanavati had kept on the cabinet nearby. But Nanavati reached it first. Ahuja suddenly gripped Nanavati's hand and tried to take the revolver by twisting Nanavati's hand. During the struggle, two shots went off.

Already, *Blitz* had found a sensational angle to the trial and a bias for Nanavati.

The following week, the trial was on *Blitz*'s front page. A bold headline, "Tragedy of the Eternal Triangle," illustrated with the photographs of Nanavati, Sylvia, and Ahuja, was followed by the story— "Sylvia Nanavati Tells Her Story of Love and Torture." It reported a scene of hysterical excitement in the packed courtroom among the surging crowds who gathered to hear Sylvia's testimony and to catch a glimpse of Nanavati, smartly attired in a starched white naval uniform. Given Hahn's report, *Blitz* did not have to invent the hoopla. But the tabloid ratcheted up the public frenzy another notch by its reports. It gleefully reported college girls losing their hearts to the handsome commander. Some swooned at his sight. Others reportedly sent him hundred-rupee bills smeared with lipstick. "A few love-

5.2. *Blitz* front page: "The Tragedy of the Eternal Triangle." Source: *Blitz*, October 17, 1959

lorn nymphets have even made him offers of marriage, anticipating divorce." While the crowd in the courtroom listened attentively to the counsels, "there [was] another mute and eyeless 'spectator' present—AHUJA'S SKULL, an exhibit in the case, which [stood] on the table near the press benches, grinning sinisterly."

Sylvia was described as the attractive blue-eyed British wife of the commander, clad in a white sari and blouse—an image of purity—and speaking in a voice choked with emotion. The article then proceeded to selectively reproduce dramatic elements of her four-

and-a-half hours of testimony as a defense witness, beginning with a scene of domestic bliss.

"On April 27, before lunch," Sylvia deposed, "we were sitting in the sitting room, my husband and I and the children."

Bliss was broken by trouble.

"My husband came and touched me. I asked him not to do it. I asked him not to touch me as I did not like him."
Defence Counsel: "Why did you not like him?"
Sylvia: "At that time I was infatuated with Ahuja."

Sylvia testified that Nanavati just sat dazed when she confessed that she had been unfaithful. Then:

Suddenly he got up rather excitedly and said that he wanted to go to Ahuja's flat and square things up. I became very alarmed and begged him not to go. I said: "Please don't go anywhere there, he may shoot you!" My husband said, "Please do not bother about me. It does not matter. In any way, I will shoot myself."

When my husband said this, I got hold of his arm and tried to calm him down. I said: "Why do you shoot yourself? You are the innocent one in this!"

After calming down, Nanavati asked if Ahuja was willing to marry her and take care of the children.

I avoided that question as I was too ashamed to admit that I felt that Ahuja was trying to avoid marrying me.

Sylvia deposed that Nanavati offered to forgive her if she promised to never see Ahuja again.

I hesitated to give an answer as I was still infatuated with Ahuja. As this was a question which affected my whole future I could not give an answer at the moment.

Sylvia admitted frequenting Ahuja's apartment. Ahuja's sister, Mamie Ahuja, knew of the affair and had allegedly agreed to serve as her alibi if Nanavati came to know of his wife's visits to their residence. This account of subterfuge was followed by the mention of Sylvia's revelation that Ahuja drank liquor. This disclosure was meant to draw attention to the discovery of twenty-three bottles of liquor in Ahuja's apartment, a quantity far larger than that permitted in Prohibition-era Bombay. The defense used this revelation to paint Ahuja as an immoral playboy who habitually threw parties, where he plied women with liquor. Sylvia went along with the defense's insinuation. More was to come. Sylvia said that Ahuja had promised to marry her several times before 1958—"the year of intimacy between the two." But this, according to her testimony, changed a month or two after they had sex, when he tried to back out of his promises.

> The deceased had given me to understand that he loved me and wanted to marry me and then he tried to back out of his promises. Having broken my marriage, I thought it was only right that he should marry me.

When challenged by the prosecutor to document Ahuja's disavowal of his promise, she read out from a letter she had written on May 24, 1958:

> Last night when you spoke about your need of marrying, about the various girls you may marry, something inside me snapped and I knew I could not bear the thought of your loving and being close to someone else.

The morality tale was set. On one side was an upright naval officer, and on the other, a liquor-drinking Don Juan. Caught in between was a remorseful wife duped into sexual intimacy by the immoral playboy's false promise of marriage.

THE VERDICT

On Wednesday, October 14, Karl Khandalawala addressed the jury, asking it to return a verdict of not guilty. For two days, he dissected the evidence to argue that the charge of premeditation was unproven; Ahuja's death, he stated, was an accident. He ended his spirited address boldly: "Commander Nanavati has committed no offence in the eyes of God nor any offence under the law of this country. I ask for no sympathy and no mercy. I ask for a decision on the facts of the evidence." Chief Prosecutor Trivedi followed. Summarizing his interpretation of the evidence, he declared that the evidence proved that Commander Nanavati had committed a cold-blooded murder. He discounted the defense theory of a struggle, asserting that there was ample proof of intention. However, he conceded that, given the exceptional circumstances and the "sordid story" underlying the killing, the jury could return a verdict of guilty of culpable homicide not amounting to murder.[29] After the prosecutor completed his rebuttal of the defense, Judge Mehta addressed the jury, patiently analyzing the evidence and instructing it of its responsibility.

After the judge finished his summation on October 21 at 4:30 p.m., the jury immediately retired to consider its verdict.[30] An hour passed, then another, as the tense spectators waited in the courtroom. The crowd swelled outside as office workers stayed to hear the decision. When it got dark, lamps were switched on inside the courtroom. Then, a little after the clock struck seven, the jury returned to announce its verdict: Nanavati was not guilty of murder. By an eight-to-one majority, it also rejected the charge of culpable homicide not amounting to murder.

The courtroom erupted in cheers. But Sessions judge Mehta brought the noisy celebration to an abrupt halt. He declared that the jury verdict was "perverse" in light of the evidence marshaled in the trial and referred the case to the Bombay High Court, the highest court in the province, "in the interests of justice."[31]

5.3. The accused commander. Source: *Blitz*, October 24, 1959.

The news of the verdict was the first time that the case made the front page of the *Times*. But it was a different story with *Blitz*. Having already elevated the case as its front-page story for weeks, *Blitz* greeted the verdict with nine pages of what it called a pictorial record of the case and a bold, front-page headline: "THREE SHOTS THAT SHOOK THE NATION."[32]

Bang ... Bang ... Bang:—Three shots ring out one by one in succession. The shrill crash of window panes is followed by a wild scream. The scene is the ultra-modernly furnished bedroom of a young Bombay businessman on the second floor of a palatial building called "Jeevan Jyot"—"the flame of Life."

A brief summary of the case was followed by a sympathetic profile of the naval officer, accompanied by his photograph in uniform. "Commander Kawas Maneckshaw Nanavati, exactly six feet tall, well-built and handsome, has spent eighteen and half years of his thirty-seven year old life in the Navy." It went on to recount his training at the Royal Naval College in England, his war service, and Lord Mountbatten's recommendation that he be trained for service in aircraft carriers. In England, Nanavati met and fell in love with the "delicately built, attractive, blue-eyed, brunette Sylvia." After a month of courting, they were married in London and returned to India, where she bore him three children. He was promoted as the second in command of the Indian Navy's flagship, *Mysore*. Aboard the ship during his last time at sea, the "thought of reunion with his pretty wife and three lovely children and meeting his aged parents fill[ed] his mind. His mind was overjoyed at the prospect of a new highly coveted post."

But Nanavati's world came apart when Sylvia confessed her affair with Ahuja. He drove to the ship to get medicine for his sick dog. But instead, he ended up securing a revolver from the ship's stores. "I just wanted to shoot myself and I thought I would do that by driving far, far away from my children." Then a sudden urge took him to Ahuja. In a rage, he entered Ahuja's bedroom, shouting, "You filthy swine," and questioned him about his intentions. *Blitz* then went on to repeat Nanavati's claim that a struggle had ensued, during which the gun went off accidently, killing Ahuja. The article ended with the question: "WHAT IS THE TRUTH?"

The answer was supposedly contained in the story entitled "This Is What Happened in the Bedroom of Ahuja." It was a dramatic retelling of the "Eternal Triangle Murder Trial," illustrated with the photographs of the main dramatis personae, the witnesses, attorneys, and the swarming crowd. *Blitz* boasted that the picture of Nanavati

5.4. Crowd gathered outside the court. Source: *Blitz*, October 24, 1959.

entering the court in his full naval regalia was an exclusive. Homi D. Mistry, the deputy editor, breathlessly recounted how he had scooped the pictures of a smartly uniformed Nanavati exiting the court. The problem was that the famous accused was whisked so briskly in and out of the navy car at the court's rear entrance that there was no clear view of him. He had meekly offered this as an excuse to Karanjia in explaining the near impossibility of obtaining a picture. But Karanjia would not take no for an answer. "Nothing is impossible for a Blitzman," he roared. A chastened Mistry and his photographer set about accomplishing the impossible. Help came unexpectedly. A man offered to stall the car long enough for the *Blitz* cameraman to snap pictures of a waiting Nanavati. In return, this unnamed angel did not want money but only a copy of the photograph. A delighted Mistry agreed. One day, while the police beat back the surging crowd and Nanavati waited at the entrance for the car stalled by *Blitz*'s photo-seeking trickster, the cameraman snapped pictures at "machine-gun" speed. These photographs became part of *Blitz*'s pictorial feature. The story depicted the homicide scene with arrow marks on the pictures of Ahuja's apartment building, bedroom, and bathroom. The mise-en-scène of the trial was set with the "cosmopolitan" crowds milling about, stretching from the courts to Flora Fountain.

5.5. The murder scene. Source: *Blitz*, October 24, 1959.

With photographs, *Blitz* presented the visual drama of the court-room entry of "the handsome, smartly uniformed Commander Nanavati, with an array of seven medals glittering on his breast, but sad-eyed and quiet." Every time he was spotted going in and out of the court, accompanied by naval officers, the crowd would shout "Nanavati Zindabad" (Long Live Nanavati) and "good luck." The tab-loid recounted the details of the case built by "the learned, soft spo-ken, thin-lipped, and bushy-browed" chief prosecutor Trivedi and the alternative theory put forward by the defense. It reminded readers of the prosecution's case for premeditated murder, substantiated by the evidence of the servants, the ballistic expert, and the police surgeon, who stuck to his view that three successive shots could not go off acci-dentally. The image of Mamie Ahuja was recalled to once again retell the defense's assertions about Ahuja's alleged affairs and love letters. The readers were reminded of Commander Samuel's testimony that Nanavati had looked dazed and disoriented, muttering "fight, fight" when he appeared at the provost-marshal's residence. This was to bol-ster the argument that the gun had gone off in a struggle.

Blitz noted the drama of Nanavati's appearance as defense witness number one. Sylvia was once again portrayed as a pretty, blue-eyed, and remorseful wife, painfully recounting her act of betrayal. *Blitz* reminded readers that senior naval officials, including the navy chief, Admiral Katari, had appeared as defense witnesses. Citing the jury's not guilty verdict and its dismissal by the judge, it closed the recapitulation of the trial by quoting Judge Mehta: "I think our whole law is on trial and that our whole Constitution is on trial." It was now for the Bombay High Court to decide, *Blitz* declared, whether Commander Nanavati is "GUILTY OR NOT GUILTY."

The trial was over, but the next week *Blitz*'s front page was still asking: "NANAVATI: What Next?" People, the article claimed, were eagerly awaiting the answer to this question. Popular excitement ran high. There were rumors among the "gullible" and the "superstitious" that Ahuja's ghost was stalking the city. Street hawkers were selling replicas of Nanavati's revolver and Ahuja's towel. The public sentiment was decidedly pro-Nanavati. Reportedly, the city teenagers put new words to the tune of "Hang Down Your Head Tom Dooley":[33]

> You're not going to hang, Nanavati,
> you don't have to cry;
> Hold up your head, Nanavati, 'cause you
> ain't going to die.

Blitz boasted that its print order had soared to 152,000 to meet the huge demand, which had reportedly led the newspaper hawkers to scalp the tabloid at as much as eight times the price. The date on the newspaper's masthead was Saturday, but impatient readers rushed to the newsstands, which received the tabloid on Friday. Old city residents remember that copies circulated among friends. It was as if *Blitz* had traversed the whole of Bombay, creating a print city through its circulation. A film journalist, who was then a schoolboy in the city, remembers cutting school and traveling ticketless on the suburban train from Kandivli to Churchgate to catch a glimpse of Nanavati and Sylvia. Nanavati appeared to him as a hero—a portrayal, he now understands, shaped by the tabloid.[34] As far away as the railway bookstall in Madras, the arrival of the *Blitz* from Bombay was eagerly awaited.[35]

Blitz roused and shaped the popular imagination with its aggressive coverage of the case. Front-page headlines, sensational stories, and exclusive photographs became regular features of its reporting of the case. In the lull before the case was taken up by the High Court, *Blitz* tried to keep the interest alive and its circulation up by somehow bringing up the issue. It even commissioned a palmist-astrologer to interpret Nanavati's horoscope to foretell his legal fate. While predicting auspicious developments in the domestic sphere, the fortune-teller announced that since the case was sub judice, he had placed his legal prediction in a sealed envelope in custody of *Blitz*, to be opened after the court's verdict.[36] The movie correspondent published an article, "L'Affaire Nanavati—Hollywood Version," discovering the resonance of the case in the 1959 film *Anatomy of a Murder*, starring Jimmy Stewart, Lee Remick, and Ben Gazzara. Illustrated with movie stills, the article highlighted the film's fascinating depiction of the trial of an army lieutenant charged with murdering his wife's rapist.

A week before the case opened before the High Court, *Blitz* published another summary of the case, illustrated with photographs and graphic representations of the prosecution and including defense theories of the murder. In an era before television, this was the closest the public could get to the case as a compelling visual drama.

THE DENOUEMENT

Blitz's coverage of the case went into high gear as the High Court took up the lower court's referral on February 8, 1960. Over the year and half that the case was deliberated in the High Court, before it moved on to the Supreme Court, there were numerous legal twists. Through it all, Karanjia relentlessly publicized its factual, legal, and moral dimensions. By the end, he had turned Nanavati into a cause célèbre.

Unlike the drama of witnesses and cross-examinations in the trial, the issues before the High Court concerned the interpretation of law and rules of evidence. Still, the public interest remained undimmed. The courtroom was overcrowded, and police forces lined the High Court corridors on each floor to regulate entry. Once again, legal luminaries were ranged on opposite sides. Y. V. Chandrachud, the government pleader and later the chief justice of India, led the prosecution. A.S.R. Chari, a leading Bombay lawyer, appeared for the defense. *Blitz* announced the importance it attributed to the High Court proceedings by publishing the photographs of the main cast of characters. There were the by-now familiar pictures of the famous accused and the victim—Commander Nanavati in his naval uniform and Ahuja in a suit. But also illustrating the story were portraits of the two counsels and the High Court justices, Naik and Shelat, in their legal robes.

The accompanying articles drew the readers' attention to the main points in Sessions judge Mehta's reference. First, the Sessions judge had ruled that the jury verdict was "perverse" because it had no reasonable basis in the evidence presented. He highlighted several facts that undermined the theory of an accidental shooting. He pointed out that had there been a struggle, the towel would not have remained in place on Ahuja's body. The defense had also failed to explain, according to him, how Ahuja knew that Nanavati's envelope contained a revolver when he allegedly lunged for it. Second, his opinion was that Nanavati was guilty of culpable homicide not amounting to murder. In view of Nanavati's excellent record of service, however, Judge Mehta recommended a nominal sentence.

The defense's first move was to challenge the dismissal of the jury's verdict. It contended that the High Court should rule only on the Sessions judge's reference, not on Nanavati's guilt or innocence. It was overruled. The government pleader claimed that the Sessions judge's instructions to the jury contained severe "misdirections" and "non-directions" that had tainted the verdict. Therefore, he argued, the court should rule on Nanavati's guilt. The High Court agreed and asked the government to argue the case on the merits of the evidence. For the next three weeks, the prosecution and defense counsels battled over the interpretation of evidence.

Blitz fully covered the courtroom tussle between the prosecution and the defense, but it also published juicy tidbits. Chief among these were Sylvia's letters to Ahuja, full of love and longing. "I want to love you in every way—with love and quietness and with passion. I want to cook for you, sew for you (poor you!). I want to look after you when you're ill, bear your children and be with you always. Please say you'll have me, please say you want me." With his wife deeply in love with another man and planning to leave him, Nanavati appeared as a grossly wronged husband. Ahuja, by contrast, was portrayed as an immoral playboy, callously playing with the emotions of an impressionable and lonely wife.

On March 9 the High Court resumed the delivery of the judgment that it had begun the previous day. "There is nothing surprising or abhorrent in the step Nanavati took in avenging his injuries," observed Justice Shelat, but, he continued, "the law of the country did not permit the avenging of a wrong by taking law into one's own hands." The verdict? "The accused is convicted under Section 302 I.P.C. (Murder) and is sentenced to rigorous imprisonment for life."[37] The judge had rejected the theory of sudden provocation and ignored the trial judge's recommendation that Nanavati be charged with culpable homicide not amounting to murder. Tension broke in the hushed courtroom. Many rushed out to flash the news of the bombshell judgment to the thronging crowd outside.

The front-page headline in *Blitz* read: "NANAVATI ... What Next?"[38] A dispirited report speculated on Nanavati's options—appeal to the nation's highest court, the Supreme Court in New Delhi, undergo the sentence, and a pardon by the state governor or the president of India. A prominent boxed item on the front page read: "Love Letters of Mrs. ? to Ahuja," with the question mark covering a woman's face. The letters were frank and intimate, with sentiments such as "I shan't see you for a very long time—ten days at least. I shall probably die in that time. What is there to live for, if I can't see you, hear you, touch you?"[39] Defense Counsel Chari had brought these letters to the court's attention to assert that they proved that Ahuja lived dangerously and was aware of the consequences of such a life. It is for this reason, the counsel argued, that the court should accept Sylvia's evidence that she had seen Ahuja with a revolver and had warned Nanavati that her lover might shoot him. Supposedly, this was why Nanavati had gone armed with a gun to Ahuja's residence.

The defense's arguments for Nanavati's innocence had failed to move the High Court, but all was not lost. On March 11 Sri Prakasa, the governor of Bombay, invoked the constitution of India to direct that Nanavati be held in naval custody pending disposal of his appeal to the Supreme Court. The order was issued even before the Sessions judge could issue a warrant for Nanavati's arrest following the conviction by the High Court, ensuring that the commander did not go to jail at all.[40] Prime Minister Nehru acknowledged that, in response to the appeal by the navy chief and with the clearance of the law minister, he had advised the governor to suspend the sentence and remand Nanavati to naval custody.[41] Both the governor's decision and Nehru's intervention in a provincial matter were unprecedented and were construed as unwarranted executive interference in the judiciary. The controversy raged in the Parliament, the provincial legislature, newspapers, and among lawyers. Even the Communist Party, with which *Blitz* was friendly, condemned the governor's action.[42] The High Court picked up the gauntlet as well. After rejecting Nanavati's petition seeking leave to appeal his conviction before the Supreme Court, it appointed a full bench of seven judges to consider the constitutionality of the governor's action.[43]

A sensational case of adultery and murder was now a high-stakes legal spectacle. The trial, the jury verdict, Nanavati's conviction by the High Court, and the governor's suspension of his sentence had escalated the case into a constitutional tangle. Brought into view was a crisis in the liberal constitutional order's management of society. The very idea of equality before the law as the means of governing social conflicts was being tested. On trial was the ability of the principle of separation of powers between the executive and the judiciary to check the abuse of power.

Blitz jumped into the legal fray with a column by Ramesh Sanghvi, a barrister.[44] He wrote that the case was no longer just a matter of the death of a rich businessman and the life of a naval officer. Hitting high rhetorical notes in the law, he declared that the battle concerned issues much bigger than the fate of one man; it was about the fate of countless Indians who have no medals to bedeck their chests but depend on the supremacy of the jury system. He pointed out that no judge could discard the decision of the jury in Britain. In importing this system into colonial India, however, the British had introduced the provision for an appeal against the jury verdict to the High Court. This anachronism in the law permitted Englishmen, who were invariably the High Court judges, to maintain control over Indians. In using this anachronistic provision in the Indian criminal law to reexamine the evidence and convict Nanavati in the High Court, the prosecution had perpetuated the colonial violation of justice. It was a clear case of double jeopardy.

The constitutional card was not the only one that *Blitz* played. Its trumps were morality and patriotism. Karanjia bylined a lead story headlined "Let the People Rally to the DEFENCE OF NANAVATI!" He began by asking a series of rhetorical questions. Why did the governor intervene? Why did Nehru offer advice? Why did the jury return a verdict of not guilty? "Finally, what magnet or magic brought some 20,000 citizens to crowd around the Bombay High Court to 'Jai' [felicitate] the man charged with killing, four times everyday of the long trial?" The answers, Karanjia claimed, lay in the "greatly derided and heavily ridiculed middle-class morality." According to him, everyone, barring the members of the upper strata and an "amoral minority of the intelligentsia, hails Nanavati as the man who fired those shots on HIS BEHALF—that is, on behalf of the sanctity of his home and honour of his family—against the plague of corruption, be it of the financial or moral variety, that is eating into the body, mind and soul of the nation." Ahuja, he suggested, had come to stand for the wealthy, corrupt, immoral, and "unsocialist" forces ranged against the country, whereas Nanavati had become a symbol of the "avenging conscience of humanity." It was a popular revolt against the corruption of public life, not an expression of communal solidarity, for those who regularly gathered at the trial were not only Parsis but included Hindus, Muslims, Christians, and even Sindhis. The people had risen against the enemies of the nation.

Ratcheting up the sensational twist to the morality angle, *Blitz* published a copy of a letter allegedly sent to Nanavati by "Mrs X," a "beautiful 30-year old Anglo-Indian married woman." Mrs. X wrote that she and her husband met Ahuja at lunch at a friend's house. During the absence of her husband, who spent days away from home on work, she often went to Ahuja's apartment for parties. At one of those parties, he plied her with drink and broke down her resistance. He stripped her naked and "proceeded to satisfy his lust." When she woke up, filled with guilt and a hangover, Ahuja offered her a packet of yellow powder to cure the hangover. This cleared her mind, and she went home. Despite the guilt and a resolve never to repeat the experience, she succumbed the moment he called a few days later. She fell under his spell, like a "woman possessed." She went to his house, where, "once more, he satisfied his lust and I meekly submitted." This occurred several times. Mrs. X could not understand why she could not resist him, until a South Indian gentleman told her about a mysterious love potion commonly used in his part of the country. Apparently, this potion's magical effect lasted only when the object of love was present; it became dormant when the person was away. This explained to Mrs. X her mood swings. Armed with this precious knowledge, she broke up with Ahuja. "Something tells me," she told Nanavati, "that what happened to me happened to your wife too." She implored him to inquire if such a thing happened to Sylvia before judging her. After all, the culprit was not a charming seducer but a love potion–dispensing villain who preyed deviously on unsuspecting married women to satisfy his lust.

Not content with playing the morality card, *Blitz* also tugged at the heartstrings. It published a story about "the agony of the family." Nanavati's eldest son, Feroze, had become the butt of cruel jokes in school. His six-year-old daughter, Tannaj, and three-year-old Jimmy had to be withdrawn from school. Nanavati was forced to sell his car, refrigerator, camera, and Sylvia's sewing machine and jewelry to pay for his legal costs.

By this time, *Blitz* had dropped all pretense of only reporting the story. The tabloid had openly become a protagonist in the legal, political, and moral theater it had helped to stage. It appealed to readers to sign and mail its draft letter of support to the governor. It exhorted them to attend a public meeting in Nanavati's support. The weekly triumphantly reported that people responded enthusiastically. The hall was packed with thirty-five hundred people, and five thousand waited outside, jostling to get in. But plans for rousing speeches had to be put off. Karanjia explained to the expectant crowd that the government had advised him to adjourn the meeting because the matter was sub judice. Then he pointed to Commander Nanavati's portrait and thundered, "The struggle will continue." Accompanying the jubilant report on the meeting was a dark front-page story by Karanjia, alleging that certain political forces had manufactured the controversy over the governor's action in their plot against Prime Minister Nehru and Defense Minister Krishna Menon. Nanavati was a mere pawn in their game. Doing their bidding was "an insignificant Bombay weekly edited by a Parsi stooge." The poison pen was aimed at his archrival D. F. Karaka, against whom Karanjia had fought and won a defamation suit in 1952. Karaka's endorsement of Nanavati's conviction provided Karanjia with an irresistible opportunity to strike once again at his Parsi foe.

Meanwhile, the High Court upheld the governor's order as constitutional but regretted his use of extraordinary powers.[45] It worried that the suspension of Nanavati's sentence would convey the impression of special treatment for a particular person. Clearly, the court was unhappy. But not *Blitz*. It celebrated the decision with the headline "vox populi ... vox dei! Full Bench Upholds Governor's Order."[46] Accompanying the story was a photograph of Karanjia and Sanghvi, both smartly dressed in suits, presenting two petitions: one with a "wide and cosmopolitan range" of fifty thousand signatures, and the second signed by a group of Sindhis in Bombay. It also published a spoof piece on the deliberations of a fictitious club determined to combat the menace of Nanavatism. The members of the club were moneybags and "Chupo Rustoms" (Judas-like men) who had gathered to denounce the violations of their fundamental right to prey on army and navy wives.[47]

The celebration proved short-lived. The Supreme Court used Nanavati's special leave to appeal his conviction petition to deliberate on the constitutionality of the governor's order. The legal drama took a twist when Attorney General M. C. Setalvad and Solicitor General C. K. Daphtary excused themselves from defending the governor's order. The explanation was that they were members of the Supreme Court Bar Association, which had criticized the governor's order. In their absence, H. M. Seervai, the advocate general of Maharashtra, rose to defend the governor's order. For several weeks, the court heard opposing arguments on the order in relation to the principle of the separation of powers between the executive and the judiciary. Finally, the Supreme Court ruled on September 5: While the constitution gave the governor the power to suspend sentence, it also empowered the court to enforce its rules. In this situation, a "harmonious" construction of the respective constitutional powers of the executive and the judiciary required that Nanavati surrender before his petition of special appeal against his conviction by the High Court could be heard.[48] The court had averted a clash with the executive while protecting its domain.

On September 8 a deflated *Blitz* published a photo story capturing Nanavati's journey to jail.[49] The newspaper's spirit was down, but not its instinct for theater. Nanavati, dressed in a suit, was shown leaving naval custody in a car, a large crowd lining the motorcade. According to the story, a "cool, calm, but sad-faced" Nanavati bade farewell to Commander Samuel, kissed a sobbing Sylvia good-bye, and took a seat in the car that drove him in the afternoon to Arthur Road Prison. There, a huge crowd stood waiting for him. Amid cries of "Nanavati Zindabad!" (Long live Nanavati) and flashing camera bulbs, the "tall, handsome, cool" Commander Nanavati came out of the car, "determined to face his destiny." After a fleeting look at the formidable jail, he bent gracefully to enter the tiny wooden door and disappeared from view. A momentary silence hung in the air. Then, mayhem, as the crowd dashed toward the door, shouting "Nanavati Zindabad! Nanavati Zindabad!"

The Supreme Court commenced its consideration of Nanavati's appeal on October 9. The murder case had now escalated into a national legal spectacle. Back onstage were star jurists. Once again, long lines formed outside the courtroom. G. S. Pathak, an eminent lawyer who later served as India's vice president, led the defense team. M. C. Setalvad, the attorney general, represented the government. Reiterating the theory of an accidental shooting, Pathak asserted the matter concerned not law but fact, which only the jury could decide. The High Court, he argued, was wrong to overrule the jury and to try the case de novo. Setalvad defended the High Court's decision to overrule the jury and its finding of Nanavati's guilt. While the legal battle went on for several weeks in the Supreme Court, *Blitz* ran a tireless campaign. Week after week, it splashed "the Case of the Eternal

NANAVATI: JOURNEY TO JAIL

"THE WRIT TO BE ISSUED AS PRAYED" .... With this brief order, Mr. Justice V. S. Desai and Mr. Justice V. A. Naik ordered on September 8, the re-issue of the writ for due execution of the sentence of imprisonment imposed by the Bombay High Court upon Commander Kawas Nanavati. It took more than six hours for the issue and execution of the warrant when three police officials, Superintendent Kanga, Deputy Inspectors Dakshankar and D'Souza came to INS Kunjali in a black Chevrolet Sedan No. BMY 1701 followed by a jeep station wagon carrying Sessions Court clerk and peon. It was 5-22 in the evening when they entered the gates of Kunjali (left) surrounded by a large crowd waiting impatiently since morning. Calm, cool but sad-faced Nanavati bid farewell to sturdy Provost Marshal Samuel under whose custody he had been for 17 months, kissed his sobbing wife Sylvia goodbye and took his seat in the car (centre) which drove out at 5-47 with the crowd shouting "Nanavati Zindabad."

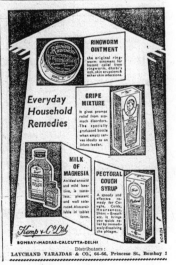

As the police car started speeding towards Arthur Road, Commander Nanavati, dressed in a cream coloured suit and brown tie, sat cooly and collected ruminating over the crowded months that changed his life ever since that fateful day of April 27, 1959.

At Arthur Road, he was given a hero's welcome (top) as people who had been waiting since morning in sunshine and rain, hungry, tired and impatient, suddenly broke the police cordon and made a dash towards the police cars shouting "Nanavati Zindabad". As the car came to a halt, press photographers, tirelessly waiting since morning, came into action, Bulbs started flashing all over when the door was swung open. The crowds pressed closer, the police too forgot the crowd and out came Commander Nanavati, tall, handsome cool, already determined to face his destiny. Taking a fleeting look at the formidable gates of the jail which was going to be home now, he walked calmly towards the door. Bending gracefully, he entered the prison through the tiny wooden door of the gate. Slowly the gate closed behind him. And then, there was silence. But only for a moment when the crowd suddenly made a dash at the closed gate shouting, "Nanavati Zinda-bad", "Nanavati Zindabad !"

5.6. Nanavati goes to jail. Source: *Blitz* September 17, 1960.

Triangle" on its front page, illustrated with photographs of the three protagonists.

On Friday, November 24, the Supreme Court delivered its judgment: Nanavati was guilty. In a unanimous judgment, the four-member Supreme Court bench upheld the right of the High Court to overrule the jury decision and consider the evidence afresh. The murder was deliberate and calculated.[50] *Blitz* responded to the decision with a front page emblazoned with an eye-catching headline, "MERCY FOR NANAVATI! An Appeal to the President for Pardon."[51] In the lead article, Karanjia was careful not to challenge the Supreme Court's confirmation of Nanavati's conviction. But he cited mitigating circumstances to plead for a pardon. Nanavati was a brilliant and patriotic naval officer; his only crime was that he had avenged his honor. Articles by its legal experts echoed the editor's argument. It was a Grecian tragedy, involving the destruction of the life of an honest officer by a notoriously "gay Lothario."[52] Ahuja's conduct represented an invasion of "unprotected homes" by the rich. The defense had bungled the case, it argued, by offering the accidental-shooting theory. This plea, according to the tabloid, denied the psychological shock underlying Nanavati's action and had lowered the brave officer in public esteem.

Invoking all these moral and patriotic reasons, *Blitz* launched a mass petition campaign for mercy. To buttress the grounds for mercy, it consolidated the story line that its coverage had developed over two and half years. This was presented in a series that it published over several weeks, comprehensively recapitulating the chain of events leading up to the murder and conviction.[53] With photographs and illustrations—now ever more creative—this series once again presented the case as a story of the tragic unraveling of a patriotic naval officer's life. It described Nanavati's illustrious career; the romance with the "beautiful, blue-eyed, brunette" Sylvia in England; the happy family life with three children; the Garden of Eden disturbed by the snake Ahuja; the news of the shocking betrayal and

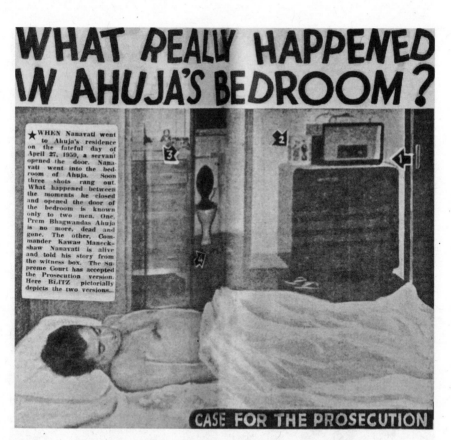

WHAT REALLY HAPPENED IN AHUJA'S BEDROOM?

★ WHEN Nanavati went to Ahuja's residence on the fateful day of April 27, 1959, a servant opened the door. Nanavati went into the bedroom of Ahuja. Soon three shots rang out. What happened between the moments he closed and opened the door of the bedroom is known only to two men. One, Prem Bhagwandas Ahuja is no more, dead and gone. The other, Commander Kawas Maneckshaw Nanavati is alive and told his story from the witness box. The Supreme Court has accepted the Prosecution version. Here BLITZ pictorially depicts the two versions...

CASE FOR THE PROSECUTION

5.7. Case for prosecution. Source: *Blitz*, December 2, 1961.

the murder; and the two and half years' legal ordeal ending in a fourteen-year sentence. This series and the pardon campaign capped the tabloid's successful effort to transform a quotidian urban episode into a national legal and moral spectacle.

SEX, LAW, TABLOID, AND THE CITY

The Nanavati case's life as a media event is a quintessentially modern story of the entanglement of the city, mass culture, and law in a single circuit. But it is a story located at a particular juncture in the cultural modernity of Bombay. There was something very specific

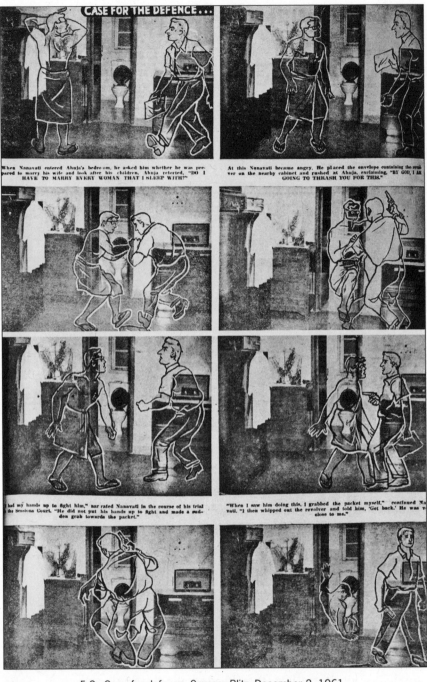

5.8. Case for defense. Source: *Blitz*, December 2, 1961.

about the city that the case brought into view. So too were the modes of the case's circulation in mass culture and the issues of the law, society, and politics it raised.

The sensational media coverage brought to the surface the elite milieu of the late-colonial and early-postcolonial city, a milieu rooted in the colonial experience. Here, English was the mode of communication. An anglicized and colonial lifestyle was utterly normal. It is the Bombay evoked in Salman Rushdie's fictionalized story of his childhood in the city. It is also the city of the golden fifties, which are nostalgically remembered today. Daily life in this world included visits to the trusty department stores on Hornby Road and Mahatma Gandhi Road—Evans and Fraser, Whiteway Laidlaw, and the Army and Navy Store. The hair salon Fucile and cafés and confectionaries—Cornaglia, Mongini, Comba, Bertorellis, and Bombellis—were familiar spots.[54] Clubs and dinner parties, bearers and servants, were fixtures of elite life. Going to an afternoon show of *Tom's Thumb* at the Art Deco Metro Theatre was not out of the ordinary. The exclusive enclaves of Cuffe Parade and Malabar Hill, the locus of the drama of adultery and murder, were well known in the elite geography of the city. Ahuja and Sylvia's affair, the love letters, and the details of the daily lives of the main protagonists did not appear exceptional in this setting.

It is this elite city that *Blitz* presented on its pages. Its relentless attention to the story was remarkable, given that this was a period of very important political developments. The Bombay State was divided into the linguistic provinces of Gujarat and Maharashtra in 1960. The border dispute between India and China was heating up at this time, and *Blitz* covered these developments as well, with front-page headlines and special features. *Blitz* also published the usual stories on political and financial malfeasance. But the Nanavati case was *Blitz's* mission. It turned what could have been a tawdry revenge killing in Bombay's upper-class social circuit into something more. It enlisted patriarchal and nationalist sentiments to forge populist support for Nanavati. In its framing of the story, the rich did not just oppress the poor but threatened the very moral fiber of the nation, which *Blitz* identified with the armed services. Thus, a routine upper-class drama of sex and murder became a spectacle of patriarchal honor and law in the modern, cosmopolitan city. If Nanavati was guilty of anything, it was of honor killing. Ahuja got what he deserved.

Blitz was not alone in prominently covering the case, but it alone was loud and partisan, in contrast to the sober and impartial dailies such as the *Times of India*. The bourgeois public sphere may well be an arena for speaking truth to power, but the speech had to be colorful, vivid, and visual. It confronted the elite discourse of cold reason with a populist politics expressed in the culture of sensations and emotions. Thus, it played the Nanavati case with classic tabloid techniques—screaming headlines, exciting stories, rumors, photographic scoops, and graphic illustrations. Reporting the case as a big-city scandal, it claimed to unearth the moral and political perversions that lurked under the surface of the city's elite life. Glossing over the fact that Nanavati was a member of this elite and had received special treatment since the time he walked into Lobo's office, Karanjia cast him as a hero of the "people," someone who stood for patriarchal and patriotic values. Drawing on its self-representation as a radical paper, *Blitz* pointed fingers at the right-wing forces allegedly determined to use the case to embarrass Nehru. Accounts of cheering crowds and petition campaigns for Nanavati were used to construct a "people" ranged on the naval officer's side.

Everyone appeared to have played along in a public drama that was largely stage-managed by *Blitz*. Nanavati was superb in his role as a patriotic naval officer and a devoted husband and father. Sylvia came across as a duly repentant wife who had strayed temporarily. Ahuja's image as a villainous playboy hung over the case, with the replica of his skull in the courtroom—according to *Blitz*—"grinning sinisterly" at the proceedings. Star attorneys dressed in their court uniform uttered high-sounding dialogues on law, evidence, and the constitution. The pronouncements of the judges from their bench cast an aura of order. The Gothic Revival buildings of the Sessions and High Courts in Bombay, and the imperial Indo-Saracenic architecture of the Supreme Court in Delhi, provided weighty authority to the spectacle in which the law strained to assert its supremacy over society. The teeming crowds shouting "Nanavati Zindabad" and college girls swooning at the sight of the commander also played their part in this riveting public theater.

Karanjia mobilized mass culture to influence the legal theater. Against the "people" whom the state claimed to embody in bringing the case against Nanavati, *Blitz* assembled an alternative collective body. On one side was the abstract citizen of the law; on the other side were flesh-and-blood "people." In the confrontation of these rival conceptions of the "people," patriarchal and patriotic values asserted their superiority over the interests of law and order. This assertion appeared momentarily successful when the jury gave a not guilty verdict. Although subsequent court decisions went against Nanavati, *Blitz* raised the stakes by its persistent orchestration of the public opinion. Under the glare of the media, the case became a spectacle of the law's capacity to resolve social conflicts. The law offered the premise of "sudden provocation" to justify the unlawful act of murder as a crime of passion.[55] Popular sentiment, summoned by *Blitz*, also goaded the courts in this direction by portraying the murder as an honor killing. Ironically, Karanjia's public campaign to influence the legal process helped the judicial system to assert itself emphatically in the theater of mass culture.

But it was a Pyrrhic victory. Commander Nanavati enjoyed powerful support. The entire naval hierarchy, including the navy chief, was in his corner. Governor Sri Prakasa and Prime Minister Nehru had already intervened on his behalf. The government had provided funds for his legal defense. After his conviction, Sylvia petitioned the governor, imploring him to pardon her husband, who was paying the price for her "stupid infatuation and selfishness."[56] Nanavati's parents and his son Feroze also submitted mercy petitions. Spearheaded by Karanjia, *Blitz* launched its mass petition for pardon.

The liberal order buckled under the populist pressure mounted in favor of the powerful. But the government feared antagonizing the Sindhi community. A behind-the-scenes intrigue developed.[57] Sylvia and Rajni Patel, Nanavati's lawyer, who was an influential power broker, visited Ram Jethmalani, a prominent Sindhi lawyer who had represented Mamie Ahuja. Patel offered a deal. The government was prepared to pardon Bhai Partap, a well-known Sindhi businessman convicted for financial fraud. The condition was that Jethmalani secure the concurrence of the Sindhi community for Nanavati's pardon. This also meant obtaining Mamie's consent. The deal was struck. Ahuja's sister gave it in writing that she had no objection to Nanavati's release from prison. With the communal calculus settled, Viyalakshmi Pandit, Nehru's sister and Maharashtra's governor, pardoned both simultaneously.

On March 17, 1964, Nanavati was released from Sundown, the small bungalow in Lonavla where he had lived for six months on a month-to-month parole.[58] He had spent less than three years in prison. A few years later, he left for Canada with Sylvia and the children, never to return or be heard from again. He passed away in 2003.

As for Karanjia, he delighted in Nanavati's release and continued to edit *Blitz* with his characteristic aplomb for the next several decades. But long before the tabloid ceased publication in 1998 and his death in 2008, *Blitz*'s Bombay had changed. The elitist late-colonial and early-postcolonial urban milieu and the legal theater that it had brought into prominence never again achieved such spectacular cultural influence. It was the mythic Bombay's last hurrah, facilitated by Karanjia, also a member of the classic cosmopolitan set.

Ironically, it was also Karanjia and his *Blitz* that inaugurated the politics of the "people" that was to hammer the nail in the coffin of the city's mythic openness and sophistication. The stage was set for Bal Thackeray and his Shiv Sena.

6

FROM RED TO SAFFRON

On the night of Friday, June 5, 1970, Krishna Desai was stabbed to death. By all accounts, he was a popular trade union and political leader. Well known and admired in the city's working-class districts, he had been a member of the Bombay Municipal Corporation for most of the period from 1952 to 1967. At the time of his assassination, he was a Communist representative in the Maharashtra Legislative Assembly.

The murder made front-page news.[1] The government appointed a senior police official, R. S. Kulkarni, deputy police commissioner (Crime Branch), to oversee the investigation. The arrests were swift. By Monday, June 8, seven suspects were apprehended. In all, sixteen youths, all members of the right-wing nativist party, the Shiv Sena, were charged and convicted.[2]

The Communist weekly, *Yugantar,* pointed fingers at the Shiv Sena and its chief, Bal Thackeray.[3] The pro-Communist *Blitz* alleged that Desai's murder was "Nazi-type tactics to liquidate the Left."[4] As evidence, it cited the "SS chief" Thackeray's speech, delivered five days prior to the murder, exhorting his supporters to liquidate the Communists.[5] Indeed, since its inception in 1966, the Sena had opposed the Communists, and Thackeray frequently aimed vitriolic rhetoric against them. This was met with an equally sharp Communist riposte, alleging that Thackeray was a pawn of the Congress chief minister, V. P. Naik, and that the Sena was nothing but a gang of Fascist storm troopers acting at the behest of mill owners. Thackeray denied complicity, but in the charged atmosphere after the murder, accusations and counteraccusations flew fast and furious.

The Desai murder signaled a far-reaching transformation in the city. While the Communists grappled with the loss of an immensely popular leader with deep roots in the working-class community, the Shiv Sena established itself as a powerful, intimidating force. Today the color saffron is ubiquitous in the city. Golden yellow is the upper band of the Indian national flag, but it is more generally associated with the Hindus and Hindu nationalists and is also the color of the Shiv Sena. You can spot the Sena's saffron flags fluttering at virtually every important street corner. Its billboards, and slogans are visible everywhere. The portraits of Bal Thackeray and his son, Uddhav Thackeray, greet you on major streets and crossroads. Even the breakaway Maharashtra Navnirman Sena (MNS), formed by Raj Thackeray, the Sena chief's nephew, who earned his spurs by sparking a violent outburst against North Indian immigrants to the city, now enjoys a significant presence.

The saffronization of Bombay is an oft-told story. Many read and lament it as an assertion of Hindu communalism and regionalism in a city that remains multireligious and multiethnic. The Shiv Sena's rise in alliance with the Hindu nationalist Bharatiya Janata Party (BJP) and the communal riots of 1992–93 lend support to this narrative of a growing Hinduization and nativism and a vanishing cosmopolitanism.

Undoubtedly, the city's ideological color has changed since the sixties. Both the Sena's supporters and its detractors agree the city looks and feels different. Though red flags did not flutter much beyond the mill gates, they signified the working class's claim on the city. Workers, intellectuals, and political activists saw radical urban dreams expressed in the color red. Behind the saffronization of the city is the story of the destruction of its working-class politics, the extinction of the red city dreamed up by the Communists and trade union activists. But this transformation was not only ideological. Saffron displaced red not just by crushing radical thought but also by fashioning and entrenching an urban political culture of populism. Karanjia's invocation of the "people" and his endorsement of Nehru as the leader offered a glimpse of this populism, albeit from a diametrically opposite ideological spectrum. Of course, his effort was episodic, and he was not engaged in leading and building a political movement. The Sena took up this task in earnest, successfully establishing populism as a coherent and effective style of mobilization of the street. Its populist politics divided society into two rival camps—the "people" and their "enemies." Positing a direct relationship between the people and their leader, the Sena installed the crowd as a forceful political actor and unleashed it on the streets to slay the "enemies" of the "people." Scorning "business as usual," Thackeray openly advocated and deployed direct and violent methods to advance the cause of the "people." With the Communist red flag lowered, Bombay was swathed in Sena saffron.

VILLAGE OF THE MILLS

The story of Bombay's saffronization began in the mill districts. It was there, in the densely packed working-class neighborhoods of Parel and Lalbaug, that the Communists dreamed of coloring the city red.

The area was known as Girangaon, or Village of the Mills. The name registered the concentration of textile mills in the area and the rural origins of its inhabitants. Most were migrants from the villages of western Maharashtra and the Konkan coast and from farther afield in North and South India. The labor migrants were also predominantly male. This was not only the result of patriarchal control over women's mobility and employment, but also because the mill owners preferred male workers due to restrictions on the hours of women's work and their entitlement to maternity benefits. With limited employment opportunities in the mills, the women who migrated to the city because of desperate circumstances in the village, widowhood, or to escape family control in the countryside were consigned to low-status and low-paying casual jobs. This included running *khanavals*, or dining spaces, where male workers gathered to eat home-cooked meals. Away from their native villages, laboring men would meet regularly over meals to gossip, exchange information, and discuss problems and shared experiences, developing a heavily male-oriented working-class culture. The khanavals provided not just a place to eat but also a space of friendship and community.

The migrants to the city came to earn a livelihood, but low wages and insecure employment rendered their position precarious.[6] With transportation expensive and inadequately developed, they congregated in the mill neighborhoods, where housing consisted of packed chawls and jerry-rigged shacks erected by mill owners and landlords. As many as twenty men would cram into a single room, often less than six square meters, in the timber-built chawls. One group of workers would vacate the sleeping spaces for the next when the shift changed in the mill, and they all shared a common bathroom at the end of the hallway. To secure even this space in shifts, they had to rely on caste, village, and kin links. The same was true in securing employment, housing, and credit. The need for credit also connected them to the grocer and the moneylender, many of whom were Pathan migrants from Afghanistan, who also acted as muscle for the mill owners. Finally, there was the Dada, the neighborhood tough guy. Known for his physical prowess, the Dada ran *vyayamshalayas*, or gymnasiums, commanded musclemen, organized religious festivals, and acted as a neighborhood patron.

With work and neighborhood so closely connected, the workers were not just an industrial proletariat determined solely by their status as wage earners; the web of neighborhood ties also shaped them. The densely packed living conditions blurred the lines between the street and the home, the public and the private, fostering a sense of community in Girangaon.

Neighborhood organizations played a part in this process. Chawl committees took care of the welfare of the residents, settled disputes, represented the tenants before landlords and municipal authorities, and organized religious festivals. Among them was the popular Ganeshutsav Festival. Traditionally, this had been a domestic ceremony. But in the early twentieth century, the nationalist leader Bal Gangadhar Tilak turned it into a public celebration. Since then, it has become a widely observed celebration, which ends with a public procession for the immersion of the elephant-headed god Ganpati's idol in the sea. Chawls and neighborhoods took a lead in mobilizing people in this celebration of Ganesh, the benevolent and imperfect elephant god.[7]

Popular cultural forms and performances also imparted a distinct flavor to Girangaon's working-class milieu. Street entertainment, folk art, the *loknatya* (popular) theater tradition, dance dramas, and devotional music flourished.[8] Accomplished singers, called shahirs, drew large audiences. Tamasha, a bawdy and improvisational theatrical form drawn from the countryside, was wildly appreciated. Madhukar Nerale recalls that there were already many tamasha theaters in the city when his father founded Hanuman Theatre in 1946. Mill workers flocked to these performances, which used no written script; the performer would draw upon characters from the epics and improvise on the spot. Tamasha, which had developed in the Deccan districts, coexisted with theatrical forms from other rural areas. Initially, artists were invited from the countryside to perform in the city, but over time Girangaon developed its own band of performers.[9]

Clearly, rural cultural forms and the social ties of caste, village, and kin were the glue binding the migrants into clusters of community. But Girangaon, despite its name, was no simple extension of the village into the city. The working-class neighborhoods of Parel and Lalbaug were irreducibly urban. The migrants patched together a distinctive collective urban identity from bits of the countryside, reflecting the circumstances of their industrial recruitment and conditions of survival. The reference to the village in the name and the invocation of rural kin and caste links served as a meaningful means to cope with and implicitly critique the difficult conditions in the city.

DREAMING RED

A collective identity forged from the neighborhood ties of village, caste, and kin did not automatically translate into a proletarian mobilization against capital. It was one thing to find workers bound together through shared cultural and social conditions, but quite another to mobilize them as a revolutionary force for socialism. This was the challenge that the Communists faced when they began their activities in Girangaon in the 1920s.

Although the Communist Party of India was founded in 1920 at Tashkent under the direction of the Comintern, the first conclave of Communist activists in India took place in Kanpur in December 1925. Out of this conference came the Workers and Peasants Party, the name of the Communist Party at that time. Absent from the conference was S. A. Dange, one of the leading Communists. Born in 1899 to a Maharashtrian Brahmin family, Dange had started his political career as a follower of the nationalist leader Tilak. But like several other nationalists of his generation, he gravitated to Marxism after the Bolshevik Revolution. In 1921 Dange published a pamphlet, *Gandhi vs. Lenin*, reflecting his conversion to revolutionary politics. A year later, he started an English journal called the *Socialist* with the help of a sympathetic flour-mill owner.[10] Strikes by workers drew him to Girangaon, where he began spreading Marxist ideas among labor activists. The British took note of his Communist activities and threw him into prison in 1924, charging him with conspiracy to overthrow his majesty's government.

At that time, the principal trade union was the All India Trade Union Congress (AITUC). Founded in 1920 by Congress leaders, the AITUC was by no means a revolutionary organization. Nor was the Girni Kamgar Mahamandal, the main trade union founded by mill clerks and jobbers during the 1924 general strike. The opportunity for the Communists came in 1927.[11] The mill owners introduced "rationalization" schemes, developed by Henry Ford in the United States and admired by businessmen and efficiency experts throughout the world. As elsewhere, rationalization raised the workload and created fears of unemployment and lower wages. The workers became restive.

The protest began at Sassoon Mills, one of the largest and most advanced manufacturing units.[12] Soon, the workers struck in mill after mill. As industrial action spread to the industry as a whole and spilled into the public sphere of the street and the neighborhood, the Marxist anticapitalist ideology provided the workers with a robust rallying point. Unlike the established labor leadership, which had particular neighborhood and political connections to defend, the Communists were unconstrained; they championed a general strike for larger political reasons. Dange, who had just been released from jail in 1927 after serving three years for his conviction in the "Bolshevik Conspiracy" case, returned to Bombay and plunged into labor activism.[13] While the established labor leaders wavered, Dange and his comrades pressed for a general strike.

A police firing on a workers' procession added fuel to fire. Inflamed by the shooting, which felled one of their comrades, the mill workers went on a general strike in 1928 that lasted for six months. The Communists worked furiously to keep up the workers' morale, organizing eight hundred public meetings.[14] They raised a strike fund from trade unions in Russia, Britain, and Europe and collected money in India.[15] Dange and the Communist leadership fashioned a system under which grain was collected, bought, and distributed for consumption among the striking workers. Even small grocers in Girangaon contributed grain, reflecting the strike's impact on the balance of power in the neighborhood.[16]

Passions ran high. Black legs, or scabs, were not welcome. Once, the workers heard that two Bhaiyyas (North Indians) had broken the strike. The striking workers lay in wait for the Bhaiyyas to emerge from the mill, nabbed them, painted their faces black, and tied them to a tree. Women activists, sporting red ribbons, picketed the mill gates, daring anyone to break the strike. The Communist leaders would roam the streets of Girangaon from 5 a.m. until late at night, overseeing the strike and boosting the workers' spirits. Their idea of uplifting the morale was to deliver speeches that sought to inspire the strikers with alluring portrayals of the Soviet Union as a proletarian paradise.[17]

The Communist militancy paid dividends. The Girni Kamgar Mahamandal, the existing trade union of mill hands, split in 1928, and the Communist Girni Kamgar Union (GKU) emerged as the dominant force. According to Dange, the growing Communist influence was a product of the strike, not its cause: "The strike was not our creation, but we were the creation of the strike."[18] Emboldened by the general strike, the GKU led several lightning strikes against the rationalization schemes. By January 1929 its membership shot up to one hundred thousand.[19] The GKU established several centers that fostered tight connections between the union, the mill committees that had sprung up during the general strike, and the neighborhood. As Dange was later to claim, the strike and the GKU's rise led to a new source of power, one that bent the neighborhood ties in the direction of worker militancy.[20]

The British government once again went after Dange, charging and convicting him in the Meerut Conspiracy Case for plotting to establish the Comintern in India. He was imprisoned from 1929 to

1935. The GKU's influence, however, remained unaffected. A wave of strikes in 1933–34 further consolidated its presence in Girangaon. Through chawl committees and party cells in mills, the Communists were able to mobilize both the workplace and the neighborhood against their employers. They matched the coordination among the employers through the Millowners' Association, with the organization of workers scattered in individual mills as a militant class force.

In this class confrontation, there was no question about the Communist commitment to workers. Their ideology was to champion the working class, shunning any accommodation with the mill owners. Nominated to no legislature, seated in no royal commission, they carried no stigma of association with the state. Their opposition to the British government as an imperialist force resonated with the workers, who saw the colonial state on the side of the employers. They viewed police repression in the name of maintaining law and order as a ruse for supporting the mill owners. The discriminatory excise policies of the government, designed to favor Manchester over the Bombay textile industry, appeared to confirm the colonial state's hostility to their interests. This favoritism was one of the reasons that several mill owners threw their support behind the Gandhi-led Congress's nationalist campaign in the early1920s.[21] But this only seemed to reaffirm the Communist claim to be the only party solely on the workers' side. The CPI, like the mill owners, supported the Congress-led nationalist campaigns against the British, but it mobilized the working class as a political force ranged against both capitalism and imperialism.

The Communists turned Girangaon into a red bastion not just with industrial actions but also with attempts to forge a progressive culture. The formation of the Indian People's Theatre Association (IPTA) in 1942, following the establishment of the All India Progressive Writers' Association (PWA) in 1936 by leftist intellectuals, was a step in this direction. Whereas the IPTA's central squad consisted of middle-class intellectuals and artists, the performers in Girangaon were drawn largely from the working class. The legendary performers in the working-class districts were Amar Sheikh, Anna-bhau Sathe, and D. N. Gavankar. Sheikh, a Muslim, had worked as a menial bus cleaner before becoming a celebrated singer and performer. Sathe was a Dalit and had worked as a mill hand.[22] Only Gavankar belonged to the middle class. He had earned a BA degree before getting involved in nationalist activities and joining Sheikh and Sathe in founding Lal Bawta Kalapathak (Red Flag Artists' Group).[23] Drawing on tamasha (a folk form of drama that combines song and dance), these performers fashioned loknatya, a people's theater form that spoke to the conditions of working-class lives. Sathe's song "Majhi Maina Gavavar Rahili, Majha Jeevachi Hotiya" (My Beloved Is Left behind in the Village, My Heart Aches for Her) spoke to the homesickness of migrant workers. His "Mumbaichi Lavni" (Mumbai's Song) evoked the workers' city, their daily struggles to survive, and their hopes of the good life in Bombay.[24]

Sheikh, Sathe, and Gavankar formed part of a worldwide phenomenon of radical working-class cultural resistance against capitalism. Similar protests against the exploitation of workers were articulated, for example, by the activists in the Workers' Theatre movement in Britain and agitprop theater in the United States.[25] Like their revolutionary compatriots elsewhere, the Bombay trio never achieved international or even national fame. Their lives and activities are not commemorated in official histories and monuments; that honor is reserved for opium kings such as Jamsetjee Jejeebhoy. But they played a vital role in Bombay's working-class life as the trio sat together regularly to experiment and compose songs for theatrical performances and political meetings. Sathe wrote the lyrics for the songs that Gavankar and Sheikh sang.[26] They were a popular group, often performing at Kamgar Maidan, the Girangaon venue where the Communists held big political meetings. Sheikh Jainu Chand remembers one such meeting at Kamgar Maidan that began with the trio singing without microphones. The large crowd joined them. When Dange arrived, firecrackers greeted his appearance. Chand found his speech mesmerizing. "It was not a speech; it was as if a worker was speaking."[27] Dange was known to have an uncanny ability to communicate with the workers. He would use his knowledge of Sanskrit and the epics to explain issues of class injustice. The workers from the Konkan coast affectionately called him Dango in their language.[28]

Women were at the forefront of this politically militant army in Girangaon. Middle-class women, radicalized by Marxist ideals and by their Communist family members, became activists in the trade union. Marxism's modern outlook also freed them from customary constraints and sparked their activism. Usha Dange, Ahilya Rangnekar, Kusum and Vimal Ranadive, Kamal Donde, Tara Reddy, and many others were deeply involved in working-class activism. Leaders also emerged from the ranks of women mill workers. Among them was Parvatibhai Bhor, who rose to become the vice president of GKU. Women activists would go to the mill gates and sing songs. The mill hands coming off their shift were exhorted to "lift high the flag of revolt, the blood red flag steeped in our blood." Songs depicting class injustice were addressed to women mill workers: "My son Raghu has to go to school, but he has no clothes to wear, and he is cold, my hunger is the reminder of the red flag."[29] During strikes, women activists stood at mill gates and spat betel juice at strikebreakers. The women khanavals smuggled pamphlets and leaflets into the mill—concealed under the food baskets—and pasted them on the walls.[30]

The color red figured heavily in the Communist iconography. Red flags were planted on factory and mill gates, at road corners, and in playgrounds. During strikes, red flags, banners, and placards were ubiquitous. In processions, everyone carried small red flags. *Torans* (strings with little triangular colorful papers) of the red flag were created and hung on walls and street corners.[31] Inside the mill, the workers would celebrate May Day right outside the manager's office, putting up portraits of Marx, Lenin, and Stalin and hoisting red flags. The workers would come and bow before the portraits as if they were worshiping a Hindu deity.[32]

Industrial actions and cultural activism kept the red flag fluttering in Girangaon through the 1940s, and Dange was its undisputed labor leader. He led a strike in 1939, for which he was imprisoned. Released after four months of rigorous imprisonment, he led another strike in 1940 and was thrown back in jail. In 1943–44 he was elected the chairman of the AITUC. In part, this was because of Dange's popularity as a militant trade unionist. But it was equally due to the imprisonment of the nationalist leaders by the British, leaving the AITUC open for a Communist takeover. The colonial authorities spared the CPI and allowed it to function legally because of its sharply changed stance on World War II.

When World War II broke out in 1939, at first the Communists denounced it as an "Imperialist War." The nationalist leadership, however, was sympathetic to the Allies and opposed to the Nazis. Winston Churchill's stirring words promising nothing but "blood, toil, tears, and sweat" in the fight against tyranny earned him plaudits in Britain and the United States but appeared deeply hypocritical in colonial India. The nationalists demanded self-government in exchange for supporting the war effort. In March 1942 the British sent a delegation headed by Sir Stafford Cripps, offering full dominion status after the war. Dismissing the proposal as a "post-dated cheque on a failing bank," Gandhi called for a mass movement to force the British to "Quit India" in August 1942. A wave of repression followed. Gandhi and other nationalist leaders were promptly jailed. Churchill thundered in the House of Commons that he had not become "the King's First Minister in order to preside over the liquidation of the British Empire."

The "Quit India" movement proved to be immensely popular. Indians responded to Gandhi's call by paralyzing the colonial administration. With the top leadership imprisoned, the initiative passed to the lower ranks, who radicalized the movement. The youth, in particular, took to the streets. The CPI stood isolated from this nationalist ferment. Following the Comintern line that the Nazi attack on the Soviet Union in 1941 had suddenly turned the "Imperialist War" into a "People's War" in defense of the socialist republic, the Communists found themselves running against the popular nationalist tide. Overnight, strikes were out, and in came full-throated calls for raising agricultural and industrial production in support of the war effort.[33] The British rewarded them by legalizing the CPI, which had hitherto functioned as an underground organization. Operating openly, the party leaders were able to establish IPTA, their cultural organization, and carry out their trade union work without repression. But they paid a high price in terms of popular support, one from which they could never quite recover.

An opportunity for partial redemption came during the mutiny by the naval ratings of the Royal Indian Navy (RIN) in 1946. On February 18 the Indian sailors on HMIS Talwar, which was docked in Bombay, rose up in revolt against the bad food and racist treatment by their British officers.[34] News of the naval mutiny spread to other ports on the subcontinent, sparking strikes by sailors stationed on ships and on shore. On February 19 the mutineers formed the Central Strike Committee, led by M. S. Khan, a Muslim, and Madan Singh, a Hindu. The naval barracks in Bombay joined the mutiny and unfurled the Congress tricolor, the Muslim League's green, and the Communist red flags. The British were alarmed; the mutiny brought a frightful reminder of the 1857 revolt when their authority nearly collapsed in North India. The Congress and the Muslim League leaders were none too happy to see a spontaneous revolt in the armed services, particularly when they were getting close to a negotiated achievement of their goals.

The Communists, however, wholeheartedly embraced the mutiny. They viewed it as a popular insurrection and a miraculous expression of Hindu-Muslim unity at a time when communal divisions were rife. Tara Reddy, then a young Communist, remembers that the CPI printed and distributed hundreds of thousands of leaflets overnight, calling workers to strike in support of the naval ratings.[35] From the early morning of February 20, workers from Girangaon and Byculla up to Naigaon began gathering on the streets. And not just mill workers; students and the middle classes from Dadar, small traders from Bhuleshwar and Kalbadevi, and Muslims from the Mohammad Ali Road, a broad swath of the city's population, came out in support of the sailors. Reddy remembers it as a war, with British troops patrolling the city in trucks and tanks, their guns trained at the insurgent population. "February 22nd was the bloodiest day; nearly three hundred workers and comrades died in police firing."[36]

Any hope that the bloody confrontation sparked by the mutiny would escalate into a revolutionary insurrection quickly vanished when the nationalist leaders intervened and mediated a compromise between the sailors and the British government on February 22. The sailors withdrew their strike in return for a promise of improved conditions and leniency in the treatment of the mutineers. The Communists were not pleased with the Congress leaders' mediation.

Unhappiness turned to outright opposition after independence and the partition of India in 1947. The CPI moved sharply to the left in its Second Congress, held at Calcutta in February 1948. Jawaharlal Nehru, who had hitherto appeared as an anti-imperialist ally, now became a lackey of the imperialists, big business, and landlords. "What has come in the replacement of a British Viceroy and his councilors by an Indian President and his ministers, of white bureaucrats by brown bureaucrats," declared the party election manifesto in 1951, is "a bigger share in the loot of Indian people for the Indian monopolists and collaborating with the imperialists."[37]

In the long, zigzagging Communist history of tortured ideological lines, the slogan "Yeh azaadi jhoothi hai (This freedom is a hoax) represented yet another new turn. The popular front line was out, and the goal now was to foment an armed insurrection, following the Bolshevik model. Leaders associated with the previous policy were forced to undergo "self-criticism," and those promoting the new line assumed control. After the Chinese Revolution, the emphasis shifted from the Bolshevik to the Maoist model of peasant revolution. As the party jumped wholeheartedly into armed struggles in Telangana and Bengal, a new group of "left" leaders, advocating the "peasant thesis," emerged.[38]

It was one thing to lead workers in strikes and quite another to turn them into revolutionaries. Militant trade unionism kept the red flag fluttering in Girangaon, enabling the Communists to bend the complex neighborhood ties in favor of labor activism. But when it came to achieving their larger goal of ratcheting up militant trade unionism to revolutionary consciousness, they came up short. The blind devotion to the Soviet Union did not help. Nor did clinging dogmatically to the idea that class interests would naturally unite workers divided by religion, region, language, gender, and caste and forge them into a revolutionary force. This naive belief in the revolutionary proletariat ran up against the competing nationalist mobilization of the population as Indians. For this reason, the CPI always struggled with defining its relationship with the Gandhi and Nehru-led Congress. So long as the British ruled India, the conflict with the "bourgeois" Congress could be muted in the interests of anticolonialism. But once India won independence and the Congress assumed power, the clash with the ruling party took center stage. In the trade union field, the GKU had to contend with the Rashtriya Mill Mazdoor Sangh (RMMS), affiliated with the Congress-led Indian National Trade Union Congress (INTUC). In addition, the socialist trade union Hind Mazdoor Sabha (HMS) also emerged as a significant competitor.[39]

The Communists remained important in Girangaon, but they no longer dominated. The slogan that national freedom was a hoax left them isolated, and the about-face to the left and the slogan of armed struggle invited government repression. As the left and right wings of the CPI became locked in disagreements, the Communist influence dwindled. Alarmed by the CPI's "left adventurist" opposition to Nehru, whose foreign-policy pronouncements won Soviet appreciation, party leaders from both wings were summoned to Moscow in 1951. Stalin ruled that Mao's revolutionary path held good for China alone; he warned the Indian Communists against following a radical path and counseled a patient and flexible approach toward Nehru. Heeding the "fraternal advice" of the Communist Party of the Soviet Union, the CPI line changed. The "left adventurist" leadership was dethroned in favor of a "centrist" one. Back in favor, Dange, sidelined previously as "right wing," searched for ways to deploy the working class for a wider political cause. He found it in the struggle for the linguistic state of Maharashtra.

DREAMING MARATHI

> Soo ché? Saru ché!
> Danda lé ké maru ché!
>
> How are you?—I am well!
> I will take a stick and thrash you to hell!

The year is 1957.[40] Bombay is rocked by linguistic regionalism. A political procession demanding the creation of the linguistic state of Maharashtra is passing by the neighborhood of Saleem Sinai, the protagonist in Salman Rushdie's *Midnight's Children*. The neighborhood children are watching the procession from the top of a lane that slopes sharply down to Warden Road. But ten-year-old Saleem is not interested in slogan-shouting mill hands and shopkeepers carrying black flags; his attention is elsewhere. He is going around and around on his sister's bicycle, trying to impress an American girl. The girl gives his bicycle a hard shove, sending Saleem hurtling down the slope. He lands smack in the middle of the procession. When the throng sarcastically asks him in Marathi to join them, he demurs. The crowd assumes that the upper-class boy is Gujarati and asks him to recite something in his tongue. All Saleem knows is a nonsense rhyme used in his school to torment Gujarati boys. The crowd is thrilled by the ridicule of the Gujarati language. They lose interest in the boy and shout out the doggerel "Soo ché? Saru ché."

The political cauldron that Saleem unwittingly rode into had been simmering. The Congress had committed itself to redrawing state boundaries to correspond with linguistic divisions as early as 1921.[41] After independence, demands grew for reorganizing the administrative divisions inherited from the British Raj. But the government wavered because Prime Minister Nehru viewed linguistic states as detrimental to national unity. Reluctantly responding to rising tensions, it created the state of Andhra in 1953 by separating the Telugu-speaking districts from the old Madras Presidency. This was the first linguistic state. In 1953 the government appointed the States Reorganization Commission (SRC) to study and recommend the redrawing of state boundaries in light of not just language but also economy and geography. One of the most contentious issues that the SRC had to deal with was the linguistic state of Maharashtra.

In 1951 the Marathi-speaking population of about twenty-seven million was scattered among three states. Nearly sixteen million were in the Bombay State, and the rest were in Vidarbha and Hyderabad. The Bombay State, which emerged from the colonial Bombay Presidency and included Gujarat and the Deccan princely states, was multilingual. While Marathi speakers constituted 44 percent of the population, Gujarati and Kannada speakers accounted for 32 and 12 percent, respectively.[42] Creating a single state for Marathi speakers, who had never been historically unified, meant dealing with both their scattered distribution and the multilingual nature of the Bombay State. As if this was not challenging enough, there was the added complication of the city of Bombay, which was also multilingual. While the Marathis formed nearly 45 percent of

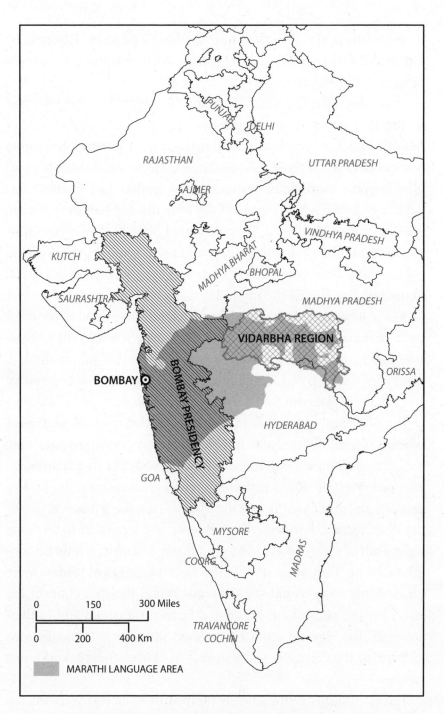

RAJASTHAN

PUNJAB

DELHI

UTTAR PRADESH

AJMER

VINDHYA PRADESH

KUTCH

MADHYA BHARAT

BHOPAL

SAURASHTRA

MADHYA PRADESH

VIDARBHA REGION

BOMBAY

BOMBAY PRESIDENCY

ORISSA

HYDERABAD

GOA

MYSORE

COORG

MADRAS

0   150   300 Miles

0   200   400 Km

MARATHI LANGUAGE AREA

TRAVANCORE
COCHIN

6.1. Bombay State in 1951. Courtesy: Tsering W. Shawa.

its population, the Gujaratis counted for 18 percent, followed by Hindi and Urdu speakers, who together also constituted 18 percent of the city's population.[43]

In dealing with this complex linguistic geography, the SRC had to also take into account the growing demand for a unified state of Marathi speakers, or Samyukta Maharashtra. Animating Samyukta Maharashtra was a powerful belief in the Marathi-speaking people's glorious past. Nationalist historians and leaders had fostered this belief by identifying impressive achievements and heroes in the region's precolonial history. They projected Shivaji, the seventeenth-century Maratha chieftain, as the preeminent symbol of the region's golden past. Thanks to leaders such as Tilak, Shivaji the historical figure became Shivaji the myth. He was no longer a Maratha chief locked in a battle with the Mughals to defend and extend his domain but a national hero. Never far from this image was also the suggestion that he was a Hindu champion against Muslim domination. A symbol of national and Hindu greatness, Shivaji became an emotive force in the movement for Samyukta Maharashtra.

The SRC ran up against the Samyukta Maharashtra sentiment when it submitted its report in 1955. It recommended maintaining the existing composite character of the Bombay State with three exceptions: First, it would include Kutch and Saurashtra, the former princely states of Gujarat, and the Marathi-speaking districts of Hyderabad; second, Kannada districts would be separated to form the independent state of Karnataka; and third, Vidarbha would be constituted into a separate state.[44] The Gujarati political leaders were pleased; not only would the Gujaratis retain their position in the state, but the addition of Kutch and Saurashtra would add to their strength. The Marathi activists, however, saw the recommendations as favoring the Gujaratis and planned to cut Marathi speakers down to size.

The Communists immediately jumped into the fray. Viewing the Soviet Union as an exemplary multinational federation, they were ideologically committed to the formation of linguistic states. But their commitment was not only ideological. Dange, in particular, was deeply emotional about Samyukta Maharashtra.[45] Thus, the day after the report was made public, the Communists held a mass meeting on October 11, 1955, on Chowpatty Beach, vowing to make a bonfire of the report.[46] The secretary of the CPI's Bombay branch warned darkly of the coming battle for the creation of Maharashtra. The unrest that the Communists whipped up put the Congress activists in a bind. They supported the demand for a unified state for Marathi speakers but had to heed the call for reason and discipline made by the leadership in New Delhi, which saw the desire for linguistic states as narrow-minded and divisive.

Unburdened by any constraint, the Communists and Socialists fanned the flame of linguistic nationalism. Dange, the Socialists S. M. Joshi and M. R. Dandavate, and the noted Marathi writer and journalist Acharya Atre emerged as the principal leaders of the movement for Maharashtra. They formed the Samyukta Maharashtra Kriti Samiti (SMKS) to fight for the unified state of Maharashtra. The new organization drew into its fold prominent intellectuals such as Keshav Sitaram Thackeray, the father of Bal Thackeray, who later founded the Shiv Sena. The leftists also recruited Senapati Bapat, a legendary Gandhian nationalist, and announced plans for a demonstration on November 21, 1955. Not even Khrushchev and Bulganin's impending visit to the city on November 23 deterred Dange. In response to SMKS's call, six hundred thousand workers struck work on November 21. The city witnessed huge demonstrations. Violence and riots broke out. The police resorted to firing on the demonstrators, killing ten and injuring three hundred. Order was restored only when Joshi was allowed to hold a meeting on Chowpatty, reiterating the demand for Samyukta Maharashtra but asking for calm.

Although the city was tense, the Soviet visit went off without incident two days later. Momentarily overlooking Moscow's growing coziness with Nehru, the Communists cooperated with the govern-

6.2. Communist leader Dange addresses a meeting for Samyukta Maharashtra. Courtesy: Taken from the collection of Com. Prakash Reddy.

ment to ensure that their Soviet comrades were warmly welcomed. Once the visit was over, the hostilities resumed. The secretary of the CPI's Bombay committee declared in December that the "final and decisive stage of the struggle for Samyukta Maharashtra is fast approaching."[47] Dange floated a new organization, the Samyukta Maharashtra Poorak Samiti (SMPS), to steer the movement in a more militant direction.[48]

The Nehru government was unbending. On January 16, 1956, it announced the decision to form three states—Maharashtra, Gujarat, and the city of Bombay, which would be administered from New Delhi. Anticipating opposition, the government arrested the leftist leaders, including Dange. The workers went on strike, and violence gripped the city for the next several days. The police opened fire in several localities. According to an official report, seventy-five people were killed in the disturbances, whereas the pro–Samyukta Maharashtra writers claimed that more than a hundred had died of police bullets. The government alleged the Marathi-speaking rioters had committed widespread violence against the Gujaratis and their commercial establishments and molested Gujarati women, a charge hotly contested by the Samyukta Maharashtra leaders. But they did not deny that the Gujaratis were attacked and feared for their lives.[49]

An alliance of opposition parties formed the Samyukta Maharashtra Samiti (SMS) in February 1956 to oppose Nehru's January decision. For the next nine months, while the SMS gathered strength by organizing satyagrahas and marches, the Congress was forced to play defense. Pressure from the Maharashtra Congress leaders mounted on Nehru. Ultimately, the central government announced a face-saving formula to create a bilingual state consisting of all the Marathi- and Gujarati-speaking areas and including Bombay City. This mollified the SMS but angered the Maha Gujarat Parishad.

While protests convulsed Gujarat, the SMS, flush with a partial victory, prepared for the 1957 general elections. Despite bitter fights between the Communists and the Socialists, the SMS candidates did remarkably well in the Marathi-speaking areas of the state.[50] The Congress was alarmed, particularly by what it saw as the threat of a Communist "takeover." New Delhi realized that the only way to check the rising Communist influence was to cede the demand for linguistic states. Accordingly, the Congress Working Committee passed a resolution in 1959 recommending the formation of Maharashtra, including the city of Bombay, and Gujarat. This took the wind out of the sails of the SMS, which was already buffeted by the bitter conflict between the Communists and the Socialists. Having achieved its goal of creating Maharashtra, the SMS collapsed.

Maharashtra came into existence on May 1, 1960. The government accepted Dange's suggestion that the new linguistic state come into existence on May Day.[51] But this was small satisfaction. As a political party, the CPI saw its influence grow. But the same could not be said of its ideology of class struggle. Whatever strength it had gained during the agitation had come not from organizing the workers as a class but from mobilizing all Marathi speakers, regardless of their class, caste, gender, and religious and political divisions, as a community. Because the majority of workers were Marathi speaking and the capitalists were Gujaratis, the Communists portrayed the struggle for Maharashtra as a class issue.[52] Dange saw the influence of big business at work in the SRC's recommendations, which, according to him, were designed to deny the "legitimate national claim" of Maharashtrians. "It seems Maharashtra can exist only as a serf nation in the service of the Commerce of Bombay City or the Commerce of the Delhi Empire."[53] Rejecting the charge that the movement for a linguistic state was a "reactionary" regional outlook against a wider national one, he characterized the Samyukta Maharashtra movement as an expression of "democratic nationalism" of the "working class, the peasantry, and the toiling middle-classes." The bilingual state, by contrast, was a form of "landlord-capitalist serfdom."[54]

Battling for Maharashtra meant going to war with the capitalists by other means, such as language and identity. During the colonial era, the strikes against mill owners had helped the Communists to mobilize Girangaon's social and cultural ties in the interests of trade-union struggles. But during the 1950s, the working-class culture forged during these decades of trade-union struggles was deployed for Maharashtrian, not proletarian, power.

When Saleem Sinai crashed into a procession of mill workers, he unexpectedly supplied them with a slogan ridiculing the Gujaratis. Off they went, crying "Soo ché? saru ché," raising slogans for Marathis, not revolution. Their symbol was not the red flag but Shivaji. Communist and Socialist writers took to portraying the seventeenth-century Maratha warrior as antifeudal and secular. Experiences of inequality and exploitation were summoned and deployed to bring a community of Marathi speakers into political existence. Their efforts were successful. But it was left to the Shiv Sena to de-

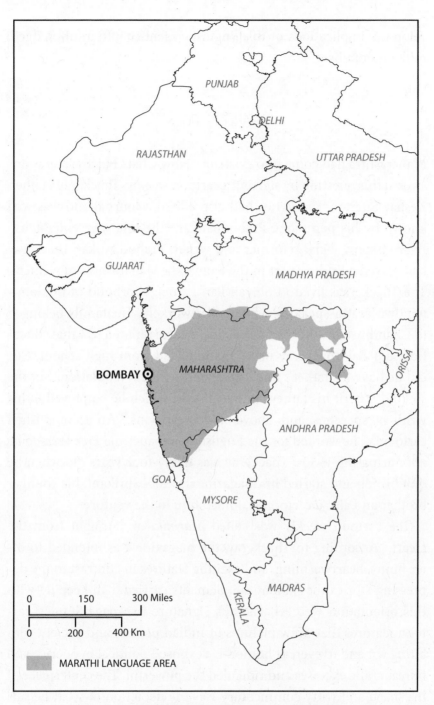

6.3. The state of Maharashtra. Courtesy: Tsering W. Shawa.

velop the implications of this linguistic identity into a full-fledged, militant populism.

SNARLING TIGER

Maharashtra had come into existence. Now what? Bal Thackeray answered this question by starting a cartoon weekly. Thackeray's father, Keshav Sitaram Thackeray, had also edited a journal and was well known by his pen name Prabodhankar, "the one who enlightens." A prominent social reformer and writer, Prabodhankar Thackeray had played a leading part in the Samyukta Maharashtra movement. The Thackerays lived in Shivaji Park, a neighborhood of predominantly Marathi-speaking white-collar workers. The family belonged to Chandraseniya Kayastha Prabhus, a caste reputed to value education, but Bal Thackeray never matriculated from high school. Nor did he have his father's intellectual and political reputation. But the son did inherit his father's pungent style, which he employed in his writings, speeches, and, above all, his cartoons. An accomplished cartoonist, he worked for the English newspaper the *Free Press Journal* during the 1950s. Thackeray was thirty-four years old when he quit his job and started his magazine in 1960. Shrikant, his younger brother and also a cartoonist, joined him in the venture.

The cartoon weekly was called *Marmik*, or "Straight from the Heart." According to Thackeray, the magazine was intended to offer funny, heartwarming, and exciting features in contrast to the depressing stories the Sunday supplements carried.[55] In keeping with this orientation were Thackeray's signature two-page Sunday cartoon features that drew pictures of Indian politics and society with biting wit and irreverent humor. He exposed political hypocrisy and bureaucratic excesses and ridiculed the powerful. The centerpiece of his sharp and witty commentary was the depiction of what he saw as the plight of the Marathi *manoos*, or the Marathi people. Week after week, he showcased the oppressed state of the Marathi and railed against the "outsiders"—initially the South Indians and Communists and later the Muslims. The magazine struck a chord, and its circulation soared to forty thousand by 1966.[56]

Emboldened, Thackeray founded the Shiv Sena in June 1966. The inaugural public meeting of the Shiv Sena, announced in *Marmik*, was held in Shivaji Park on October 30, the day of the Dushera Festival. Nearly half a million people swarmed the open ground, surprising everyone.[57] Thackeray's father spoke to the assembled crowd, exhorting them to restore Maharashtrian cultural purity. Other speakers followed. The last was Bal Thackeray, the featured speaker. He was not a great orator, but his wit and sarcasm captivated the crowd. He likened *rajkaran* (politics) with *gajkaran* (ringworm), playing on the phonetic similarity of the two words to rail against politics and politicians. He declared that the Shiv Sena was not a political party but, as the name suggested, an army inspired by Shivaji. The goal of this army, according to Thackeray, was to advance the cause of the Marathi manoos by smashing its way past the intrigue-ridden realm of politics. He uttered no deep political philosophy or complex set of principles, but only a stirring nativist appeal on behalf of the oppressed Marathi manoos. This went over well with the audience.[58]

Soon, Thackeray emerged as a force to reckon with in Bombay, and his meetings, accompanied by an elaborate dramaturgy, always roused the audiences. A contemporary report describes one such meeting.[59] "Thunderous cheers break out from a mammoth audience, as a slight figure, in thick-rimmed glasses, a high-collared coat and trousers and chappaled [slippered] feet, strides to an elaborate stage, bedecked with saffron flags and pennants." Accompanied by cheers, Thackeray took his seat on the stage, at the center of which was a table with a heavily garlanded bust of Shivaji. Proceedings opened with martial songs that swelled into a "mass chorus in which the audience join with gusto, and is punctuated by blasts of the 'tu-

6.4. The snarling tiger and the Sena chief. Courtesy: *Indian Express*, October 26, 2001.

tari,' [a buglelike instrument] to the martial notes of which Shivaji's legions galloped to battle." Thackeray spoke to the audience alternately in tones of affection and chiding, exhortation and indignation, dwelling on the injustice Maharashtrians suffered in their own state. Then the mood changed abruptly. Scolding them for their inertia and indifference, he thundered at them for "looking on helplessly while their 'rights and privileges' are 'stolen' from them under their very noses." In a crescendo, he exhorted them: "Wake up, wake up, before it is too late." By the time he ended, the audience was thoroughly riled up, and the "meeting conclude[d] with a storm of applause and 'jais' [cheers] for Shri Chhatrapati Shivaji and Bal Thackeray." Roused by the leader, the snarling tiger, the Sena's mascot imprinted on its flags, began to the stalk Bombay.

Despite Thackeray's reference to the sorry state of Maharashtrians, economic distress did not drive the rise of the Marathi manoos' sentiment. Between 1960 and 1965, Bombay attracted a significant increase in capital investment, and Indian industrial growth registered a robust 7.7 percent per year between 1951 and 1965.[60] Recession hit Bombay, like the rest of the country after 1966, but office jobs rose by 28 percent between 1962 and 1967—a period of strong economic growth, when *Marmik's* commentary on the plight of the Marathi manoos found a receptive audience.[61] The bright employment prospects, however, coincided with an extraordinary growth in the number of qualified applicants. There was a phenomenal rise in the number of matriculating males from high school, and the enrollment in Bombay University soared.[62] It was this that made Bombay's job market tight for young educated males. With the literates constituting nearly 59 percent of the city's population by 1961—twice as high as the state's—the power of *Marmik's* printed word found a receptive audience among the disaffected Marathis.[63]

The educated and unemployed young men provided a fertile ground, but to represent their frustrations in terms of Maharashtrians versus non-Maharashtrians required political intervention. No straight correlation can be made between a tight job market and the rise of the Marathi manoos' ideology. Expressing the discontent of the unemployed in nativist terms, and channeling their frustrations into a torrent of ethnic grievances, required a populist turn. Of course, the Samyukta Maharashtra movement had mobilized Marathi speakers as a political entity, but it was Thackeray who successfully deployed it as an anti-immigrant, populist force. There was no inherent reason for counting the unemployed in ethnic terms. Religion, class, caste, region, gender, and age could have served as equally valid classificatory categories. But Thackeray calculated employment figures in ethnic terms to claim the underrepresentation of Maharashtrians. In Thackeray's definition of who was a Maharashtrian, domicile alone, for however long, was not enough. Nor did the ability to speak Marathi, as many immigrants did. One had to be born a Marathi speaker to be a Maharashtrian.

Politics, not economics or culture, was in command. No socioeconomic reality, no cultural tradition, sufficiently explains the emergence of the Marathi manoos. It was Thackeray's political creation, despite his claim that the Sena was nonpolitical. To suggest that the Sena chief merely expressed—or cynically exploited—the groundswell of discontent among the Marathi youth is to underplay the radical significance of his populist intervention. Thackeray's "postpolitical" populism transformed the political landscape of the city and the state.

Underlying Thackeray's populism was the claim that the Marathi manoos was a transcendental subject. The "people" were not reducible to particular demands but something altogether more general.[64] Accordingly, Thackeray invoked grievances over language and unemployment not to seek their redress but to produce the Marathi manoos as a universal political subject. He referred to the injustices, real or imagined, suffered by the Marathi speakers in order to constitute them as the only legitimate "people." The claim was that a part of society, the oppressed underdogs, was its whole; the Marathi manoos was the sum total of the community. This strategy is evident in a satirical *Marmik* essay depicting a writer's visit to the guest of honor on a special day in the year 2065, when South Indians rule the roost in Bombay.

In the calm and quiet of the night, I went to the house of Ganpati Maratham, and greeted him with Namaskar, informing him that I had come to take his interview. Ganpati looked at me with surprise and said: "Oh, after so many years the old Marathi language is again spoken today. How do you know this language?" "I took the subject 'Old Marathi language' for my Ph.D.,"—I replied. He said, smiling, "Nowadays this language is never heard. In my childhood, Marathi was spoken in pure form; now that pure language is heard only in a small habitation of Chambal valley. A hundred years ago in Bombay, Madrasi governors, mayors, and sheriffs were appointed. The Marathi people of the time used to call these people outsiders. Then, the Madrasi lungi [a garment worn around the waist] was a topic of fun. Today everyone wears a lungi."[65]

The Marathi speakers, oppressed and overwhelmed, were the authentic and legitimate "people" held back by the illegitimate South Indian elites. "South Indian" or "Madrasi" was how Thackeray referred generally to immigrants from southern provinces, though he had Tamil and Malayalam speakers particularly in mind, and he took pleasure in ridiculing their language and dress. The mix of envy and contempt he felt for them made their supposed dominance all the more galling. But the belief in their dominance was real. So strongly felt was the grievance and the belief in a conspiracy against the Maharashtrians that the Sena published a diatribe in English to make its case. Entitled *Shiv Sena Speaks: Official Statement*, it explained that the publication was necessitated by the "scurrilous attack" on its true mission. It likened the "South Indian controlled English language Press" in Bombay to the "octopus emitting black fluid" to blur the prey's vision before tightening its grip and killing the victim.[66] The publication denied that the Sena encouraged violence against non-Maharashtrians and charged that the allegation was a lie. Behind the lie were the South Indians who wished to malign the Sena because it defends the "sons of the soil." They monopolized not only the top positions in the government and private corporations but also the clerical service. "Maharashtrian boys" were not even granted interviews, let alone hired. The Sena was a revolt against the "rabid communalism" of South Indians, who were flooding Bombay and forming slums that had become dens of bootleggers and criminals. "The dense cloud of intruders from outside has deprived the blossoming generation of Maharashtra of its ancestral zeal and enthusiasm to fight out the battles of life with determination and chivalry."[67] The Sena was founded to restore this zeal, to expose the conspiracies hatched by "outsiders" against the "people."

In fact, there was no sudden increase in the number of immigrants, either from South India or anywhere else. The South Indians constituted less than 9 percent of the city's population, scarcely more than Hindi speakers and less than half of Gujaratis. Nor did the South Indian share of white-collar jobs rise abruptly; in fact, the Gujaratis had a greater share of higher-status jobs than either South Indians or Marathis.[68] Yet, Thackeray seized on the South Indians' larger representation relative to Marathis in higher-paying jobs to target them as the enemy. In identifying South Indians as responsible for the plight of the Marathi manoos, he implied that there was nothing inherently wrong with the prevailing order; it was the intrusion of the alien matter, the corruption of the system by an external agent, that accounted for the injustices and oppressions of the "people." Once excised of these "outside" elements, justice, purity, and health would return to the social and political order, and the Marathi manoos would regain his rightful place.

To identify the intrusion of alien elements, Thackeray compiled lists of top corporate officials—many with South Indian names— from a telephone directory and published them in *Marmik*. These lists served as "proofs" of the discrimination against the Marathi manoos. The captions accompanying the lists instructed the readers to "read and keep quiet" and "read this and think."[69] He derisively referred to South Indians as "lungiwallahs," making fun of their clothing, and lampooned the phonetic patterns of their languages by calling them "yandugundu." When Sena supporters attacked South Indian restaurants, Thackeray rewarded them with praise.[70] When the theaters in Tamil-speaking Madras stopped screening Hindi films during the throes of anti-Hindi agitations in 1968, Thackeray retaliated. The Sena activists prevented the Bombay theaters from screening films produced in the south.[71]

If South Indians were aliens, so were the Communists. Although Dange had been Keshav Thackeray's associate in the Samyukta Maharashtra movement, Bal Thackeray had nothing but contempt for him. Playing on his name, Thackeray repeatedly referred to Dange as Dhonge, a hypocrite.[72] In 1965 *Marmik* published a cartoon on its cover that showed Bharatmata, or Mother India, in a state of misery and helplessness, while Dange, the pro-Communist Acharya Atre, and the Socialist George Fernandes looked on gleefully.[73] The reaction was swift. The supporters of the insulted leaders marched to Thackeray's Shivaji Park residence, which also served as *Marmik's* office. They raised slogans against Thackeray and the Sena, threw stones, and made a bonfire of the copies of the offending magazine. Thackeray's father was forced to plead with the demonstrators to forgive his son, whom he called a donkey.[74]

But Thackeray was not to be deterred. He continued to hurl insults at the Communists and their sympathizers. Ideology was part of the reason for his visceral hatred for the Communists. Thackeray saw them as antinational, and he was opposed to their language of class struggle. But the battle for the control of the city was an equally important reason for his vitriol.[75] Though a shadow of their former strength, the Communists were still powerful in the mill districts. Eager to engage them in battle, the Sena got an opportunity in 1967. V. K. Krishna Menon, who had served as defense minister in Nehru's cabinet, was denied the nomination to contest the election by the Congress, despite having won a seat in the Parliament from Bombay in 1962. Menon decided to contest the election as an independent candidate, with Communist support. The situation was tailor-made for Thackeray. Here was Menon, whom Thackeray scorned as a South Indian with "rhinoceros skin," in alliance with the Communists. The Sena threw its support behind the Congress candidate. The election was bitterly fought. There were frequent violent clashes between the Sena and Communist activists. Atre, the legendary leader of the Samyukta Maharashtra movement, came out strongly for Menon and dared the Sena to disrupt his rally. And disrupt it they did. They hurled stones and shoes at him and made bonfires of red flags. Atre managed to escape with his life, but his car was smashed. This was the Sena's retribution for the demonstration at Thackeray's residence.[76] To add salt to the wound, Menon lost the election to the Sena-supported Congress candidate.

No self-respecting right-wing populist movement in India can succeed without targeting the Muslims as alien to the nation. Accordingly, the Shiv Sena spiked its nativism with an anti-Muslim Hindu nationalism. Although this was to become much more prominent in the 1980s, Thackeray was thundering against the Muslims soon after the Sena's foundation. In 1969 he delivered an inflammatory speech, calling Muslims antinational and referring to Bhiwandi, a Bombay suburb, as a second Pakistan. The Muslims of Bhiwandi, he said, were committing such shameful acts that he was embarrassed to mention them in the presence of ladies.[77]

Bhiwandi is a small town north of Bombay, with nearly half of its population comprising Muslim immigrants from North India who worked as weavers in its thriving hand-loom and power-loom industry. As well known as it was for its industry in the 1960s, the town later became notorious for the rising Hindu-Muslim hostilities produced by municipal politics. These hostilities got mixed up with the conflict surrounding the Shiv Jayanti Festival.

This celebration of Shivaji had been a domestic festival until 1964, when it became a public event organized by a committee that excluded Muslims. Tensions started building the following year when Hindu activists insisted on leading the celebratory procession past a mosque, playing music and throwing *gulaal* (colored powder). In the run-up to the 1970 celebrations, tensions mounted. Both Hindu and

Muslim activists held meetings, denouncing the evil designs of each other. The Sena and right-wing Hindu activists lit the powder keg of communal violence on May 7, 1970, when the procession again marched past the mosque. They shouted provocative slogans—"Gali Gali Mein Shor Hai, Musalman Chor Hai" (In every street there is an outcry that Muslims are thieves), "Shiv Sena Zindabad" (Long Live Shiv Sena), "Musalman Murdabad" (Death to Muslims), and "Hamse Jo Koi Poochegaga, Uski Ma Ko Chodega" (Whoever questions us, we will fuck their mother). Altercations, followed by stone throwing, looting, and arson, ensued. Bhiwandi burned for the next three days. When the violence was over, fifty Muslims and seventeen Hindus lay dead.[78]

Violence against its enemies was not an unfortunate by-product of Shiv Sena's activities but an essential method. The Sena distinguished itself from all political parties by presenting itself as an organization committed to action.[79] Its words were direct and hard-hitting, and its actions were immediate. Society had to be purged of the alien matter, promptly and completely. The submission of petitions and charters of demand could not achieve this end. The "people" could not depend on the bureaucracy and the political process. Thus, ridiculing terms such as *consensus and public opinion*, Thackeray declared in 1968 that if the central government did not cede the Marathi-speaking districts of Karnataka (then Mysore) to Maharashtra, he would ban New Delhi leaders from entering Bombay.[80] He carried out his threat in February 1969, when Morarji Desai, the deputy prime minister, visited Bombay. As Desai's motorcade attempted to avoid the Shiv Sena crowd, all hell broke loose. The Sena activists pelted stones, and the police charged the crowd with batons. Soon, the city became a battlefield between the police and the Sena. Thackeray and other Sena leaders were arrested. The news of the arrests spread like wildfire. The Sena activists went on an angry rampage, burning shops, torching buses, and attacking police stations. The police had to open fire to maintain order.[81] When the police were unsuccessful, the army was put on alert. The Congress government stood helpless. Ultimately, it had to suffer the ignominy of requesting Thackeray to issue an appeal for peace. Smelling victory, Thackeray consented and signed a statement from his prison cell, expressing his anguish that the army had been deployed to maintain order instead of guarding the nation's frontiers. He appealed to his Shiv Sainiks to restore peace and not to allow their struggle "to be exploited by the communists."[82] The government published and distributed his statement. After four days of violence, which claimed forty-four lives, order returned.[83] The snarling tiger had become the keeper of the zoo.

The Marathi manoos's abject state demanded concrete deeds and instant results. As opposed to *lokshahi*, or democracy, he advocated *thokshahi*, or the rule of force. His organization was Shivaji's army, and he was called the Senapati, or commander in chief. He structured the Sena into *shakhas*, or branches, like the paramilitary structure of the Hindu supremacist group Rashtriya Swayamsevak Sangh (RSS). The imitation of the RSS's militaristic order and discipline, however, did not mean that Thackeray shared its ascetic ideology. He thought of the RSS as a collection of glum old men.[84] The Sena chief, by contrast, appealed to youthful, masculine virility. Only forty years old when he founded the Shiv Sena, Thackeray presented himself as a fearless, youthful leader of a new type, one able to bend feckless bureaucrats, the older generation, the elites, and evil enemies to the force of his will. Unlike most political leaders, he did not advocate asceticism and sacrifice. He expressed feelings that most disaffected young men may have felt but dared not articulate. Openly advocating material acquisition and pleasure, he absolved "them from their feelings of guilt for failing to support their families or for their attractions to the hedonistic pursuits of life." He embodied "their desire to speak their minds, to be violent, fearless, self-made men."[85]

The Sena struck a chord with the unemployed youth in poor neighborhoods, where it organized self-help ventures and employment agencies. But the secret of its success was that it wove itself into the urban fabric. It was not averse to dealing with extortionists, bootleggers, smugglers, importers and exporters, and builders, as well as the official economy.[86] It developed a close relationship with the slum dwellers, where its ideology of masculinity, virility, and action found resonance in the struggles for survival.[87]

The Sena mobilized the youth with a plebeian ideology of open defiance to authority. The exhilaration of direct action offered them a fantasy of freedom from the malaise of reality. This was clearly the case in the Sena-led violence during the 1969 agitation to incorporate Belgaum and other Karnataka districts into Maharashtra. The Shiv Sainiks descended on the streets of Bombay and bonded as a "people" to violently reclaim the city. In place of the norms of liberal-democratic politics of reasoned discussion and debate, what drove the Sena-mobilized crowd were feelings of virility, hatred for the enemies of the Marathi manoos, and strong emotional bonds with each other and their Senapati, Thackeray. In place of process and protocols, the "people" advanced the populist reason of direct action as the dominant currency of politics.

ANNIHILATING THE REDS

The Sena threw the city into tumult. The liberal-democratic and leftist politicians were appalled by its open and unapologetic violation of established norms of politics. They saw the Sena as an unruly force set to unravel the political processes and protocols that were already under great pressure. The economic downturn aggravated a sense of crisis in the late 1960s. After 1965, industrial growth dwindled to 3.6 percent.[88] Budget and trade deficits, followed by the cutoff of U.S. foreign aid, forced a devaluation of the rupee in 1966. Politically, Nehru's death in 1964 had created a void at the center. Lal Bahadur Shastri stepped into the breach, but barely a year later, India was at war with Pakistan. After a United Nations–mandated cease-fire, he traveled to Tashkent in January 1966 to sign a Soviet-brokered peace, but he died in Tashkent soon after signing the agreement. Indira Gandhi succeeded him, but she had yet to consolidate her power. In the 1967 elections, the Congress governments suffered defeats in a number of states. The postcolonial Nehruvian order was imperiled.

In Maharashtra the Congress's electoral hold remained intact, but Bombay was in a state of turmoil. The newspaper headlines of the late 1960s paint a picture of relentless crisis and upheaval. Collapsing infrastructure and municipal dysfunction, rising crime statistics, exposés of corruption, political and economic scandals, strikes and lockouts in mills, and simmering unrest and outbreaks of political violence dominated the newspaper pages.

This maelstrom was both the context and the product of an intense contest to establish political hegemony. Different political groups and ideologies vied for influence and control. Among them were the Dalit Panthers. Drawing a leaf from the Black Panthers, the radical Dalit intellectuals mounted a militant challenge to the centuries-old oppression of the so-called untouchable castes. Influenced by Marxism, they penned biting critiques of the existing order and wrote influential poems and essays. But their challenge was largely literary and intellectual; the political leadership among the Dalits remained fragmented. The Communists pressed on with trade-union militancy and led strikes in the mills. Dange was elected to the Parliament in the 1967 elections, and the CPI won three seats to the state legislature from Bombay's working-class districts. The Shiv Sena's nativist campaign won legitimacy among the Marathi-speaking middle class and the unemployed youth in poor neighborhoods and slums in the city.

The Congress's response to this roiling political crisis was administrative. For the ruling party, managing the city with an enormous population of poor and politically energized people was a matter of administration and planning. Accordingly, the state's strategy was to deploy municipal regulation and planning to keep the city function-

6.5. Cartoon war 1. A Thackeray cartoon showing the Sena slaying the Communist giant.

ing as an industrial organism. To cope with the political demands of the population, the Congress depended on intrigues and manipulations, using the Shiv Sena to tame the Communists.

Critics routinely charge that Thackeray owed his rise to covert support by the state Congress leaders, particularly V. P. Naik, the chief minister, and the mill owners, who were keen to finish off the Communists. There is some truth to this argument; the Congress and the mill owners did find the Sena's anticommunism useful. But this notion underestimates Thackeray's political brilliance and misreads the Sena's character. The Shiv Sena was no cat's paw, and Thackeray was his own master. Feeding on the political and economic crisis, the Sena acted decisively to disgorge the populist force of the Marathi manoos on Bombay streets, changing the political landscape.

The Communists had to eat humble pie when Menon lost the election in 1967. They could momentarily take comfort in the fact that Dange had won a seat to the Parliament and the CPI had performed well in Girangaon. Among its elected legislators was the firebrand Krishna Desai, from working-class Lalbaug. But Thackeray's sights

6.6. Cartoon war 2. A Communist cartoon showing Thackeray performing cabaret for the elite.

were set on them. On September 10, 1967, he declared in Marmik that his object was the "emasculation of the Communists." Three months later, the Sena activists attacked the CPI's Dalvi Building office in Parel.[89] They burned files and threw out the furniture. It was an audacious attack, brazenly carried out to strike at the very heart of the enemy. What was the Communist response? Nothing.

Desai was not satisfied with inaction. At a meeting of the CPI state council in Aurangabad to discuss its response to the attack, he, along with others, argued for a counterattack. But they were overruled by a majority, which concluded that counterviolence would only invite police repression. Undeterred, Desai returned to Lalbaug from the meeting and founded the Lok Seva Dal (People's Service League), a volunteer corps of young men, to confront the Sena.[90]

Starting a volunteer force was entirely in keeping with Desai's militant personality. Small but strongly built, he was known and feared as a combative leader. Born in 1919 in Ratnagiri District, he came to Bombay when he was twenty.[91] Starting work in the Finlay Textile Mill, he immediately plunged into labor activism, leading a strike in 1940. Two years later, he was busy working with the underground nationalist leaders of the 1942 Quit India movement in the city. This brought him to the attention of the police. During the naval mutiny in 1946, he was thick into the popular upsurge. He led young men from Lalbaug in pitched battles with the British troops, firing on them with one of their own machine guns, which he had snatched away.[92]

Wanted by the police for his actions during the naval mutiny, Desai went underground. But he did not remain there for long, according to the autobiographical reminiscences of Dinanath Kamat, who was a schoolboy in 1946 and tagged along everywhere with his mentor, Desai. What drew Desai out of hiding was the Hindu-Muslim violence that broke out on August 16, 1946, when Jinnah called for its observance as Black Day. Many Muslims fled their homes to escape Hindu rioters. Muslim rioters entered Desai's neighborhood and killed several young men in a gymnasium. Never one to shy away from a fight, Desai attacked Muslim hoodlums in several neighborhoods. He even invited the RSS, the paramilitary Hindu right-wing group, to join him in the attack. This was not all. Accompanied by Kamat, Desai set upon sword-wielding Pathan rioters and attacked them with hand grenades.[93]

Desai's brush with violence continued when his close friend became embroiled in a clash between two rival gymnasiums and was killed by a well-known neighborhood hoodlum, Moses Dada. Immediately afterward, Dada and his bodyguards were attacked. The bodyguards took to their heels, but Dada was killed. A gang war followed, resulting in many deaths. The suspicion fell on Desai. Already wanted by the police for his role in the violence during the naval mutiny, the gang violence put Desai in hot water. With the help of a worker comrade, he was spirited away to Calcutta. There, he was sheltered by members of the Revolutionary Communist Party (RCP), a group that had broken off from the CPI in the 1930s. The stay in Calcutta and his participation in RCP's militant activities radicalized Desai. Upon his return to Bombay in 1947, he formed a branch of the RCP in the city and became involved in trade-union organization.

Desai had become a revolutionary, but he was not one who engaged in arcane ideological disputes and sectarian fights. A tough and militant activist whose feet were firmly planted on the rough Lalbaug streets, he itched for action and political and physical battles. Thus, when Goa's liberation from Portuguese rule became an issue after Indian independence, he promptly got involved in procuring arms through a European Trotskyist. In 1948 he went to Goa in disguise and lobbed hand grenades at police stations.[94] Ideological differences did not prevent him from joining hands with the Socialist leaders in trade-union activities. But when the RCP split into three factions, and the leader of one rival faction was killed in 1953, Desai was arrested as a suspect and spent a year in jail. He was expelled from the Municipal Corporation and replaced by a member of the Congress.[95] When he got out of jail, Desai plunged into the movement to create the linguistic state of Maharashtra. He marched in processions and led rallies in his neighborhood. Riding on the crest of the popularity of the movement for Samyukta Maharashtra, he won back his seat in the Municipal Corporation in 1957.

His participation in the movement for the linguistic state drew him close to the CPI, which he joined in 1962, finding it a natural home for militant labor politics. When the party split in 1964, he remained with Dange and the pro-Moscow wing. Desai was a great asset to the CPI. Drawn from the ranks of the working class, he was a militant activist with deep connections to the social networks of the mill districts. The election to the Maharashtra legislature in 1967 dulled neither his militancy nor his attachment to his working-class roots. He continued to live with his family in their cramped room in a Lalbaug chawl, remaining actively involved in trade-union and Communist Party activities. He maintained ties with the gymnasiums in Lalbaug and Parel and enjoyed close relations with young men with whom he played chess and carom. Occasionally, he would watch English films for entertainment, but his daily life consisted of trade-union and political work in the neighborhood. He made it a habit regularly to visit the homes of workers, listening to their problems, offering help, and engaging in chitchat.

Alive to the pulse of the working-class neighborhood, Desai was well aware of the Sena's appeal among the youth. He founded the Lok Seva Dal as much to counter the Sena's ideological appeal as to confront its physical force. With these twin purposes in mind, the Lok Seva Dal held political-education classes as well as organized physical exercise programs and games.[96] Since the party leadership offered no support, Desai raised money locally to pay for expenses. To build their esprit de corps, he would take the young volunteers to camps outside the city. Two to three hundred young men would get into buses and travel to weekend spots such as Lonavla for overnight camps. Once there, they would be given training in sword fighting and firearms.

Violence was not new to Bombay's politics. Keshav Borkar, or Borkar Dada, was notorious from the 1920s to the 1950s for his strong-arm tactics in the trade-union field on behalf of the Congress. But the establishment of the Lok Seva Dal signified the growing intensity of violence in urban politics. Desai did not view the attack on the Dalvi Building as an isolated incident because the Sena's activists frequently tried to disrupt Communist activities. In 1968 the formation of its trade-union wing, Bharatiya Kamgar Sena (BKS), which opposed the idea of class conflict and sought to broker peace between the mill owners and workers, rendered the trade-union field even rougher.[97] According to his family members, the Sena had physically attacked Desai during the 1967 election campaign. He escaped with his life by using his briefcase as a shield.[98] Apparently, Desai knew he was a target. A feared trade unionist and a political leader with deep roots in the neighborhood, Desai stood between the Sena and Girangaon. Anticipating an attack, he decided to send his family away to safety to his village in Ratnagiri. As for himself, he planned to go underground and take the fight to the Sena.

On June 5, 1970, Desai, as usual surrounded by Anil Karnik and others, was winding down for the day in his one-room hutment.[99] His wife had laid out the dinner. Desai took off his shirt and was about to sit down to eat when he was summoned. His party associates wanted to discuss the next day's planned Lok Seva Dal camping trip. Telling his wife and Karnik that he would be back shortly, Desai walked a few hundred yards down the winding lane to the office of a rice mill.

A mentally challenged man from the neighborhood interrupted Desai's conversation with his comrades in the office, informing him that some workers wanted to meet him. The assembled group looked out toward the open field that faced the rice mill office. The power was off, and it was raining lightly. At the head of the narrow lane that led out from the field, the silhouettes of a few men were visible. Desai called out to ask who they were. A voice shouted "Jai Bharat" (Hail to India) in response. Desai's young comrade Prakash Patkar walked toward them. As he neared the group, Patkar saw a few men standing by a car. One of the assembled men had a gupti, a long-bladed weapon, tucked under his shirt. Patkar shouted out a warning to Desai, who rushed instantly to his side. Patkar was stabbed. Within seconds, Desai was surrounded and stabbed in the back, with his liver slashed. Having achieved their purpose, the attackers vanished into the darkness. Miraculously, Desai walked to the nearby house of a friend, who rushed him to the hospital, but he succumbed to the fatal wound.

6.7. Funeral procession for Krishna Desai. Source: *Yugantar*, June 14, 1970.

This was an audacious murder. After all, Desai was a member of the Maharashtra legislature. The GKU, of which Desai was the vice president, called for a strike to protest his killing. Nearly twenty-five mills observed a complete strike. Shops in Lalbaug pulled down their shutters. The word on the street was that the Shiv Sena had finished off the Communist leader. A twenty-five-thousand-strong funeral procession marched to Shivaji Park, the Sena stronghold, shouting anti-Shiv Sena slogans. The leaders of several political parties and trade unions denounced the Sena at a huge public meeting held at Nare Park, Parel.[100]

Under its crack detective R. S. Kulkarni, the police arrested nineteen suspects, all of them school dropouts and some with criminal records. Almost all were members of the Sena. The leaders of the group broke down under Kulkarni's interrogation and confessed, spilling out the details of the murder conspiracy.[101] The pro-Communist *Blitz* report on the discussion in the legislature following the arrests was headlined "SS Charged with Political Murder."[102] Thackeray denied any complicity in the murder, and none was proven.

Ram Jethmalani, a high-profile criminal lawyer, defended the suspects, of whom three were acquitted; the rest were convicted.

In an attempt to make up for Desai's loss, the CPI nominated his widow, Sarojini Desai, as a candidate for the special election held in October 1970. A thirteen-party combination, including the ruling Congress Party, supported her candidature. The Sena put up Wamanrao Mahadik, a sitting member of the Bombay Municipal Corporation, who was once a clerk in the municipal body. Right-wing parties came out in support of Mahadik. The election was symbolically important, and it was bitterly fought.

Mary Katzenstein, an American scholar who visited the Sena and CPI offices two days before the election, provides telling portraits of the two offices.

> The Sena offices were jubilant, crowded, and noisy. The CPI ofice was half-empty, the workers muted. The contrast could not have been more stark. At the Sena office, the first object to meet the eye—as in most Sena offices—was a garlanded print of Shivaji. ... The walls were plastered with photos of Mahadik and Thackeray. ... Only a couple of those present appeared older than forty. The rest were young boys in their teens and early twenties. Constant chatter—all in Marathi—jokes, and an occasional excited command filled the office. A few workers exclaimed in a manner reminiscent of the ebullience of an athletic competition: "We'll show them—the red flag will never fly again in Bombay."
>
> The visit to the CPI headquarters revealed an entirely different scene. A half-dozen workers sat around a table. ... A handful of children and young teenagers came in—and were introduced as the children of several of the party workers. The workers were almost all in their forties and fifties. On the walls were several posters, including one, slightly yellowed at the edges, of Lenin as a young man. ... The party workers sitting in the office included

several women—a marked contrast to the all-male group in the Sena office. The atmosphere was somber and studied. Two men debated a point about the campaign procedure—in English, although both were Maharashtrians. The visitors were quickly asked to sit down and tea was immediately brought. ... Those gathered around were uninterested in making predictions or even in engaging in the usual campaign denunciations of the other party; instead, a tense discussion was struck up about the historical role of the party in the Bombay trade union movement. Two workers vehemently and openly disagreed—an occurrence almost never witnessed in public view in a Shiv Sena office.[103]

There it was, the stark contrast between the youthful, populist politics of the Sena and the politics of reason in the Communist Party office. When the election results were announced on October 18, 1970, Mahadik had narrowly edged out Desai's widow by 1,679 votes out of the nearly 62,000 votes cast.[104] The Sena had gained its first legislator, at the expense of the Communists.

Desai's murder was a turning point. The Communists were never again to claim Girangaon as a red city. The political landscape of the city was transformed. The Left and liberal intelligentsia bemoaned the death of the city of reasoned discussion and debate. A new mode of politics, whose adherents spouted populist reason, had made a decisive entry. The Sena's critics denied that Thackeray's outfit was a political party, deriding it as a gang of the lumpen proletariat. Ironically, Thackeray too claimed that the Shiv Sena was not a political party, stating that it was antipolitics and antipoliticians. According to him, the Shiv Sena was an upsurge of the people. This upsurge did not achieve a dominant presence until the late 1980s, when it made common cause with the anti-Muslim Hindu nationalist politics. But by 1970, it had served notice that its style of antidemocratic and populist politics of the Marathi manoos was here to stay. It was a mode of political mobilization that absorbed individuals in the collective "popular will" and unleashed it against the "outsiders" and elites to realize the fantasy of a Marathi Bombay.

The chief architect of this fundamental change in Bombay's political landscape was Thackeray. Supremely contemptuous of the prevalent political order, he was the original "angry young man." Long before the superstar Amitabh Bachchan made the screen image of the young underclass urban vigilante famous in the 1970s, Thackeray had made a forceful entry into the city as an angry, irreverent, and defiant voice of the people.

7

PLANNING AND DREAMING

In 1965 *MARG*, a Bombay journal of art and architecture, published an issue entitled "Bombay: Planning and Dreaming." Showcasing plans prepared by three young professionals, Charles Correa, Pravina Mehta, and Shirish Patel, the issue proposed the development of a twin city for Bombay. The editorial by Mulk Raj Anand, an acclaimed writer and the journal's editor, implored the city to pick up the courage to dream up a worthy metropolis. He wrote that dreaming was no idle activity, for "in dreams begins responsibility."[1] The responsibility to plan Bombay's future, therefore, had to begin as dreams, and planning was dreaming.

Anand issued this incitement to dream an ideal city at a time when independent India was less than two decades old. The national mythology, which still enjoyed authority at that time, held that the village, and not the city, defined India. According to the nationalist myth, this was not simply because most Indians lived in the countryside but because the village epitomized India's cultural essence. Although nationalism took shape in cities and the leaders lived in urban areas, the cultural imagination of India identified the soul of nationhood in the village. Gandhi, as is well known, regarded the city as the expression of a modern civilization alien to India. For him, the nation's true spirit resided in the simple human relations of the village community.[2] Even Nehru was not exempt from this thought, writing of the mythic "Bharat Mata" (Mother India) in the countryside, among the peasantry.[3] Though no longer a self-contained community, "the village still holds together by some invisible link and old memories revive."[4]

Yet, if villages were where India existed in all its vividness, where "fine types" of men and beautiful women reminded him of the ancient frescoes that had endured, they were also places of backwardness and superstition. In a letter to Gandhi in 1945, Nehru wrote: "I do not understand why a village should embody truth and nonviolence. A village, normally speaking, is a backward environment."[5] The village may have represented India's soul, but its existence as a modern nation required industrialization and urbanization.[6] Interestingly, Nehru sings no paeans to the city, for it was not in the existing city but in a planned urbanization spearheaded by a modernizing state that he saw India's future. Urbanization meant something larger and more abstract than what could be found in the existing city. Though Bombay, Calcutta, Madras, and other cities had served as cradles of modern thought and life, Nehru saw them as expressions of colonial history; they were not incipient, even if imperfect, blueprints for the future. The shining example of the future was Chandigarh, the modernist city commissioned by the nation-state and designed by Le Corbusier. As the expression of an abstractly conceived model of urbanization, it represented a higher rationality than did any existing Indian city. The source and instrument of this true and universal reason was the nation-state, which stood poised to steer India toward modern nationhood through industrialization and urbanization.

With the nation-state defined as the realization of the modern nation, planning emerged as the key instrument for achieving this condition. Chandigarh demonstrated this faith in planning. Even if there was only one Chandigarh, or only one Brasilia, underlying it was the authority of the modernist ideal of a rationally planned urban organism. Planning enjoyed the imprimatur of science; it was viewed as a technical exercise, fashioned by experts and governed by scientific principles that could be applied just as easily to economic and social structures as it was to nature. The cultural prestige of science extended to urban planning as well, and urban planners and architects claimed authority as experts engaged in reengineering space by applying their scientific knowledge. The Athens Charter of the Congrès International d'Architecture Moderne (CIAM), published by Le Corbusier in 1942, was an expression of this modernist claim. Aimed at engineering the city as an industrial product, as a machine with social functions, the Athens Charter projected planning as a scientific enterprise designed to reengineer urban life rationally and efficiently.[7] This vision of manufacturing urban life took shape and struck a chord in the immediate postwar era, which was characterized by unprecedented urbanization throughout the world.[8] Chandigarh and Brasilia were its most spectacular expressions because they were built from scratch, but urban planning's authority and influence extended well beyond these two experiments.

The exuberant spirit of planning also gripped Bombay's urbanists. Leading intellectuals, architects, and planners breathlessly promoted the idea of the twin city as a rational solution to Bombay's problems of haphazard growth and urban congestion. They challenged the state to dream big. Only bold planning, they argued, could build an orderly and efficient urban society. Utilizing their status and influence as experts, the urban planners enlisted the modernizing state in its dream of New Bombay. But their dream repressed the reality of politics and society. And most crucially, they forgot the powerful force of greed.

TOWARD URBAN PLANNING

As in other countries, India also experienced rapid urbanization after Independence and Partition in 1947. With men and women flocking to cities and towns in search of economic opportunities,

Bombay's population grew from 1.49 million in 1941 to 2.3 million in 1951.[9] A share of this increase was also due to the influx of refugees who were fleeing from the Partition violence. The surging urban population and expanding city sharpened the sense of an urban crisis, already reverberating in the early 1940s. J. F. Bulsara, a commentator on urban affairs, bemoaned "two hundred and eighty seven years of unplanned building."[10] His text catalogs Bombay's problems—its haphazard growth, the "cheerless chawls and bleak block-houses," the amorphous architectural map, and a "preponderant illiterate population" that lacks the art of living together in the city and whose "primitive mental condition" aggravates the problems of filth. He paints a picture of ethnic groups living in ethnically segmented neighborhoods—Gujaratis, Banias, Bhatias, and Jains in Kalbadevi, Bhuleshwar, Ghatkopar, and Borivili; the Maharashtrian middle classes at Girgaum, Thakurwar, and Shivaji Park; the South Indians at Matunga; the Muslims at Mohammad Ali Road, Bhendi Bazaar, and Abdul Rahman and Sheikh Memon Streets; the Parsis at Colaba, Tardeo, and Dadar; the Jews at Israel and Samuel Streets; and the Europeans in Colaba and Malabar and Cumbala Hills. These communities found spiritual enjoyment in their places of worship and culture, but not in the fractured civic life. The unplanned and shapeless city offered only the "spurious attractions" of glittering lights, the silver screen and celluloid entertainment, the excitement of the racecourse and gambling, "the universal craze for getting rich," and the "soul-destroying chase of overnight fortunes."[11]

Bulsara continues his litany, moving from detailing the problems of housing, to spatial disorganization, to community divisions, to "spurious" attractions in the city. It is a picture of whole-scale urban crisis. This was not peculiar to him; the newspapers of the period regularly highlighted the mounting disorder in the city. Bombay, which went through a building boom in the thirties and the forties, had a sizable number of engineers and architects who also expressed concern about the city's future. Their concern was reflected in the *JIIA* (*Journal of the Indian Institute of Architects*) and *MARG*. Both journals published a number of articles that kept up a steady drumbeat of warnings about the impending urban disaster caused by unplanned growth. The solution to Bombay's problems, Bulsara argued, lay in systematic planning, based on a scientific survey of the city's problems taken as a whole.

A particularly passionate advocate of modernist planning was *MARG*, under Mulk Raj Anand's editorship. A writer and novelist in the tradition of social realism, Anand had published an impressive social realist novel, *Untouchable*, in 1935, followed by *Coolie* in 1947, both of which evoked the national and class ferment in Bombay. Anand was not only a novelist but also a cosmopolitan intellectual. He had studied in England in the 1920s, earning an undergraduate degree from University College, London, and a doctorate in philosophy from Cambridge University. After completing his education, he remained in London, pursuing a literary career. He worked for T. S. Eliot's journal *Criterion* and Leonard Woolf's Hogarth Press, fraternized with the Bloomsbury writers, turned to Marxism, and drafted the manifesto of the Indian Progressive Writers' Association.[12]

On his return to India in 1945, Anand became an important part of Bombay's intellectual circuit. His circle included the painters Francis Newton Souza, S. H. Raza, M. F. Hussain, and K. H. Ara and the sculptor S. K. Bakre of the Progressive Artists' Group. Supported by exiled Central European Jewish intellectuals and Indian benefactors in Bombay, these artists, all of whom were migrants to the city, were beating down the doors of the city's art establishments with their modernist work. In place of the spiritualism and revivalism of the nationalist artists of the Bengal School and the academicism of the colonial school, they saw their artwork, following the German Expressionists, as conceptual "expressions" of their inner emotions and concepts. Rather than articulating the nation's cultural essence, they viewed themselves as artists participating in the universal discourse of art. Their modernism avoided the Indian/Western trap by balancing nationalism with universalism, by inhabiting a form of cosmopolitanism that assumed India's national sovereignty and equality in a world of nations.[13] It was national without being anticosmopolitan, and it was cosmopolitan without being antinational.

Anand founded *MARG* in 1946 with precisely this idea of nation-based cosmopolitanism. Its mission was to promote modern, progressive thinking on art, architecture, and modern life in the future free Indian nation. Accordingly, it was a platform for the art produced by the Progressive Artists Group in Bombay. The same impulse drove its advocacy of modernist urban planning. The word *marg* means "pathway" in Hindi, but it was also an acronym for the Modern Architectural Research Group, a name that was modeled after the Modern Architectural Research Society of architects and planners in London.[14] To highlight the promise of modern architecture and urban planning, *MARG* published the Athens Charter of *CIAM* as well as contributions from Le Corbusier and other prominent international architects and planners.[15] Apparently, it was Anand who planted the idea of building Chandigarh and recommended Le Corbusier's name as the architect for the project.[16]

While being partly responsible for the first of the two largest urban projects undertaken in postcolonial India, Anand was also laying the foundation for the second—New Bombay (now Navi Mumbai)—by heavily promoting the cause of modern architecture and planning. In an editorial published in 1947, Anand extolled the virtues of American architects such as Frank Lloyd Wright for revolutionizing urban planning by incorporating science and industry in their designs.[17] He argued that what India needed was planning from this new perspective. The Bombay architects, engineers, and intelligentsia associated with *MARG* and *JIIA* breathed the heady air of a big city in the throes of change. If the city's problems were immense in their eyes, so was the power of urban planning, whose cause they zealously championed.

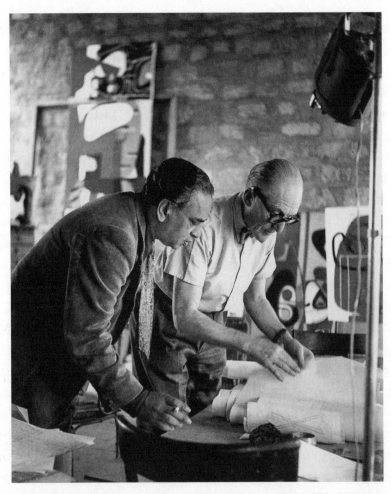

7.1. Mulk Raj Anand with Le Corbusier in the architect's studio in 1953. Courtesy: Shirin Vajifdar.

As the modernist intelligentsia began to press for urban planning, the government moved in the same direction. In 1945 the government appointed the Bombay City and Suburbs Post-war Development Committee to deal with the issue of "Greater Bombay" and town planning of the suburbs. Composed largely of government officials, the committee appointed three subcommittees on town planning, housing, and traffic and railways, asking each to prepare a report. Even before the panel on town planning published its report, criticism came forth fast and furious. The *JIIA* berated the committee for not seeking the expertise of architects and town planners. How could the Bombay Municipal Corporation (BMC) develop an organic plan to tackle the problems of slums, filth, overcrowding, and traffic congestion without the expert advice of planners? "Instead of eradicating the disease at the center, the fungus [was] being allowed to spread outward." The target of their ire was the BMC, which was accused of being blissfully ignorant of the benefits of planning.[18] When the town planning panel eventually published its report, *MARG* roundly criticized it for "disjointed planning" and for overlooking the needs of "the city as an organic unit."[19] Sarcastically applauding the recommendation for the preparation of a master plan, the journal noted that it was something that "the enlightened architects in the city had been urging the authorities [to do] for a long time."

MARG and *JIIA* got what they wanted when N. V. Modak, a BMC engineer, and Albert Mayer, an American town planner and architect, prepared an outline for a master plan in 1948. This was a significant development. The clamor for experts had been heard and heeded. The BMC had long claimed its authority over planning as a representative body of the citizenry. However limited this assertion may have been under colonial rule, there is no denying the fact that the BMC had exercised its authority over Bombay's development as a public body. Faced with the torrent of criticism that greeted its initial efforts, however, it ceded the domain of urban knowledge to the technocratic elite. Experts, not the urban citizenry, were to decide Bombay's future.

PLANNERS AS DREAMERS

The elevation of the planners' authority, ironically, came close on the heels of independence in 1947. The nationalists assumed power claiming that the nation, not alien rulers, must exercise authority over India. But once India was independent, the power to decide Bombay's future was ceded to the technocrats, bypassing the citizens. *MARG* had been pushing the case for architects even before independence. In the editorial of the inaugural 1946 issue, entitled "Planning and Dreaming," Anand wrote in soaring rhetoric about dreaming a future: "Planning is like dreaming—dreaming of a new world." Architects and urban planners were to dream of ways to usher in the good life, to produce "the blue prints of a new social order." The future lay with architects because they could plan India's cities on a scientific basis. "It is because an architect seems to us a symbol of the resurgent India, that the Modern Architectural Research Group has come forward to sponsor this magazine of architecture and art."[20]

In the dream world of planners, Bombay appeared primarily as a configuration of industries, buildings, houses, and streets, a system of production, communication, and circulation. This was evident from the very beginning of urban planning in Bombay. Thus, when the panel on town planning issued a report in 1946, it bemoaned the magnitude of urban problems: disorganized growth; acute traffic congestion; narrow and crooked lanes and side lanes; insufficient, unsanitary, and overcrowded housing; congested and obsolescent areas; unsightly buildings; and inadequate public infrastructure for water and sewage.[21] The existence of these problems reflected unplanned growth and required, according to the committee, a regional "master plan" that would impart coherence to Bombay's future development. A regional master plan was expected to achieve the objective of ordered development by reorganizing the physical space. In the committee's view, Bombay's problems of congestion, overcrowding, unsightly buildings, and unsanitary and inadequate housing were fundamentally spatial. The committee used symbolically rich images of sewage and waste, densely packed slums, and traffic-snarled city streets to express a sense of India's shortcomings as a nation. On the one hand, there was a deep belief in the nation's existence; on the other hand, the emotively charged images of poverty, congestion, and filth questioned the fullness of identity and prepared the ground for the manipulation of urban space according to a set of functions and needs. "Every acre of land must be rightly used to balance the everyday requirements of the population in respect of work, industry, housing, recreation (both physical and mental), transport and communication and amenities."[22]

The French theorist Henri Lefebvre writes that planners, urbanists, and social engineers operate with what he calls representations of space.[23] Such representations conceptualize space according to self-referential understandings and ideologies linked to production relations. Specific spatial forms of society and the lived experience of space appear through the lens of concepts and codes appropriate for the dominant social order. Under capitalism, planners represent particular social spaces—factories, offices, homes, schools, and so on—and the symbolic forms through which such spaces are lived as points on a grid of abstract space. Leached of practices and meanings, space appears abstract because capitalism erases qualitative distinctions and reduces them into homogeneous units of exchange value. Land comes into view as undifferentiated space, ready for the planners' cartographic pencil, so that the city can be visualized as a well-coordinated and balanced organism of capitalist industrialization.

Just such a concept of space lay behind the Bombay planners' dissatisfaction with the city's unplanned growth. Expansion without regional master planning meant that urbanization and industrialization could not occur efficiently. *Efficiency* and *organization* were the keywords of planners, who saw inefficiency and confusion everywhere in Bombay. They noted that industrial units were being established in the suburbs, which would be followed by the construction of housing, creating visible disorganization and inconvenience. The specter was urban sprawl. "What waste! What inconvenience!" Modak and Mayer exclaimed. They warned that the situation was worsening so speedily that unless a regional master plan was adopted,

"Bombay will grow just as an industrial enterprise used to grow, adding a building here and a shed there and a godown somewhere else—the result—inefficient and obsolete development competitively at a handicap with modern industries."[24]

The metaphorical comparison of the city with industry was no accident; the planners were consciously planning the city as a space of industrial capitalism. Organizing such a space required the strict control of land use because land was "the basic commodity in which the town planner deals."[25] Control over land use permitted the planners to outline the projected city as orderly and efficient. There was attention to questions of zoning—the location of the heavy and light industries, the site for stables and tanneries—and provision for green spaces. The problem of housing received prominent attention. This was no surprise in a city where the housing shortage was dramatized by densely packed chawls. Both colonial officials and the Indian intelligentsia had long lamented the lack of adequate housing for the poor. Given the self-representation of nationalist planning as a project for the "people," the plan could not and did not ignore this issue. Describing housing as the "dynamics of planning—the core of planning,"[26] it projected the construction of a substantial number of low-income housing units, surrounded by parks and schools, to improve the "health and morals" of the poor. Bombay's open spaces and suburban towns were expected to accommodate the growing population, with an efficient transportation system linking the suburbs to the city. Modak and Mayer imagined Bombay as a city in motion and recommended the expansion of east-west transportation links to foster an orderly westward settlement and the development of satellite towns.

Although Modak and Mayer modestly stated that their plan was not a "final detailed blue-print" but an "envelope" to be filled with details,[27] there is little doubt about its ambition. The idea was to reengineer an organic urban space to meet the needs of capitalist industrialization. Naturally, such a project of planning was a dream of the city as a grid of functions. Efficiency, need, function, and order were its watchwords. Plans for housing addressed a need, rather than the rich and symbolic sense of home. The provision for the expansion of rail and road networks was meant to answer the demand for the efficient movement of people and the orderly development of the industrializing city, rather than speaking to the cultural experience of mobility and speed. Zoning was aimed at the spatial organization of work and life, and not the practices and experiences of daily living. Unsuited to dealing with the practices and experiences of space and time, the language of the planners focused on systematic and orderly functions and the needs of industrial urbanization. Social problems appeared through the lens of space, and their resolution seemed to rest in the reorganization of the built environment. The ideal city, from the planners' perspective, consisted of a closely coordinated mechanism of life, work, recreation, education, shopping, business, industry, and transportation—an efficiently functioning organism.

The planners' dreamscape of Bombay may appear rational and cold, but their emotional energy is palpable in the plan. Exclamation points punctuate their proposals, and the language pulsates with calls to transform the messy and muddled city into a metropolis that would function like a well-oiled machine to power India's modern nationhood. "We must vastly improve and modernize, not de-Indianize," wrote Modak and Mayer.[28] Bombay was to be both a modern and an Indian metropolis. The claim was that modernist ideas were consistent with the nation, that applying Western urban planning methods to Bombay did not undermine its Indianness. So, Modak and Mayer presented their plan as a product of Indian knowledge and foreign experience. They said little about the content of Indian knowledge, except to state that the plan took into account India's and Bombay's conditions while proposing "the most modern solutions" that avoided the mistakes committed in Europe and the United States.

The master plan shared and expressed the nationalist fantasy of modernization. India's nationalist leaders visualized the fulfillment of the independent nation in the industrial modernization of society through planning.[29] This fantasy was a response to their view that India's poverty, economic underdevelopment, urban congestion, and transportation bottlenecks reflected the nation's shortcomings—the lack of full-scale industrialization, the absence of scientific agriculture, the deficiency of modern infrastructure, and so on. Planning was the means to overcome these deficiencies; it was to be the instrument of the desire to overcome "backwardness" and to realize the pleasure of the modern nation. India was to be modern and different, at once embodying national traditions and industrial and technological modernity because the two were, in fact, compatible.

One way in which the planners incorporated Indianness in their imagined metropolis was to treat it as a matter of architectural design and aesthetics. In *JIIA* and *MARG*, architects frequently debated the merits of revivalist versus modern architecture. Most rejected a return to precolonial architectural styles, but almost everyone agreed that modern architecture must maintain a link to India's past: Modern housing must express the character of the place in its style. Geography was yet another way for urban design to incorporate the character of the place. Thus, urban planners returned again and again to representing the dream metropolis as a city nestled between the hills and the sea. In 1948 Modak and Mayer urged a creative use of the sea and the hills to formulate a plan with emotional and aesthetic appeal: "People want to live in a great City, a City of dignity, grace, and inspiration; not only an efficient City."[30]

Seventeen years later, Charles Correa, Pravina Mehta, and Shirish Patel returned to the image of the city on the water and offered their plan for New Bombay as an alternative that would overcome the sense of lack expressed by images of congestion, crowding, and sprawl.[31]

In 1964 the BMC issued a development plan for Bombay.[32] The municipal plan, meant to update the Modak and Mayer master plan, was preceded by the publication of a report by a study group appointed by the government to study the problems of the city. Headed by S. G. Barve, secretary of the Public Works Department, the group included N. V. Modak, the housing commissioner, the director of industries, the deputy secretary of the Public Works Department, and representatives of the BMC, Railways, Indian Merchants' Chamber, and Port Trust. As the group's composition suggests, the government's guiding concern was to improve the city as an industrial space. Accordingly, the group was instructed to consider problems relating to traffic congestion, scarcity of housing and the lack of open spaces and playing fields, and the overconcentration of industry in the metropolitan and suburban areas.[33] The group concluded that most of the city's problems were created by "drift," but that they were surmountable by "a planned approach and machinery for bringing about the necessary measure of coordination."[34] As the group noted, its proposals were not new; the novelty lay in their offer of an overall framework for understanding the problems and of suggesting a coordinated plan for implementing measures to realize a lower population density, decentralization of industry, an efficient communication system, and an increase in housing and open spaces.[35]

The BMC plan of 1964 went over the same ground. Like the study group, it focused on industry, transportation, housing, and open spaces. Declaring that the city had grown much beyond what the 1948 master plan had visualized, the municipal authorities advanced their proposal as the means for realizing "Bombay the beautiful."[36] Once again, the culprit identified was haphazard and unplanned development. The BMC plan acknowledged and listed previous attempts to shape and order growth but stated that none had been comprehensive. Even the Modak and Mayer plan of 1948, it argued, "was not a complete Master Plan but a preliminary guide for further detailed study of the areas earmarked for different purposes."[37] As opposed to these earlier attempts, the BMC plan proposed a full-scale restructuring of the Greater Bombay region by zoning, developing suburbs to absorb population growth, decentralizing industry, and developing the urban infrastructure. Together, these proposals were presented as "elements of a single community design."[38]

The critics were not impressed. A newspaper article derisively declared that the municipal master plan was "no master plan at all" but "a pot-pourri of various regional and district survey maps grouped together incoherently with a palliative sprinkling of unimportant land-use recommendations such as for car parks, municipal schools, graveyards and dumpyards."[39] Correa, Mehta, and Patel were not impressed either; they wrote a letter to the municipal authorities—taking the invitation for public comment seriously—and laid out an alternative plan for building a twin city on the mainland.[40] Their letter went unanswered.

Possibly India's best-known architect today, Charles Correa studied architecture at the University of Michigan and MIT and established a practice in Bombay in 1958. Shirish Patel, a civil engineer, was educated at Cambridge and established his engineering consultancy firm in Bombay in 1960. Pravina Mehta, an architect and planner trained in the United States, formed the third member of this team of young urbanists who deeply believed in their fresh, modernist planning ideals. Even before the BMC plan was published, Correa and Patel began discussing Bombay's problems. They agreed that the issue was not population growth but the constraints imposed by the narrow strip of land on which the city was situated. "One look at the map, and you knew that the answer was to strike eastwards onto the mainland rather than perpetuate the existing North-South axis."[41] Correa and Patel started discussing the alternative and brought in Mehta, whom they knew as a thoughtful planner. After the BMC published its plan, the three experts agreed that it was flawed in persisting with the north-south tunnel vision of the city. They wrote to the municipal authorities suggesting a twin city on the mainland instead. The BMC ignored their letter, but an assistant editor at the *Times of India* who knew Mehta agreed to publish it. After its publication,[42] Mulk Raj Anand offered to showcase an expanded version as an alternative in a *MARG* issue devoted to the consideration of the BMC plan.[43]

Correa, Patel, and Mehta advanced their plan for the twin city of New Bombay as a comprehensive and radical alternative to the existing planning ideas on Bombay, all of which proposed extending the city northward. They rejected the 1948 proposal by Modak and Mayer to build satellite towns encircling the Island City as a practical and effective measure to develop Bombay as a metropolitan region. They believed that satellite towns would be impractical and, without expensive civic facilities, would become shantytowns. The 1964 BMC plan was no better, for it too was burdened with the idea of northward growth.

The idea of striking out eastward to the mainland was not new. The first to suggest it was H. Foster King, a prominent Bombay architect and a partner in the firm of Gregson, Batley and King, who was elected several times as the president of the Indian Institute of Architects. In an address to the institute on June 14, 1945, he said: "Would it not be wiser to boldly strike out laterally in an eastward direction across the harbour to the inviting mainland beyond rather than unimaginatively persist in increasing our civic problems of traffic, population trends, zoning and health by not deviating from a vertical northerly advance which leads appreciably further and further away from the heart of the city?"[44] It is not clear whether Correa and his associates were aware of King's suggestion, but they certainly knew of the Barve study group's recommendation in 1959 to build a bridge over the Thane Creek to connect the city and the mainland, and they seized on it to propose the twin city.

Though the idea was not new, no one had previously proposed building an entirely new urban system. There was something breathtakingly bold about the plan to create another metropolitan center, one with equal prestige and importance to the Island City, which would bring about equilibrium. The authors outlined the idea of the new city with numerous charts, graphs, and maps and offered comprehensive proposals to link the island with the mainland by rail, roads, and bridges, projecting Bombay as an integrated metropolitan industrial region. A regional plan based on the idea of the twin city, their plan promised, would rescue millions from the asphalt jungle in which they currently lived and make Bombay once again the splendid "city on the sea" that it once was. People who spent most of their lives in the interior of the island would experience the harbor and the sea as part of their daily lives. With the Elephanta Caves standing at the center of the twin cities and exuding a sense of the past, one would enter the harbor to see the city on both sides—"on the one side extending over the island, and on the other rising above its shores into the hills beyond."[45]

The New Bombay plan was a richly embroidered dream text. A visual feast of beautifully produced maps, charts, and graphs, it presented the planned metropolis in the alluring image of the city by the water. A society imagined as a physical space integrated by ferries, bridges, rail, and road and organized into parks, new housing, business centers, and industrial regions was the stuff of dreams.

Not surprisingly, the New Bombay plan received the full-throated endorsement of Anand. Ruefully noting that the city had neglected the "orchards of azure sea water around the island," he enthusiastically endorsed the idea of a twin city connected by the ocean.[46] He implored his readers to think of Bombay's future with vision.

Let us not build blind alleys. Let us open out to gardens, vistas, utilities, gathering places, schools, hospitals, on the hitherto neglected spaces, away from the congested "Fort" of the bygone era,

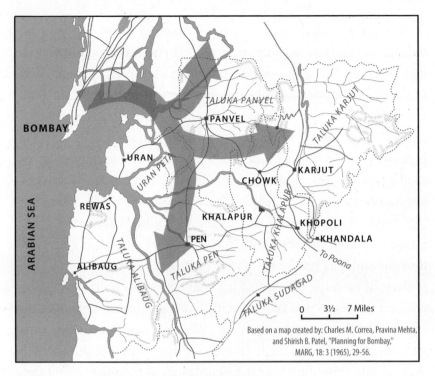

0   3½   7 Miles

Based on a map created by: Charles M. Correa, Pravina Mehta, and Shirish B. Patel, "Planning for Bombay," MARG, 18: 3 (1965), 29-56.

7.2. The Twin City plan.

until many "Xanadus" grow beyond the dream of Kubla Khan, nearer our own dreams for a city worthy of an emergent new world, beyond the concepts of London, Paris and New York, to our own inner aspirations towards the "city beautiful." Let us have the courage to dream: For in dreams begins responsibility.[47]

Over the next several years after the publication of the New Bombay Plan in *MARG*, support for the twin city idea grew.[48] A number of government-appointed bodies incorporated its suggestions, but no concrete steps to implement it were taken until Patel and Correa had a chance conversation by the swimming pool with V. Srinivasan, an Indian Administrative Service (IAS) officer.[49] When Patel complained that the plan was tied up in committees, Srinivasan, who headed the State Industrial Corporation of Maharashtra

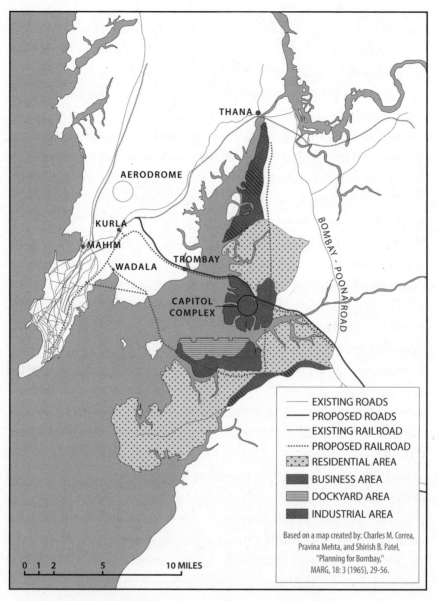

EXISTING ROADS
PROPOSED ROADS
EXISTING RAILROAD
PROPOSED RAILROAD
RESIDENTIAL AREA
BUSINESS AREA
DOCKYARD AREA
INDUSTRIAL AREA

Based on a map created by: Charles M. Correa,
Pravina Mehta, and Shirish B. Patel,
"Planning for Bombay,"
MARG, 18: 3 (1965), 29-56.

THANA

AERODROME

KURLA
MAHIM
WADALA
TROMBAY

CAPITOL
COMPLEX

BOMBAY - POONA ROAD

0 1 2   5   10 MILES

7.3. The Twin City transportation network plan.

(SICOM), came up with a solution. In 1970 he created the City Industrial Development Corporation (CIDCO) as a subsidiary of SICOM, charged with implementing the New Bombay plan. J. B. D'Souza, an upright IAS officer, was appointed as CIDCO's managing director, with Shirish Patel as the chief planner.

CIDCO began the project in earnest in 1973. In the project's favor was the bridge across the Thane Creek, connecting it to the Island City, and the plan for developing an advanced port at Nhava Sheva on the mainland side of the bay. Blessed with these advantages, D'Souza set about realizing the planners' dream of developing New Bombay on nearly 135 square miles of land across the water from Bombay as a countermagnet. He shared with the planners the objective of diverting the growing population away from the Island City to the new city. New Bombay, they estimated, would reach a population of two million by 2000. "A large part of that population would have otherwise come to Bombay—or so we naively believed," D'Souza writes. "And so we tried to convince everyone interested in urban management."[50] They planned to accelerate the development of Nhava Sheva and attract commercial houses, and they even thought of persuading the state government to relocate its offices. CIDCO would restrict industrial development and encourage the service sector as the growth engine of New Bombay. Lands acquired at the market rate for agricultural fields, then developed and sold at commercial rates, would finance the whole development project, including the cost of building roads and railway lines.

The plan was not without its critics. No sooner was CIDCO founded than K. A. Abbas charged that New Bombay would be built on lands seized from poor peasants to provide "a metropolis for the industrialists, the capitalists, the traders, the hoteliers, the building contractors, the architects, the interior decorators, and other species of the profit making professions."[51] A year later, *Blitz* accused CIDCO of ignoring the problem of congestion and slums in Bombay and denounced it for building a "neo-Manhattan" as a playground for monopolists and speculators.[52] There were also less colorful criticisms.[53] It was pointed out that the plan would fail to create a countermagnet to relieve congestion in Bombay; instead, the new city would merely extend the jurisdiction of the metropolitan region to include the territory across the harbor as yet another suburb. Critics also argued that the new city would do nothing to relieve Bombay's chronic problem of congestion and excess population.

Undeterred, the project moved ahead. The dream was too seductive. New Bombay would reorient the Island City to the water. The harbor would hum with the sound of boats ferrying people and goods between the twin cities. Oil tankers and ships would line up on the sea-lane to Nhava Sheva. Built from scratch and protected from industrial pollution, New Bombay would be a clean, planned city providing affordable accommodations to its residents. Efficient and sensible planning, narrowing the distance between work and home, would reduce commuting time, and the separation of vehicular roads from pedestrian paths would provide mobility without traffic snarls. Everything would be clean and orderly—a utopia realized.

THE DREAM SOURS

It was not to be. New Bombay never became a countermagnet. The population growth and congestion in Bombay continued unabated. What is more, the Backbay reclamation raised its ugly head again, now crowned by soaring towers.

CIDCO's singular success was that it realized its goal of achieving financial self-sufficiency by selling plots it had acquired at low agricultural land rates, which provoked protests and conflicts. On other counts, the results have been, at best, mixed. A new city was built, with settlements organized around planned nodes, supporting a population of 785,000 by 2001. Nearly two-thirds of the city's residents are employed in offices. The housing stock has provided decent and affordable living space for its inhabitants, the majority of whom are migrants from the Island City. But with regard to acting as a countermagnet, it has come up severely short.[54] The new city has turned into a dormitory to absorb distress migrants and has fueled the speculative real estate market.[55] This was not what the planners had in mind in their projection of the ideal city of New Bombay as modern society.

Sensing that things were going wrong, Patel resigned as chief planner as early as 1975. He felt that the project lacked full government support. This was evident in its refusal to move the state offices and the legislature complex to the new city, something on which the planners had hung their hopes—too highly, they acknowledge in retrospect.[56] Looking back now, Patel thinks that an undoubted factor in the government's refusal to move its offices to the mainland must have been the fear that if Bombay ceased to be the seat of state power, the Island City could become a Union Territory.[57] Against the background of the violence-ridden struggle for Maharashtra and for the Maharashtrian claim over Bombay—just over a decade old at the time—this would have been a likely apprehension. Back then, however, he believed that their ideas would prevail through the "sheer force of logic."[58]

The most distressing sign of the failure of the "sheer force of logic" was the decision to revive the Backbay reclamation, which had stalled in the late 1920s amid cost overruns, mismanagement, and accusations of high-handedness and graft. Only blocks 1 and 2 (at the Chowpatty end of Marine Drive) and block 8 (occupied by the defense services) were successfully reclaimed; blocks 3 to 7, amounting to 550 acres, were left unreclaimed (see fig. 7.4). But as Marine Drive, flanked by Art Deco buildings, arose in the 1930s and the 1940s and became a prestigious and picturesque address, the abandoned blocks looked increasingly like a gold mine. This included the unreclaimed area immediately south of Marine Drive, which the postcolonial government had named Nariman Point to honor

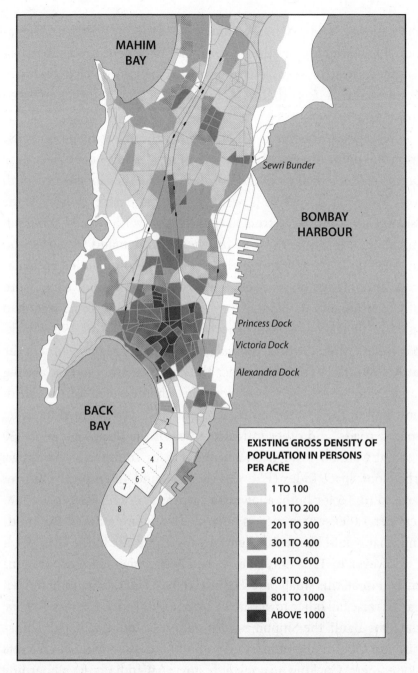

MAHIM
BAY

Sewri Bunder

BOMBAY
HARBOUR

Princess Dock

Victoria Dock

Alexandra Dock

BACK
BAY

1

2

3

4

5

6

7

8

**EXISTING GROSS DENSITY OF
POPULATION IN PERSONS
PER ACRE**

1 TO 100

101 TO 200

201 TO 300

301 TO 400

401 TO 600

601 TO 800

801 TO 1000

ABOVE 1000

7.4. Unreclaimed Backbay blocks. Source: *Bombay Development Plan* (Bombay: Government Central Press, 1964).

the nationalist whose muckraking had turned the 1920s reclamation into a scandal. But the lofty spirit of nationalism was no match for the powerful scent of money. Land sharks circled Nariman Point, ready to close their jaws on any speck of land that emerged from the sea.

Reclamation was back on the agenda, though it made no sense from the point of view of urban planning.[59] Additional office space on the reclaimed lands would only accentuate the city's north-south axis. More office workers traveling to the southern extremity of the Island City would add stress to the already overburdened suburban rail system, to say nothing of the increased demand for water and power. The Barve Committee in 1959 had recommended reclamation, but only for open spaces and for housing slum dwellers, both of which the city desperately needed. Just as the colonial state had used the fig leaf of a housing shortage to embark on the 1920s Backbay reclamation, the postcolonial government of Maharashtra in the early 1960s did exactly the same. The government began reclaiming lands, which were then auctioned. The scheme called for the sale of only half of the 550 reclaimed acres; the rest were allotted for open spaces, roads, and other infrastructure. Of the disposable plots, 60 percent were for residences, and the rest for commercial buildings. The Floor Space Index (FSI) was set at 3.5 and 4.5 respectively, later revised to 3.5 for both, allowing a carpet area of 35,000 square meters per 1,000 square meters of land. This figure allowed for buildings that would be much taller than anywhere else in the city.

However, by 1968 only 64 acres had been reclaimed. Corporations rushed in on this small parcel of land to buy plots at auctions and began to raise tall office towers. One by one, Air India, Express Towers, the State Bank, the Shipping Corporation of India, Mafatlal, Somanis, and Oberoi Sheraton raced to build a dense jungle of concrete skyscrapers. Cocking a snook at history, Air India hung a hoarding on its twenty-four-story building that read: "Nariman had a point and we are on it."[60] The irony was cruel.

Criticisms poured in from urban planners, architects, and government-appointed committees. In a four-volume confidential report assessing the development plan, which it submitted to the Maharashtra government, the World Bank expressed its disapproval.[61] But the government was undeterred. It flaunted the state coffers, which were overflowing with auction money. While some politicians looked at the waves washing over the remaining planned reclamation area and saw the potential for a rich harvest of bribes, the well-connected land sharks and builders saw the potential for vast profits. The situation was ripe for crony capitalism to work its black magic.

On January 29, 1972, the Bombay weekly *Current* ran an explosive story asking "Why No Tenders, Mr. Naik, for Backbay Plots?"[62] Quoting an "anonymous informant," it reported that in a sudden departure from past practice, the government was allotting commercial plots on the Backbay without a public tender. It named the builders who were the beneficiaries of the government's sudden change of heart: the Mittal Group, Maker and Jolly Builders, Gupta and Company, and Somani. Without claiming that it had any proof, *Current* invited the government to respond to the charge of a dark builder-politician conspiracy suggested by its informant's allegation.

The response was immediate. The director of publicity of the Maharashtra government issued a statement acknowledging the allotment of unreclaimed lands without public auction but denied that there was any ground for suspicion. The clarification, published in its entirety in *Current*, justified the allotments as a way to encourage reclamation, which was necessary to increase the supply of land in the space-starved city.[63] The rationale was uncannily similar to the one the British had advanced in the 1920s. But whereas the colonial government had undertaken the reclamation work itself so the profit would also accrue to the state, Maharashtra had decided to entrust that job to "reputed" private builders. This was because the government had found very little demand for the lands it had reclaimed. In fact, it had to induce corporations such as Air India to lease the reclaimed plot.

Therefore, it abandoned reclamation, deeming it too expensive. But since public interest demanded the augmentation of the city's land supply, it decided to sell unreclaimed plots to builders with the financial and executive wherewithal. Private parties, unencumbered by the time-consuming procedures that the government had to follow, could move faster and more efficiently. Finally, the government spokesman claimed, the rates at which allotments had been made were "very attractive." There was no reason to suspect any foul play; it was all done in the public interest by an enlightened government.

The government's explanation did not satisfy *Current*. It rejected the claim that the private sales had been made at "attractive rates." The tabloid noted that a public tender forced by its exposé had attracted twenty-six offers. It also fetched more than three times the price earned by private sale—Rs 12,829 versus Rs 4,000 per square meter. Granted that the unreclaimed plot sold by public tender included approval for a cinema theater, the price offered, according to *Current*, exposed the hollowness of the government's claims. The writer of the story ended by smugly noting that the tabloid's exposure of private sales had led to the resumption of public tenders and had resulted in a substantial gain to the state treasury.

The satisfaction was short-lived. A year later, *Current's* front page screamed: "V. P. Naik to Sell More Backbay Plots—without Public Tenders Again!"[64] Quoting "reliable construction sources," the editor D. F. Karaka reported that the chief minister was back to his old habits, preparing to allot fifteen to seventeen plots without a public tender to so-called reputed builders. These builders were actually "fly-by-nights who have arisen out of the rubble into which Naik and his ruling party threw ingots of gold so that men like these can become rich." The whole Backbay affair stank, demanding Naik's ouster from power. *Current's* editor, an inveterate anti-Communist, stated that he was aware that there was a "Commie conspiracy" to capture the government. Nonetheless, so foul was the stench of the scandal that Chief Minister Naik had to go.

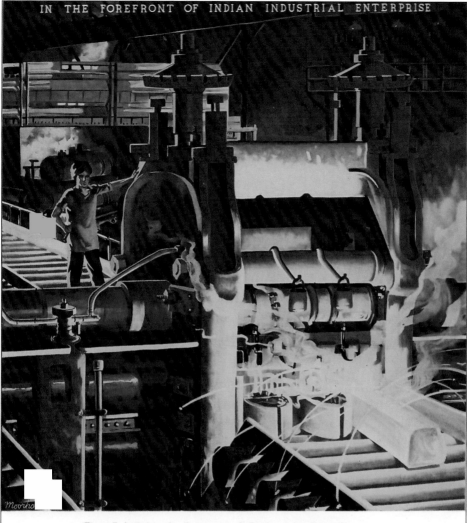

1. Steel and Art Deco. Source: Times of India Annual, 1935.

2. Doga and Suraj. Courtesy: Raj Comics.

3. Planning violence. Courtesy: Raj Comics.

4. Doga's pathology. Courtesy: Raj Comics.

1997

देश में शान्ति व व्यवस्था बनाए
रखने के लिए जरूरी है कानून –

कानून की रक्षा के लिए
जरूरी है पुलिस –

पुलिस पर नियंत्रण के लिए
जरूरी है नेता –

यानी देश का आधार है...

खाकी
और
खद्दर

• लेखक
तरुण कुमार वाही
• कथानक
संजय गुप्ता,
विवेक मोहन
• चित्रांकन
मनु
• सम्पादन
मनीष गुप्ता

©RAJA POCKET BOOK

1

5. The opening page of *Khaki Aur Khaddar*. Courtesy: Raj Comics.

6. Monica forced to watch atrocities. Courtesy: Raj Comics.

7. The comic-book panels scrambled by the chaos of violence. Courtesy: Raj Comics.

8. Doga fights the rioters in vain. Courtesy: Raj Comics.

9. The superhero is assailed by self-doubt. Courtesy: Raj Comics.

10. The superhero despairs at the loss of humanism. Courtesy: Raj Comics.

11. *Luxurious 1,2&3 BHK Flats*, by Meera Devidayal. Mixed media on canvas, 40 x 30 in. Courtesy: Meera Devidayal.

12. Taxi stickers.

13. *Objects in the Mirror Are Closer than They Appear*, by Meera Devidayal. Mixed media on canvas, 30 x 42 in. Courtesy: Anant Art Gallery, New Delhi.

14. *Altamount Road*, by Meera Devidayal. Digital print, oil, enamel, and epoxy galvanized steel sheet, 49 x 36 in. Courtesy: Meera Devidayal.

15. Free enterprise in Dharavi. Author's photograph.

16. Collectors of discarded history in Chor Bazaar. Author's photograph.

17. Atul Dodiya, *Bombay Buccaneer*. Courtesy: Atul Dodiya and Peabody Essex Museum, Salem, Massachusetts. Acc E301042.

While Karaka merely insinuated backroom deals, J. B. D'Souza was a witness to the goings-on. Along with his responsibilities as the managing director of CIDCO, the upright officer was also the secretary of the Department of Urban Development. In his memoir, D'Souza writes that one day he found himself rushed into approving leases for fifteen plots of land that were still under the sea.[65] Unbeknownst to him, the government had abandoned the system of public auctions and had decided to conclude deals with builders without a competitive process. Aghast at this development, he still managed to raise the price by 20 percent—from approximately Rs 4,000 to Rs 5,400 per square meter. Showing a fine sense for bureaucratic wile, he got the new rate approved by the finance secretary. Immediately, he was summoned by the revenue minister, H. G. Vartak, huddled with the builders chosen for leases. The minister upbraided him for "spoiling" the deal that had already been settled with the chief minister, Naik. After the builders trooped out, the revenue minister reiterated that the rate had been set and approved by the chief minister. When D'Souza argued that the builders should be squeezed for more, since the land was in an expensive neighborhood, the minister blurted out: "We have already squeezed them!"

D'Souza also felt the pressure applied by Rafiq Zakaria, the suave and reputed Bombay politician and the Urban Development minister. Zakaria summoned D'Souza and the finance secretary to his office. He was subtler than the revenue minister. Addressing his ministerial colleague, who hovered in the room, Zakaria noted that their decision ran the risk of going against the opinion of two senior government officers, unless, of course—he cannily added—the officers chose to reconsider. "At this stage," D'Souza writes, "we both got absorbed in the fascinating view outside the Minister's room."

The plucky civil servant had won a small victory. The government was forced to conclude the deal with the builders at an enhanced rate. But D'Souza was not done yet. He encouraged a lawsuit against the government. Piloo Mody, a member of the Parliament, joined by two others, filed a case in June 1974.[66] It named the State Government, the Union Government, the Municipal Corporation, the chief minister, the ministers for Revenue and Urban Development, and the builders who had been allotted the lots as respondents. The petitioners charged that the allotment was in violation of the government's constitutional and statutory obligations and mala fide. The private lease of lands, without a public tender, amounted to a collusion between the government and builders, which had produced an insufficient price charged for the land. As citizens of India and as the city's taxpayers, the petitioners claimed, the government's decision had harmed them. Therefore they requested the court's intervention.

THE STATE ON TRIAL AND THE CITY OF CONSPIRACY

Justice J. M. Gandhi of the Bombay High Court heard the case from April to September 1975. He took one month to deliver the judgment, which ran to 953 double-spaced typed pages.[67] It is a remarkable document, not just for its length but also for its content. On the face of it, the issue before the court was relatively straightforward—whether or not the government had a right to allot Backbay lands privately. But the consideration of this matter placed on trial the very nature of the state, the extent of the executive's powers, the jurisdiction of the judiciary, and the rights of citizens. The court witnessed an extremely learned legal contest. Opposing counsels cited precedents from different courts and authorities extending from India to Britain to the United States. Justice Gandhi was equal to the task. Presenting the opposing arguments meticulously and comprehensively, his judgment carefully and systematically analyzed legal issues that go to the heart of the definition of state power. The judgment stands as a record of what transpired in the court—the trial and defense of the modern liberal-democratic state against its agents. But it also documents the failure of the effort to make the state live up to its ideal as an instrument of general good, above powerful, private interests. This failure produced the idea of the city as a conspiratorial space. Backroom deals, not transparent transactions, constituted Bombay's reality.

The judgment begins on a low key. It offers a brief summary of the opposing arguments, a history of Backbay reclamations, and a factual account of allotments made by the government. But the stakes rise the moment the court considers the petitioners' contention that the government was lawfully bound to allot lands through public auction. The advocate general of Maharashtra asserted that the allotment was a contract between the state and private parties. This contract, according to him, was an executive act and outside the court's purview. The state could dispose of its property as if it were an individual, without any limitation and not subject to judicial review. To buttress this argument, the counsel cited case precedents in the United States that upheld the power of the Congress over public lands without the court's review of the manner of its administration.[68] He acknowledged constitutional limitations but went on to assert that there were no restrictions on the state's disposal of property and its contractual agreements. It could dispose of property for any purpose, even other than public purpose, without the interference of the court.

Opposing the state's extravagant claim, the petitioner's counsel, Askok Desai, argued that the state owns property on behalf of the people. He cited an American case judgment that held that the United States does not and cannot hold property like a monarch for private and personal purposes. This principle must also apply to the state of Maharashtra, he argued.[69] The Indian Supreme Court had affirmed that the state must be guided by the principle of public interest. The constitution gives wide powers and discretion to the officers and agents of the state, but it enjoins them to act for the public good. In the Backbay case, this principle demanded a public auction, not the disposal of plots through private sale as if the state were an individual or a monarch. Underlying the question of a public auction, then, was the larger issue of the very nature of the state. According to Desai, the state must stand above private interests to advance the general good. This is what distinguished a liberal-democratic state from a monarchy and autocracy. The Indian constitution enjoined even the executive to act for the state's purpose, which could be no other than the public purpose. The property held by the state must be regarded as that of the community, the people, or the public. Therefore, all state transactions must be for the people's benefit.

Justice Gandhi rejected the extreme claims the government and the builders made for the state's unfettered right. He sided with Desai in holding that the officers of the government held lands as trustees for the state, not for the benefit of private persons. Hence, their power to dispose of property could not be like that of an individual owner. According to him, a reading of the revenue laws and codes enacted by the legislature made clear that it was the state's public duty and statutory obligation to realize market price when disposing of land. This implied a public auction, since it was a proven method to ascertain market price. He did not mean that the government was obliged to accept the highest bidder's price; he allowed that the bid could be rejected for public policy reasons. The government could even offer the land for free or at concessional rates in the public interest. The executive retained discretion, but this did not free it from constitutional and statutory obligations. Taking these into consideration, the judge ruled that the government could not dispose of property without inviting public tenders.

This was not the end of the dispute over the meaning and functions of the liberal-democratic state. A counsel representing some of the builders cited the British political theorist Harold Laski's argument that the millions of citizens the modern state organizes cannot be expected to participate in daily deliberations.[70] They can express their hopes and provide general direction, but they cannot expect a voice in the day-to-day decision making. That was possible in the direct democracy of the Athenian city-state, but not now. In the modern state, a limited number of representatives act as trustees and governors of the whole. It is up to them to glean the needs of the people and translate them into policies. In other words, representative government demanded that the determination of the public interest be left to the elected executive, whose decisions could not be second-guessed.

The counsel for the *Free Press Journal,* which had been allotted a plot, made an even more forceful claim for the exemption of state's decisions from being questioned. The state, he argued, was a distinct legal entity. It was an artificial person, a juridical personality with sovereign power. This sovereignty owed its origin to *Patria Potestas*—the supreme power of the father in the family over life and death. The state's commanding force and its absolute power over property, according to him, originated in patriarchal authority. Given this origin of sovereign power, the state cannot accommodate the idea of a trust. Even in a modern democracy with representative government, where sovereignty is dispersed and exercised through different agencies—executive, legislature, and judiciary—the concept of the state's obligation to the people is contrary to its origin and character. Those who act for the government make their best efforts to hold resources for the benefit of the people. It is an ideal, but one that gives no right to the inhabitants as beneficiaries under a trust.

The extreme leaps of these arguments indirectly affirmed the fact that the agents of the state had acted against its ideals. So palpable was their violation that the defense had to argue for unfettered executive power. But the judge was having none of it. He ruled that there was no constitutional provision that granted absolute power to the executive, thus permitting it to alienate property in any manner it liked. On the contrary, constitutional history made it abundantly clear that the transaction must be for the benefit of the state, whether or not its legal personality included the people. This meant that none of its limbs, no officer, could alienate it for private benefit. That would be an arbitrary or capricious act.[71] This did not question the state's right to make policy. Rejecting Desai's argument that the Backbay reclamations were contrary to the existing laws on town planning, Justice Gandhi ruled that the executive was entitled to make that decision. But what the existing laws and statues did not permit were transactions without any effort to ascertain the market price for land. In the absence of a public auction, the government's conduct was mala fide.

Mala fide, but with no proof of collusion. The judgment documented that the private agreements violated the state's constitutional and statutory obligations. It meticulously established that even though there were sixty-six bids for unreclaimed lands between 1969 and 1972, the government chose to make allotments to a small gang of builders—Dr. Maker, the Jolly group, the Mittals, Tulsiani Builders, Dalamal, Somani, and Raheja. The decision to abandon public tenders and enter into private agreements with this gang of builders was made in secret. The judge dismissed the publication of the government's explanation in *Current* in 1972, holding that lands were disposed in a "secret and surreptitious manner."[72] He also ruled that the collector, the administrator in charge of making allotments, was directed to do so under the express orders of Chief Minister Naik, Revenue Minister Vartak, and Urban Development Minister Zakaria. The result of this secret and surreptitous decision making was a gross, not merely marginal, undervaluation of lands. And but for the vigilance of the secretary of urban development— meaning D'Souza—the extent of undervaluation would have been even greater. Given this finding, he directed the builders to pay a higher amount—33 percent more—for their allotments. The government's counsel questioned the court's right to determine the price and to judge the executive's action mala fide. But the judge stuck to his guns, declaring that his task was to determine if there was gross undervaluation, not to fix the price. Given the executive violation of the law, its "secret and surreptitious" decision, he justified his ruling of mala fide. But Justice Gandhi backed away from finding collusion between the government officials and the builders. Mere suspicion could not substitute for proof.

The judge may have been restrained in finding collusion, but not the media. Even before the judgment was delivered, a swirl of rumors about graft and public criticism of the project floated in the city. The court served as a venue for defending the ideals of the liberal-democratic state. It affirmed the citizen's right to question the state, acknowledging their *locus standi* and establishing the principle of public-interest litigation. But the standards of law that prevented it from finding collusion served only to confirm that powerful private interests worked in secret to thwart the public good. What was seen on the surface was not real. The city was a space of conspiracy.

The *Times of India*, the *Free Press Journal, Blitz*, and other newspapers carried regular reports, describing the reclamation as a disaster for urban planning and a colossal scam involving politicians and builders.[73] The Save Bombay Committee was formed to agitate against the government's misadventures. Forced on the defensive, the government appointed a committee to review the Backbay development. The committee recommended the continuation of reclamations, raising the share of commercial buildings, and, as a sop to critics, the creation of a pond for recreation.

The critics were not mollified.[74] The committee was seen as unrepresentative and blind to the views of citizens, most notably to fishermen, who were directly affected by the scheme but whose opinions were never solicited. The amount of reclamation was slightly reduced, but its basic thrust remained. The towers would proliferate on reclaimed lands at Nariman Point and Cuffe Parade. The north-south axis of the city would be reinforced, and the pressure on the traffic arteries would grow. The prospect of New Bombay's emerging as a countermagnet to the Island City seemed more distant than ever. The tall towers rose up on the Backbay, representing the broken

7.5. Nariman Point towers in the 1990s. Photo by Rahul Mehrotra. Courtesy: Sharada Dwivedi and Rahul Mehrotra, *Bombay: The Cities Within* (Bombay: India Book House, 1995).

dreams of the twin city. To the critics, the government offered a sop by offering to create a pond on Nariman Point—"a little more suffering, a little more style."

REPRESSION, DISGUISE, AND DISPLACEMENT

What went wrong? How did the dream of building a twin city sour? Correa and Patel have offered explanations—their political naïveté, a flawed implementation of the plan, the wrongheaded Backbay reclamation, the development of commercial and industrial centers in the suburbs and the north, and the lack of will to do what was necessary. These are reasonable explanations, but were these all? Was there something more fundamentally flawed in the planners' dreams? Freud suggests that intentions produce dream images, but they are not immediately accessible; interpretation is required to reveal the intentions repressed, disguised, and displaced by images. What did the dream images of a rationally ordered and organic city repress and disguise?

One clue exists in the image of the overcrowded phantom city that clings to the dream of the "city beautiful." Again and again, planners and their supporters returned to denounce the asphalt jungle that had smothered the city on the sea. Disorganization and disorder haunted their dreamscape. Anand's article in *MARG* calling for planning as dreaming ended with a series of photographs of congestion, unsanitary conditions, unplanned growth, and dirt and filth in the city with telling captions—"Two views of hell" and "If there was no 'black hole' of Calcutta, then here is an entrance to one in Bombay."[75] These images of dirt and dysfunction were meant to refer to the actual city. In fact, they acted as screens concealing the daily social practices and symbolic experiences of work and life in Bombay. The city's spatial organization by capital remained hidden; class inequality and conflicts and elite-subaltern divides were kept out of view. The experience of the city as a place of encounter, difference, struggle, enjoyment, and aspiration disappeared behind the ghostly image of Bombay's unplanned sprawl and congestion. In the clean and orderly urbanism proposed for the nation, there was no place for the heterogeneous and conflict-ridden urban life, no room for chawls as spaces of community and memory, and no provision for the rich and varied life on the streets. The dream city of clear lines and coordinated functions repressed the knowledge of the city as society; the visually rich image of the city by the sea projected the ideal of an urbanism without urbanity. Bombay was to be nothing more than an industrial metropolis, a cog in the wheel of the industrializing and urbanizing nation.

If the nationalist fantasy of modernization found its expression in the dream image of a planned industrial metropolis, this was not surprising. Jonathan Raban writes that town planning since Patrick

Geddes and Lewis Mumford has abandoned the real city and vested its hope in techniques; since love and reason had failed, a stew of science, technology, and bureaucratic administration was offered as the recipe for achieving an ideal city.[76] The modernist manifestos offered a brave new world, but they were really no more than a "shrilly puritanical backlash" to the actual conditions in the city.[77] Their ideal of a rationally planned city held up the lure of order and harmony in the face of the unpredictability and chance of the actual city. The dream of a new city, where spatial design was expected to shape a society of harmony and goodness, could be only a "flight into Utopia," the "creation of a preferred reality far removed from the complexities of urban planning for an existing city."[78]

Crucial to this project was the persistent demand for delegating planning to experts. I do not mean to suggest that there was a conspiracy to circumvent democracy, but only that there was a touching faith in the power of reason, in its inherent force to cut through the webs of society, property interests, speculators, and political calculations to transform reality. Having displaced and concealed the city as a social space in order to plan Bombay as a spatial machine, the dream text of planning saw the murky and unpredictable world of politics and society as an obstacle that the force of reason could overcome. Anand's comments on this issue are telling. Exhorting his readers to think big, to envision Bombay as one of the major cities in the "One World" of the future, he acknowledged that this may be difficult because the intelligentsia "lives in a democracy, where the vote has been given to illiterate peoples, who have so far been deprived of the knowledge of their own self interest."[79] What was required, then, was a spirited campaign by the intelligentsia to articulate and advance the interests of those who did not know them.

Remarkably, the campaign was successful. The very manner in which CIDCO came into being is revealing. No sustained public conversation, no democratic participation, and no consultation with the peasants whose lands were to be acquired preceded the formation of a body that was to undertake the building of a new city. Instead, the publication of the letter from Correa, Mehta, and Patel through an acquaintance in the *Times of India*, followed by Anand's enthusiastic endorsement in *MARG*, counted for the public conversation. A chance poolside conversation with a senior IAS officer substituted for democratic procedures. Access to the state proved useful in getting the plan set into motion. But then the agents of the state were entangled in a dense web of political and economic interests. If these ultimately proved to be the undoing of the dream, then the basic problem was that the compact between the state and technocratic elites had failed. Politics and society, which the planners had suppressed, returned with the rage of the repressed to sour the modernist dream of postcolonial geography.

The wonder is not that New Bombay failed to achieve its objectives, but that its failure and the stinging judgment by Justice Gandhi on the Backbay deals have not prevented the powerful private interests to relentlessly undo the liberal state's ideal to promote the public good. Because modernist planning aimed to achieve a more efficient and rational urban space rather than to address social desires and needs, its failure eroded the faith in the ideal of the state as an expression of general interests. Walk around Nariman Point and Cuffe Parade, and you will see the ruins of this ideal in tower after tower named after a limited group of builders. Venture into the old mill districts with its silent machines, and you will hear the sound of bulldozers demolishing chawls to make way for tall apartment towers, shopping malls, and commercial buildings. With the growing influence of the neoliberal faith in the market, builders are racing to erect towers to "rehabilate" slum dwellers—and make a tidy profit. The city is dotted with World Bank–funded projects to improve the infrastructure and forge an efficient transportation network to serve the globalizing economy. New Mumbai may be resigned to its status as a bedroom community serving contemporary Mumbai, but the elites continue to sell the dreams of newness.

Meanwhile, the *Human Development Report* retails an unremittingly dismal picture for the majority of the citizens. Malnourishment, cramped and unhygienic housing, diminishing open space, and ever more crowded suburban train travel to work characterize their lives.[80] Is it any wonder that the city appears as a space of conspiracy by the few behind the backs of the rest?

8
AVENGER ON THE STREET

A jeep careens recklessly through Bombay's streets. It is filled with ruthless goons of the notorious Panther gang. They mow down pedestrians without pausing, braking only when they find their target. The man, a witness in a case against the Panthers, is beaten senseless while onlookers watch impassively. They do not intervene, leaving the bruised and battered victim where he falls. An old man cries out in despair, "Who will help? The hearts of these people have been turned to stone."[1] This is *Bombay Dying*.

Suddenly, a tall and muscular masked figure in a bodysuit appears, guns blazing. It is Doga, Bombay's very own superhero. An adept boxer, proficient in karate and firearms, he hunts down and annihilates criminals with a gusto to match that of his quarry. He conceals his identity by wearing a dog mask. Unmasked, he is Suraj, a mild-mannered physical instructor at the Lion Gym (plate 2).

In the popular comic-book series named for him, Doga is a ferocious and ruthless killing machine clad in a body-hugging circus suit that accentuates his imposing physique. The mask and the name Doga evoke the quality of loyalty associated with man's best friend to proclaim the superhero's commitment to protecting and serving the city. He respects the police but freely breaks laws and defies authority to blow criminals away. He is a loner, an angst-ridden man with memories of a violent past that propel him into sociopathic rampages against gangsters and evildoers. His motto is "Doga does not seek to solve problems, he eliminates them."

Doga's mission is to save Bombay from the scourge of criminals running rampant in a city out of control. The street—an archetypal urban space of freedom and public life—is rife with danger and violence. Crime lords oppress ordinary citizens. The common folk going about their daily business to earn an honest living are defenseless against the unscrupulous forces that conspire against them. The law is helpless. The state's authority is corroded. The police force is riddled with corruption. The few honest officers are vastly outnumbered by the ever-growing power of menacing criminals. Besides, they are stymied because they have to follow the law, whereas the outlaws have no such constraints. But neither does Doga. Matching bomb for bomb and AK-47 for AK-47, Doga is the only one who can protect Bombay's beleaguered law-abiding citizens. A creature of the street, he dispenses street justice.

In the nearly 150 issues published since 1993, Doga has annihilated numerous criminal gangsters, unscrupulous builders and businessmen, terrorists, corrupt politicians, and instigators of communal riots. Remarkably attentive to contemporary events, the comic book's supervillains are often ripped from newspaper headlines. Sometimes their names rhyme with those of real underworld dons. At other times the stories derive from actual events. Doga is often preachy, drawing clear moral lines while fighting his adversaries. Enemies of the nation, Pakistan-backed terrorists, violators of communal harmony, oppressors of the poor, double-faced politicians, crooked policemen—all face Doga's righteous tongue and deadly power.

Doga is clearly a nationalist, but Bombay is the scene of his superhero exploits. An urban imagination underwrites the series, both as a form of storytelling and as a specific representation of Bombay. The actions take place in Bombay's neighborhoods, which are often named. The superhero's primary goal is to safeguard the urban society from its enemies, foreign-backed or indigenous. The comic book sells approximately seventy thousand copies per issue at the suburban railway station bookstalls and through direct subscriptions. This sales figure underestimates the actual readership because each comic book is passed along from reader to reader. Its online availability in more recent times has vastly increased the readership, as is evident in discussion forums and fan clubs on the Internet. This widely circulated comic series invites us to see the city through the eyes of its ferocious urban vigilante.

THE UNRULY CITY

There is a background to Doga's dark city. The series portrays a widely shared view of Bombay as a lawless space, where state and police authority routinely succumbs to criminal predators. It is a view that has developed since the late 1960s when Bal Thackeray and the Shiv Sena fired the opening salvo against lawful authority. As the Sainiks repeatedly took the law into their own hands on the grounds that it was rigged against the Marathi manoos, they forcefully thrust the street against the authority of the postcolonial liberal order. The Nehruvian model of modernization and national development, based on the edifice of law and parliamentary government, faced a serious challenge from the assault mounted from below.

Close on the heels of the Sena's assault came the declaration of the National Emergency by Indira Gandhi on June 26, 1975.[2] Citing a "deep and widespread conspiracy" against her progressive policies and India's integrity, she suspended civil rights, censored the press, and cracked down on her political opponents. Actually, it was Indira, not India, who was under threat. But since the Congress's slogan was "India is Indira, and Indira is India," it proceeded to arrest several prominent opposition leaders. Among them was Jai Prakash Narayan, the aging Gandhian socialist who spearheaded a popular upsurge against her regime. Ironically, his movement's call for the summary dismissal of unpopular but elected provincial governments was fundamentally anticonstitutional. That the constitutional order was attacked from rival political sides, both invoking the "people," was telling commentary on the state of India's liberal democracy.

In Bombay the Emergency's slogan of discipline and order received full-throated support from Thackeray, who had already displayed his impatience with democracy. Also in the cheering section, albeit from the opposite end of the political spectrum, was Karanjia's leftist *Blitz*, which lauded Indira Gandhi's promise to deploy her newly seized power to implement progressive policies. As elsewhere in the nation, Bombay's Congress regime censored the press and hunted down political dissenters.[3] However, unlike elsewhere, Bombay was saved from the pet projects of Indira's son Sanjay Gandhi—the dreaded roving sterilization vans equipped to perform on-the-spot vasectomies and the ruthless slum demolitions for beautification.[4] Though the city escaped the worst excesses, the Emergency inspired Rohinton Mistry's unremittingly Dickensian novel *A Fine Balance* (1995), which paints a city thrown out of balance, the equilibrium of its diverse population upset by the anarchy let loose by the exercise of arbitrary power.

Indira Gandhi got her just desserts when she lifted the Emergency and called for elections in 1977. In an intense anti-Indira wave, the incensed electorate washed her out just as thoroughly as the 1971 pro-Indira wave had carried her to power. The Congress was trounced in much of North India and lost all five parliamentary seats in Bombay. Constitutional order was restored, but it concealed a deeper transformation. The street had emerged as a powerful force. The politics of the people, championed by both the JP (Jai Prakash) movement and Indira Gandhi in their different ways, had permeated the soul of the body politic. The image of the state as an institution standing above the everyday hustle and bustle of politics stood battered.

But nothing darkened Bombay's mood more enduringly than the collapse of the textile industry, which began in the late 1970s. Several factors contributed to the fall of the cotton mills.[5] One was the failure to update technology. World War II brought huge profits to the mill owners, but instead of investing in new machinery, they used the money to pay handsome dividends to their shareholders. Three decades later, nearly half of the machines were forty years old. Sanguine in their protection by tariffs, the industry failed to embrace the high-growth ready-made sector of the garment industry.[6] The cotton mills' share of employment dropped from 28 percent in 1976–77 to 13 percent in 1991; approximately 133,000 jobs were lost.[7]

The rapid growth of power looms compounded the industry's decline. The mills, based on eight-hour shifts and unionized workers, could not compete with power looms, which operated on twelve-hour shifts and paid lower wages to its unorganized labor force. As capital-intensive but technologically backward mills faltered before the competition from the unorganized power looms, a process of deindustrialization set in. The government took over the management of several "sick" Bombay mills, which were subsequently nationalized, but this only confirmed the malaise in the industry. The 1982–83 workers' strike dramatized the fall of the cotton mills from the exalted position they had occupied for a century in the city's history.

The leader of the strike was Dr. Datta Samant. He was reviled by critics as a terrorist thug and lauded by supporters as an uncompromising leader of workers; his name dominated the newspaper headlines in the late 1970s and the 1980s. By this time, the Communist AITUC, previously the dominant trade union among mill workers, was a spent force. The murder of its most militant leader, Krishna Desai, in 1970 and the pounding by the Sena had taken its toll. The Sena's influence, in turn, had dwindled because it resisted the workers' militancy. The Congress-affiliated Rashtriya Mill Mazdoor Sangh (RMMS) unions enjoyed official recognition, but there was intense competition for influence among mill workers. Datta Samant flourished in this environment. Though no revolutionary, he enjoyed a well-earned reputation for being combative and uncompromising. His chosen methods were direct action, with little regard for legal niceties and negotiated settlements. Interunion rivalry suited him just fine; it provided an opportunity to browbeat his opponents with violence and intimidation.[8] A series of electrifying strikes and work stoppages between 1977 and 1980 turned him into the leader to go to for militant industrial action.

In their struggle for higher bonuses and wages and the regularization of casual workers, the mill hands turned to Samant.[9] On January 18, 1982, his newly formed Maharashtra Girni Kamgar Union declared an indefinite strike. Nearly 250,000 workers downed their tools. Datta Samant's union was clearly supported by a majority of workers, but the Congress government, eager to protect its labor union, denied it recognition. The red-flag unions, never enthusiastic about the economic focus of workers' agitations, lost the little support they enjoyed. Datta Samant studiously avoided infusing politics into the strike, focusing exclusively on the economic demands. In return, he received the workers' enthusiastic support.

Backed by militant workers, the strike was total. But the mill owners dug in their heels, and violence broke out between the strikers and strikebreakers. As the months wore on, the workers' militancy flagged. Samant had miscalculated, believing that the mill owners would retreat in this war of attrition. Instead, they sent their inventories for weaving to the power looms (a decision they would soon sorely regret). The workers were defeated. Though the strike was never officially called off, the mill owners, the government, and the Congress-affiliated union declared it over on August 2, 1983. The mills reopened but never recovered their former vitality. More than one hundred thousand workers were never rehired. In the ensuing decade, as Bombay's textile industry steadily lost ground, the city lost not just an industry but an entire way of life.

Since the late nineteenth century, the mills had formed the city's backbone. King Cotton provided steady employment to immigrant workers and made great fortunes for mill owners, producing both legendary capitalists and trade-union leaders and creating vibrant neighborhoods and stately mansions. The manufacturing compounds, the factory chimneys, and the chawls packed with workers were the principal threads in the city's social and mental fabric.

As the collapse of the mills tore apart Bombay's urban fabric, there emerged an ominous web of connections between real estate, the underworld, and politics. The murder of Sunit Khatau in 1994 brought this to light.[10] Khatau was a scion of a family that had owned mills for over a century. When the textile industry went into crisis, he decided to sell his mill but was stymied by the opposition from mill workers. Determined to go ahead, he entered into a devil's contract, with criminal muscle, to browbeat the workers into agreeing to the sale of the mill lands. Khatau successfully engineered the defeat of the existing union leader, paving the way for the infiltration of the underworld. Influential politicians were roped into the conspiracy, tempted by the huge sums of money involved. Datta Samant alleged that the mill owner had even enlisted Dawood Ibrahim, the dreaded don who fled Bombay in the 1980s and set up shop in Dubai. But the scheme fell apart when two gangsters on a motorcycle drew alongside the textile tycoon's car at a traffic signal and pumped eleven bullets into his body. Apparently, it was a targeted hit by a rival gang.

Violence and intimidation had always been part of the trade-union scene in Bombay, but the collapse of the mills scaled everything up. The defunct mills stood on highly prized lands in a space-starved city. Builders and real estate speculators hovered over the mill districts like vultures while the government and the planners debated the fate of the land. The stakes soared even higher as the real estate sector boomed in the early 1990s, largely due to the massive investments by Indian developers and, to a lesser extent, some inflow of foreign capital following globalization and economic liberalization.[11] Bombay's criminals were nimble in adjusting to the market.

Like any other city, the criminal underworld had always been part of Bombay's urban life. From time to time, the newspapers, tabloids, and magazines would titillate readers with sensational exposés of crime, which, until the 1970s, centered on smuggling, distilling illegal country liquor and bootlegging, drug trafficking, illegal gambling called *matka*, protection rackets, and prostitution.[12] In response to Prohibition (gradually dismantled in the seventies and eighties) and antigambling and antismuggling policies, enterprising criminals formed powerful gangs.[13] The leaders of these gangs in the sixties and the seventies were Vardharajan Mudaliar and Haji Mastan (both of whom were Tamil migrants), Yusuf Patel, and Karim Lala. Emerging and recruiting their foot soldiers from the slums and poor neighborhoods of the city, the gangsters bought the services of corrupt police officials to facilitate their criminal enterprises. The Pathan gangs, headed by Karim Lala, were the lords of violent crime. In the late seventies, however, they crossed paths and swords with an emerging gangster named Dawood Ibrahim.

A police constable's son, Dawood began his life of crime in 1974 when a fledgling political outfit called the Young Party, of which he was a loyal member, was left without support by its patron.[14] In a desperate bid to fund the organization, he turned to robbery. He was arrested, but the court acquitted him. The constable's son then turned to *palti*, a con game that involved showing a gold biscuit or an imported wristwatch for sale to a customer, and then switching it for something worthless, with the hapless customer realizing only too late that he had been swindled. But Dawood soon left these petty crimes behind. He graduated to transporting, protecting, and delivering smuggled goods, turning the Young Party into a criminal gang. Karim Lala was not amused. His decision to teach the aspiring gangster a lesson led to skirmishes between the Pathans and Dawood.

It soon turned into vicious gang warfare in 1981 when Dawood's brother was killed on the orders of two Pathan brothers, Alamzeb and Amirzada Khan. Dawood avenged his brother's assassination by hiring a killer, who brazenly shot Amirzada in a courtroom. Karim Lala tried to forge a truce, but Dawood was adamant; he finished off the Pathan don's nephew in 1984 but then fled to Dubai in 1985, as he was wanted by the police.

In Dubai, Dawood established a legitimate construction and trading company. From his Gulf residence—called the White House—he organized Bombay's gangs into the most feared and dominant crime syndicate in the city. Haji Mastan had retired from smuggling and turned to politics and films. Hounded by the police, Vardharajan Mudaliar left the city. He died in Madras in 1988. Karim Lala bought peace from Dawood and withdrew from the crime scene. Through his hirelings, Dawood enforced his control over several gangs in the city, with distance posing no obstacle. The diminishing cost and ease of communication enabled him to exert tight control from Dubai over his criminal enterprise in Bombay, popularly known as the D Company. With a strong network of foot soldiers and lieutenants, accountants, agents, lawyers, corrupt police personnel, and judicial officials to manage the gang's legal hurdles, D Company rose to the top of the underworld by the early 1990s.[15] Real estate provided it with a golden opportunity to extort money from builders and enter into partnerships with them. Lording over a powerful business and criminal empire, Dawood hosted and consorted with Bombay film stars and even moved into film production through his associates. Like the public, the underworld was fascinated by the glamour of the tinsel town. In equal measure, the Bombay stars found hanging out with a feared don irresistible.

In the popular imagination, Dawood has become not merely a criminal but a gangster, a mythical figure of terrible daring and lurid artistry. If you walk into the neighborhood of Dongri, people will point to his house with awe. He is viewed as a classic Bombay figure, one bred by the illicit opportunities that the city offers and adept at creating others out of its pulsating daily life. Legends about how he used his skills in exploiting cracks in the gangland to become its lord are as much about him as they are about the city. So are stories about his use of violence to mow down rivals and traitors and the murderous control he currently exercises from Dubai over his criminal network in Mumbai. These accounts lend a fablelike quality to both the criminal world of the city and Dawood as a gangster. Not surprisingly, newspapers regularly report his sightings—now in Dubai, then in Karachi, but always allegedly nostalgic about his native city. Surrounded by glamorous personalities, he is a figure of glamour himself. In the gangster film *Company* (2002), Dawood's rise to the top and his murderous enmity with his onetime associate Chota Rajan acquires a legendary status. So does the idea that the city provides a space for conspiracy, that cops and criminals, politicians and builders, plot and scheme behind everyone's back to render Mumbai a place of crime and murder.

The rise of Dawood Ibrahim and his criminal network coincided with the collapse of the mills. The mill workers, who remained jobless after the prolonged strike of 1982–83, were targeted for recruitment by the gangs as foot soldiers. The densely packed chawls became their hideouts.[16] As the Khatau Mills case shows, the underworld infiltrated the unions to grab a piece of the defunct mill lands. It was against this background of growing lawlessness and a complicit state authority that the communal riots of 1992–93, followed by the serial bomb blasts, tore apart the city.

On December 6, 1992, a right-wing Hindu mob razed the sixteenth-century Babri Masjid in Ayodhya. Television footage repeatedly beamed the destructive act, showing exultant Hindu militants dancing on the mosque's debris. A thousand miles away in Bombay, jubilant Shiv Sainiks celebrated the demolition by holding a rally in Dharavi, twisting a knife in the wounded Muslim psyche. The city, already on edge with months of Hindu nationalist propaganda and the retaliatory calls to defend Islam, exploded in bloody violence.[17] The Muslims attacked Hindu temples and shrines and struck out at the police in retaliation for the official inaction during the Babri Masjid's demolition. The Hindus assaulted mosques and looted and set fire to Muslim-owned shops. In the mill districts, which seethed with the disaffection and frustration of laid-off workers, the Sena, like the underworld, found willing recruits for its violence against the Muslims.[18] Knives and swords flashed while stones and Molotov cocktails rained down. The sky darkened with the smoke from burning shops, hutments, and motor vehicles. The police resorted to firing, ostensibly to maintain order, but they ended up killing many more Muslims than Hindus. "This was not a Hindu-Muslim riot, but a police-Muslim riot," said an eyewitness.[19]

The violence took a break for a few weeks after December 12 but was unleashed again in full force on January 6, 1993. For nearly two weeks, murder and arson raged across the city. Unlike previous communal clashes, the 1992–93 riots were not confined to particular neighborhoods but engulfed the entire city. Bal Thackeray stoked the fire by publishing inflammatory editorials.[20] Armed with voter lists identifying the apartments where Muslims lived, the Sena gangs stalked the high-rise buildings in upscale neighborhoods. Terrified residents removed nameplates from the lobbies of their buildings to avert attacks. The Muslims felt threatened by the Sena-led mobs and did not trust the police to protect them. "I feel like a Jew in Nazi Germany," said a Muslim.[21] Thackeray thought that this was only fitting. In an interview with *Time* at that time, he said if the Muslims behaved like the Jews, "there is nothing wrong if they are treated as Jews were in Germany."[22]

When it was all over, the official estimate was that nine hundred residents had lost their lives and many more were injured in the communal violence and police firings. Unofficial estimates counted many more killed and injured. Everyone agreed that the overwhelming majority of the victims were Muslims. There were many instances of the police's anti-Muslim bias. A Muslim woman who phoned a police station for help when a Hindu mob attacked her chawl was told: "Landyabai Chup baitho, Abhi kuch nahi hua!" (Shut up, you circumcised pricks' woman. Nothing has happened yet!). To her horror, when the policemen did show up, they assisted the Hindu rioters.[23] In case after case, the police displayed rank indifference to the Muslims under attack, fired excessively at them, and collaborated with the Sainiks.[24]

The violence-scarred city barely had a chance to recover before it was battered once again. On March 12, 1993, ten bombs—plastic explosives packed in cars—targeted the busy commercial district and other prominent city sites. The aftermath of Black Friday presented gruesome scenes: charred bodies, blood-splattered severed limbs, mounds of shattered glass, and flattened cars. The serial bomb blasts killed over three hundred people, leaving the city engulfed in chaos and fear.

The police investigations subsequently revealed a conspiracy hatched in Dubai, Bombay, and Pakistan that used the underworld to plan and execute the blasts.[25] After the 1992–93 riots, Dawood received a package in Dubai from Bombay. It contained red and green glass bangles with a mocking note in Urdu that read: "Jo bhai bahen ki izzat ki hifazat na kar sake use ye tohfa Mubarak" (A brother who cannot protect the chastity of his sisters deserves this gift).[26] With this challenge to his manhood, the plot to avenge the attacks on the Muslim community was born. Now even the underworld was communalized.

The chief mastermind of the plot in Bombay was Tiger Memon, who had quickly risen from the ranks as a major smuggler. Tiger had his own motivation. During the riots, his office was burned to cinders. Inflamed by his loss, Tiger joined the conspiracy to hit India's commercial capital in order to deliver a message to the Hindus—lay off, or else. The plan involved the transport of explosives to a landing spot on the rocky coast that was a smugglers' haven. Teams of gang members were recruited to assemble and plant bombs. Many of them were sent to Pakistan via Dubai for training. The targets included the Bombay Stock Exchange, the Air India building, luxury hotels, the Bombay Municipal Corporation building, and the Shiv Sena headquarters. Once everything was in place, Tiger fled with his family to Dubai on an early-morning flight on March 12, just hours before the blasts.

That it took the underworld to act on behalf of the Muslim community was a telling commentary on the state of the rule of law. If any further evidence of the liberal order's breakdown was needed, it was provided by the fate of the judicial commission instituted to inquire into the riots. The Congress-led Maharashtra government appointed the commission only when it came under intense public pressure and in an effort to restore the state's image as an institution standing above social divisions. Justice B. N. Srikrishna, a retired High Court judge, was named to head the commission of inquiry. But when the Sena–Bharatiya Janata Party alliance rode to power in 1995, it tried to disband the inquiry. Only loud public protests and pressure from the central government forced it to restore the commission. However, the Maharashtra government hindered the process at every turn and, in an effort to blunt the expected findings against the Sena, saddled the commission with investigating both the riots and the bomb blasts.

Any hope that the government would uphold the rule of law went up in smoke when the Srikrishna Commission issued its two-volume report in 1998. The state government, first under the Sena-BJP alliance and later under the Congress, ignored the commission's recommendations for prosecuting the guilty political leaders and police officials involved in the communal riots. Meanwhile, the investigation and prosecution of the perpetrators of the bomb blasts proceeded expeditiously, leading critics to charge that the government was quick to act against Muslims while letting Hindu activists and police officials with blood on their hands go scot-free.

The Srikrishna Commission concluded that the bloody spectacle of a sustained pogrom against the Muslims was carried out with the police looking the other way or assisting the rioters. "The police," the commission concluded, "by their own conduct, appeared to have lost moral authority over the citizens and appeared to evoke no fears even in the minds of criminal elements."[27] The state had buckled under the pressure of Hindu majoritarianism. If the Srikrishna Commission stood out as a courageous assertion of liberal norms, its findings, disregarded by the government, demonstrated the abject failure of the rule of law.

The image of Bombay as a liberal city ruled by law and reason turned out to be a chimera. It is for this reason that the Sena-BJP government's official renaming of Bombay as Mumbai in 1995 was not a simple matter of reclaiming the city from its colonial heritage. It was also an act of populist insurgency, a forcible takeover of state power to deliver the city to the people. Behind this story of the populist and communalist mobilization of the street lies the broader narrative of the crisis of the liberal order. The state's authority, in spite of Justice Srikrishna's valiant attempt, stood hollow. The combination of the Shiv Sena's populism, the Congress's resort to political expediency, the collapse of the mills, and the rise of the underworld and Hindu nationalism had taken its toll. Choking in a polluted atmosphere of bitterness and distrust, the city faced seemingly intractable political, social, and economic problems that had rendered it lawless and disorderly. The rhetoric of liberal democracy that filled the official realm of politics increasingly appeared unreal. The reality seemed to be corruption and violence, riots and murders. Conspiracies, hatched by politicians, builders, criminals, Hindu militants, and Muslim dons, appeared to be the underlying dynamic of the city. Anger and violence ruled the street. It was into this tortured city that Doga arrived to deliver street justice.

Crime offers a perceptive optic for viewing the state of law. Thus, imaginative practices return again and again to the scene of lawlessness. Novels, detective fiction, pulp, cinema, and comic books turn to the disorder produced by crime to represent the functioning of order. What is at issue in their depictions of murder, robbery, intrigue, kidnapping, blackmail, and extortion is the state of law. In courtroom dramas, what is on trial is not the criminal order but the legal one. When the detective carefully pieces together clues in crime fiction, he or she identifies and assembles the system's dysfunctions. Typically, such dysfunctions are located in the city, for it is in the urban space that modernity finds its most concentrated expression. It is there that society is fabricated, pieced together, rather than formed organically. The modern city is forged by the operations of the capitalist economy and the practices of everyday life. Its built environment—the grid of transportation, streets, neighborhoods, tenements, shops, and businesses—is produced by modernity. The social spaces of the city express and are formed by modern political, cultural, and psychological forces. Above all, it is in the modern city that law functions to constitute and regulate society.

Not surprisingly, literature and cinema locate their crime fictions in the modern city. Consider Raymond Chandler's hard-boiled detective novels, which register the breakdown of class and racial orders in Los Angeles. Or take Hollywood film noir, with its characteristic shadows and highlights, which reveal urban wastelands of gangsters, tainted judges, femme fatales, brothels, and shysters. Crime has also served as a lens to represent urban society in India. There is an established tradition of detective pulp fiction in Hindi. In addition, Hindi cinema of the 1950s produced a spate of "crime melodramas," such as *Baazi* (1951), *Aar Paar* (1954), *Taxi Driver* (1954), and *CID* (1956).[28] Using noir style, these films depict Bombay as an ambiguous and crime-ridden space for the confrontation between law and crime, family and money. Bombay turns darker in the "angry young man" films of Amitabh Bachchan in the 1970s and the 1980s. The city appears racked by the breakdown of citizenship and the legal order. Bachchan's underclass vigilante emerges from the depths of urban crisis to singlehandedly avenge injustice.[29]

Like the 1950s crime melodramas and the Bachchan films, Doga views Bombay through the lens of lawlessness. But the comic book is a different medium.[30] Like cinema, as a graphic form, it produces representations in images. But its boxed panels, combining text with images, constitute a specific form. Unlike cinema, there is no synchronicity between words and pictures. We view the visual and read the text sequentially. The reader makes the connections, determining their meanings and that of the narrative as it progresses from panel to panel. This makes the comic book an interactive medium, as does its handcrafted appearance. Its preindustrial look requires us to suspend disbelief much more radically than the realist illusion of the photograph and the cinema screen. We are invited to participate in the comic book's fantastic storytelling and enlisted to establish the meanings of its words and pictures. Inexpensive and published as a series, like pulp detective and romantic fiction, comic books are published month after month, extending the narrative with new episodes. Readers buy, borrow, trade, and collect these graphic narratives, forming long-lasting relationships with them. Like pulp fiction, comic books circulate widely in popular culture, perhaps the reason why they are viewed as lowbrow commodities.

When Doga appeared in 1993, the comic-book market in India was already developed. *Superman* and *Batman* were familiar superheroes in the big cities. But the first series to be published in India was the *Indrajal* comics. Published between 1964 and 1989, these, in the main, were adaptations of Phantom stories. Eventually, Phantom acquired an Indian name, Veytal, but the exploits of this comic-book superhero in distant Africa did not find an enduring readership in India. Far more successful has been *Amar Chitra Katha* (*ACK*), which began publication in 1967. Its stories are drawn from epics and historical myths. Cast in a Hindu nationalist mould, the ACK series has become an iconic artifact of popular culture. Even as its location in contemporary cultural politics is clear, *ACK* is dressed heavily in classical and historical garb and views itself as teaching children their cultural heritage.[31] Those who do not have a taste for *ACK*'s Hindu nationalist history can turn to another wildly popular comic book, *Chacha Chaudhary*. Published in several languages, *Chacha Chaudhary* recounts the adventures of a superhero with no special powers. He is an old man, armed only with a stick and his incredible wit, which he uses to foil thieves and robbers.

While all of these graphic narratives express the vital place of visuality in modern life, the Doga series is strikingly different. Its focus is decidedly on the modern city. This is evident not just in its narratives and their setting in Bombay but also in its close attention to visual surfaces. Of course, this is understandable, since it is a visual medium. But what is significant is the attention it pays to the city as a visual spectacle. Streets, buildings, apartments, shop windows, and bodies—all are drawn with an eye to their aesthetics. Buildings are not just buildings but shiny towers of glass and concrete. The apartments of the rich exude luxury and are filled with expensive-looking furniture and decorative goods, whereas the dens of criminals appear menacing. Advertising signs and shop-window displays present visual spectacles. Even the bodies of the comic characters—underworld dons in stylized clothing and police officials in crisp uniforms—point to the comic book's attention to the city's visual surfaces.

Writing about Berlin in the 1920s, Siegfried Kracauer identified urban modernity in its "surface-level expressions."[32] He argued that the emergence of mass society in the modern city under capitalism rendered aesthetic forms and spectacles vital to urban life. Commodity exchanges take place by packaging goods with an alluring exterior so that similar products can be distinguished. Advertising, shop signs, and architectural forms turn the city into a space of man-ufactured spectacles.

It is seeing Mumbai as just such a city of spectacle that inspired *Doga's* creators to locate the comic-book series there. According to Sanjay Gupta, the studio head of Raj Comics, who conceived and de-veloped the concept in collaboration with Vivek Mohan and Tarun Kumar Wahi, the idea was to create a comic-book series aimed at big cities.[33] Mumbai seemed an obvious choice because of its "khaas chamak" (special shine).[34] It is a place of high finance, big deals, and a fast life. The city also sparkles with glamorous film stars. The "cha-mak," adds Gupta, extends to its underworld. Though crime is not Mumbai's exclusive preserve, in the city the scale appears immense. The complexity and vast organization of Mumbai's crime syndicates are scaled to match the high stakes. The creators decided that the su-perhero would not only fight Mumbai's criminal world but must also be brushed by it; Doga had to partake of the environment even as he acts on the side of the angels.

Thus, Doga was born as an urban warrior who fights violent crim-inals with violence. Like many superheroes, he is estranged from so-ciety, an angst-ridden loner, and an orphan with no siblings or other family.[35] Halkan Singh, a notorious and ruthless dacoit of the Cham-bal Valley, found him abandoned as an infant in a garbage heap. The dacoit brings up the orphan but treats him no better than a stray dog. He is even called a dog and forced to accompany the dacoit on his criminal forays. The boy simmers with revulsion as he witnesses Hal-kan's bloody actions. His disgust with the criminal's brutality reaches a breaking point when the dacoit kidnaps a young girl named Sonu. The young Doga frees the girl and escapes with her. A grateful Sonu names him Suraj (Sun) before drowning in a river while escaping from the gangsters who are in hot pursuit. (Actually, she survives and appears later in the series as Suraj's love interest.) Haunted by Sonu's anguished cries before she apparently perishes, the boy goes to the police and spills out the dacoit's secrets. The police attack the gang, but Halkan gets away and flees to Bombay, where he establishes himself as a gang lord. Meanwhile, the boy also arrives in the city, looking for Halkan. He gets a job at the Lion Gym, growing into adulthood as Suraj, a young man with a fabulous muscular body.

As Suraj, he has an adopted family of four uncles.[36] Under the supervision of Adrakh Chacha (Uncle Ginger), the head of the Lion Gym, Suraj turns his muscles into steel. Dhaniya Chacha (Uncle Coriander) teaches him boxing, Haldi Chacha (Uncle Turmeric) is his karate instructor, and he becomes an expert in firearms under the tutelage of Kaali Mirch Chacha (Uncle Black Pepper). They not only train him but also save his life when he is shot and bleeding profusely, in urgent need of a massive blood transfusion. Since his blood group is different from that of the uncles, all four troop into a blood bank, where they open their veins in exchange for a supply of Suraj's blood type.

With this rebirth, the orphan acquires a fictive family. But religion does not mark this family. We do not know Doga's religion, but his adopted name, Suraj, is Hindu. The person closest to him, the only one who knows his secret identity, is Adrakh Chacha, a Muslim. But he is named after a spice, as are his brothers. According to Gupta, the creators named the uncles after spices as much to give them catchy and memorable monikers as to avoid the "baas" (stench) of communal identity. As a consequence, while the comic book identifies the religion of Doga's adopted uncles, it also places his fictive family beyond the most identifiable social identity.

As an orphan, Doga is already on the margins of society. But even when he acquires an adopted family, Suraj remains an outsider. Because of this outcast status, he adopts the secret identity of Doga to deal with the searing memory of Halkan's horrific cruelties. Social alienation is not uncommon with superheroes, as in the case of Bruce Wayne or Clark Kent. But the rejection of a religious identity to signify an anomalous relationship with society is significant in the Mumbai context of Hindu-Muslim conflicts. In this respect, it is noteworthy that this comic-book series appeared in 1993, that is, in the wake of the riots and the bomb blasts. It is as if the burst of communal violence gave birth to a superhero altogether beyond communities.

Being an outsider, Doga is free of society's prejudices. His close relationship with his spice uncles, signifying a bond with nature, magnifies his estrangement from culture. So do the dog mask and his unique relationship with the canine world. Doga is assisted by an army of stray dogs, a dependable pack who arrive when they hear his ultrasonic whistle, a sound that is inaudible to others. When summoned, the dogs attack his adversaries. When he is injured in fights, they drag Doga to the safety of underground sewers, where they nurse him back to health. He does not have supernatural powers but does possess keenly developed senses that bestow on him an uncanny ability to become one with the instinctual animal world. His muscular physicality and his extraordinary strength and indestructibility enhance his power as a force of nature. He is essentially human but elemental. Simplicity, directness, and honesty define him.

Doga has a single mission: ridding Mumbai of criminals. It is his defining character. His adversaries may be as powerful and lethal as he is, but they do not have his moral compass. Haunted by the anguished cry of the girl he believes he failed to save from the dacoit Halkan, Doga is motivated by a sense of duty to avenge injustice. But Mumbai is so overrun by outlaws that he must deliver street justice, exterminating the immoral and the lawless. This makes for an ambiguous relationship with the authorities. He is deferential toward the police, but their protocols hinder his mission to avenge injustice. For him, matters are clear and the choices are obvious—law versus the lawless, good versus evil, justice versus injustice. He flouts laws in fighting criminals. He shoots and throws hand grenades at the evildoers, rather than handing them over to the police. Never squeamish about killing his adversaries, Doga's violence is fierce. He does not invoke self-defense to justify his ferocity because the annihilation of criminals, not their reform and rehabilitation, is his aim.

His violent vigilantism invites a vicious response from the criminals. They hunt for him, lay traps, and unleash their guns and goons on him. When he is temporarily captured, Doga has to endure unbelievable torture. Violence meets with violence, cruelty with cruelty. The only difference between the two is the morality that motivates Doga's bloody actions.

Even as the police recognize Doga's essential goodness, they cannot condone his vigilantism because that would mean acknowledging their own weakness and accepting an alternative authority. This makes for an ambiguous relationship between the two. The authorities persistently try to apprehend him for taking the law into in his hands, but the superhero successfully ducks their grasp and manages to protect his secret identity. This cat-and-mouse game between the police and the superhero keeps alive Doga's position as an outsider. As an agent outside the social and legal order, he is able to do what the police cannot—defend society against criminal predators. But even more important, because Doga's enforcement of justice is extralegal, the legitimacy of the state as the lawful authority is affirmed.

THE PATHOLOGY OF URBAN VIOLENCE

Crime never stops in Doga's Mumbai. It has no beginning and no end, but it endlessly changes its form. No sooner has Doga slain one criminal mastermind than another one emerges. In the city that never sleeps, crime also does not take a break. Lawlessness is a constant feature of the urban landscape; it touches the lives of ordinary people and makes their lives a living hell.

Genda, for example, is about the havoc wreaked on the lives of poor slum dwellers by the real estate developer Dinanath.[37] In public life, he is a respectable businessman, but secretly he is the ruthless gang lord Genda (Hippopotamus). His modus operandi is to get his goons to set fire to shantytowns, clearing the land for his real estate ventures. Then, feigning sympathy, he appears as Dinanath before the displaced residents and gifts them petty amounts of cash. Having lost everything, the poor slum dwellers are happy to get any little crumb. They go away, singing Dinanath's praises, while he builds luxury hotels and apartment towers on lands cleared by arson. The gangster's hirelings escape police dragnets by capturing a brave police officer and threatening to kill a hostage. Fortunately, Doga comes to the rescue. He not only frees the officer but also goes after Genda. After finishing off his goons, the superhero ensures poetic justice for the developer-cum-gangster. He ties the crooked hypocrite to a chair in his mansion and sets it on fire. The homeless do not get their homes back, but their oppressor meets with a fiery end.

The story strikes a chord. It is an experience that is familiar in Mumbai. The poor come to the city from all parts of India, looking for a livelihood. They build shantytowns, often on marshes, and make the land habitable. As the population grows and the slum becomes a thriving neighborhood, the municipal authorities are forced to extend some minimal civic facilities, even if the settlement is illegal. But once the poor have made the land livable, it becomes a valued commodity. The residents are evicted, often by force, or a combination of muscle and political power, and the lands are cleared for the construction of apartments and office buildings. The poor develop the land, but it is the unscrupulous builders who reap the profits. This process reached a fever pitch during the real estate boom of the 1990s. With stakes escalating, the builders hired gangsters to clear lands for construction by evicting slum dwellers. The underworld, crooked builders, and corrupt politicians made hay while the poor suffered.

There are plenty of accounts of the builder-criminal nexus in Mumbai. In the comic book's show *and* tell, however, the story acquires other layers of meaning. Drawings and words attract attention to their surface, resisting realist mystifications and inviting the reader to imagine the scene, to explore the interaction between the text and the images. Consider, for example, the first scene of a crime depicted in the opening pages of *Genda* (plate 3). Three gasoline tankers appear, each in a separate panel. It is night, and no one is around. The meaning of the tankers' images is made clear by the accompanying text, which tells us that they are converging on a shantytown under the cover of darkness. The text and the pictures together suggest that something ominous is afoot. The following two panels enhance this suggestion. The woman jumping out of her tanker notes with satisfaction that everyone is asleep, making the job easy. The nature of the job is made plain by the picture of a man reeling out a hose from his tanker. The balloon expressing the man's hope that his accomplices are also doing the same thing establishes that it is a coordinated plan. This would not be apparent from the drawing itself. In this sense, the pictures are not self-sufficient. But neither is the text, for the words would not make sense without the drawings of the tankers. Words also function graphically. Thus, in the second row of panels, each thought balloon spills beyond the gutters and occupies a space in an adjacent box. These indicate that the woman and the man are working in coordination and that a third person is also part of the conspiracy. This meaning is produced as much by the words as by their placement in balloons that violate the panel borders. In the bottom two panels, we see the further execution of the diabolical plan—the third conspirator and the woman are dousing the hutments with gasoline. While the man marvels at the ease with which gasoline gushes forth, the woman revels in its intoxicating smell.

Words and visuals together depict a heinous crime in operation. While the innocent slum dwellers sleep in their hutments, the goons engage in an evil conspiracy against them. They feel no sympathy for their intended victims while executing their inhuman plan. Their criminal pathology can be understood as a grotesque manifestation of the indifference to strangers, or what Georg Simmel called the "blasé outlook," characteristic of the cold and calculating modern capitalist metropolis. Tracing the psychic effects of money, Simmel argued that commodity exchange erases the qualitative distinction between things, hollows out their specific values and meanings by reducing them to their monetary equivalents, breeding an attitude of indifference.[38] Fleeting and anonymous social relations produce the bystander who looks away from the suffering of others. The criminal is only a perverted expression of this indifference in the modern city. Thus, the gangsters plotting to burn down the shantytown do not look away but take a cruel pleasure in their violence on strangers. The comic book's show-and-tell description throws a spotlight on the social psychology that underpins criminal violence.

Doga himself is no shrinking violet. He also takes pleasure in pulverizing and killing his enemies. In close-ups showing him bashing gangsters' heads together, accompanied by exclamatory sounds, we see not only the display of his extraordinary strength but also his murderous desire. The images of faces twisted in pain and words expressing the sounds of Doga's fist smashing into the gangster's head enlist the reader in imagining the deadly intent and the terrible intensity of violence. If capitalist excess produces greedy criminals who run riot in the city, taking pleasure in arson and murder, then Doga must respond with a greater burst of bloodshed. Justice is served not by locking up the evildoers but by countering their twisted cruelty with more intense and decisive violence. It requires a response that is commensurate with the deep psychic alienation that underpins the criminals' brutality in the modern capitalist city.

Thus, Doga not only slays the crooked developer but also delights in the deed (see plate 4). In the first panel, he towers over the cowering Dinanath seated on a couch, while a battered goon lies prostrate on the floor. The text characterizes the scene as a verbal confrontation between a triumphant Doga and a defeated adversary who issues empty threats. Without showing the intervening actions, which the reader has to imagine, the next panel shows Dinanath tied up and the masked superhero determinedly walking away. While his captive pleads for mercy, Doga gleefully announces that a fiery death awaits him. In the following panel, Doga holds a flame and is about to set fire to Dinanath's mansion. The picture of his bloodthirsty vengeance is modified by his utterance that his action is in response to the thousands burned to death by Dinanath. With the morality of his action established, Doga swaggers off triumphantly. His steps do not falter, and he does not look back. The vigilante superhero does not feel any qualms about leaving the gangster to his fiery fate.

DEMOCRACY DESECRATED

Genda is finished, but Doga's work is not over. In issue after issue, he encounters yet another evil villain. Being a superhero series, the comic book naturally treats each encounter from Doga's point of view. We are offered his appraisals of the contemporary city and his perceptions of what is wrong with its legal and political order. The villains are not only underworld dons and crooked builders but also corrupt policemen and politicians. This theme recurs in the series, but *Khaki Aur Khaddar* offers a particularly withering critique of the hypocrisy and treachery of public servants.[39]

Khaki Aur Khaddar opens with a picture that covers most of the page (see plate 5). A portly man in the Indian politician's traditional uniform—*khaddar* (homespun cloth) kurta pajama, Nehru jacket, and Gandhi cap—stands with his back to a police officer in khaki. The accompanying text intones that peace and order in the country require law, that protection of the law needs the police, and to control the police a politician is needed. The statuelike images and the declarative sentences portray a solemn and universal ideal. But on the very next page, all hell breaks loose. The police are raining bullets at a car on a crowded Mumbai street. The shots crack the windshield and the windows. The Opel Astra sedan careens out of control, banging into a roadside fence before coming to a halt, blood spilling out of the doors. The policemen converge on the car, whose occupants lie felled by bullets. Prem Singh, a constable, turns over a dead passenger to identify him. His face contorted with shock, the constable exclaims that the slain man is not Lion, the dreaded gangster. Other constables add with shocked realization that the remaining dead passengers are not Lion's henchmen either. The enormity of the blunder registers on Inspector Arjun Singh, the supervising officer. The tip that Lion and his hirelings would be traveling in the car has turned out to be false; they have killed innocent people.

This killing scene reprises the infamous "encounter" that the Mumbai police have used routinely since the 1990s to kill underworld gangsters. The police force has several specialists who triumphantly proclaim the number of criminals they have "encountered." Charges swirl that "encounter" is another name for the cold-blooded killings of alleged gangsters by a police force under pressure. Civil libertarians have charged that the police—frustrated by gang wars, contract killings, and the underworld's ability to manipulate the judicial system—resorted to encounters as a way to combat crime. A culture of killing took hold, and officers were decorated and promoted on the basis of the number of alleged criminals they had encountered. There were also rumors that the underworld bosses had used friendly police officers to "encounter" their rivals.

Using the thread of these charges and rumors surrounding the encounter, *Khaki Aur Khaddar* weaves a story about the criminalization of politics. As the story progresses, it turns out that the false tip was planted by Constable Prem Singh at Lion's behest. Inspector Arjun Singh, an honest police officer, was a thorn in Lion's hide, raiding the gangster's warehouse and seizing his smuggled goods. Through Prem Singh, Lion plants false information about the car, confident that the officer will take the bait to promote his career through the encounter. Instead, when innocent people are killed, Arjun Singh will lose his uniform. Lion's plot is successful. Arjun Singh is dismissed from the police force. When another honest police officer figures out the plot and arrests Prem Singh and Lion, the ever-resourceful criminals remain undaunted. The now-jailed Prem Singh stands for election and wins with the help of Lion's thugs, who silence the opposition. The rule of law becomes a mockery as Prem Singh becomes a minister in the government and has the police at his command. Democracy and political citizenship stand grossly perverted.

Where is Doga? Why does he not put an end to the oppression of the criminal-turned-politician and the law-turned-lawless? Tragically, Doga is dead. Suraj has killed his secret superhero identity because his girlfriend, Monica, hates the violent Doga.[40] This twist in the story permits the full portrayal of the reign of terror let loose by Prem Singh and Lion. Suraj watches helplessly as shantytowns are burned to make way for the politician's luxury hotel. He seethes with anger as the police are turned into Lion's agents. As a law-abiding citizen, he can do nothing but watch the dance of lawlessness. The injustice also disturbs Monica, but she still has faith in the law and nonviolence. As if to mock her naïveté, Suraj invites her to a fashion show. When she expresses her surprise that he would invite her to something so frivolous, he responds that domestic life means going to clubs, shopping, fashion shows, and wandering aimlessly. On the way to the fashion show, they run into Lion's goons, who, with police assistance, beat up people and set fire to their shantytown. Monica is horrified at the sight and says that she cannot see such injustice. Suraj insists that she must watch the tyranny that runs riot on the street (see plate 6). In the panel, he directs her to observe the smoldering slums, a blood-spattered body, and the anguished face of a fleeing resident. Suraj says: "Just watch, but see it like a fashion show. Not through the eyes of the law, not from the viewpoint of violence that Doga unleashes after seeing such oppression. See it through the eyes of a terrorized citizen."

Monica remains unmoved by Suraj's anguished plea. She refuses to abandon her faith in law and democracy even as the sight of a vast gap between the ideal and the experience of the liberal-democratic state stares her in face. It is only when repression and tyranny break all bounds that Monica cries out for Doga's return. Suraj once again dons the dog mask and tight bodysuit and reappears as Doga. He goes after Lion, tearing through the gangster's protective armor of law. The coup de grace is getting Prem Singh to sign his death warrant by unknowingly ordering the police to shoot at his own official car. The criminal career that began with an encounter also ends with one.

The criminalization of politics is a familiar story in Indian politics, and the encounter killings of Mumbai gangsters became a routine news item in the 1980s and the 1990s. In their comic-book rendering, these well-known stories are given a twist. Law and politics have not just been turned upside down but have been desecrated. What we see are not violations but the complete perversion of norms and ideals. This point is driven home when a character, a former police officer, is locked up illegally and tortured. He implores an officer who is reluctant to participate in Prem Singh's illegal activities not to stain khaki and khaddar. "These two are holy like the Ramayan [the ancient Sanskrit epic], Bible, and the Quran."[41] His appeal to the sacred image of the democratic state is in vain. The police have no recourse but to follow the elected representative's orders. The ordinary citizens are also helpless. Protests against official conduct are brutally suppressed. The twist in the plot, involving Doga's absence, allows the display of a completely defiled legal and political system.

By the time Suraj becomes Doga again, the idealized image of khaki and khaddar lies in total ruins. Corrupted to the core, the democratic state is thoroughly distorted; it has become an agent of despotism and oppression. Gloom and despair prevail among the citizenry. Only the superhero can rescue the city from its misery and hopelessness. But Doga does not lead the citizens to a popular revolution. He is a vigilante, but no rebel. He accepts the democratic state's ideal as an abstract institution, standing above concrete private interests. In his eyes, the state's aura appears intact; only its agents look rotten and ineffective. Faced with the gap between this ideal and its actual experience, he seeks to close the breach by performing functions that the state cannot, due to either corruption or legal constraints. By embracing the extralegality of his actions to secure justice, Doga provides supplementary support to the legitimacy of the liberal-democratic state.

BLOOD AND COMMUNITY

The relief, however, is ephemeral. Yet another criminal, and then another, appears and terrorizes the city. In recounting the superhero's exploits from issue to issue, the *Doga* comic books show a remarkable attention to Mumbai's political landscape. The corruption of politics and the police, which figures prominently in the public discourse, remains an enduring theme in the series. So is the question of Hindu-Muslim relations. An anticommunal thrust is a constant presence in the series, expressed through Doga's relations with Adrakh Chacha, who frequently invokes Allah's blessings for the superhero. But in a recent set of issues, the comic book also tackles the question of communal conflict head on.[42]

Like most *Doga* comic books, the series on communal conflicts also begins with declarative statements in the opening page that set the moral parameters of the narrative. A living body needs a heartbeat, a heartbeat needs blood, and blood needs oxygen. A living city needs the law, the law needs honesty, and honesty needs humanity. Thus begins *Doga Hindu Hai* (Doga Is Hindu). This analogical opening sets a fundamental relationship between blood and humanity, echoing the sentiment in Shylock's question "If you prick us, do we not bleed?" Underneath the differences of religion, we are all human. Blood does not differentiate between Hindus and Muslims. When this universal belief is challenged, the Doga series on the Hindu-Muslim conflict tells us, a communal bloodbath engulfs us.

The story concerns a blood bank, whose manager is in league with a fiendish criminal, Bloodman. To obtain blood, the manager has to be bribed. The money goes to Bloodman, who replenishes the supply by his tie-up with a drug pusher, Smackbhai (Brother Smack). Smackbhai lures workers into his drug den, where they blow their monthly paychecks on smack. While they are lost in their drug-induced dreamworld, blood is drained out of their veins and sold at a premium at the blood bank. Doga intervenes when the corrupt blood bank manager denies blood for children injured in a school-bus accident. He beats up the manager and the Bloodman's thugs. In response, the enraged criminal lays a deadly plot. He shoots several of his own Muslim hirelings, leaving three Hindus alive. His men spread the rumor that Doga killed only Muslims and spared the Hindus because he is a Hindu himself. Communal tensions grip the city. These escalate into open warfare as a result of another conspiracy hatched by Bloodman.

Doga is invited to a Hindu wedding in Dharavi. The bride insists that the superhero escort her to the palanquin after the wedding. Treating her as his sister, Doga willingly does the deed and leaves. As the newly wed bride departs from her natal home in a palanquin, Muslim rioters block the path. They attack the Hindu wedding party but flee when they see Doga. Hindu rioters react by attacking a Muslim wedding, which is occurring at the same time, also in Dharavi. The Muslims' hopes soar when they spot Doga; they are sure that the superhero will come to their rescue. But Doga sits frozen in a corner, paralyzed by the spiked dessert that he has eaten at the Hindu wedding. It is later revealed that the woman who gave it to him is Bloodman's plant. But meanwhile, Doga's frozen state convinces the Muslims that Doga is on the Hindu side. His image as a superhero transcending community identity is tarnished. The Muslim bride spits at him, and the city rings with cries denouncing Doga as a Hindu communalist.

The Hindu-Muslim violence rages on in the city. When arson and killings take over, the army is summoned to restore order. Such is the scale and intensity of the chaos and carnage that the artist dispenses with the square panel—the meter of comic books (see plate 7). It is as if the anarchy has thrown even the comic-book format out of alignment, unable to contain the disorderly energy of sectarian violence. Doga plunges into the cauldron to extinguish the fire, but he is helpless, unable to decide whom to thrash and whom to spare (see plate 8).

The Muslims turn on Doga, convinced that he is on the other side. A Muslim mob converges on him and pummels him when it finds further evidence—again planted by Bloodman's agents—that he is one of the Hindu assailants. Rather than defend himself, Doga meekly suffers a rain of blows by sticks and iron rods. Why should he protect his body when his reputation as a man who is above religious difference is already dead? The blows nearly kill him. Fortunately, Lomdi (Fox), a female superhero, whisks him away. As she nurses him, Doga's soul separates from his body and cries out in pain (see plate 9). The last time he has cried was as a young boy when witnessing Halkan's cruelties. A sense of duty toward others has enabled him to suppress pain. But how can he withstand the pain of being seen as a betrayer of trust? His soul sobs inconsolably. Lomdi tries to coax him back to life, but Doga's soul resists. Why does she want to save him? How can he live with the burden of communal slaughter? Doga is dead, and the dead cannot be brought back to life.

The sociological and political phenomenon of the communal bloodbath becomes a crisis of the soul, a deep psychic event in the comic book. The dark and foreboding artwork and the internal monologue create a picture of psychological unraveling. Despair and self-doubt overwhelm the resolute and indestructible superhero. The agents of the state can be corrupt, the politicians can be crooked, and the criminals can hatch conspiracies. But what happens when the general principle itself is placed in doubt? To the extent that Doga embodies the universal ideal, the splitting of his body and soul expresses the loss of the general principle. Mumbai is no longer Mumbai when it loses the bond of humanity underlying religious difference; it is a Hobbesian jungle of warfare and brutality.

Thanks to Bloodman's conspiracy, ranged against Doga are the city's population, the police, and the military, which has been called in to restore order. The superhero can battle his adversaries and survive physical attacks but not the destruction of his moral being. If Doga is to live, he must regain his moral reputation. His soul must rejoin his body. Fortunately for the city, this is exactly what happens. In *Doga Ka Curfew* (Doga's Curfew), the superhero rises up from the ashes. With grim determination, he imposes a curfew on the city to quell violence. Anyone venturing out, particularly those armed with weapons, is subjected to Doga's harsh justice. He enlists his faithful dogs to enforce his will. When the military sedate his faithful canine army, Doga appeals to their conscience and wills them back to action. As the superhero roams the city to enforce his curfew, he carries on an internal monologue on the effects of communal carnage (plate 10). He is puzzled by people who invite riots even though they are fully aware that these result only in destruction, orphaned children, and devastated families. Thousands are willing to die in the name of religion, but no one is willing to fight for humanity.

Doga's curfew stops the bloodshed, but there is still the matter of his besmirched reputation. How can the superhero, embodying the universal ideal of communal harmony, live with the stigma of being a Hindu communalist? He is resolute in smothering the embers of violence, but his secular heart bleeds. Fortunately, two honest policemen discover video footage that reveals how the false evidence implicating Doga as a Hindu partisan was planted. When the footage is shown in slow motion on television, the conspiracy to frame the superhero becomes clear to Mumbai's residents. Stricken with guilt for having doubted Doga, they once again embrace him. Bloodman dies a bloody death when Doga orders that no blood supply be made available to revive the bleeding, bullet-riddled body of the merchant of blood.

The superhero format requires a villain, a definite cause for criminal mayhem, which must be annihilated. Thus, by killing Bloodman, Doga slays the cause of the communal bloodbath. But along the way, the comic book identifies the murderous fury of the crowd as the real agent of carnage. It is this bloody rage that splits Doga's body from his soul. It breaks apart the very embodiment of the universal ideal of human coexistence. As the superhero—the conscience of society—grieves for the damage wreaked by the frenzy of communal violence, questions of sociology and politics are reduced to the elemental level of blood and humanity. Caring for fellow human beings is portrayed as the essence of religion. Social harmony means not a society that is above religion but one nourished by religion's commitment to humanity. Thus, Adrakh Chacha expresses his Islamic identity by standing up for the welfare of all, not just the Muslim community.

Caring for other human beings, according to the comic book, is what holds an urban society together. The society plunges into crisis when vested interests hatch criminal conspiracies that incite violent passions. As the storm of communal rage engulfs the streets, the glue that binds humanity gives way. When this happens, the rule of law is the only answer. However, the state is unable to enforce the law; its power and authority are compromised. Therefore, the superhero must act.

LAW'S EMISSARY

Act he does, swiftly and decisively, to enforce the law. Battling the diabolical underworld dons, then slaying the vicious criminal in the pious garb of a politician, Doga annihilates them all. The villains' power is commensurate with that of the superhero. Though they lack Doga's immense physical strength and indestructibility, the crime lords command gangsters and have corrupt politicians and policemen dancing to their tune. The terrorists operate with the support of foreign powers. Some, like Kaal Paheliya, are devilishly devious like the Joker in *Batman*. Thus, Doga has to solve the trickster Paheliya's riddles in order to foil his criminal designs. All this helps to magnify Doga's superhero character.

The superhero's exploits against the supervillains, his relentless drive to rescue Mumbai's inhabitants, portray the predicaments of life in the modern metropolis. The challenges are many. The attractions of quick money, the lure of drugs, shortcuts to career advancement, and enticements of fame turn the city into a powder keg of pressure. The availability of technologies of killing—AK-47s, grenades, and bombs—make life precarious. With modern technologies of transportation, criminals strike with lightning speed. The density, diversity, and size of the city's population unleash conflicting forces. Now moved by one impulse, then by another, the city's crowd adds to its volatility. In Doga's eyes, Mumbai is never in a state of repose but in constant motion, moved by an excess of conflicting stimuli. The power of money runs riot, setting loose pathological violence for criminal gain. No kinship of blood binds this urban society. With its framework of law in tatters because of criminal conspiracies, it lurches from crisis to crisis.

Doga confronts the challenges of not just any modern metropolis but those of contemporary Mumbai. Much of the series' drama derives from Doga's engagement with the experiences of the last two decades—the criminalization of politics, the underworld menace, the builder-criminal-politician nexus, communal riots, and terrorist attacks. Borrowing freely from the journalistic and cinematic images of urban strife and darkness while using the popular art form of comic books, *Doga* strips contemporary events and figures down to their bare essentials and universalizes them. Its graphic retelling distills Mumbai's experiences to simple but powerful stories of the state's failure to act against injustice. We see the city stalked by the pathology of criminal violence, unrestrained by the rule of law. The criminalization of politics is the desecration of khaki and khaddar; the outbreak of communal violence is a crisis in human relations. As Doga confronts the enemies of truth, justice, democracy, and human community, the comic book's stark narrative form magnifies the moral stakes.

To its credit, though, the comic book is reflexive about Doga's moral authority. So, when the stigma of being a Hindu communalist haunts him, Doga's soul splits off from his body. How can he be a superhero when the public doubts his secular self? He may be physically indestructible, but Doga cannot be Doga against public opinion. The legitimacy of his vigilante violence depends on his maintaining the public's trust. And even then, his moral authority is not entirely secure. Why not fight crime and injustice with the law and democratic activism, instead of vigilante violence? Do the ends justify the means? When Monica poses these questions, Suraj is not entirely convinced, but he reluctantly declares Doga dead. As criminals burn shantytowns and render people homeless to make way for luxury hotels and apartment towers, an immense chasm opens between the ideal of the state as an instrument of general welfare and the reality of its agents' complicity in crime and corruption. It is a breach that only the superhero can fill. Even Monica arrives at this conclusion. Doga must kill the criminals, rather than hand them over to the police as Batman and Superman do, because the political and legal order is thoroughly corroded. He must act on the state's behalf because its agents cannot or will not. A contingent moral justification for Doga's violent vigilantism is reestablished.

Doga's power is imperishable. But he does not deploy it to establish his personal rule. He is law's emissary. If he acts outside the law to restore its authority, this is because Mumbai lives in dark, unruly times. Adopting the viewpoint of the street, Doga sees the city perverted by the illicit use of money, power, politics, and religion. The constant peril posed to the rule of law is drawn in the images of burning slums and crowd violence. Blood-splattered panels, and the drawings of evil villains voicing their poisonous plans, bring the reader face to face with the elemental meaning of lawlessness. When Doga annihilates the outlaws, he acts to rehabilitate the hegemony of law, to rescue state authority from the damage inflicted by its agents. From his actions, it is clear that the legitimacy of the liberal-democratic order depends on the probity of its functionaries. Even the superhero is not exempt from accountability.

Mumbai's society is diverse, consisting of different classes, religious communities, and neighborhoods, but it has no foundational structure, no primordial ties of kin, caste, or religion. It is a delicate mix, a "fine balance" between Hindus and Muslims, the rich and the poor, state power and ordinary citizens. The thread that holds together Mumbai's disparate social, cultural, and political fabric is the everyday practice of human interactions. But criminals, crooked politicians, and communal rioters threaten this slender thread. They hatch conspiracies every minute to achieve their nefarious aims. Mumbai teeters under this pressure, struggling to maintain itself as a just and democratic city of law. Injustice runs riot while the law stands corroded and paralyzed. Hoodlums go on the rampage, thrashing law-abiding citizens. So anonymous are social relations in the big city that bystanders do not intervene to stop the violence, and nor do the police. The comic book presents *Bombay Dying* from the point of view of the street. For it is there that injustice and violence threaten the very essence of the urban order. Fortunately, Doga is there, standing with the people and delivering street justice to restore the urban legal order.

9
DREAMWORLDS

"Haay Haay Haay Haay . . ."

On the pavement by the sea, a dark thin man is smacking his blood-spattered naked back with a whip made of rags. People have thrown coins in front of him. This is the first time that Neel has seen such an original method of earning a livelihood.

Tonight he will reach his shack. Just as a middle-class man's wife greets him with a cup of tea, this man's wife will welcome him by soothing his bloodied back with balm. He never found work as a load carrier or as a security guard. Never learnt to mend shoes, broken umbrellas, or sing with his harmonium on the local train. Never acquired the skill to pick pockets, to snatch purses and chains. He could not even manage to get hold of two-dozen bananas in a broken basket. He and his family reeled with hunger. So, he made a whip out of his torn shirt and started beating his back. After a few hours, when blood started spluttering, a pious woman threw him a five-rupee bill. Why has the President not awarded this ingenious man with a prize for India's greatest scientific invention?[1]

This is a scene from a Hindi novel about two men from North India, Neel and Bhola, who meet on a train on their way to Mumbai to seek their fortunes. "I am going to Mumbai to earn a hundred thousand rupees in two years," Bhola announces soon after making Neel's acquaintance. His plan is to land a job as a security guard in an apartment building, like many of his North Indian compatriots. Neel has set his sights higher. After all, unlike the aspiring security guard, he is educated. With his fledgling academic career in Delhi having gone up in smoke because of an affair with his PhD adviser's niece, he is in the city to make a new beginning. Money and success will come easily in Mumbai for a man of his education and youthful good looks, he has been told. In spite of the difference in class and education, Neel feels a strange closeness to the simple and generous-hearted Bhola and is happy to take him around the city that he knows from a guidebook.

Both Neel and Bhola have landed in Mumbai, drawn by its fabled opportunities. It is another matter that one will become a gigolo and the other will join the underworld. Upon arrival, they take in the tourist attractions. The sights live up to their fabulous image of the city. As they gaze upon the city from the windows of Naaz Restaurant on Hanging Gardens in Malabar Hill, the clustered towers on Cuffe Parade, then Express Tower, then the Air India building, and finally the string of buildings on Marine Drive sweeping into Chowpatty come into view. The sight of the limitless expanse of the Arabian Sea is entrancing. Waves crash into the seawall, turning into foam, then transforming back into a lacework of water drops. The crimson rays of the setting sun are reflected on the surface of the water. Neel is witness to Mumbai's doubly colonized history—the colonization of nature by culture and its formation through the British territorial conquest.[2] The fables spun by this doubly colonized history are embodied in the structures spread out before his eyes. But what are the stories hidden in this fabled city by the sea?

Neel finds the answer at the Gateway of India, an area that was witness to a furious symbolic contest to claim the city. Standing tall by the sea is the Gateway, built in 1923 to monumentalize the visit of the Prince of Wales. Nearby is the colossal statue of Shivaji on a horse, contesting the British claim to ownership of Mumbai. The immigrant duo does not notice the Maratha warrior. Instead, their eyes are drawn across the road to the opulent Taj Mahal Hotel, a tribute to the pride and wealth of its Parsi founder, Jamsetji Tata. Bhola knows the story that Tata built it when he was refused entry into a British-owned hotel. Neel patiently answers his uneducated companion's questions about the Taj and discusses its architectural merits in comparison with the Intercontinental Hotel. The thin dark man whipping his body breaks their reverie. His bloodied back wins the symbolic contest over the city. Barely a day in his new home, Neel grasps that hidden in Mumbai's fabulous history are stories of its legendary spirit of survival. You duck and weave, grab opportunities, licit and illicit, to survive. And when all else fails, you turn to your own body, whip it bloody, or become a gigolo, as Neel does, in exchange for a few coins.

Neel's life in Mumbai speaks to the essence of the city's fabled history. It evokes both its alluring promise and the mythic struggles of immigrants to survive and forge the modern city *as* society. Excess characterizes Mumbai—excesses of power and ambition, of profiteering and exploitation, of aspirations for justice and equality in the face of terrible injustice and inequality. It is, as Suketu Mehta says, a "maximum city." How could it not be? Consider its forging as a thriving metropolis out of seven islets. Power, ambition, fantasy, and violence—all had to be enlisted on an extraordinary scale. Its stories contain a surfeit of dreams and nightmares, lofty aspirations of cosmopolitan openness and violent nativist and communal passions. These are what pulsate Mumbai with energy and dynamism.

Mumbai grows unabated, a megacity devouring mangroves, swallowing the graceful line of bungalows, covering the landscape with apartment towers and shantytowns, and enveloping it all in its polluted air. The infrastructure creaks under the growing population pressure. The city appears out of control, its urbanism splintered by nativism and communalism. Where the aging Bal Thackeray and the Shiv Sena have lost some of their roar, Thackeray's nephew, Raj Thackeray, has picked up the slack. His Maharashtra Navnirman Sena (MNS) has grown from strength to strength, eating into the support of the Shiv Sena from which he broke away. A cartoonist like his uncle, Raj Thackeray rides the tiger of populist politics by targeting North Indian immigrants. These contemporary excesses produce despair and pronouncements of the city's death. But as Gillian Tindall reminds us, Mumbai's problems are due not to its weakness and decline but to its strength and dynamism.[3] The city's troubles mount because Mumbai continues to draw people by its promise.

VISION MUMBAI

If mounting problems produce despair, they also generate grand visions. A new vision for Mumbai appeared in 2003. It was based on a study conducted by McKinsey and Company for Bombay First, a nongovernmental organization of business leaders. Carried out in cooperation with the relevant government bodies, the study published a report entitled *Vision Mumbai: Transforming Mumbai into a World-Class City*. The consultants developed a database and framework for "benchmarking Mumbai" and for the "calibration" of its performance under different parameters along a spectrum—from "poor" to "average" to "above average" to "finally world class." In McKinsey's judgment, the city's slipping economic growth and quality of life placed it at the lower end of the range on a number of categories. Its recommendation? A change in Mumbai's "mind-set." Instead of the timid attempts at "incremental improvement and de-bottlenecking," it advocated bold "step jumps."[4]

The Maharashtra government promptly succumbed to the seductive vision of Mumbai's rise to "world-class" status. The chief minister appointed a task force composed of senior government officials and Bombay First's representative, which endorsed the "world-class" aspiration. Enumerating the city's woes, it painted a picture of Mumbai hovering "perpetually on the brink of collapse, with its swelling population, deteriorating environment, income disparities and lack of funds." The city risked "entering the graveyard of failed cities" unless it took command of its future. Fortunately, there was hope. It recommended seizing the potential presented by globalization for increased trade and "the transfer across geographies of investment, technology and talent" and proposed a ten-year strategic plan to improve governance, accelerate economic growth, construct affordable housing, and develop infrastructure. If financed by a $40 billion investment and fast-tracked by a series of "quick wins" to secure public support, the plan would turn Mumbai into a world-class city by 2013. "The world is watching. Mumbai is waiting."[5]

Here it is once again, an enticing planned vision of the future city. However, unlike the modernist twin-city project, this initiative comes not from architects and urban planners but from business leaders and a global consultancy firm. Echoing the ascendancy of the market-based ideology, the proposal advocates a "public-private" partnership, rather than a public undertaking. The market orientation is particularly visible in its proposals for private capital-based slum rehabilitation. Unfairly holding slums responsible for bottling up Mumbai's growth, the document recommends offering builders incentives to construct towers to house the slum dwellers. Particular attention is showered on Dharavi—"Asia's largest slum"—three sectors of which are to be cleared and developed as office and commercial space. With its proximity to the corporate Bandra-Kurla complex, Dharavi is a real estate El Dorado, prompting attempts to drive away slum dwellers. The city beautiful can be built only by chasing away the poor with the help of the market, supplemented by evictions and demolitions that miraculously followed the unveiling of "Vision Mumbai." Several critics charge that the "world-class city" is a dream sold to facilitate the corporate takeover of the city's future.[6]

The "Vision Mumbai" focus on housing is no accident. Over sixty percent of Mumbai's population lives in slums. The density of the city's population is 29,000 per square kilometer, the highest in the world—compared with 13,000 in Shanghai, 10,000 in New York City, and 5,000 in London. Break it down further, and the figure for the densest Mumbai ward climbs to over 100,000. The colonial state had resorted to the ruse of a housing shortage to launch the Backbay reclamation, a ploy that was used by the postcolonial government in the 1960s to push for further seizure of land from the sea. The aspiration to become a world-class city returned to this tried-and-tested tactic in proposing slum rehabilitation. Builders enthusiastically endorsed the move. Why would they not? The Dharavi Rehabilitation Project is a gold mine for them. As a newspaper comment points out: "Builders get 535 acres of prime land, in return for providing free housing to 52,000 families—plus hospitals, schools, international craft villages, peace parks, art galleries, an experimental theatre and a cricket museum!" But since each "apartment" measures only 21 square meters, and the minimum distance between two buildings is only 5 meters, there will be 1.8 million square meters that the builders may sell in the commercial market. Furthermore, the government has granted an unprecedented floor space index of 4.1—as opposed to the standard 1.3—to attract developers. "No wonder the sharks can't wait to bite. And with Rs 2,700 crore [*$574 million*] expected to land in the official kitty, neither can the state government."[7]

COUNTERDREAMS

Since the start of the building boom of the early 1990s, the real estate industry has aggressively sold the dream of owning a home. Glossy brochures and colorful advertisements promise richly appointed apartments equipped with the latest appliances and housed in exotically named residential complexes boasting lush green lawns and recreation facilities. Meanwhile, the developers and the government entice displaced slum dwellers with offers of marginally larger living spaces in modern towers equipped with plumbing and electricity.

Urban activists have criticized the serious shortcomings of the private capital-led makeover dreams of the city. A compelling critique also emerges in the works of Meera Devidayal, a Mumbai artist. What is different about her commentary is that it engages with the dream of a home at the level of its image. Devidayal began by collecting images circulated by newspapers and brochures from property developers. People were "being bombarded with the marketing of dreams by the media, by banks offering easy home loans, by developers offering everything from free vastu consultation [supposedly from the ancient science of construction] to British governesses."[8] Her 2003 "Dream Home" exhibition responds to the fantasies spun by real estate entrepreneurs. In canvas after canvas, Devidayal brings into view the repressed desires of the dream home. *Gold Valley* presents a lifeless, gray tenement building superimposed on a lush green landscape that is watered by a stream. The fantasy of luxuriant nature, the "Way to Gold Valley," as the sign reads at the bottom of the painting, crashes against the incongruous bleak reality of the square, cagelike tenement rooms. Through the windows, we see nature mapped as numbered property lots.

Her *Luxurious 1,2&3 BHK Flats* is dominated by the image of a blueprint of an apartment building elevation drawing (see plate 11). The bright red tulips at the bottom suggest the dream home stored in the image. Running through the smooth surface and neat lines of the elevation is a brick crack, the trace of a demolished structure. Together with the antique lamp shade on the upper left, the crack envisions or visualizes what is hidden by the blueprint, what the new will reduce to rubble.

With an ingenious superimposition of architectural drawing over the painted surface of the canvas, Devidayal suggests the complicity of architecture in the destruction of life's rich texture. Unmindful of the concrete experience of home, the real estate industry forges ahead by reducing it to the abstract space represented by geometric lines.

But are the experience and meaning of home in an immigrant city like Mumbai reducible to owning a dwelling? Feeling at home in the impersonal metropolis is always a challenge. This is even more so for immigrants in Mumbai. Because of their precarious livelihood in the city, they have traditionally maintained ties with their native places. Mumbai is just a *mahanagari*, a metropolis that poor immigrants endure to earn a living. They may live two or three generations in slums, but home is still the village or the small town they came from. Belonging is a complex emotion for those who struggle to survive amid daily injustices.

Muzaffar Ali's 1978 Hindi film *Gaman* (Departure) offers a haunting perspective on the meaning of home for immigrant taxi drivers in Mumbai. We see the city from the point of view of Ghulam, a Muslim who leaves his North Indian village after the family is cheated out of its land by the landlord. Leaving behind his ailing mother and wife, he lands at the door of Lallu, a taxi driver, who is his friend from the village. Lallu warmly welcomes Ghulam, offers him some space in his shack, and then takes him on a ride to the city's tourist attractions. Much like Neel and Bhola, they go to the Gateway, the Taj, and other sights. When Ghulam expresses his awe at Bombay's grandeur, his friend remarks that it is grand outside but rotten inside. We are warned that things are not what they seem in the city. Sure enough, when the suburban train suddenly stops because someone has died under the tracks, a passenger remarks: "Why did he die under the train? The delay is costing me money! Just drag the carcass out. Why waste time?" When Ghulam expresses shock at this indifference, his friend says: "Give it time, you will also become indifferent."

Ghulam does not become indifferent, but we see an impersonal city emerge through his eyes. Taxi drivers eke out a miserable living and suffer humiliations inflicted by haughty passengers and heavy-handed policemen. Lallu's girlfriend's old father, who drove a taxi for thirty years, is now addicted to gasoline fumes. Shots of Marine Drive and Cuffe Parade seen through the taxi window are contrasted with the squalid shantytown in which the cab drivers live. But unlike the superficial and uncaring milieu of the rich, depicted through the conversations of passengers, there is humanity and solidarity in the world of taxi drivers. Lallu not only shares his shack with his friend but also gets him jobs, first as a taxi cleaner and then as a driver. He is Hindu, and Ghulam is Muslim. But religion does not stand between their friendship. Their world is cosmopolitan. Underlying it is not some developed philosophy of cosmopolitanism but a bond formed by village links and the experience of struggling to survive in the stone-hearted city. *Gaman* shares this conception of Mumbai's vernacular cosmopolitanism with Chetan Anand's *Taxi Driver* (1954). But its style is realist, and the tone is melancholy. Unlike *Taxi Driver*'s detached observer's perspective, Ali's film evokes the city through the protagonist's experience and emotions. As Ghulam drives his taxi, lost in the anxiety of gathering enough money to send home for his mother's medical treatment, a song plays in the background:

Seene mein jalan
Aankhon mein toofaan kyon hai?
Is Shahar mein har shakhs pareshaan sa kyon hai?
. . . .
Kya koi nai baat nazar aati hai hum mein?
Aainaa humein dekh ke hairan kyun hai?

[Why] this heartburn
Why these storm-filled eyes?
Why is everyone so troubled in the city?
. . . .
Is there something new about me?
Why is the mirror aghast at the sight of me?

The merciless metropolis, the relentless routine of work, and the loneliness of separation from his wife have changed Ghulam. The cruel city even snatches his friend away when Lallu is killed by the hired goons of his girlfriend's family. They are opposed to their friendship because it threatens their designs on her as a passport to wealth. There is no limit to Bombay's inhumanity. How can Ghulam belong here? In the film's last scene, he goes to the train station to return home. But as the engine blows its whistle, we see Ghulam watching the train leave, his face framed by a row of steel bars. Bombay is not home, but that is where he lives.

What is home, then, for the immigrant taxi drivers? In her series Tum Kab Aaoge (When Will You Come), Devidayal delves into the immigrant taxi driver's imagined home in the city. The city's fleet of yellow and black taxis is manned predominantly by immigrants from North India. Most live and sleep in their taxis; it is their home on wheels. In 2004 stickers entitled "Tum Kab Aaoge" started appearing on these taxis. The images varied, but all of them pictured a pining woman against the background of a lush, green countryside and mountains, with a train engine, truck, or taxi in the foreground (see plate 12). The images, with the captions reading "When Will You Come" or "When Will You Come Home," express the immigrant's nostalgia for home. Uncannily, the question these images pose is also the one that Ghulam hears his wife ask in *Gaman* as he gazes at the green countryside through the door of the train racing toward Bombay. It is a question that his wife will keep asking in her letters throughout his stay in the city.

When she noticed the same question being asked by the image on taxi stickers, Devidayal set off to explore the fantasy homes the immigrants created in their taxis by decorating them with floral and velvet seat covers, miniature shrines, stickers, and other objects. Her paintings are not a journalistic report, nor an anthropological study of the materials she encountered in taxis. Rather, they are a "pictorial take based on a play of signs which morph reality into fantasy, fluidly erasing the boundaries between the two."[9]

Objects in the Mirror Are Closer than They Appear (see plate 13) blurs the boundaries between reality and fantasy while insisting on their difference. The swans gliding through pristine waters, seen through the windshield, spill inside the taxi, appearing as a reflection on the dashboard, invading the inside world of the vehicle. The caption declares that the dream is closer to the dreamer than we might think, but set against the colorful yet tranquil image of swans is the darkened silhouette of the taxi driver, who watches them as images on a screen. The taxi driver's figure is dislocated from the ground. You cannot place him in the dreamy image on the windshield. He views the swan scene as a movie, sitting in a darkened theater, retaining his separation from the dreamscape on the screen. This point is stressed by the picture of the woman to the left, who stands in the doorway against a black background, her face half covered by shadows. Serving as a reminder of what the taxi driver has left behind, her image suggests that the taxi is not his home; he is out of place. In other paintings in the series, the dreamworld seeps into the taxi driver's body, obliterating the distinction between the dreamscape and the dreamer.

But Devidayal does not allow illusion to overwhelm reality. There is always something that breaks the reverie—the cityscape, the conspicuous yellow and black image of the taxi, the steering wheel—and underlines the distinction between fantasy and reality. Her use of mixed media on canvas—paint, photograph, and print—underscores boundaries and distinctions. She unsettles the world the painting depicts by underlining the out-of-place nature of things, by drawing attention to the fantasy, and by her clever use of different materials. Through these methods, her work suggests that the immigrant lives his reality in the city by assembling an imaginary home with objects around him, by putting together a world with irreconcilable things. Viewed against the illusions of home sold by the wily real estate promoters, Devidayal's paintings pay tribute to the inventive survival tactics of Mumbai's lonely taxi drivers.

The portrayal of a resourceful and distinctive style of everyday, popular urbanism can be discerned in Devidayal's paintings. The world she presents in her Where I Live series is far removed from that of the architect and the urban planner. Once again, the theme is a dream home, and her subjects are poor immigrants. She does not romanticize them; nor does she share the reformer's response of recoil and outrage at the sight of their abysmally cramped and desperate living conditions. Devidayal's art represents not "slums" but homes.

Devidayal's compassionate engagement with the imagination of poor migrants, with people living on the edges of survival, is evident in the very medium of her art in Where I Live. Consisting of digitally printed photographs on recycled sheets of galvanized steel, her art incorporates the material of their lived lives, of huts fabricated with used, cast-off objects. The medium captures the "everyday alchemies of Bombay's informal sector" that "turn dross into gold, giving a second life to the broken and redundant objects of daily use."[10] She counteracts the coldness of steel by splashing its surface with color. The result is a work that not only pays tribute to the survival strategies of the poor by using recycled steel but also attributes them with richness and dynamism. Thus, in *Altamount Road* the bright photograph of a film star, affixed on a steel almirah, in striking contrast to the gray corrugated sheet, offers a cheerful portrayal of the poor's patched-together home (see plate 14). The reflected images of the television, the utensils stacked on top and beside the almirah, add a colorful dimension. Devidayal does not romanticize the life of the poor. Her use of different surfaces and the spotlight on dissimilar objects draw attention to the jagged world assembled by the poor while also recognizing their creativity and desires. The portrait that emerges is of an urbanism that turns necessity into opportunity, an imagination that squeezes color and pleasure from the gray and dreary conditions of the poor in Mumbai.

EVERYDAY TACTICS OF SURVIVAL

The clichéd description of Dharavi as "Asia's largest slum" depicts the 175-hectare tract, housing eight hundred thousand people, as a place of misery and oppression. In the corporate and middle-class visions of Dharavi, it is an obstacle in Mumbai's path to achieving a "world-class" status. It is for this reason that many critics in India accuse the Oscar-winning film *Slumdog Millionaire* of portraying Mumbai in a bad light. For them, the film is one more example of the West's obsession with poverty and wretchedness when it comes to representing India. In fact, the critics share with the film the vision of Dharavi as an abject slum, rather than a place where the poor live and work with imagination and enterprise.

Prior to the late nineteenth century, Dharavi was a swamp inhabited by the Koli fishing community. Fishing died out as the swamp was filled. Poor migrants moved in from different parts of India, making the land habitable. Their resourcefulness transformed Dharavi into a flourishing economy. The eighteen-year-old Shamsuddin, for example, traveled all the way from Tamil Nadu to Dharavi in 1948, looking for work.[11] He worked initially in his uncle's rice-smuggling business, transporting the grain from the outskirts to the city to sell it at nearly ten times the original price. The rice business ended after a few years when his uncle moved back to the village and the cousins migrated to Pakistan. Shamsuddin survived by working first for a coal company and then at a printing press. He got married, and the couple moved into a ten-by-ten room in a "settled chawl" in 1961. A little later, Hamid, a man from his native village, arrived in Dharavi and made him a proposition. "Give me space and I'll make chiki [sesame brittle]." Shamsuddin procured him a shack and went from shop to shop selling chiki and other snacks. When Hamid moved away to Calcutta, Shamsuddin and his wife took over the business. They learned how to make chi-ki, which he sold in cinemas every day, returning home late at night. They packaged it and named their product "A-1 ckiki." It grew into a successful business employing twenty workers, who lived in the two-room chiki factory's loft.

Shamsuddin's story is not exceptional. Dharavi is full of such tales of migrants making a go of their lives. Their ingenuity and spirit have transformed Dharavi into a thriving economy amid poverty and squalor. Seen through the jaundiced eyes of the middle-class re-former, the city is full of only claustrophobic density, fetid drains, garbage, and ugliness. But if you open yourself to observing the drive, the enterprise, and the spirit of survival amid the incredibly wretched physical conditions, you cannot help but be uplifted. Rare-ly do you see idleness and despair associated with this "slum." From the establishments manufacturing leather goods for export and sell-ing knockoffs of designer brands on the main street to artisanal es-tablishments in the tight inner lanes, the picture is one of pulsating energy. Recycling is a way of life and livelihood.

Dharavi is an economic success story. It has developed without any public state subsidy or assistance. Illegality thrives and is vis-ible. Until police pressure chased him out to Tamilnadu in the mid-1980s, the notorious underworld don Vardarajan Mudaliar used to distill and distribute illicit liquor from his operating base in Dharavi. Today, although all kinds of illegal activities are openly carried out in the area, it is not infested with crime and violence, as the popu-lar middle-class stereotype insinuates. Rather, Dharavi is a zone of booming free enterprise and a tribute to the ingenuity and hard work of the migrants, who come from everywhere in India (see plate 15). Tanners from Tamil Nadu, leatherworkers and artisans from Uttar Pradesh, potters from Gujarat, and migrants from Maharashtra, Rajasthan, Bihar, and elsewhere work in Dharavi's amazing variety of trades, legal and illegal. Every religion is represented. Hindus, Muslims, and Christians coexist despite bouts of communal violence. Every linguistic group is present, but the language on the street is the mongrel tongue Bambaiya. A mix of all the regions from which people come, Dharavi is "allah ka gaon [God's village]," says Khatija, the old Muslim woman who migrated from Kerala decades ago.[12] It is a cosmopolitan mix brought together by *dhandha*—business deals, clean and shady. Dharavi is pure Mumbai.

"No master plan, urban design, zoning ordinance, construction law or expert knowledge can claim any stake in the prosperity of Dharavi."[13] Though far from perfect, it represents a form of urbanism characteristic of what architect Rahul Mehrotra calls the "kinetic city." He distinguishes the kinetic city from the static city, which is composed of architecture and monuments built with permanent materials. The kinetic city represents the city of motion—"the kutcha city, built of temporary material"; it is temporal, a city in "constant flux."[14] In the apparent chaos of narrow streets crowded with people disgorged by suburban trains, in the constant making and remaking out of recycled materials in Dharavi, in the vital pulsating energy of the informal economy, in the exuberance and spectacle of wedding processions on the street, and in the multiple uses of space, he finds a dynamic urbanism. The vibrant urbanism of the kutcha city shares urban space with the static urbanism of the "pucca" (permanent, stable) city, colliding with it, provoking its wrath. The slum rehabilitation projects represent attempts to displace the kinetic city, to expunge its existence, and to order Mumbai to the dull discipline of the static city—to the delight of real estate magnates and the middle-class heritage activists. Fortunately, the kinetic city survives in Dharavi; Mumbai's legendary everyday tactic of survival with wit and enterprise stubbornly persists under the looming shadow of the bulldozers of "development."

Mehrotra's "kinetic city" is a city of layers, with multiple and successive historical slices of Mumbai coexisting in the same time and space. Henri Lefebvre wrote that urban space has a structure more like that of "flaky pastry" than like the homogeneous and isotropic space of classical mathematics.[15] This is true as much of the so-called bounded places of the cities of an earlier time as it is of the new urban constellations of shopping malls and the displaced poor.

You can get a vivid sense of this layered history in Chor Bazaar (Thieves' Market), the city's flea market. The place has intrigued me from the very first time I set eyes on it a few years ago. Since then, I have returned several times to the dense maze of shops that are located between Sardar Patel Road and Grant Road. As you traverse the narrow lanes packed tight with vendors and stores selling a bewildering array of goods—genuine antiques and knockoffs, old coins, furniture, hardware, automotive parts, records, Hollywood and Bollywood film posters and lobby cards, shoes, clothes, and just plain junk—it becomes clear that this is no ordinary flea market. An extraordinary history is on display here. The objects on sale and the people who sell them embody the heritage of Mumbai's urban life. Yes, it is a market, but the trade in the debris of commodities of modern life here tells stories about the city. To make sense of these narratives, I had to begin with the name.

"Let me tell you how Chor Bazaar got its name," said Zafar Bhai, the owner of Jubilee Decorators, a shop selling antique furniture and decorative objects in Mumbai's legendary market. The owner of another furniture shop introduced me to Zafar Bhai as an old-timer, as someone who knows and has lived through Chor Bazaar's history. One look at this man in his seventies with his courtly manners, and you knew that there was something terribly odd and inappropriate about the bazaar's name. The soft cadence of his elegant North Indian Hindustani language spoke of a sophisticated urbanity, not devilish thievery. But he good-humouredly accepted Chor Bazaar as the name for the market where he earns an honest living.

"You see, the name goes back to the time when the Gateway of India was built, when Queen Victoria visited Bombay." He continued with a tale about a theft. "When her ship docked, she discovered that her violin was missing." It was the queen who ordered that the market be rechristened Chor Bazaar after the stolen violin was found on sale on Mutton Street. "This is how the place got its name."

Of course, Queen Victoria never set foot in Bombay. The Gateway was built to commemorate the visit of the Prince of Wales in 1911 and was completed only in 1924. I did not point out these inaccuracies. To be sure, the story is apocryphal, and yet it contains a representation of the past, one that is very different from that which appears in the archives. Like the bazaar, which exists on the margins of the mainstream markets, this historical representation lurks outside the shadows of disciplinary history. There are no documentary records or commemorative plaques to substantiate this expression of the past; instead, it survives precariously in recycled stories as a faint impression, imperfect and obscure.

Enter the world of this past, and unexpected knowledge greets you. To begin with, let us take the colonial genealogy of the name suggested by the story. Flea markets are not unusual; all across the world one finds places for trade in the debris of modernity. But to my knowledge, nowhere are these places called Chor Bazaar. It is telling that this term was used in colonial cities to name sites for the trade in used goods. Delhi also had one with this name. Such bazaars probably followed the establishment of orderly markets where colonial subjects were expected to act as modern bourgeois consumers. But when commodities sold in the organized and official precincts are used up, they lose the legitimacy conferred by the shine of newness. Faded and worn out, when these artifacts returned from the dead to assume a second life as recycled goods, they probably appeared as illegitimate. To the British, Chor Bazaar must have seemed an appropriate name for a place where Indians (who, in any case, frequently appeared as untrustworthy and dishonest in colonial stereotypes) bought goods to live stolen lives. It is no wonder, then, that Zafar Bhai's story pins responsibility on the British for the naming of the market.

Chor Bazaar probably followed the establishment of Crawford Market and the founding of shopping arcades on D. N. (Hornby) Road during the late nineteenth century, when the city expanded beyond the Fort precincts. The *Gazetteer*, published in 1909, does not mention it, suggesting that the bazaar emerged only in the early decades of the twentieth century. By this time, the cotton mills had expanded, and the city was flush with poor migrants who were employed as mill workers. Its location in an area thoroughly revamped by the City Improvement Trust during the 1910s also suggests that the market made its appearance when Bombay became a thriving industrial city. Zafar Bhai's references to Queen Victoria (or the Prince of Wales) and the construction of the Gateway of India also suggest the same.

The apocryphal story, then, captures something of Mumbai's colonial heritage as a modern industrial city. But it refers to a heritage that is very different from that monumentalized in the parade of Gothic Revival buildings; rather than commemorating the self-representations of British power, it registers the colonial framing of the life cycle of commodities as they changed from their state of glittering newness in shopping arcades and established markets to their condition as old, used debris in Chor Bazaar.

Modernity and debris go hand in hand. As commodity production quickens the pace of life, it also hastens the speed of obsolescence. Not only does it label existing artifacts as traditional and thus outmoded, it quickly renders its own products out of date. Commodity production, aided by advertising, constantly strives to disseminate new styles and fashions, casting away yesterday's goods as old-fashioned, as junk. You can find these outmoded commodities in Chor Bazaar—old mariner's compasses, cuckoo clocks, Art Deco furniture and decorative objects, film memorabilia, and a baffling assortment of other goods. Each object tells you a story of Mumbai's urban life. Take, for example, old jazz records, which you find for sale in specialty stores. Besides telling us about the change in the recording technology and medium, the presence of these records in Chor Bazaar suggests a decline in the appreciation of jazz in Mumbai. Restaurants where jazz was regular fare until the early seventies either no longer exist or have moved on to other musical offerings. With the change in the social world that patronized jazz, the records too have moved on, ending up on the dusty shelves in Chor Bazaar. Look closely at the fusion music of Hindi films and Latin beats, and you will find the lost world of Goan musicians who were in the forefront of Western music in the city until the early seventies. Synthesizers and changes in musical taste in Hindi cinema have rendered this earlier form of musical cosmopolitanism obsolete. Visit the store selling old film magazines, posters, lobby cards, and songbooks, and you become aware of an earlier technology of advertisement, now overtaken by television and computer graphics. The bazaar is a rich archive of such discarded histories (see plate 16).

At first glance, the odd collection of old artifacts in the bazaar appears as just that—odd. But if you examine it carefully, you find that the arbitrariness repositions commodities; it tears them away from their original historical context and places them in a new environment. The unexpected juxtaposition of records and postcards, clocks and curios, posters and furniture, in the bazaar functions like a montage, breaking up the smooth and evolutionary surface of historical representation. You see the city's urban heritage not in a linear fashion but in the heretical arrangement of fragmentary and spatial combinations. History appears jagged and disjointed as your eyes move from old hardware parts to beautiful objects sculpted in glass, from jazz records of the sixties to knockoffs of Art Deco furniture fabricated today. The aura of heritage is broken by the arbitrary collection of commodities.

If the ephemera on sale in Chor Bazaar offer us a heretical archive of Mumbai's commodity life, they also provide glimpses into changes in the fortunes of families. Goods end up here not only when they become obsolete but also when death and disputes break up families. Chor Bazaar is the repository of changed and broken families. Interviews with shop owners suggest that this was particularly the case during the 1940s and the 1950s, when the Partition saw both a flight and an influx of people. Muslim families who moved to Pakistan sold their belongings before seeking a new home in the new country. The fact that most of the Chor Bazaar merchants are Muslim may have eased these transactions. This was also the time when the outward trickle of Europeans began. If there was an outflow of people, there was also an inflow of immigrants, particularly the Sindhis, who made Mumbai their new home. Chor Bazaar became one of the places where these refugees bought furniture sold by departing Muslims. The next two decades witnessed the departure of Parsi families to the UK, Canada, and Australia. Furniture dealers speak of these decades as Chor Bazaar's golden age, when the market was flush with quality goods. Parsis, in particular, were valued as sellers and buyers because of their strong preference for heavy, Victorian furniture. Well preserved, the exquisitely made Burma teak and rosewood furniture, designed in Victorian and modern styles, along with delicate, decorative objects, were bought from Parsis in estate auctions and household sales during the sixties and seventies. Apparently, this was when the market for used goods morphed into a bazaar for antiques.

Antiques emerge only with modernity, when mechanical reproduction deprives objects of their originality and authenticity. Devoid of any original essence and uniqueness, industrially produced goods acquire an aura only when they lose their novelty and are discarded. Then, what the city throws away as junk is recommmodified and assumes its second life as a residue of the past. As representations of a disappeared era, as condensed remainders of an elusive past, antiques do not have use value; they are valued precisely because they are useless. No one actually uses these spittoons, clocks, picture post-cards, and film posters. Even the delicate decorative furnishings you can buy at Zafar Bhai's store are valued as reminders of a bygone era and are used in film sets to evoke the past.

The aura of antiques springs from their value as remembrances, as evocations of style. For this reason, too, one finds copies of antiques in plentiful supply at the bazaar. Both owners and consumers will tell you that there are very few genuine antiques in Chor Bazaar; for those you have to go to expensive dealers elsewhere in the city who can authenticate their collections. In the bazaar, you mostly get knockoffs, which lack the aura of uniqueness and genuine essence. Yet, the bazaar is always crowded with people. While some hunt for that rare thing that they cannot find anywhere else, others eagerly acquire copies of antique furniture and replicas of old gramophones. They are in the market for style. The city is an emporium of styles. While modernity homogenizes urban life, standardizing individuals and their environment, it also creates a strong desire for differentia-tion. Style provides one way to assert individuality. The city is where you find the dandy, who draws attention to his person through fash-ion, flamboyance, and wit. "In the old days," said Zafar Bhai, "a hun-dred rupees bought you a good suit, shoes, and a tie; and with a lit-tle more money, you could throw in a bowler hat as well, and there you were—a proper city man!" Today, one does not see dandies with bowler hats in the city, but one finds Mumbaikars furnishing their lives with both genuine antiques and copies secured from Chor Ba-zaar. Surround yourself with an old gramophone, Victorian and Art Deco furnishings, film memorabilia, and jazz records, and you can rescue yourself from the modern jungle of urban anonymity and as-sert your uniqueness.

Not for nothing, then, does Chor Bazaar stand as the heretical heritage of the city. Existing in the shadows of the mainstream mar-kets and carrying an air of illegitimacy both in its name and in the goods it transacts, the bazaar represents the city's history in junk, memorabilia, antiques, copies, and kitsch. There are no stories of a rise and fall, of glory and decline, but only the debris of Mumbai's modern life. You do not find history memorialized and frozen in a museum here. The remaindered past is alive, active in the present and exerting pressure on it by breathing life into what has been discarded as junk by history.

HISTORICAL ILLUMINATION

I began the journey to Mumbai's past nine years ago to understand the source of my childhood image of the city. As a historian, I was aware that the image did not come out of nowhere but was historically produced and circulated. The examination of this historical process took me to the shards of Bombay's shattered image as a shining, cosmopolitan city. As I turned over this debris, it became clear that what was remaindered was not the city itself but a certain idea of it, a myth that history had produced and that many had lived.

This myth of the modern city was once a powerful, globally influential saga that sustained the worldwide and unequal expansion of capitalism for a century after the 1850s. In Bombay colonialism gave birth to this dreamworld. You cannot walk by the parade of nineteenth-century Gothic buildings without wondering about what the forces of this imperial display sought to suppress and overpower. The mythic life of the industrial city appears in another light as you wend your way through the mill districts and see the textile machinery covered in a film of dust and cobwebs, bringing into view the exploited immigrant laborers and their world. The soaring imagination of the city by the sea on the panoramic Marine Drive provokes thoughts about the history buried beneath. Probe the literary, cinematic, and artistic history of radical and anticolonial imaginations of the cosmopolitan city, and you become aware of its aspirations and limits. Now that the Nanavati case no longer casts the spell that it once did, the meanings of its legal and urban spectacle become clear. Visible is the twilight of Bombay's elitist cosmopolitan culture of the early post-colonial era and its vision of a rationally ordered urban society.

In delving into this history, I did not oppose myths to reality but sought to gain an understanding of their history by revealing what they hid in composing their spell. So, in the destroyed remains of the "tropical Camelot," I found an elitism that the Shiv Sena seized on to install the populist mobilization of the "Marathi manoos," muscling out a flawed but radical challenge to capitalist modernity. In this process, the Sena also defeated the aspirations that had inspired the writers and intellectuals in Bombay in the 1940s, until nationalism and Partition forced them on the defensive. Traces of their utopian hopes, now turned to dust, are mixed with the ruins of the elitist visions of cosmopolitan Bombay. So too are the aspirations of the modernist urban plans for the failed twin-city project of Navi Mumbai in the soaring towers of Nariman Point. Examine them without the spell they cast in their own time, and you encounter the political structure that permitted the planners to dream big and that also cut it down to size.

In the city wracked by assaults on the ideal of the liberal state, by crime and corruption, Doga stands on the cusp of the old and the new. The superhero inhabits a city of lawless urbanism and dispenses street justice, but he aspires only to restoring a lawful society. He still believes in the modernist ideal of the city that the others have demolished. While he seeks to restore the dead to life, the state and private capital conjure up dreams of a "world-class city" out of the ruins. In the process, they threaten to cast off "slums," the ingenuous urbanism fabricated with discarded and everyday objects, to freeze the "kinetic city," to render it obsolete. This vision rests on the idea of successive historical change from one phase to another, from Bombay to Mumbai, from "poor" city to "world-class" city. But as the historical journey shows, the people and imaginations declared out of joint and discarded contain sources for a critical understanding of the present. Just as you can dig into Marine Drive's history and find that the buried remains critically illuminate the fantasies spun by industrial modernity, the bricks appearing through the crack on the surface of the blueprint in Devidayal's *Luxurious 1,2&3 BHK Flats* take the sheen off the real estate dreamscape. Note the heretical heritage revealed by the objects in Chor Bazaar.

In Mumbai, history is not easily superseded and assigned to the museum. Even cosmopolitanism, though damaged by the communal riots of 1992–93 and officially declared dead by the renaming of Bombay as Mumbai, survives as a powerful memory and an aspiration. On the streets and in everyday life, you can observe the living presence of the city's history as a place of interactions between different communities, languages, and religions, even if this practice does not ascend to an Olympian philosophy of life.

Consider the comtemporary artist Atul Dodiya's *Bombay Buccaneer* (plate 17). The self-portrait assembles multiple fragments that share no organic connection but depend on artifice and imagination. A poster of the Hindi film *Baazigar* (1993) is its formal inspiration. In the original, the images of two female protagonists are mirrored in the sunglasses worn by the film's psychopathic antihero. *Bombay Buccaneer* replaces them with the reflections of the painters David Hockney and Bhupen Khakhar. In place of the menacing antihero, there is an ordinary office worker, collar unbuttoned and tie askew, but armed with a gun. The fixtures of everyday urban life frame the portrait— the open doorway of a suburban train, a metalled roadway, and the ubiquitous yellow and black taxi, broken down. Dodiya intermeshes art and cinema, Indian and Western, pop culture and high art, to brilliantly capture Mumbai's kaleidoscopic urban experience.

Mumbai's everyday practice rejects history written as a linear story and presents it instead as a tapestry of different, overlapping, and contradictory experiences, imaginations, and desires. It is in such a historical survival that I find the living imagination of the city *as* modern society. This renders my childhood mythic image of Bombay more compelling, enriched as it is by the historical examination of its remains.

Acknowledgments

I set foot in Mumbai nearly ten years ago as a challenge to test my childhood image of the mythic city. Contrary to expectations, the confrontation with the actual city did not unravel the myth; instead, the experience served only to heighten my awareness of its richness and compelling power. I decided to explore the history of the mythic city, to collect the stories told and understand how they were composed. It was the generosity of several institutions and individuals that made this exploration possible.

As always, Princeton University has been extremely supportive, providing time and resources to make numerous trips to Mumbai and London for research. Its grant of a sabbatical, supplemented by an award by the National Endowment for the Humanities, enabled me to spend an academic year in Mumbai, completing the research and writing of the book. The visiting fellows to the Shelby Cullom Davis Center for Historical Studies, which I had the privilege to direct from 2003 until 2008, not only cheerfully tolerated my obsession with Bombay but also helped me figure out ways to channel it productively and critically.

One among many joys of working on this book has been the pleasure of encountering the amazing kindness and warmth of people in Mumbai. If the idea that the modern city is a place for forming a human community based on chance encounters and fabricated ties—not prior family and kin links—ever needed confirmation, you will find it in Mumbai. Sally Holkar, whom I had met only once in New York, opened her home to me when I first arrived in the city.

Feroze Chandra and Chandita Mukherjee, old friends from college, insisted that I live with them as long as I wished. For several years, their lovely Colaba flat became my home away from home. Getting to know Naresh Fernandes has been one of the highlights of my experience in the city. It was an incredible blessing to be the beneficiary of his astounding readiness to help in matters both high and low, a deep knowledge of the city, including its history of jazz, and his warm friendship. Shekhar Krishnan's resourcefulness and intimate familiarity with the city, which he offered freely and frequently, were invaluable.

Rahul Mehrotra and Sharada Dwivedi were always ready to share their significant knowledge and work on the urban form of the city. Shirish Patel helped me understand some of the complexities of urban planning in Bombay. Meera Devidayal was extraordinarily generous in discussing her art and allowing me to reproduce some of her remarkable work in the book. Atul Dodiya very kindly and promptly gave me permission to use his exceptional painting *Bombay Buccaneer* as a cover image. Vivek Menezes's enthusiasm for seeing Mario Miranda's cartoons as art persuaded me to look at his work with a different eye. It was due to Nancy Adajania's initiative that Muzaffar Ali magnanimously sent me a copy of his film *Gaman*. I will remain forever grateful to Vikram Doctor for introducing me to the comic-book hero Doga. Vivek Mohan and Sanjay Gupta of Raj Comics kindly shared their experiences of creating the Doga character, and Manish Gupta unhesitatingly allowed me to use images from the comic book.

Zainab Bawa provided valuable research assistance, including helping me to navigate the world of Chor Bazaar. I am thankful to Com. Amberkar and Sarojini Desai for talking with me and re-creating the world of Krishna Desai. Many others in Mumbai provided help and advice: Arvind and Meera Adarkar, Vidhu Vinod and Anu Chopra, Darryl D'Monte, Mariam Dossal, Rupali Gupte, Anurag

Kashyap, Saeed Mirza, Deepak Rao, Kundan Shah, Prasad Shetty, and Rohan Sippy.

Meeting Philip Knightley in London at a very early stage of my research proved to be extremely helpful. I learned a great deal from his firsthand account of the city in the 1960s, told from the acutely observant journalist's point of view. Also in London, Ian Jack was kind enough to take time out from his busy schedule of editing *Granta* to talk to me about my project and his time as a journalist in Bombay. I am thankful to Homi Bhabha for sharing his memories of growing up in the city, offering his characteristically sharp perceptions of its pleasures and disappointments. Arjun Appadurai, who also grew up in the city, and established Partners for Urban Knowledge, Action, and Research (PUKAR) as a uniquely innovative organization for urban research, was generous with ideas and suggestions. Carol Breckenridge, who sadly passed away in 2009, was unfailingly stimulative with her out-of-the-box thoughts. Several colleagues and friends have read the manuscript in its different stages and made perceptive comments. These include Janaki Bakhle, Feroze Chandra, Naresh Fernandes, Michael Gordin, Molly Greene, Bill Jordan, Stephen Kotkin, Shekhar Krishnan, Mark Mazower, Ranjani Mazumdar, Ninad Pandit, and Ravi Sundaram.

I am deeply grateful to Brigitta van Rheinberg at Princeton University Press and Saugata Mukherjee at HarperCollins, India, for their enthusiasm for the book. Brigitta read the manuscript line by line and made all the right suggestions to improve it, and collaborated with me about the book's design and illustrations. I have nothing but praise for the entire production staff of Princeton University Press—Clara Platter, Sara Lerner, and Dalia Geffen. Tsering Wangyal Shawa at Princeton University spent hours working to draw maps. Michael Alexander helped to make the historical maps legible. Indra Gill worked painstakingly to improve the quality of the illustrations.

This book would not exist without the love and support of Aruna, my wife. She has lived with it as long as I have and has shared the pleasures and setbacks of my research and writing. She read the manuscript countless times, asking searching questions about the stories I wanted to tell and making vital suggestions on how to tell them. If the book is at all readable, it is largely due to her. It is to Aruna that this book is dedicated with love.

Notes

CHAPTER 1. THE MYTHIC CITY

1. Mss. Eur. C.285, Oriental and Indian Office Library and Records (OIOLR), British Library (BL).

2. Jonathan Raban, *Soft City* (London: Harvill Press, 1974), 4.

3. See, for example, his *Crazy Bombay* (Bombay: Popular Prakashan, 1991), a collection of his articles in English and translations of essays originally written in Marathi.

4. Philip Knightley, *A Hacker's Progress* (London: Vintage, 1996), 83–97.

5. Author's interview with Philip Knightley, London, June 2005.

6. Allen V. Ross, *Bombay after Dark* (New York: Macfadden-Bartell, 1971), 25, 50.

7. Captain F. D. Colaabavala, *Bombay by Night* (Bombay: Hind Pocket Books, 1977), 18.

8. "Protima's Naked Run," http://www.hindustantimes.com/news/specials/proj_tabloid/protimastory.shtml (accessed July 10, 2009).

9. See Ranjit Hoskote, "The Complicit Observer: Reflections on the Art of Sudhir Patwardhan," in his *Sudhir Patwardhan: The Complicit Observer* (Mumbai: Popular Prakashan, 2010), 7–39. See the color plates *Riot*, 107, and *Lower Parel*, 128–29.

10. Of the recent spate of novels, the two that are most acclaimed are Gregory David Roberts's *Shantaram* (London: Little, Brown, 2003) and Vikram Chandra's *Sacred Games* (London: Faber and Faber, 2006), both nine-hundred-plus pages of gangster epics.

11. Suketu Mehta, Maximum City (New York: Alfred A. Knopf, 2004).

12. Darryl D'Monte and Priyanka Kakodkar, "Bye-Bye, B'Bay?" *Outlook*, February 4, 2002.

13. Ibid., 38.

14. Rohinton Mistry, *Family Matters* (New York: Alfred A. Knopf, 2002), 263–64.

15. *Museebat mein Bambai* (Bombay: Krunal Music Company, 2005).

16. The information on bomb blasts, here and below, is compiled from the *Times of India, Bombay Mirror, Asian Age,* and *Indian Express*, July 12–18, 2006.

17. United Nations Population Division, *World Urbanization Prospects: The 2001 Revision* (New York: United Nations Publications, 2002), 1.

18. Mehta, *Maximum City*, 3.

19. Mike Davis, *Planet of Slums* (New York: Verso, 2006).

20. David Harvey, *The Condition of Postmodernity: An Enquiry into the Origins of Cultural Change* (Oxford: Blackwell, 1989).

21. Ravi Sundaram, *Pirate Modernity: Delhi's Media Urbanism* (London: Routledge, 2009).

22. Arjun Appadurai and James Holston, "Introduction: Cities and Citizenship," in *Cities and Citizenship*, ed. James Holston (Durham: Duke University Press, 1999), 1–20.

23. Partha Chatterjee, *The Politics of the Governed: Reflections on Popular Politics in Most of the World* (New York: Columbia University Press, 2004).

24. Paul Virilio, *The Lost Dimension,* trans. Daniel Moshenberg (Paris: Semiotext[e], 1991).

25. Rem Koolhaas, "Postscript: Introduction for New Research 'the Contemporary City,'" *Architecture and Urbanism* 217 (October 1988), reprinted in *Theorizing a New Agenda for Architecture*, ed. Kate Nesbitt (New York: Princeton Architectural Press, 1996), 325.

26. Rem Koolhaas and Bruce Mau, *S,M,L,XL* (New York: Monacelli Press, 1995).

27. On Walter Benjamin's method of urban archaeology, see his Berlin essays in *Walter Benjamin: Selected Writings*, vol. 2, pt. 2, ed. Michael Jennings (Cambridge, Mass.: Belknap Press of Harvard University Press, 1999), 595–637, and *Walter Benjamin: Selected Writings*, vol. 3, ed. Michael Jennings (Cambridge, Mass.: Belknap Press of Harvard University Press, 2002), 344–413. I have benefited from Graeme Gilloch's insightful discussion of the concept in his *Myth and Metropolis: Walter Benjamin and the City* (Cambridge: Polity Press, 1996), 70–78.

CHAPTER 2. THE COLONIAL GOTHIC

1. The epigraph by Namdeo Dhasal, "Mumbai, Mumbai My Dear Slut," trans. Vidyut [Bhagwat] and Sharmila, is in "Bombay in Dalit Literature," by Vidyut Bhagwat, in *Bombay: Mosaic of Modern Culture,* ed. Sujata Patel and Alice Thorner (Delhi: Oxford University Press, 1995), 123.

2. Gerson da Cunha, "The Origin of Bombay," *The Journal of the Bombay Branch of the Royal Asiatic Society*, extra number (1900): 83.

3. Cited ibid., 109.

4. Ibid., 116–19; S. M. Edwardes, *Gazetteer of Bombay City and Island* (Bombay: Times Press, 1909), 2:40–41.

5. The following account comes from *Oriente Conquistado a Jesus Christo* and is cited in Cunha, "Origin of Bombay," 151–53.

6. See Christine Dobbin, *Urban Leadership in Western India* (London: Oxford University Press, 1972), ch. 1, for details on Bombay's merchant communities.

7. Amar Farooqui, *Opium City: The Making of Early Victorian Bombay* (Delhi: Three Essays Collective, 2006).

8. John F. Richards, "The Opium Industry in India," *Indian Economic and Social History Review* 39, nos. 2–3 (2002): 168.

9. Pamela Nightingale, *Trade and Empire in Western India* (Cambridge: Cambridge University Press, 1970), 17–22.

10. D. F. Karaka, *History of the Parsis Including Their Manners, Customs, Religion, and Present Position* (London: Macmillan, 1884; repr., Bombay: Indigo, 2002), 2:57.

11. What follows is drawn from Jehangir R. P. Mody, *Jamsetjee Jejeebhoy: The First Indian Knight and Baronet (1783–1859)* (Bombay: RMDC Press, 1959); Karaka, *History of the Parsis* 2:78–88; Farooqui, *Opium City*; Asiya Siddiqi, "The Business World of Jamsetjee Jejeebhoy," *Indian Economic and Social History Review* 19, nos. 3–4 (1982): 302–24; and Christine Dobbin, *Asian Entrepreneurial Minorities* (Richmond, Surrey: Curzon Press, 1996), ch. 4.

12. Mody, *Jamsetjee Jejeebhoy*, 28.

13. Farooqui, *Opium City*, 57.

14. Siddiqi, "Business World of Jamsetjee Jejeebhoy," 307–8.

15. Cited in Edwardes, *Gazetteer of Bombay City* 2:163.

16. Ibid.

17. Dinshaw Wacha, *Premchund Roychund: His Early Life and Career*, 99, cited in Teresa Albuquerque, *Urbs Prima in Indis: An Epoch in the History of Bombay, 1840–1865* (New Delhi: Promilla, 1985), 17.

18. Albuquerque, *Urbs Prima in Indis*, 18.

19. Wacha, *Premchund Roychund*, 137, cited ibid., 19.

20. Raj Chandavarkar, *The Origins of Industrial Capitalism in India* (Cambridge: Cambridge University Press, 1994), 65.

21. Ibid., 250.

22. Ibid., 241–44.

23. Ibid., 128–29.

24. Ibid., 105.

25. Meera Kosambi, *Bombay in Transition: The Growth and Social Ecology of a Colonial City, 1880–1980* (Stockholm: Almqvist & Wiksell International, 1986), 55–56.

26. Ibid., 59.

27. Ibid., 60.

28. Ibid.

29. Cited in Edwardes, *Gazetteer of Bombay City* 1:66.

30. Ibid. 2:170.

31. Ibid. 1:68–69; 2:170.

32. Sharada Dwivedi and Rahul Mehrotra, *Bombay: The Cities Within*, 2nd ed. (Bombay: Eminence Designs Private Ltd., 2001), 92.

33. Christopher W. London, *Bombay Gothic* (Mumbai: India Book House Publishing Limited, 2002), 28.

34. For a full description of these Gothic buildings and their history, see ibid.

35. Ibid., 90–92.

36. See David Harvey, *Paris: Capital of Modernity* (New York: Routledge, 2003), and Carl E. Schorske, *Fin-de-Siècle Vienna: Politics and Culture* (New York: Vintage, 1981).

37. G. W. Stevens, "All India in Miniature," in *The Charm of Bombay: An Anthology of Writing in Praise of the First City in India,* ed. R. P. Karkaria (Bombay: D. B. Tarporevala & Sons, 1915), 82.

38. Govind Narayan Madgavkar, *Mumbaichi Varnan* (1863); translated as *Govind Narayan's Mumbai: An Urban Biography from 1863*, trans. Murali Ranganathan (London: Anthem Press, 2007).

39. Ibid., 32–33.

40. Walter Benjamin, "The Paris of Second Empire in Baudelaire," in *Charles Baudelaire: A Lyric Poet in the Era of High Capitalism*, trans. Harry Zohn (London: Verso, 1983), 9–106; *The Arcades Project*, trans. Howard Eiland and Kevin McLaughlin (Cambridge, Mass.: Belknap Press of Harvard University Press, 1999). See also Gilloch, *Myth and Metropolis*; and Anke Gleber, *The Art of Taking a Walk* (Princeton: Princeton University Press, 1999).

41. D. E. Wacha, *Shells from the Sands of Bombay* (Bombay: Bombay Chronicle Press, 1920).

42. D. E. Wacha, *Rise and Growth of Bombay Municipal Government* (Madras: G. A. Natesan, 1913).

43. Wacha, *Shells from the Sands of Bombay*, 558.

44. Ibid., 560–61.

45. Ibid., 566–67.

46. Ibid., 461–84.

47. Ibid., 318.

48. Ibid., 319.

49. What follows is based on Wacha, *Shells from the Sands of Bombay*, 82–93.

50. Henri Lefebvre, *Everyday Life in the Modern World* (New York: Harper and Row, 1971), 21.

51. Madgavkar, *Mumbaichi Varnan*, 7.

52. Ibid., 12.

53. Hari Narayan Apte, *Pan Lakshyat Kon Gheto!* cited in Meera Kosambi's "Marathi Writers," in *Bombay: Mosaic of Modern Culture,* ed. Sujata Patel and Alice Thorner (Delhi: Oxford University Press, 1997), 264.

54. Madgavkar, *Mumbaichi Varnan,* 29.

55. Benjamin, "Paris of the Second Empire," 44. See also Gleber, *Art of Taking a Walk,* 57; and David Frisby, *Cityscapes of Modernity* (Cambridge: Polity, 2001), 52–56.

56. Naoroji M. Dumasia, *A Biographical Sketch of Sardar Mir Abdul Ali, Khan Bahadur, Head of the Detective Police, Bombay* (Bombay: Bombay Gazette Press, 1896).

57. Ibid., pt. 2, p. 1.

58. Dumasia, "The Lady and the Marwaree," ibid., pt. 1, pp. 126–30.

59. Dumasia, "Double Murder at Oomerkhadi," ibid., pt. 1, pp. 188–95.

60. Stevens, *Charm of Bombay,* 82–83.

61. S. M. Edwardes, *By-Ways of Bombay* (Bombay: Times of India Office, 1912), 6–7.

62. Ibid., 9.

63. Ibid., 11.

64. Ibid., 16.

65. Ibid., 48–51.

66. Ibid., 91–95.

67. Cited in Dwivedi and Mehrotra, *Cities Within,* 209.

68. See, for example, A. R. Burnett-Hurst, *Labour and Housing in Bombay: A Study in Economic Conditions of the Wage-Earning Classes in Bombay* (London: P. S. King, 1925).

69. See Robert Alter's perceptive reading of Dickens on this point in his *Imagined Cities: Urban Experience and the Language of the Novel* (New Haven: Yale University Press, 2005), 54.

70. Gillian Tindall, *City of Gold* (London: Temple Smith, 1982), 252.

71. On colonial cities, see Anthony D. King, *Colonial Urban Development: Culture, Social Power, and Environment* (London: Routledge and Kegan Paul, 1976); Zeynep Çelik, *Urban Forms and Colonial Confrontations: Algiers under French Rule* (Berkeley: University of California Press, 1994).

72. See, for example, Tindall, *City of Gold,* 252–53.

73. Cf. Chandavarkar, *Imperial Power and Popular Politics,* 107.

74. Edwardes, *Gazetteer of Bombay City and Island* 3:174.

75. This description is taken from Parliamentary Papers, *Report of the Indian Plague Commission, 1898–99, with Appendices and Summary,* v (1902), vol. 82, cmd. 810, app. 3, 446–54. See also Ira Klein, "Urban Development and Death: Bombay City, 1870–1914," *Modern Asian Studies* 20, no. 4 (1986): 725–54.

76. What follows is taken from *Bubonic Plague in Bombay,* by A. G. Viegas (Bombay: Tatva-Vivechana Press, 1896).

77. *Bleak House,* edited with an introduction and notes by Nicola Bradbury (London: Penguin Books, 1996), 710. Robert Alter suggests that the typhus epidemics in London were very much on Dickens's mind when he wrote this. Alter, *Imagined Cities,* 67.

78. The above is taken from *Report of the Outbreak of Bubonic Plague in Bombay, 1896–97,* by P.C.H. Snow (Bombay: Times of India Steam Press, 1897), 5–6.

79. J. K. Condon, *The Bombay Plague, Being a History of the Progress of Plague in the Bombay Presidency from September 1896 to June 1899* (Bombay: Education Society's Steam Press, 1900), 130.

80. The above epigraph is from "Mumbai," in *Maze Vidyapeeth,* trans. Mangesh Kulkarni, Jatin Wagle, and Abhay Sardesai (Bombay: Popular Prakashan, 1975), reprinted in Shirin Kudchekar's "Poetry and the City," in *Bombay,* ed. Patel and Thorner, 149.

81. Daya Pawar, *Balute* (Bombay: Granthali, 1982), 132, cited and translated in Bhagwat's "Bombay in Dalit Literature," 114.

CHAPTER 3. THE CITY ON THE SEA

1. See Prashant Kidambi, *The Making of an Indian Metropolis: Colonial Governance and Public Culture in Bombay, 1890–1920* (Aldershot: Ashgate, 2007), 71–113, for a detailed account of the Improvement Trust's projects.

2. "Development of Bombay City and the Improvement of Communications in the Island," Resolution of Government, General Department, no. 3022, June 14, 1909, in Bombay Development Committee, *Report of the Bombay Development Committee, 1914* (Bombay: Government Press, 1914), app. A.

3. *Evidence Oral and Documentary Recorded by the Back Bay Enquiry Committee, 1926,* pt. 3 (London: HMSO, 1927), 5.

4. Bombay Development Committee, *Report,* xiii–xv.

5. Government of India, *Report of the Committee Appointed by the Government of India to Enquire into the Bombay Back Bay Reclamation Scheme, 1926* (London: HMSO, 1926), 7–8.

6. "Letters from Lord Lloyd to Halifax," December 22, 1918, BL, OIOLR, Mss. Eur. B.158.

7. *Proceedings of the Legislative Council of the Government of Bombay, 3rd August 1920,* 565–66.

8. Cited in Government of India, *Report of the Back Bay Enquiry Committee,* 10.

9. W. R. Davidge, "The Development of Bombay," *Town Planning Review* (1924): 273–79.

10. S. Nihal Singh, *Development of Bombay* (Bombay: Director of Public Information, 1924), 16–29.

11. Government of India, *Report of the Back Bay Enquiry Committee*, 39.

12. Ibid., 37.

13. Ibid., 53.

14. Ibid., 17.

15. Ibid., 47–48.

16. Government of Bombay, *Second ad Interim Report of the Advisory Committee Dealing with the Back Bay Reclamation Scheme* (Bombay: Government Central Press, 1925), 9.

17. *Bombay Legislative Council Debates: Official Report, Tuesday, March 3, 1925* (Bombay: Government Central Press, 1925), 546.

18. *Bombay Chronicle*, March 17, 1926.

19. Ibid., March 29, 1926.

20. Ibid., July 22, 1926.

21. Ibid., August 4, 1926.

22. Ibid., August 5, 1926.

23. *Times of India*, August 6, 1926.

24. *Bombay Chronicle*, August 23, 1926.

25. Ibid., August 25, 1926.

26. Ibid., November 6, 1926.

27. Ibid., November 13, 1926.

28. See, for example, ibid., June 14, 1927.

29. Ibid., January 28, 1928.

30. Ibid., January 30, 1928.

31. *Harvey-Nariman Libel Case,* ed. S. M. Surveyor (Bombay: S. M. Surveyor, 1927–28).

32. Government of India, *Report of the Back Bay Enquiry Committee*, 82–83.

33. Dwivedi and Mehrotra, *Cities Within*, 268.

34. Cf. Charlotte Benton and Tim Benton, "The Style and the Age," in *Art Deco, 1910–1939*, ed. Charlotte Benton, Tim Benton, and Ghislaine Wood (New York: Bulfinch, 2003), 12–27.

35. Cf. Jon Alff, "Art Deco: Gateway to Indian Modernism," *Architecture + Design* 8, no. 6 (November–December 1991): 58.

36. Ibid.; see also Amin Jaffer, "Indo-Deco," in *Art Deco,* ed. Benton, Benton, and Wood, 383–84.

37. "The Ideal Home Exhibition," *Journal of the Indian Institute of Architects (JIIA)* 4, no. 3 (January 1938): 323.

38. Dwivedi and Mehrotra, *Cities Within*, 246–47. See also their lavishly illustrated *Bombay Deco* (Mumbai: Eminence Designs, 2008), 41–45.

39. "Review of Construction and Materials," *JIIA* 1, no. 2 (July 1934): 79.

40. Editorial, *Indian Concrete Journal* 9, no. 10 (October 1935): 329.

41. Dwivedi and Mehrotra, *Bombay Deco*, 264–99. See also Kamu Iyer, ed., *Buildings That Shaped Bombay* (Mumbai: KRVI, 2000).

42. "Back Bay Reclamation Scheme," *Times of India*, July 29, 1935; and "Back Bay Reclamation Scheme: Detailed Programme of Development," *Times of India*, March 10, 1936.

43. "New Back Bay Buildings," *Illustrated Weekly of India*, January 3, 1936, iv; "Building Boom in Bombay," *Illustrated Weekly of India*, February 2, 1936, iii.

44. "Palm Trees along Marine Drive," *Indian Concrete Journal* 12, no. 2 (February 1939): 46.

45. Alff, "Art Deco," 59.

46. Editorial, *JIIA* 4, no. 3 (January 1938): 116.

47. What follows is drawn from Jon Alff, "Temples of Light: Bombay's Art Deco Cinemas and the Birth of the Modern Myth," in *Bombay to Mumbai: Changing Perspectives* (Mumbai: Marg Publications, 1997), 250–57; and Dwivedi and Mehrotra, *Bombay Deco*, 46–81.

48. "Parsi Business Man's Experiences: Mr. Cambata in Hollywood and New York," *Illustrated Weekly of India*, October 25, 1936.

49. Louis Bromfield, *Night in Bombay* (New York: P. F. Collier & Son, 1939), 94.

50. Dwivedi and Mehrotra, *Bombay Deco*, 28–32.

51. Mustansir Dalvi, "'Domestic Deco' Architecture in Bombay: G.B.'s Milieu," in *Buildings That Shaped Bombay*, ed. Iyer, 14.

52. What follows is drawn from Naresh Fernandes's painstakingly and lovingly etched portrait of jazz in Mumbai in his *Taj Mahal Foxtrot* (Calcutta: Seagull, forthcoming).

53. Dwivedi and Mehrotra, *Cities Within*, 246.

54. *Illustrated Weekly of India*, May 3, 1936, vi–vii.

55. Vikram Doctor and Alikhan, "A Century of Indian Advertising," *Advertising Brief*, December 30, 1999, 33–47. What follows is drawn from this article.

56. Government of India, *Report of the Indian Cinematograph Committee* (Madras: Government Press, 1928), 180.

57. Erik Barnow and S. Krishnaswamy, *Indian Film* (New York: Oxford University Press, 1980), 31–36.

58. Valentina Vitali, *Hindi Action Cinema: Industries, Narratives, Bodies* (New Delhi: Oxford University Press, 2008), 22–24. See also 11–55 for her analysis of the 1920s stunt films.

59. What follows is based on Rosie Thomas, "Not Quite (Pearl) White: Fearless Nadia, Queen of the Stunt," in *Bollyworld: Popular Indian Cinema through a*

Transnational Lens, ed. Raminder Kaur and Ajay J. Sinha (New Delhi: Sage, 2005), 35–69; Dorothee Wenner, *Fearless Nadia: The True Story of Bollywood's Original Stunt Queen* (New Delhi: Penguin Books, 2005); Vitali, *Hindi Action Cinema,* 56–118; and J.B.H. Wadia, "Those Were the Days" (unpublished autobiography, Bombay, 1980).

60. Wadia, "I Become a Filmmaker," in "Those Were the Days."

61. Thomas, "Not Quite (Pearl) White," 51.

62. Bromfield, *Night in Bombay,* 8.

63. Ibid., 129–30.

64. For example, J. P. Orr, *Density of Population in Bombay* (Bombay: British India Press, 1914), and A. R. Burnett-Hurst, *Labour and Housing in Bombay* (London: P. S. King, 1925).

65. Burnett-Hurst, *Labour and Housing in Bombay,* 22.

66. Cited in Dwivedi and Mehrotra, *Cities Within,* 210.

67. *Census of India, 1931,* vol. 9, pt. 1 (Bombay: Government Central Press, 1933), 81.

68. Ibid., pt. 2, 199.

69. Kosambi, *Bombay in Transition,* 165.

70. Bromfield, *Night in Bombay,* 51–52.

71. OIOLR: Govt. of Bombay, Home Department Proceedings, P/11466, "Annual Report on Traffic in Women and Children for the Year 1924," May 8, 1925.

72. Bombay Vigilance Association, *Report of the Prostitution Committee* (Bombay: Bombay Vigilance Association, 1927), 8–10, 31.

73. Claude Batley, "The Importance of City Planning," in *Bombay Looks Ahead,* ed. Clifford Manshardt (Bombay: D. B. Tarporevala Sons, 1934), 39.

74. *Illustrated Weekly of India,* February 9, 1936.

CHAPTER 4. THE COSMOPOLIS AND THE NATION

1. *Bombay Chronicle,* October 10, 1947.

2. For biographical details on Manto, I have used Jagdish Chander Wadhawan's *Manto Naama: The Life of Saadat Hasan Manto* (New Delhi: Roli Books, 1998), 13–30, and Manto's own stories, which are full of references to his life.

3. Saadat Hasan Manto, "Mammad Bhai," in *Saadat Hasan Manto: Dastavez,* ed. Balraj Menra and Sharad Dutt (Delhi: Rajkamal Prakashan, 1993), 1:343–54. For an English translation, see "A Question of Honour," in *Bitter Fruit: The Very Best of Saadat Hasan Manto,* ed. and trans. Khalid Hasan (New Delhi: Penguin Books, 2008), 249–57.

4. Saadat Hasan Manto, "Naya Qanoon," in *Dastavez* 1:241–49. For an English translation, see "New Constitution," in *Bitter Fruit,* 206–15.

5. Saadat Hasan Manto, "Babu Gopinath," in *Dastavez* 1:215–28. English translation in *Bitter Fruit*, 279–90.

6. Ibid. 1:220.

7. Ismat Chugtai, "Humlog" [We the People], in her *My Friend, My Enemy: Essays, Reminiscences, Portraits,* trans. Tahira Naqvi (New Delhi: Kali for Women, 2001), 105. The biographical details of her life are taken from "Humlog" and "Ghubar-e-Karavaan" [The Dust of the Caravan], ibid., 111–30.

8. See Shabana Mahmud, "*Angare* and the Founding of the Progressive Writers' Association," *Modern Asian Studies* 30, no. 2 (1996): 447–67.

9. Ismat Chugtai, "Lihaaf" [Quilt], trans. M. Asaduddin, in *Women Writing in India,* ed. S. Tharu and K. Lalita (New York: Feminist Press, 1993). On Chugtai, see Priyamvada Gopal, "Habitations of Womanhood: Ismat Chugtai's Secret History of Modernity," in her *Literary Radicalism in India* (London: Routledge, 2005), 65–88.

10. Chugtai, "The 'Lihaaf' Trial," in *My Friend, My Enemy*, 135.

11. For an interpretation of the sexual politics of these two and other Manto stories, see Priyamvada Gopal, "Dangerous Bodies: Masculinity, Morality, and Social Transformation in Manto," in *Literary Radicalism*, 89–122.

12. Chugtai, "Mera Dost, Mera Dushman," in *My Friend, My Enemy*, 193.

13. "Chugtai, 'Lihaaf' Trial," 131–47.

14. For Manto's account of his relationship with Chugtai, see Manto, "On Ismat," in *Ismat: Her Life, Her Times,* ed. Sukrita Paul Kumar and Sadique (New Delhi: Katha, 2000), 156–72.

15. Ahmed Ali, "The Progressive Writers' Movement and Creative Writers in Urdu," in *Marxist Influences and South Asian Literature*, ed. Carlo Coppola, South Asian Monograph Series Occasional Paper No. 23, vol. 1 (East Lansing: Michigan State University, 1974), 36.

16. See Sajjad Zaheer, "Reminiscences," in *Marxist Cultural Movement in India: Chronicles and Documents (1936–1947),* ed. Sudhi Pradhan, vol. 1 (Calcutta: National Book Agency, 1979), 33–46; and Carlo Coppola, "All India Progressive Writers' Association: The European Phase," in *Marxist Influences*, ed. Coppola, 1:1–34, for an account of the PWA's founding efforts in Europe.

17. Coppola, "All India Progressive Writers' Association," 7.

18. What follows is largely based on Hafeez Malik, "The Marxist Literary Movement in India and Pakistan," *Journal of Asian Studies* 26, no. 4 (1967): 649–64.

19. Ali Husain Mir and Raza Mir, *Anthems of Resistance* (New Delhi: Roli Books, 2006), 37.

20. Saadat Hasan Manto, "Taraqqipasand," in *Dastavez* 1:287–95; and "To My Readers," in *Bitter Fruit*," 657.

21. Khwaja Ahmed Abbas, *I Write as I Feel* (Bombay: Hind Kitabs, 1948), 30.

22. Ibid., 30–31.

23. "Indian People's Theatre Association," *Bulletin No. 1*, July 1943, in *Marxist Cultural Movement*, ed. Pradhan, 1:124–42. On the formation of IPTA, see Nandi Bhatia, "Staging Resistance: Indian People's Theatre Association," in *The Politics of Culture in the Shadow of Capital*, ed. Lisa Lowe and David Lloyd (Durham: Duke University Press, 1997), 432–60.

24. "Provincial Reports Bombay," in *Marxist Cultural Movements*, ed. Pradhan, 1:145.

25. "Bombay," ibid., 260.

26. Khwaja Ahmed Abbas, *I Am Not an Island: An Experiment in Autobiography* (New Delhi: Vikas Publishing House, 1977), 97–98. I have drawn details of Abbas's biography from this text and from his *Bombay, My Bombay: The Love Story of the City* (Delhi: Ajanta Books International, 1987).

27. Balraj Sahni, *Balraj Sahni: An Autobiography* (Delhi: Hind Pocket Books, 1979), 17. For his biography, I have also relied on Bhisham Sahni, "Balraj, My Brother," in *Balraj Sahni: An Intimate Portrait*, ed. P. C. Joshi (Delhi: Vikas Publishing House, 1974), 16–49.

28. Sahni, *Balraj Sahni: An Autobiography*, 23–26.

29. Uma Anand and Ketan Anand, *Chetan Anand: The Poetics of Film* (Mumbai: Himalaya Films—Media Entertainment, 2007), 9–10.

30. Ibid., 17.

31. Sahni, *Balraj Sahni: An Autobiography*, 46–47.

32. What follows is based on Sahni, *Balraj Sahni: An Autobiography*, 51–56.

33. "Diary of Margaret C Godley," C 827/3, June 29 to July 7, OIOLR: Mss. Eur. C.827.

34. Raj Thapar, *All These Years* (New Delhi: Seminar Publications, 1991), 4.

35. Ibid., 12.

36. Ibid., 6–7.

37. Ibid., 6.

38. "Diary of Margaret C Godley."

39. Thapar, *All These Years*, 20.

40. Secy, Home (special), G. G. Drewe to Governor of Bombay, September 3, 1946, "Fortnightly Reports from the Governor of Bombay, 1946," BL, OIOLR, L/PJ/5/167.

41. J. C. Masselos, "The City as Represented in Crowd Action: Bombay 1893," *EPW* 28, no. 5 (1993): 182–90.

42. The full details of the violence are contained in Government of Bombay, *The Police Report on the Bombay Riots—February 1929* (Bombay, 1929).

43. Patrick Kelly, Commissioner of Police, Bombay, to Secretary, Government of Bombay, Home Department, September 29, 1932, BL, OIOLR, L/PJ/7/371.

44. Mss. Eur. F97/26, BL, OIOLR, Brabourne Collection.

45. The account of violence in the city is contained in "Fortnightly Reports from the Governor of Bombay" for the years 1946 and 1947.

46. The effect of the circulation of rumors is mentioned ibid.

47. A. C. Clow, Governor, to Archibald Wavell, Viceroy, September 17, 1946, "Fortnightly Reports from the Governor of Bombay, 1946."

48. Abbas, *I Am Not an Island*, 277.

49. Saadat Hasan Manto, *Stars from Another Sky: The Bombay Film World of the 1940s,* trans. Khalid Hasan (New Delhi: Penguin Books, 1998), 74–75.

50. Ibid., 76.

51. Chugtai, "Mera Dost, Mera Dushman," in *My Friend, My Enemy*, 209.

52. Aamir Mufti, *Enlightenment in the Colony: The Jewish Question and the Crisis of Postcolonial Culture* (Princeton: Princeton University Press, 2007), 207–8.

53. Saadat Hasan Manto, "Toba Tek Singh," in *Dastavez* 2:192–98.

54. Manto, *Stars from Another Sky*, 73.

55. Saadat Hasan, "Mozail," in *Dastavez* 2:249–67. The English translation appears in *Bitter Fruit*, 26–38.

56. Abbas, *I Write as I Feel*, 315–16.

57. Chugtai, "Communal Violence and Literature (Fasaadat aur Adab)," in *My Friend, My Enemy*, 3–5.

58. The above two are cited ibid., 6–7.

59. Abbas, *I Am Not an Island*, 289.

60. Abbas, *I Write as I Feel*, 317.

61. Cited and translated in Mir and Mir's *Anthems of Resistance*, 122.

62. Erik Barnouw and S. Krishnaswamy, *Indian Film*, 2nd ed. (New York: Oxford University Press, 1980), 155.

63. I have drawn on the following: Rashmi Varma, "Provincializing the Global City: From Bombay to Mumbai," *Social Text* 81, vol. 22, no. 4 (2004); Gopal, *Literary Radicalism*, 123–62. See also Madhav Prasad, "The State in/of Cinema," in *Wages of Freedom: Fifty Years of the Indian Nation-State,* ed. Partha Chatterjee (New Delhi: Oxford University Press, 1998); and Ravi Vasudevan, introduction to *Making Meanings in Indian Cinema,* ed. Ravi Vasudevan (New Delhi: Oxford University Press, 2000), 1–36.

CHAPTER 5. THE TABLOID AND THE CITY

1. John Lobo, "Now It Can Be Told—the Nanavati Story," in *Leaves from a Policeman's Diary* (New Delhi: Allied Publishers, 1992), 21. Unless stated otherwise, what follows is taken from Lobo's account, 21–22.

2. In September 1958 the Law Commission of India had already recommended the abolition of the right to trial before jury, which in any case was confined to the

old presidency towns of Bombay, Calcutta, and Madras. See Government of India, *Law Commission of India: Fourteenth Report*, vol. 2 (Delhi: Ministry of Law, 1958), 873. The Nanavati trial appeared to have sealed the case for abolition.

3. "For the Love of Sylvia," *Time*, March 28, 1960, http://www.time.com/time/magazine/article/0,9171,826134,00.html (accessed April 15, 2008); Emily Hahn, "Commmander Nanavati and the Unwritten Law," *New Yorker*, November 26, 1960, 188–205.

4. Salman Rushdie, *Midnight's Children* (London: Jonathan Cape, 1980), and Indra Sinha, *The Death of Mr. Love* (London: Scribner, 2002). The case was also loosely fictionalized in Hindi in Tapan Ghosh's *Nanavati ka Mukadama va Anya Kahaniyan* [Nanavati's Case and Other Stories] (New Delhi: Vishwa Sahitya, 2002).

5. Vijaya Sharma, "Prem Bhagwandas Ahuja," http://www.hindustantimes.com/news/specials/proj_tabloid/nanavati1.shtml (accessed April 15, 2008).

6. P. Sainath, "R. K. Karanjia: Living through the Blitz," http://www.hindu.com/2008/02/06/stories/2008020652441100.htm (accessed February 28, 2010).

7. The following description of Karanjia's family background is taken from his brother's autobiography. See B. K. Karanjia, *Counting My Blessings* (New Delhi: Penguin Books, 2005), 1–15.

8. Homi D. Mistry, "The Young Rebel," in *Blitz: Four Fighting Decades* (Bombay: Blitz Publications, 1981), 3. What follows is drawn from this article, 3–4.

9. "To Our Readers, February 1, 1941," cited in *Blitz*, February 25, 1961.

10. "Mighty All-Party Rally Felicitates Editor Karanjia," *Blitz*, February 27, 1965.

11. *Blitz*, June 25, 1960. Below the main story was another headline: "Did US Spy Chief Dulles Meet [the Naga leader] Phizo?"

12. Ibid., April 16, 1960.

13. "Festival of Indo-Arab Amity," *Blitz*, July 3, 1965.

14. "Great Morarji Fraud," *Blitz*, January 19, 1952.

15. Cited in Homi D. Mistry's "Sins of Shri No. 2," in *Blitz: Four Fighting Decades*, 97.

16. "U.S.A. Welcomes Indian Mediation in Korea," *Blitz*, July 19, 1952.

17. A summary account of the case appears in "Chester Bowles Forgery Case," by Homi D. Mistry, in *Blitz: Four Fighting Decades*, 54–55.

18. *Blitz*, October 4, 1952.

19. Ibid., August 1, 1953.

20. Cited in "The Racket-Buster," *Blitz*, February 25, 1961.

21. These headlines are from *Blitz*, December 2, 1961, and March 13, 1965.

22. The following description comes from "Naval Officer Says He Is Not Guilty," *Times of India*, September 24, 1959.

23. John Lobo, "Now It Can Be Told: The Nanavati Story," in *Leaves from a Policeman's Diary*, 28. The excluded testimony appears in his memoir.

24. "Nanavati Says He Did Not Kill Intentionally: 'Bullets Went Off during the Struggle for Revolver,'" *Times of India*, October 6, 1959.

25. "'Reason for Bringing Gun from the Ship Was to Shoot Myself': Commander Nanavati Is First Defence Witness," *Times of India*, October 7, 1959.

26. "Prem Ahuja Tried to Avoid Marrying Accused's Wife: Mrs. Nanavati's Evidence in Murder Case," *Times of India*, October 14, 1959.

27. Hahn, "Commander Nanavati," 194–95.

28. *Blitz*, October 31, 1959. Unless stated otherwise, what follows is from *Blitz*, October 10, 17, and 25, 1959.

29. For the defense address, see "No Offence Committed by Accused, Says Defence Counsel: Address to Jury in Ahuja Murder Case," *Times of India*, October 15 and 16, 1959; for the prosecution address, see "Lesser Offence Suggested by Prosecution: 'Jury Entitled to Return Verdict of Homicide,'" *Times of India*, October 17, 1959.

30. The following description comes from R. P. Aiyar, "The Full Story of the Trials of Nanavati … the Ahuja Murder Case," *Blitz*, January 6, 1962.

31. "Nanavati Is Not Guilty, Says Jury. Judge Disagrees: Refers Case to High Court," *Times of India*, October 22, 1959.

32. *Blitz*, October 24, 1959. Unless stated otherwise, what follows is from *Blitz*, October 24 and 31, 1959.

33. "For the Love of Sylvia."

34. Mohan Deep, "Line of Fire," http://www.hindustantimes.com/news/specials/proj_tabloid/lof1912.shtml (accessed April 15, 2008).

35. V. Gangadhar, "Dial M for Murder," http://www.rediff.com/style/1998/mar/14gang.htm (accessed April 15, 2008).

36. *Blitz*, November 7, 1959. Unless otherwise stated, what follows is from *Blitz*, February 6, 13, 20, 27, and March 5, 1960.

37. "Commander Nanavati Found Guilty of Murder," *Times of India*, March 10, 1960.

38. *Blitz*, March 12, 1960.

39. Ibid.

40. "Naval Custody for Nanavati till Appeal Is Heard," *Times of India*, March 12, 1960.

41. "Mr. Nehru Says He Advised Governor," *Times of India*, March 15, 1960.

42. "Suspension of Sentence Deplored: Resolution Adopted by C.P.I. Secretariat," *Times of India*, March 17, 1959.

43. "Full Bench of High Court May Hear Writ Issue Tomorrow," *Times of India*, March 16, 1960.

44. *Blitz*, March 19, 1960. What follows is from *Blitz*, March 19 and 26, 1960.

45. "High Court Says Governor's Order Is Valid," *Times of India*, March 31, 1960.

46. *Blitz*, April Fool number, 1960.

47. Ibid.

48. "Governor Has No Power to Suspend Life Sentence: Supreme Court Ruling in Nanavati Case," *Times of India*, September 6, 1960.

49. *Blitz*, September 17, 1960.

50. "Nanavati's Plea Dismissed by Supreme Court," *Times of India*, November 25, 1961; for full judgment, see 1961 INDLAW SC 397 [Supreme Court of India], State of Maharashtra v. K. M. Nanavati.

51. *Blitz*, December 2, 1961.

52. Ibid. Another article by its "constitutional expert" also made similar arguments.

53. R. P. Aiyar, "The Full Story of the Trials of Nanavati ... the Ahuja Murder Case: Great Trials That Rocked India. . . ." The first installment appeared in *Blitz*, December 2, 1961, and continued for every subsequent week until January 13, 1962.

54. Gerson da Cunha, "Decline of a Great City," *Seminar* 528 (August 2003): 15.

55. Aarti Sethi, "The Honourable Murder: The Trial of Kawas Maneckshaw Nanavati," in *Sarai Reader 05: Bare Acts*, ed. Monica Narula, Shuddhabrata Sengupta, Jeebesh Bagchi, and Geert Lovink (Delhi: CSDS, 2005), 444–53.

56. *Blitz*, April 7, 1962.

57. The following details come from Nalini Gera, *Ram Jethmalani: The Authorized Biography* (New Delhi, Viking, 2002.

58. *Blitz*, March 21, 1964.

CHAPTER 6. FROM RED TO SAFFRON

1. *Times of India*, June 6, 1970.

2. *Times of India*, June 9, 1970; Vaibhav Purandare, *The Sena Story* (Mumbai: Business Publications, 1999), 145.

3. *Yugantar*, June 14 and June 21, 1970.

4. *Blitz*, June 13, 1970, 10.

5. Ibid., June 20, 1970, 1.

6. Raj Chandavarkar, *The Origins of Industrial Capitalism in India* (Cambridge: Cambridge University Press, 1994), ch. 5. What follows draws heavily from this meticulously researched work.

7. See the transcript of the oral testimony of Khatu, a retired mill worker, in Neera Adarkar and Meena Menon, *One Hundred Years, One Hundred Voices* (Calcutta: Seagull, 2004), 107–8.

8. Raj Chandavarkar, "From Neighborhood to Nation," ibid., 24–25.

9. See the transcript of Madhukar Nerale's oral testimony in Adarkar and Menon, *One Hundred Voices*, 121–24.

10. The pamphlet *Gandhi vs. Lenin* and the journal *Socialist* are reprinted in S. A. Dange, *Dange: Selected Writings*, vols. 1 and 2 (Bombay: Lok Vangmaya Griha, 1977).

11. What follows draws on Raj Chandavarkar's *Imperial Power and Popular Politics: Class, Resistance and the State in India, c. 1850–1950* (Cambridge: Cambridge University Press, 1998), 129–31.

12. S. V. Ghate, "Girni Kamgar Hadtaal," in CPI, *Jan Sangharshon ki Amar Gaathaayen* (Delhi: New Age Printing Press, 1975), 10–11 (in Hindi). This text consists of the reminiscences of Ghate, a prominent trade union and Communist activist in the mills, recorded in 1971.

13. Dange provided a detailed description of his involvement in the labor movement at this time in his statement at the Meerut Conspiracy Case trial in 1931 and 1932. See the text of his statement, running over three hundred pages, in S. A. Dange, *Dange: Selected Writings*, vol. 3 (Bombay: Lok Vangmaya Griha, 1979).

14. Ghate, "Girni Kamgar Hadtaal," 11.

15. Dange, *Selected Writings* 3:154–66.

16. Adarkar and Menon, *One Hundred Voices*, 156; and Ghate, "Girni Kamgar Hadtaal," 12.

17. Ghate, "Girni Kamgar Hadtaal," 12–13.

18. Dange, *Selected Writings* 3:55.

19. Ibid., 227.

20. On mill committees, their formation, functions, and influence, see Dange, *Selected Writings* 3:191–201, and Chandavarkar, *Imperial Power and Popular Politics*, 132.

21. See A.D.D. Gordon, *Businessmen and Politics: Rising Nationalism and a Modernizing Economy in Bombay, 1918–1933* (Columbia, Mo.: South Asia Books, 1978), particularly chs. 5 and 6.

22. Adarkar and Menon, *One Hundred Voices*, 133.

23. "Shahir Com Da. Na. Gavankar," *Saaptahik Yugaantar* (Marathi), April 4, 1971, 3.

24. Adarkar and Menon, *One Hundred Voices*, 131.

25. See David Bradby and John McCormick, *People's Theatre* (London: Rowman and Littlefield, 1978).

26. "Shahir Com Da. Na. Gavankar," 3.

27. Sheikh Jainu Chand's oral testimony's transcript in Adarkar and Menon, *One Hundred Voices*, 140.

28. Kusum Ranadive's oral testimony transcript, ibid., 161–62.

29. Ahilya Rangnekar's oral testimony transcript, ibid., 159.

30. Prema Purav's oral testimony transcript, ibid., 163.

31. Author's interview with Tara Reddy, September 1, 2005.

32. Sitaram Jagtap's oral testimony transcript, in *One Hundred Voices*, by Adarkar and Menon, 165.

33. On CPI's policies during the war, see M. R. Masani, *The Communist Party of India: A Short History* (London: Derek Verschoyle, 1954), 76–86.

34. On the mutiny, see Subrata Banerjee, *The RIN Strike* (New Delhi: People's Publishing House, 1954).

35. Interview with Tara Reddy.

36. Ibid.

37. *Documents of the History of the Communist Party of India*, vol. 8, ed. Mohit Sen (New Delhi: People's Publishing House, 1977), 65.

38. For an account of the shifts in the CPI's policies, see Gene D. Overstreet and Marshall Windmiller, *Communism in India* (Berkeley: University of California Press, 1959), 276–93.

39. See H. Van Wersch, *Bombay Textile Strike, 1982–83* (Bombay: Oxford University Press, 1992), 66–70.

40. The epigraph is from Rushdie, *Midnight's Children*, 228.

41. Marshall Windmiller, "The Politics of States Reorganization in India: The Case of Bombay," *Far East Survey* 25, no. 9 (1956): 129. See also Jyotindra Das Gupta, *Language Conflict and National Development* (Berkeley: University of California Press, 1970), 116–17.

42. Windmiller, "Politics of States Reorganization," 130.

43. Kosambi, *Bombay in Transition*, 129.

44. Windmiller, "Politics of States Reorganization," 131.

45. Y. D. Phadke, *Politics and Language* (Bombay: Himalaya Publishing House, 1972), 20, 61–62.

46. Windmiller, "Politics of States Reorganization," 132. Unless indicated otherwise, what follows is based on this article.

47. Cited ibid., 138.

48. Phadke, *Politics and Language*, 149. Chapters 3–7 contain a detailed account of the different phases of the Samyukta Maharashtra movement.

49. Ibid., 154–58.

50. Adarkar and Menon, *One Hundred Voices*, 255.

51. Ibid., 261.

52. See the transcripts of Ahilya Rangnekar and G. L. Reddy's oral accounts, ibid., 230, 234.

53. Cited in Windmiller, "Politics of States Reorganization," 139.

54. S. A. Dange, "People of Maharashtra Have Rejected Bilingual State," *Blitz*, April 13, 1957, 15.

55. *Marmik*, May 25, 1997, 4. Purandare, *Sena Story*, 21.

56. Mary Fainsod Katzenstein, *Ethnicity and Equality: The Shiv Sena Party and Preferential Policies in Bombay* (Ithaca: Cornell University Press, 1979), 49.

57. Purandare, *Sena Story*, 40.

58. The account of the public meeting is drawn from Purandare's *Sena Story*, 41–45. See also Jayant Lele, "Saffronization of the Shiv Sena: The Political Economy of the City, State and Nation," in *Bombay: Metaphor for Modern India,* ed. Sujata Patel and Alice Thorner (New Delhi: Oxford University Press, 1995), 187.

59. A. N. Confectioner, *The Shiv Sena: Why? And Why Not?* (Bombay: Popular Prakashan, 1967), 8–10.

60. Lele, "Saffronization of the Shiv Sena," 189, and Sujata Patel, "Bombay and Mumbai: Identities, Politics, and Populism," in *Bombay and Mumbai: The City in Transition,* ed. Sujata Patel and Jim Masselos (New Delhi: Oxford University Press, 2003), 10.

61. Katzenstein, *Ethnicity and Equality*, 76.

62. Ibid., 76–77.

63. Ibid., 48, 51.

64. My analysis of Thackeray's politics draws on Ernesto Laclau's discussion of populism in his *On Populist Reason* (London: Verso, 2005).

65. "The Interview of Purnashambu for Marmikam," *Marmik*, August 15, 1965, cited and translated in Katzenstein's *Ethnicity and Equality*, 50.

66. Kapilacharya, *Shiv Sena Speaks: Official Statement* (Bombay: Marmik Cartoon Weekly, 1967), 3.

67. Ibid., 24.

68. Katzenstein, *Ethnicity and Equality*, 66, 79.

69. Ibid., 48–49.

70. Purandare, *Sena Story*, 66.

71. Ibid., 75–78.

72. "Shabbas Pralhadkhan Atre! Anantali Bhide," *Marmik*, March 12, 1961, 4.

73. *Marmik*, August 29, 1965.

74. Purandare, *Sena Story*, 70.

75. Cf. Ram Joshi, "The Shiv Sena: A Movement in Search of Legitimacy," *Asian Survey* 10, no. 11 (1970): 975.

76. Purandare, *Sena Story*, 69.

77. Justice D. P. Madon, *Report of the Commission of Inquiry into the Communal Disturbances at Bhiwandi, Jalgaon and Mahad in May 1970*, excerpted in Sabrang, *Damning Verdict* (Mumbai: Sabrang Communications and Publishing, 1998), 264. Unless indicated otherwise, the following account is drawn from the excerpts on 252–323.

78. Ibid., 292. For details of events leading to the conflagration, see 280–93.

79. Cf. Julia Eckert, *The Charisma of Direct Action: Power, Politics, and the Shiv Sena* (New Delhi: Oxford University Press, 2003). See also Gérard Huezé, "Cul-

tural Populism: The Appeal of the Shiv Sena," in *Bombay: Metaphor for Modern India*, ed. Patel and Thorner, 211–47, and Thomas Blom Hansen, *Wages of Violence: Naming and Identity in Postcolonial Bombay* (Princeton: Princeton University Press, 2001), 56.

80. Purandare, *Sena Story*, 107–8. What follows is drawn from 103–31 and E. S. Modak, *Sentinel of the Sahyadris (Memories and Reflections)* (Delhi: Originals, 2001), 115–22.

81. *Times of India*, February 9 and 10, 1969.

82. Ibid., February 11, 1969.

83. Ibid., February 12, 1969.

84. Purandare, *Sena Story*, 60.

85. Hansen, *Wages of Violence*, 60.

86. Lele, "Saffronization of the Shiv Sena," 199.

87. Huezé, "Cultural Populism," 236.

88. Sujata Patel, "Bombay and Mumbai," 10.

89. Purandare, *Sena Story*, 85.

90. Author's interview with Anil Karnik, Mumbai, November 23, 2008. Karnik was Desai's associate and served as the secretary of the Lok Seva Dal.

91. Details of his personal and political life are drawn from "Krishna Desai Was a Militant Leader," *Times of India*, June 6, 1970, 6; Prabhakar Vaidya, *Com. Krishna Desai Aani Tyanche Khooni* [Marathi] (Mumbai: Maharashtra State Council of the CPI, 1970); and from author's interviews with Karnik; Sarojini Desai, his widow; and Ajit Desai, his son; November 23, 2008.

92. Dinanath Kamat, *Ladai Prasthapitanshi* [Marathi] (Mumbai: Shilalekh Printers and Advertisers, 2004), 115.

93. Ibid., 17–19. What follows is based on 20–44.

94. Ibid., 32–34.

95. Ibid., 44–45.

96. Interview with Anil Karnik.

97. Purandare, *Sena Story*, 84–86.

98. Interview with Sarojini Desai and Ajit Desai.

99. What follows has been compiled from interviews with Karnik and Sarojini Desai; "Communist MLA Murdered," *Times of India*, June 6, 1970, 1; "Krishna Desai: The First Victim of Fascist Plot," *Blitz*, June 13, 1970, 3; and Ramakant Kulkarni, *Footprints on the Sands of Crime* (Delhi: Macmillan, 2004), 64–76. Kulkarni was the police officer entrusted with the investigation of this high-profile case.

100. The above account is compiled from Purandare's *Sena Story*, 141–44; *Times of India*, June 6, 7, and 8, 1970; *Blitz*, June 13, 1970; and *Yugantar* (Marathi), June 14, 1970.

101. Kulkarni, *Footprints on the Sands*, 70–71.

102. *Blitz*, June 13, 1970.

103. Katzenstein, *Ethnicity and Equality*, 112–13.

104. *Times of India*, October 20, 1970.

CHAPTER 7. PLANNING AND DREAMING

1. Mulk Raj Anand, "Editorial: In Dreams Begins Responsibility," *MARG* 18, no. 3 (1965): 2–3.

2. Speaking of cities as evil, Gandhi wrote: "Bombay, Calcutta and other chief cities of India are the real plague spots." M. K. Gandhi, *Hind Swaraj and Other Writings*, ed. Anthony J. Parel (Cambridge: Cambridge University Press, 1997), 130. For his views on the village as the authentic expression of India, see 150–51.

3. Jawaharlal Nehru, *The Discovery of India* (1946; repr., Delhi: Oxford University Press, 1985), 50–51.

4. Ibid., 523.

5. "Nehru's Reply to Gandhi," October 9, 1945, in Gandhi, *Hind Swaraj and Other Writings*, 152.

6. Nehru wrote that "the fundamental problem of India is not Delhi or Calcutta or Bombay but the villages of India. … We want to urbanise the village, not take away the people from the villages to towns." Cited in *Chandigarh: The Making of an Indian City*, by Ravi Kalia (Delhi: Oxford University Press, 1999), 30.

7. See James Holston, *The Modernist City: An Anthropological Critique of Brasilia* (Chicago: University of Chicago Press, 1989), 51, 52.

8. Norma Evenson, *The Indian Metropolis: A View toward the West* (New Haven: Yale University Press, 1989), 183.

9. K. C. Zachariah, *Migrants in Greater Bombay* (Bombay: Asia Publishing House, 1968), 12.

10. J. F. Bulsara, *Bombay: A City in the Making* (Bombay: National Information and Publications, 1948), 5.

11. Ibid., 62.

12. See Geeta Kapur's "Partisan Modernity," in *Mulk Raj Anand: Shaping the Indian Modern*, ed. Annapurna Garimella (Bombay: Marg Publications, 2005), 28–41, for the details on his biography and intellectual formation.

13. Karin Zitzewitz, in "The Aesthetics of Secularism: Modernist Art and Visual Culture in India" (PhD diss., Columbia University, 2005), 34, 39–45, 87–139, has an illuminating discussion on the cosmopolitan world of the Progressives. See also her *Perfect Frame: Presenting Modern Indian Art; Photographs and Stories from the Collection of Kekoo Gandhy* (Bombay: Chemould Publications and Arts, 2003). On Progressives, see also Vasudha Dalmia, *The Moderns: The Progressive Artists' Group and Associates* (Bombay: National Gallery of Modern Art, 1996) and *The Making of Modern Indian Art: The Progressives* (New Delhi: Oxford Uni-

versity Press, 2001), as well as Kekoo Gandhy, "Beginnings of an Art Movement," *Seminar* 528 (August 2003).

14. Charles Correa, "Mulk Raj Anand at 100," in *Mulk Raj Anand*, ed. Garimella, 66–67.

15. The following articles are all in *MARG*. "The Charter of Athens: A Treatise on Town Planning," 3, no. 4 (1949): 10–17; "Le Corbusier," 2, no. 4 (1947): 9–11; Le Corbusier, "Yesterday, Today and Tomorrow," 2, no. 4 (1947): 12–19. In addition, there were several articles in the journal during the 1950s and 1960s by Le Corbusier and by others on him and his urban plans. For examples, see "Le Corbusier on Town Planning," 6, no. 3 (1953): 2–3, and "Urbanism," 6, no. 4 (1953): 10–18; Balkrishna Doshi, "A Note on Le Corbusier," 6, no. 4 (1953): 8–9. A number of articles were on Le Corbusier's Chandigarh plan.

16. Mustansir Dalvi, "Mulk and Modern Indian Architecture," in *Mulk Raj Anand*, ed. Garimella, 61, 65.

17. "Architecture and Planning," *MARG* 1, no. 3 (1947): 23–28.

18. *JIIA*, January 1945, 1–2.

19. *MARG* 2, no. 1 (1947): 28.

20. Ibid. 1, no. 1 (1946): 1–2.

21. Bombay City and Suburbs Post-war Development Committee, *Preliminary Report of the Development of Suburbs and Town Planning Panel* (Bombay, 1946), 10.

22. Ibid., 7.

23. Henri Lefebvre, *The Production of Space* (Oxford: Blackwell, 1991), 38.

24. N. V. Modak and Albert Mayer, *An Outline of the Master Plan of Greater Bombay* (Bombay: Bombay Municipal Printing Press, 1948), 3.

25. Ibid., foreword.

26. Ibid., 14.

27. Ibid., 4.

28. N. V. Modak and Albert Mayer, *Master Plan for Greater Bombay: First Progress Report* (Bombay: Bombay Municipal Printing Press, 1949), 2.

29. For a fuller discussion of this point, see my *Another Reason: Science and the Imagination of Modern India* (Princeton: Princeton University Press, 1999), ch. 7.

30. Modak and Mayer, *Outline of the Master Plan*, 10.

31. Charles Correa, Pravina Mehta, and Shirish Patel, "Planning for Bombay," *MARG* 18, no. 3 (June 1965): 29–56.

32. Municipal Corporation of Greater Bombay, *Report on the Development Plan for Greater Bombay, 1964* (Bombay: Government Central Press, 1964).

33. Government of Bombay, *Report of the Study Group on Greater Bombay* (Bombay: Government Central Press, 1959), 1.

34. Ibid., 93.

35. "We are indeed conscious that most of the ideas and lines of activity recommended herein are trite and have been often mentioned before and many of them

indeed 'leap to the eye' as the obvious solutions to different problems. Perhaps only the various pieces have been set up within a single comprehensive framework for the first time." Ibid.

36. Municipal Corporation of Greater Bombay, *Report on the Development Plan*, xii–xii.

37. Ibid., xxxi.

38. Ibid., xvii.

39. J. H. Ghadiali, "Plan for Bombay: Another View," *Times of India*, July 12, 1964.

40. Charles Correa, "Evolution of the Concept," *Architecture + Design* 14, no. 2 (1997): 124–26.

41. Shirish Patel, author's interview, Bombay, July 20, 2009. See also Correa, "Evolution of the Concept."

42. "Twin City on the Sea," *Times of India*, March 29, 1964.

43. Charles Correa, "New Bombay: MARG as an Urban Catalyst," in *Bombay to Bombay: Changing Perspectives,* ed. Pauline Rohatgi, Pheroza Godrej, and Rahul Mehrotra (Bombay: MARG Publications, 1997), 312–13.

44. H. Foster King, "Editorial: Greater Bombay—across the Harbour," *JIIA* 12, no. 1 (1945): 2.

45. Correa, Mehta, and Patel, "Planning for Bombay," 44.

46. Mulk Raj Anand, "Splendors and Miseries of Bombay," *MARG* 18, no. 3 (1965): 16.

47. Anand, "In Dreams Begins Responsibility," 3.

48. Annapurna Shaw, *The Making of Navi Bombay* (New Delhi: Orient Longman, 2004), 74–79.

49. Shirish Patel, interview.

50. J. B. D'Souza, *No Trumpets or Bugles: Recollections of an Unrepentant Babu* (Bombay: Allied Publishers, 2002), 168.

51. "Last Page: Will the Twin City across the Harbour Be a Better Bombay?" *Blitz*, July 11, 1970.

52. "Bombay's Neo-Manhattan Twin City: Playground for Monopolists and Speculators," *Blitz*, June 5, 1971.

53. Shaw, *The Making of Navi Bombay*, 80–81.

54. The above is based on Shaw, in *The Making of Navi Bombay*, 251–64.

55. See the special issue of *Architecture + Design* 14, no. 2 (1997), devoted to the reassessment of "Navi Bombay."

56. Shirish B. Patel, "The Thirty-Year Journey," *Architecture + Design* 14, no. 2 (1997): 120.

57. Shirish Patel, interview.

58. Patel, "Thirty-Year Journey," 120.

59. "A Little More Suffering, a Little More Style," *Economic and Political Weekly* 11, no. 30 (July 24, 1976): 1101–6, contains an overview of the reclamation in the 1970s.

60. "Inside Bombay's Concrete Jungle ... Hell for Six Millions," *Blitz*, June 10, 1971.

61. B. B. King et al., "Main Report," in *Urban and Regional Report No. 73–6: Report on Bombay* (Washington, D.C.: World Bank, Development Economics Department, Urban and Regional Economics Division, 1973), 11.

62. *Current*, January 29, 1972.

63. Ibid., 1972.

64. Ibid., May 19, 1973.

65. What follows is based on D'Souza's *No Trumpets or Bugles*, 168–73.

66. The following details are taken from "A Little More Suffering, a Little More Style," 1104.

67. Bombay High Court, Original Side, Misc. Petition no. 519 of 1974; *Piloo Mody and Others v. State of Maharashtra and Others*.

68. *Piloo Mody and Others v. State of Maharashtra and Others*, 319–21.

69. Ibid., 382–83. See also 396–439 for Desai's arguments on this point.

70. Ibid., 503–4.

71. Ibid., 583–84.

72. Ibid., 604.

73. For examples, see "The Backbay Blight," *Times Weekly*, December 9, 1973; "NCPA: Big Plans, Small Returns," *Times Weekly*, February 17, 1974; "Naik Govt's Newest Racket: Super-Skyscrapers without Tenders," *Blitz*, March 26, 1973; "King's Ransom for Queen's Barrack," *Free Press Journal*, April 18, 1972.

74. "A Little More Suffering, a Little More Style," 1105–6; Atul D. Ranade, "What Has Gone Wrong at Backbay?" *JIIA* 42, no. 4 (1976): 14–18.

75. Anand, "Splendours and Miseries of Bombay," 19–20.

76. Raban, *Soft City*, 16.

77. Ibid., 20.

78. Rahul Mehrotra, "From New Bombay to Navi Bombay: The Twenty-Five Years," *Architecture + Design* 14, no. 2 (1997): 22.

79. Anand, "Splendours and Miseries of Bombay," 17.

80. Municipal Corporation of Greater Mumbai, *Human Development Report, Mumbai 2009* (Mumbai: Municipal Corporation of Greater Mumbai, 2009).

CHAPTER 8. AVENGER ON THE STREET

1. *Bombay Dying* (Delhi: Raj Comics, 2001)

2. There is a vast literature on the Emergency, written largely by journalists and by Mrs. Gandhi's opponents. For a recent balanced and synthetic account, see

Ram Chandra Guha, *India after Gandhi: The History of the World's Largest Democracy* (New York: HarperCollins, 2007), chs. 21, 22.

3. Author's interview with Kalpana Sharma, April 14, 2009. Sharma was then the editor of a feisty weekly, *Himmat*, which, like all other publications, was subjected to censorship.

4. See Emma Tarlo, *Unsettling Memories: Narratives of the Emergency in Delhi* (London: C. Hurst, 2003).

5. What follows is based largely on Darryl D'Monte's *Ripping the Fabric: The Decline of Mumbai and Its Mills* (Delhi: Oxford University Press, 2002), 85–105, which very usefully summarizes and analyzes the extensive literature on the decline of the textile industry.

6. Nigel Harris, "Bombay in the Global Economy," in *Bombay: Metaphor for Modern India*, ed. Patel and Thorner, 50.

7. Mumbai Metropolitan Regional Development Authority, *Draft Regional Plan for the Bombay Metropolitan Region, 1996–2011* (Mumbai: MMRDA, 1995), 109, cited in D'Monte's *Ripping the Fabric*, 82.

8. Sandip Pendse, "The Datta Samant Phenomenon," pts. 1 and 2, *Economic and Political Weekly* 16, no. 16 (1981): 695–97 and 16, no. 17 (1981): 745–49; and H. van Wersch, *The Bombay Textile Strike, 1982–83* (Delhi: Oxford University Press, 1992), 95–100.

9. What follows is drawn from Wersch, *Bombay Textile Strike*, 95–233.

10. See D'Monte, *Ripping the Fabric*, 153–86, for a detailed account of this murder and for the gangland wars over the mill lands.

11. Jan Nijman, "Mumbai's Real Estate Market in the1990s: Deregulation, Global Money and Casino Capitalism," *Economic and Political Weekly* 35, no. 7 (2000): 575–82.

12. See, for example, "The Other Bombay: Some Glimpses of the City's Underworld," *Illustrated Weekly of India*, September 9, 1959, 11–13; "The Matka Menace," *Illustrated Weekly of India*, February 11, 1968, 8–11; "Operation Gold I" and "Operation Gold II," *Illustrated Weekly of India*, May 24 and June 7, 1970; "Dubai Daredevils Defy Bombay Customs Dragnet," *Blitz*, November 14, 1970, 12–13; and "The New Golden Triangle," *Times Weekly*, January 6, 1974, 7.

13. Greater Bombay Police (Crime Branch), "The Growth of Gangsterism in Greater Bombay" (unpublished report, Bombay, 1994), 147. What follows is drawn from the richly detailed information in this report.

14. The details of Dawood's career are drawn from Greater Bombay Police (Crime Branch), "Growth of Gangsterism," 7–42.

15. The deposition to the police by Pradeep Narayan Madgaonkar, also known as Bandya Mama—an agent of Chota Rajan, who was then with Dawood but fell out later—offers a detailed portrait of the gang's network. Greater Bombay Police (Crime Branch), "Growth of Gangsterism," 45–68.

16. Ibid., 149.

17. For a detailed account of the riots, see Clarence Fernandez and Naresh Fernandes, "The Winter of Discontent" and "A City at War with Itself," in *When Bombay Burned*, ed. Dileep Padgaonkar (New Delhi: UBS Publishers' Distributors, 1993), 12–41, 42–108.

18. Ibid., 33.

19. Quoted ibid., 35.

20. Rajdeep Sardesai, "The Great Betrayal," in *When Bombay Burned*, ed. Padgaonkar, 199–200.

21. Quoted in "A City at War with Itself," by Fernandez and Fernandes, 74.

22. "Kick Them Out—No Compromise with the Muslims: The Rhetoric of Hatred from Shiv Sena's Bal Thackeray," *Time*, January 25, 1993.

23. *Report of the Srikrishna Commission Appointed for Inquiry into the Riots at Mumbai during December 1992–January 1993 and the March 12, 1993 Bomb Blasts*, vol. 1, in *Damning Verdict* (Mumbai: Sabrang Communications and Publishing, 1998), 49.

24. Ibid., 40, 42.

25. S. Hussain Zaidi provides a detailed and riveting account of the conspiracy in his *Black Friday* (New Delhi: Penguin Books, 2002). Anurag Kashyap's film of the same title (2005) is based on this book.

26. Zaidi, *Black Friday*, 28.

27. *Srikrishna Commission Report* 1:25.

28. The term "crime melodrama" comes from Ravi Vasudevan, "Shifting Codes, Dissolving Identities: The Hindi Social Film of the 1950s as Popular Culture," in *Making Meanings in Indian Cinema*, ed. Ravi Vasudevan (Delhi: Oxford University Press, 2000), 99–121.

29. Ranjani Mazumdar, *Bombay Cinema: Archive of a City* (Minneapolis: University of Minnesota Press, 2007), 1–40.

30. On the comic-book form, see Scott McCloud, *Understanding Comics: The Invisible Art* (New York: Harper Perennial, 1993); Mila Bongco, *Reading Comics: Language, Culture, and the Concept of the Superhero in Comic Books* (New York: Garland Publishing, 2000); Stephen Weiner, *Faster Than a Speeding Bullet: The Rise of the Graphic Novel* (New York: Nantier Beall Minoustchine Publishing, 2001); and Roz Kaveney, *Superheroes! Capes and Crusaders in Comics and Films* (London: I. B. Tauris, 2008).

31. For a study of *Amar Chitra Katha*, see Nandini Chandra, *The Classic Popular: Amar Chitra Katha, 1967–2007* (New Delhi: Yoda Press, 2008).

32. Siegfried Kracauer, *The Mass Ornament*, trans. and ed. Thomas Y. Levin (Cambridge, Mass.: Harvard University Press, 1995), 74.

33. The information that follows is drawn from the author's interviews with Vivek Mohan, January 2006, and Sanjay Gupta, April 2009.

34. Sanjay Gupta, interview.

35. The first three issues establish the superhero's character and his backstories. See *Curfew* (Delhi: Raj Comics, 1993); *Yeh Hai Doga* [It's Doga] (Delhi: Raj Comics, 1993); and *Main Hoon Doga* [I Am Doga] (Delhi: Raj Comics, 1993).

36. The story of his training under four uncles appears in *Adrakh Chacha* (Delhi: Raj Comics, 1993).

37. *Genda* (Delhi: Raj Comics, 1993).

38. Georg Simmel, "Metropolis and Mental Life," in *On Individuality and Social Forms* (Chicago: University of Chicago Press, 1971), 324–39.

39. *Khaki Aur Khaddar* (Delhi: Raj Comics, 1997).

40. *Sher Ka Bachcha* [The Lion's Cub] (Delhi: Raj Comics, 1997).

41. *Khaki Aur Khaddar*, 37.

42. *Doga Hindu Hai* [Doga Is Hindu] (Delhi: Raj Comics, 2008); *Apna Bhai Doga* [Our Brother Doga] (Delhi: Raj Comics, 2008); *Doga Haay Haay* [Down with Doga] (Delhi: Raj Comics, 2009); *Ro Pada Doga* [Doga Breaks Down] (Delhi: Raj Comics, 2009); and *Doga Ka Curfew* [Doga's Curfew] (Delhi: Raj Comics, 2009).

CHAPTER 9. DREAMWORLD

1. Surendra Verma, *Do murdon ke liye guldasta* [Bouquet for Two Corpses] (Delhi: Radhakrishna, 1998), 22. All translations are mine.

2. Ibid., 20.

3. Gillian Tindall, *City of Gold* (Delhi: Penguin Books, 1982), 3–4.

4. McKinsey and Company, *Vision Mumbai: Transforming Mumbai into a World-Class City* (Mumbai: Bombay First, 2003), vii.

5. Government of Maharashtra, *Transforming Mumbai into a World-Class City: First Report of the Chief Minister's Task Force* (Mumbai: Government of Maharashtra, 2004).

6. Darshini Mahadevia and Harini Narayan, "Slumbay to Shanghai: Envisioning Renewal or Takeover?" in *Inside the Transforming Urban Asia: Processes, Policies and Public Actions* (New Delhi: Concept Publishing House, 2008), 94–131, particularly 121–27.

7. Farah Baria, "A Pile of Dirt Worth Its Weight in Gold," September 24, 2006, http://www.indianexpress.com/news/a-pile-of-dirt-worth-its-weight-in-gold/13295/2 (accessed July 20, 2009).

8. Cited in Meher Pestonji's catalog essay in *Dream Home* (Mumbai: Chemould Gallery, 2003).

9. Nancy Adjania, "*Gaman/Aagaman*: The Interstitial Spaces between Departure and Arrival," in *Tum Kab Aaoge* (exhibition catalog) (New Delhi: Anant Art Gallery, 2005).

10. Nancy Adjania, "Narrative Geographies: Meera Devidayal's Map of Bombay," *Where I Live* (exhibition catalog) (Mumbai: Chemould Prescott Road, 2009).

11. Kalpana Sharma, *Rediscovering Dharavi: Stories from Asia's Largest Slum* (Delhi: Penguin Books, 2000), 76–78. Sharma's sensitive and insightful account demolishes the stereotypical image of the area as a miserable slum of squalor and crime.

12. Ibid., 36.

13. Matias Echanove and Rahul Srivastava, "Taking the Slum Out of 'Slumdog,'" New York Times, February 21, 2009.

14. Rahul Mehrotra, "Learning from Mumbai," *Seminar* 530 (October 2003).

15. Henri Lefebvre, *The Production of Space*, trans. Donald Nicholson-Smith (Oxford: Blackwell, 1991), 86.

Index

China: Communist revolution in, 218, 219; opium trade with, 36–39; political theater in, 132; yarn export to, 40

Chor Bazaar (Thieves' Market), 340–46, 348

Christianity, 33–34

Chrysler Building, New York City, 96

Chugtai, Ismat, 118, 125–27, 131, *139*, 143–44, 147; "Lihaaf" (Quilt), 126–27

Churchgate Street. *See* Veer Nariman Road

Churchill, Winston, 215

CID (film), 9, 78, 156–57, 303

Cine Blitz (magazine), 8

cinema: advertising and, 106–7; angry young man films, 304; Bombay origins of, 107–8; comic books compared to, 304; crime melodramas, 154–57, 303–4; novelty of, 115; post-Partition, 148–57; studio system for, 128; stunt films, 108–11; tramp films, 150–54; underworld and, 297; writers for, 128, 135, 148. *See also* Hindi cinema

cinema theaters, 101–2

cities: crime and, 303, 322; criticisms of, 19–21, 251–52; *Doga* comic books and, 305–6; generic, 21–22; kinetic vs. static city, 339–40; modernity and, 20–21, 303, 305; visuality of, 305–6. *See also* urban life

citizenship, 150–51

City Improvement Trust, 342

City Industrial Development Corporation (CIDCO), 270–71, 286

class, Indian-British relations and, 60–61. *See also* working class

Clow, A. C., 142

Colaabavala, F. D., *Bombay by Night*, 8

Colaba, 80, 99

Colaba Causeway, 28, 101

Coleman, Bill, 104

colonialism: architecture and urban planning expressive of, 48, 50; attempted erasure of, 25–26, 29–30; persistence of, 26–27. *See also* British colonialism; Portuguese colonialism

colonization, double, 51–52, 73–74, 326

comic books, 304

Comintern, 13, 130, 209, 211, 216

commerce: Bombay natives and, 103; British colonization and, 35–43; Victoria Terminus as symbol of, 47–48

Communist Party of India (CPI): cultural activities of, 212–13; decline of, 218–19, 240–50; Desai and, 241–42, 244–45; founding of, 209; goals of, 205–6; after Independence, 217–18; labor activities of, 210–12, 214, 240; left adventurist wing of, 217–19; legalization of, 215, 216; and linguistic states, 222–23, 225, 244; mutiny supported by, 216–17; and Nanavati case, 189; opposition of, to British colonialism, 212; and Partition, 148; return to center of, 219; revolutionary goals of, 218; right-wing nationalists vs., 204–6; rise of, 209–10; Shiv Sena opposition to, 235, *241*, 241–43, 245–49; and World War II, 215–16; writers and artists associated with, 130–32, 137–39

Company (film), 298

Confectioner, A. N., 370n59

Congrès International d'Architecture Moderne (CIAM), 253, 256

Congress. *See* Indian National Congress

Contractor, Behram (pen name: Busybee), 5

conversion, to Christianity, 34

Coppola, Carlo, 362n16, 362n17

Correa, Charles, 251, 263, 265–66, 268, 284, 287

corruption, in real estate and construction, 76, 88, 91–92, 94, 274–84, 287–88, 295, 297, 309–10

cosmopolitanism: art and, 256; of Bombay/Mumbai, 3, 11, 56, 117–19, 154–56, 161, 333; breakdown of, 11, 24, 348; cinema and, 152, 154–56; in Dharavi, 339; Hinduization vs., 205; ideal of, 348; imperialism and, 117–18; of India, 152, 154; mercantile, 35; Nanavati case and, 161; nationalism vs., 118; nation-based, 256; race and, 109; vernacular, 333

cotton mills, 11, 29, 40–43, *42*, 293–95, 298. *See also* textile mills

cotton trade, 39–40, 44

Crawford Market, 29, 342

Cricket Smith Band, *105*
crime: in Bombay/Mumbai, 57–60, 154–57, 324; cities and, 303, 322; detectives and, 57, 59–60; in *Doga* comic books, 290, 308–13; film melodramas about, 154–57; state of law revealed through, 303. *See also* underworld
Cripps, Stafford, 215
Criterion, 255
Cuffe, T. W., 79
Cuffe Parade, 79–80, 283, 287
cultural modernity, 110, 197
culture, colonization of, 51–52
Cumbala Hills neighborhood, 99, 100
Cunha, Gerson da, 31, 367n54
Cunha, Nuno da, 30–31
Current (newspaper), 166–67, 275–76, 282
Customs House, 27

Dadabhai Naoroji Road (Hornby Road), 29, 47, 342
Dadar, 99
Dadas (neighborhood gangsters), 121–22, 207
Daily Mirror (London newspaper), 163
Dalit, 10, 72
Dalit Panthers, 10, 240
Dalmia, Vasudha, 372n13
Dalvi, Mustansir, 360n51, 373n16
Dandavate, M. R., 223
dandies, 345
Dange, S. A., 209–15, 219, 223–26, *224*, 235, 240, 241, 244; *Gandhi vs. Lenin*, 209
Dange, Usha, 214
Daphtary, C. K., 193
Das Gupta, Jyotindra, 369n41
Davar, Kavasji Nanabhai, 40
Davidge, W. R., 83, *84*, 85, 95
David Sassoon Library and Reading Room, 51
Davis, Mike, 354n19
D Company, 297
Delhi, 10, 120, 341. *See also* New Delhi
democracy: erosion of, 10, 292; frustration with, 19; ideals of, 283; as obstacle to rational ideal of urban planning, 22, 280–81, 286; representative, 281; Shiv

Sena's rule of force vs., 238, 292
Desai, Askok, 279–80, 282
Desai, Krishna, 204, 241–47, *247*, 293
Desai, Morarji, 166–67, 237
Desai, Sarojini, 248, 249
detective pulp fiction, 303
detectives, uncovering of reality by, 57, 59, 170
Development Department, 83, 85, 87–89, 92
Development Directorate, 82
Devidayal, Meera, 331, 334–37, 348; *Altamount Road*, 336; "Dream Home" exhibition, 331; *Gold Valley*, 331; *Luxurious 1,2&3 BHK Flats*, 331; *Objects in the Mirror Are Closer than They Appear*, 335; "Tum Kab Aaoge" (When Will You Come) series, 334–36; "Where I Live" series, 336
Devoted Wife (film), 107
Dharavi, 12, 329, 337–39
Dharavi Rehabilitation Project, 330
Dharti ke Lal (Children of the Earth) [film], 136–37
Dhasal, Namdeo, 10, 25, 29–30
Dhawan, Prem, 147, 149
Diamond Queen (film), 109
Dickens, Charles, *Bleak House*, 69
Diler Daku, or *Thunderbolt* (film), 109
Dilruba Daku, or *Amazon* (film), 109
Direct Action Day, 141
Ditchburn and Mistri, 102
D'Monte, Darryl, 353n12, 376n5, 376n10
D. N. (Hornby) Road. *See* Dadabhai Naoroji Road
Dobbin, Christine, 355n6, 355n11
Doctor, Vikram, 360n55
Doga comic book series, 289–91, 304–24, 347; city as setting for, 305–6; communal conflict in, 317–20; crime in, 290, 308–13; the hero of, 289–90, 306–7, 318–21, 323; law in, 308, 313, 315–16, 321, 323–24; and Mumbai, 289–90, 306–10, 317–24; readership of, 291; religion in, 307; social alienation in, 307–9; violence in, 306, 308–9, 312–13, 315, 318–21
Doga Hindu Hai (Doga Is Hindu) [comic book], 317–20

Girni Kamgar Mahamandal, 210, 211
Girni Kamgar Union (GKU), 211–12, 214, 218, 247
GKU. *See* Girni Kamgar Union
globalization, 20–21, 329
Goa, 244
Goans, 105
Godley, Margaret C., 137, 139–40
Gopal, Priyamvada, 362n11, 364n63
Gordon, A.D.D., 368n21
Gothic Revival architecture, 29, *47*, *48*; architect of Bombay's, 101; Art Deco vs., 99; colonial connotations of, 44, 46–48, 50
Government of India Act (1935), 122–23
Green's (music venue), 105
Gregson, Batley and King, 266
Guha, Ram Chandra, 376n2
Gujarat, 30, 31, 35, 222, 224–25
Gujarati language, 220, 222
Gun Sundari (Why Husbands Go Astray), 107
Gupta, Sanjay, 306–7
Gupta and Company, 275

Haffkine, Waldemar, 69
Hahn, Emily, 174–76
Hanuman Theatre, 208
Hansen, Thomas Blom, 371n79, 371n85
Harding, Gilbert, 134
Harris, Nigel, 376n6
Harvey, David, 354n20, 356n36
Harvey, Thomas, 92
Haussmann, Georges-Eugène, 48
Hazaribagh, 4, 5
Hepper, Lawless, 88, 90–91
High Court building, 47
Hindi cinema: golden age of, 148–49; impact of, 4; and Marine Drive, 77–78; music of, 343; origins of, 107. *See also* cinema
Hindi language, 128, 130, 222
Hind Mazdoor Sabha (HMS), 218
Hinduism: in Bombay, 43; saffron as color of, 205; violence between Muslims and Hindus, 10, 141–43, 205, 236–37, 243, 298–302, 307–8, 317–20

Hindustan Times Tabloid, 160
history, in flea markets, 340–46
Hitler, Adolf, 163–64
HMIS *Talwar*, 216
Hogarth Press, 255
Hollywood films, 105, 107
Holston, James, 354n22, 372n7
home, meaning of, 330–37
home ownership, 330–32
Hopkinson, Frederick, 91–92
Hornby, William, 44
Hornby Road. *See* Dadabhai Naoroji Road
Hornby Vellard, 44
Horniman, Benjamin Guy, 89, 163
Horniman (Elphinstone) Circle, 27, 45, *46*, 50
Hoskote, Ranjit, 353n9
housing: apartment complexes, 100–101, 113; development justified by need for, 81–83, 274, 329–30; immigrants', 64–65, 67, 336; and meaning of home, 330–37; in New Bombay, 271–72; of the poor, 70, 111–12; urban planning and, 261; Vision Mumbai and, 329–30; working-class, 64–68, 112–13, 207
Huezé, Gérard, 370n79, 371n87
Human Development Report, 288
Hunterwali, or *The Lady with the Whip* (film), 108, 109
Hurricane Hansa (film), 109
Hussain, M. F., 255
Hutatma Chowk (Flora Fountain), 27

Ibrahim, Dawood, 295–98, 300
Ideal Home Exhibition (Bombay, 1937), 97, *98*
identity: under colonialism, 118; of Marathi manoos, 232–33; as national citizen, 118, 150–51; working-class neighborhood, 207–9
Illustrated Weekly of India (magazine), 6–7, 105, 115
immigrants: to Bombay/Mumbai, 10–11, 23, 234; British colonial commerce and, 36; as cab drivers, 334–37; living conditions of, 64–65, 67, 207, 336; meaning of home for, 332–37; as mill workers, 42–43, 206–7; neighborhood

Mumbai: bombings in, 16–18; as city of artifice, 75–79, 100; colonial past of, 74; cosmopolitanism of, 10–11, 333; crises in, 11–20, 329; diversity of, 10–11, 35, 324, 339; *Doga* comic books and, 289–90, 306–10, 317–24; excess as characteristic of, 327; global features of, 22; historical fragments of, 340–48; images of, 22–24, 77–78, 306, 328–30, 337; map of, *ii*; modernity of, 10, 77; naming of, 11, 302; population of, 10–11, 12; siting of, 26–27; as society, 23–24, 75, 327, 348; terrorist attacks in, 16–19; vision for, 328–30. *See also* Bombay; Navi Mumbai

Mumford, Lewis, 286

Municipal Corporation, 82, 244

Municipal Corporation Building, 47, *48*

Museebat mein Bambai (Bombay in Trouble) [music video], 14–15

music, 104–6

Muslim League, 140–41, 216

Muslims: belongings discarded during Partition by, 344; in Bombay, 43, 117–18; under British colonization, 36; as merchants, 56; police bias against, 299–300, 302; under Portuguese colonization, 33; Shiv Sena opposition to, 236–37, 249, 298–99; underworld and, 300–301; violence between Hindus and, 10, 141–43, 205, 236–37, 243, 298–302, 307–8, 317–20; women, 125–26

Mussawar (journal), 120

mutiny, 216–17, 243

Nadia (Mary Evans), 108–11, *110*

Nadkarni, Dinkar V., 163, 169

Naik (High Court justice), 187

Naik, V. P., 205, 241, 276–77, 282

Nanavati, Kawas Maneckshaw, 158–62, 171–202

Nanavati, Sylvia, 159–61, 171–72, 174–79, 182, 185–86, 188–89, 192, 194, 196, 199–200, 202

Nanavati case, 158–62, 171–202, *177, 181, 183, 184, 195, 197, 198*

Naoroji, Dadabhai, 26

Narayan, Harini, 378n6

Narayan, Jai Prakash, 10, 291

Nargis, 151

Nariman, Khurshed Framji, 87–88, 115–16, 274

Nariman Point, 272, 274, 283–84, *284*, 287, 347

Nasser, Gamal Abdel, 165

National Emergency, 10, 291–92

nationalism: and the body, 108; cinema and, 149–50; and homogeneity, 118; and land reclamation opposition, 82, 87–90; linguistic, 219–28; Marathi-speaking people and, 222; saffron as color of, 205; Shiv Sena and, 236, 249; urban planning and, 263; and World War II, 215–16

Native States, 103

nativism, 9, 15–16, 204–5, 229, 231, 240. *See also* saffronization

nature, colonization of, 51–52, 73–74, 326

naval mutiny, 216–17, 243

Navi Mumbai, 256, 287

Nazis, 129, 132, 215, 216

Neecha Nagar (Lowly City) [film], 136

Nehru, Jawaharlal, 118, 130, 133, 138, 140–42, 148, 149, 165–67, 189, 190, 192, 200, 201, 206, 217, 219, 220, 223–25, 239, 251–52

neighborhood organizations, 208

Nerale, Madhukar, 208

Netherlands, 34

New Bombay, 251, 253, 256, 263, 265–72, *268, 269*, 287

New Cuffe Parade, 79

New Delhi, 4, 5. *See also* Delhi

New Mumbai. *See* Navi Mumbai

newspapers, 164. *See also* tabloids

New Yorker (magazine), 160, 174

Nijman, J., 376n11

Nightingale, Pamela, 355n9

Oberoi Sheraton, 274

obscenity, 126–27

Odets, Clifford, *Waiting for Lefty*, 139

opium, 36–39, 62

Oriental Spinning and Weaving Company, 40

Orient Club, 162

Village of the Mills. *See* Girangaon

violence: in Bombay politics, 245; in *Doga* comic books, 306, 308–9, 312, 315, 318–21; Hindu-Muslim, 10, 141–43, 236–37, 243, 298–302, 307–8, 317–20; Krishna Desai and, 243–44; linguistic states issue–related, 223–25; Partition-related, 117, 141–47; Shiv Sena use of, 15–16, 204–5, 223–25, 233–39, 242, 246–47, 291, 299. *See also* bombings; terrorism

Virilio, Paul, 21, 354n24

Vision Mumbai, 328–30

visuality, 60, 305–6

Vitali, Valentina, 360n58, 361n59

Vithal, Master, 108

Wacha, Dinshaw, *Shells from the Sands of Bombay*, 53–55

Wadhawan, Jagdish Chander, 361n2

Wadia, Homi, 108–9

Wadia, J.B.H., 108–9, 361n59, 361n60

Wadia, Mrs. (workers' theater group member), 132

Wadia family, 37, 38, 41, 108–9

Wahi, Tarun Kumar, 306

Wales, Prince of, 28, 327, 341

Walker, Johnny, 4, 9, 78, 155, 156

Weber, Max, 52

Weiner, Stephen, 377n30

Wenner, Dorothee, 361n59

West Bengal, 5

White, Pearl, 108

Wilkins, Henry St Clair, 46

Windmiller, Marshall, 369n41, 369n42, 369n44, 369n46

women: employment restrictions on, 207; labor activities of, 214; social roles for, 109–11, 125–26

Woolf, Leonard, 255

Workers and Peasants Party, 209

Workers' Theatre, 213

working class: Communist support of, 210–19; entertainment of, 208, 213; living conditions of, 64–68, 112–13, 207–8; and politics, 205–6; response of to modernity, 66–67; strikes by, 210–12, 214–15, 223–24, 240, 247, 293–94. *See also* poor, the

World Bank, 275, 287

World War II, 215–16, 293

Worli embankment, 44, 51–52

Wright, Frank Lloyd, 256

writers: in Bombay, 119–40; Hindi, 128, 130; and politics, 128–31, 147–48; Urdu, 128, 130–31

Yeh Raaste Hain Pyaar Ke (These Are the Pathways to Love) [film], 160

Young Party, 296

Yugantar (newspaper), 204

Zachariah, K. C., 372n9

Zaheer, Sajjad, 129–30, 147

Zaidi, S. Hussain, 377n25

Zakaria, Rafiq, 277, 282

Zitzewitz, Karin, 372n13

Zoroastrianism, 35